ŚRĪMAD BHĀGAVATAM

Eighth Canto

"Withdrawal of the Cosmic Creations"

(Part One—Chapters 1-8)

With the Original Sanskrit Text,
Its Roman Transliteration, Synonyms,
Translation and Elaborate Purports

by

His Divine Grace
A.C. Bhaktivedanta Swami Prabhupāda
Founder-*Ācārya* of the International Society for Krishna Consciousness

THE BHAKTIVEDANTA BOOK TRUST
New York · Los Angeles · London · Bombay

Readers interested in the subject matter of this book
are invited by the International Society for Krishna Consciousness
to correspond with its Secretary.

International Society for Krishna Consciousness
3764 Watseka Avenue
Los Angeles, California 90034

Library of Congress Catalogue Card Number: 73-169353
International Standard Book Number: 0-912776-90-0

First printing, 1976: 20,000 copies

Printed in the United States of America

ALL GLORY TO ŚRĪ GURU AND GAURĀṄGA

ŚRĪMAD BHĀGAVATAM

of

KṚṢṆA-DVAIPĀYANA VYĀSA

सत्त्वेन प्रतिलभ्याय नैष्कर्म्येण विपश्चिता ।
नमः कैवल्यनाथाय निर्वाणसुखसंविदे ॥

sattvena pratilabhyāya
naiṣkarmyeṇa vipaścitā
namaḥ kaivalya-nāthāya
nirvāṇa-sukha-saṁvide (p. 84)

BOOKS by
His Divine Grace A. C. Bhaktivedanta Swami Prabhupāda

Bhagavad-gītā As It Is
Śrīmad-Bhāgavatam, Cantos 1–8 (24 Vols.)
Śrī Caitanya-caritāmṛta (17 Vols.)
Teachings of Lord Caitanya
The Nectar of Devotion
The Nectar of Instruction
Śrī Īśopaniṣad
Easy Journey to Other Planets
Kṛṣṇa Consciousness: The Topmost Yoga System
Kṛṣṇa, the Supreme Personality of Godhead (3 Vols.)
Perfect Questions, Perfect Answers
Dialectic Spiritualism—A Vedic View of Western Philosophy
Transcendental Teachings of Prahlād Mahārāja
Kṛṣṇa, the Reservoir of Pleasure
Life Comes from Life
The Perfection of Yoga
Beyond Birth and Death
On the Way to Kṛṣṇa
Rāja-vidyā: The King of Knowledge
Elevation to Kṛṣṇa Consciousness
Kṛṣṇa Consciousness: The Matchless Gift
Back to Godhead Magazine (Founder)

A complete catalog is available upon request

International Society for Krishna Consciousness
3764 Watseka Avenue
Los Angeles, California 90034

Table of Contents

Preface

We must know the present need of human society. And what is that need? Human society is no longer bounded by geographical limits to particular countries or communities. Human society is broader than in the Middle Ages, and the world tendency is toward one state or one human society. The ideals of spiritual communism, according to *Śrīmad-Bhāgavatam,* are based more or less on the oneness of the entire human society, nay, on the entire energy of living beings. The need is felt by great thinkers to make this a successful ideology. *Śrīmad-Bhāgavatam* will fill this need in human society. It begins, therefore, with the aphorism of Vedānta philosophy (*janmādy asya yataḥ*) to establish the ideal of a common cause.

Human society, at the present moment, is not in the darkness of oblivion. It has made rapid progress in the field of material comforts, education and economic development throughout the entire world. But there is a pinprick somewhere in the social body at large, and therefore there are large-scale quarrels, even over less important issues. There is need of a clue as to how humanity can become one in peace, friendship and prosperity with a common cause. *Śrīmad-Bhāgavatam* will fill this need, for it is a cultural presentation for the re-spiritualization of the entire human society.

Śrīmad-Bhāgavatam should be introduced also in the schools and colleges, for it is recommended by the great student devotee Prahlāda Mahārāja in order to change the demonic face of society.

kaumāra ācaret prājño
dharmān bhāgavatān iha
durlabhaṁ mānuṣaṁ janma
tad apy adhruvam arthadam
(*Bhāg.* 7.6.1)

Disparity in human society is due to lack of principles in a godless civilization. There is God, or the Almighty One, from whom everything emanates, by whom everything is maintained and in whom everything is merged to rest. Material science has tried to find the ultimate source of creation very insufficiently, but it is a fact that there is one ultimate source of everything that be. This ultimate source is explained rationally and authoritatively in the beautiful *Bhāgavatam* or *Śrīmad-Bhāgavatam.*

Śrīmad-Bhāgavatam is the transcendental science not only for knowing the ultimate source of everything but also for knowing our relation with Him and our duty towards perfection of the human society on the basis of this perfect knowledge. It is powerful reading matter in the Sanskrit language, and it is now rendered into English elaborately so that simply by a careful reading one will know God perfectly well, so much so that the reader will be sufficiently educated to defend himself from the onslaught of atheists. Over and above this, the reader will be able to convert others to accept God as a concrete principle.

Śrīmad-Bhāgavatam begins with the definition of the ultimate source. It is a bona fide commentary on the *Vedānta-sūtra* by the same author, Śrīla Vyāsadeva, and gradually it develops into nine cantos up to the highest state of God realization. The only qualification one needs to study this great book of transcendental knowledge is to proceed step by step cautiously and not jump forward haphazardly as with an ordinary book. It should be gone through chapter by chapter, one after another. The reading matter is so arranged with its original Sanskrit text, its English transliteration, synonyms, translation and purports so that one is sure to become a God realized soul at the end of finishing the first nine cantos.

The Tenth Canto is distinct from the first nine cantos, because it deals directly with the transcendental activities of the Personality of Godhead Śrī Kṛṣṇa. One will be unable to capture the effects of the Tenth Canto without going through the first nine cantos. The book is complete in twelve cantos, each independent, but it is good for all to read them in small installments one after another.

I must admit my frailties in presenting *Śrīmad-Bhāgavatam,* but still I am hopeful of its good reception by the thinkers and leaders of society on the strength of the following statement of *Śrīmad-Bhāgavatam.*

tad-vāg-visargo janatāgha-viplavo
yasmin pratiślokam abaddhavaty api

nāmāny anantasya yaśo 'ṅkitāni yac
chṛṇvanti gāyanti gṛṇanti sādhavaḥ
(*Bhāg.* 1.5.11)

"On the other hand, that literature which is full with descriptions of the transcendental glories of the name, fame, form and pastimes of the unlimited Supreme Lord is a transcendental creation meant to bring about a revolution in the impious life of a misdirected civilization. Such transcendental literatures, even though irregularly composed, are heard, sung and accepted by purified men who are thoroughly honest."

Oṁ tat sat

A. C. Bhaktivedanta Swami

Introduction

"This *Bhāgavata Purāṇa* is as brilliant as the sun, and it has arisen just after the departure of Lord Kṛṣṇa to His own abode, accompanied by religion, knowledge, etc. Persons who have lost their vision due to the dense darkness of ignorance in the age of Kali shall get light from this *Purāṇa*." (*Śrīmad-Bhāgavatam* 1.3.43)

The timeless wisdom of India is expressed in the *Vedas*, ancient Sanskrit texts that touch upon all fields of human knowledge. Originally preserved through oral tradition, the *Vedas* were first put into writing five thousand years ago by Śrīla Vyāsadeva, the "literary incarnation of God." After compiling the *Vedas*, Vyāsadeva set forth their essence in the aphorisms known as *Vedānta-sūtras*. *Śrīmad-Bhāgavatam* is Vyāsadeva's commentary on his own *Vedānta-sūtras*. It was written in the maturity of his spiritual life under the direction of Nārada Muni, his spiritual master. Referred to as "the ripened fruit of the tree of Vedic literature," *Śrīmad-Bhāgavatam* is the most complete and authoritative exposition of Vedic knowledge.

After compiling the *Bhāgavatam*, Vyāsa impressed the synopsis of it upon his son, the sage Śukadeva Gosvāmī. Śukadeva Gosvāmī subsequently recited the entire *Bhāgavatam* to Mahārāja Parīkṣit in an assembly of learned saints on the bank of the Ganges at Hastināpura (now Delhi). Mahārāja Parīkṣit was the emperor of the world and was a great *rājarṣi* (saintly king). Having received a warning that he would die within a week, he renounced his entire kingdom and retired to the bank of the Ganges to fast until death and receive spiritual enlightenment. The *Bhāgavatam* begins with Emperor Parīkṣit's sober inquiry to Śukadeva Gosvāmī:

> "You are the spiritual master of great saints and devotees. I am therefore begging you to show the way of perfection for all persons, and especially for one who is about to die. Please let me know what a man should hear, chant, remember and worship, and also what he should not do. Please explain all this to me."

Śukadeva Gosvāmī's answer to this question, and numerous other questions posed by Mahārāja Parīkṣit, concerning everything from the nature of the self to the origin of the universe, held the assembled sages in rapt attention continuously for the seven days leading to the King's death. The sage Sūta Gosvāmī, who was present on the bank of the Ganges when Śukadeva Gosvāmī first recited *Śrīmad-Bhāgavatam*, later repeated the *Bhāgavatam* before a gathering of sages in the forest of Naimiṣāraṇya. Those sages, concerned about the spiritual welfare of the people in general, had gathered to perform a long, continuous chain of sacrifices to counteract the degrading influence of the incipient age of Kali. In response to the sages' request that he speak the essence of Vedic wisdom, Sūta Gosvāmī repeated from memory the entire eighteen thousand verses of *Śrīmad-Bhāgavatam*, as spoken by Śukadeva Gosvāmī to Mahārāja Parīkṣit.

The reader of *Śrīmad-Bhāgavatam* hears Sūta Gosvāmī relate the questions of Mahārāja Parīkṣit and the answers of Śukadeva Gosvāmī. Also, Sūta Gosvāmī sometimes responds directly to questions put by Śaunaka Ṛṣi, the spokesman for the sages gathered at Naimiṣāraṇya. One therefore simultaneously hears two dialogues: one between Mahārāja Parīkṣit and Śukadeva Gosvāmī on the bank of the Ganges, and another at Naimiṣāraṇya between Sūta Gosvāmī and the sages at Naimiṣāraṇya Forest, headed by Śaunaka Ṛṣi. Furthermore, while instructing King Parīkṣit, Śukadeva Gosvāmī often relates historical episodes and gives accounts of lengthy philosophical discussions between such great souls as the saint Maitreya and his disciple Vidura. With this understanding of the history of the *Bhāgavatam*, the reader will easily be able to follow its intermingling of dialogues and events from various sources. Since philosophical wisdom, not chronological order, is most important in the text, one need only be attentive to the subject matter of *Śrīmad-Bhāgavatam* to appreciate fully its profound message.

The translator of this edition compares the *Bhāgavatam* to sugar candy—wherever you taste it, you will find it equally sweet and relishable. Therefore, to taste the sweetness of the *Bhāgavatam*, one may begin by reading any of its volumes. After such an introductory taste, however, the serious reader is best advised to go back to Volume One of the First Canto and then proceed through the *Bhāgavatam*, volume after volume, in its natural order.

This edition of the *Bhāgavatam* is the first complete English translation of this important text with an elaborate commentary, and it is the first widely available to the English-speaking public. It is the product of the scholarly and devotional effort of His Divine Grace A. C. Bhaktivedanta Swami Prabhupāda, the world's most distinguished teacher of Indian religious and philosophical thought. His consummate Sanskrit scholarship and intimate familiarity with Vedic culture and thought as well as the modern way of life combine to reveal to the West a magnificent exposition of this important classic.

Readers will find this work of value for many reasons. For those interested in the classical roots of Indian civilization, it serves as a vast reservoir of detailed information on virtually every one of its aspects. For students of comparative philosophy and religion, the *Bhāgavatam* offers a penetrating view into the meaning of India's profound spiritual heritage. To sociologists and anthropologists, the *Bhāgavatam* reveals the practical workings of a peaceful and scientifically organized Vedic culture, whose institutions were integrated on the basis of a highly developed spiritual world view. Students of literature will discover the *Bhāgavatam* to be a masterpiece of majestic poetry. For students of psychology, the text provides important perspectives on the nature of consciousness, human behavior and the philosophical study of identity. Finally, to those seeking spiritual insight, the *Bhāgavatam* offers simple and practical guidance for attainment of the highest self-knowledge and realization of the Absolute Truth. The entire multivolume text, presented by the Bhaktivedanta Book Trust, promises to occupy a significant place in the intellectual, cultural and spiritual life of modern man for a long time to come.

—The Publishers

His Divine Grace
A. C. Bhaktivedanta Swami Prabhupāda
Founder-Ācārya of the International Society for Krishna Consciousness

PLATE ONE

By the arrangement of providence, a strong crocodile once became angry at Gajendra, the King of the elephants, and attacked his leg in the water. Pulling one another in and out of the water, the powerful elephant and the crocodile fought for one thousand years. Because of being pulled into the water and fighting for many long years, Gajendra became diminished in his mental, physical and sensual strength. The crocodile, on the contrary, being an animal of the water, increased in enthusiasm, physical strength and sensual power. At last, Gajendra saw that he was helpless, and he prayed to the Lord for release. Understanding the elephant's awkward condition, and moved by his heartfelt prayers, the Supreme Personality of Godhead, Nārāyaṇa, who lives everywhere, appeared before Gajendra accompanied by the demigods, who were also offering prayers to Him. Gajendra had been forcefully captured by the crocodile in the water and was feeling acute pain, but when he saw that Nārāyaṇa, wielding His disc, was coming in the sky on the back of Garuḍa, he immediately took a lotus flower in his trunk, and with great difficulty due to his painful condition, he uttered the following words: "O my Lord, Nārāyaṇa, master of the universe, O Supreme Personality of Godhead, I offer my respectful obeisances unto You." *(pp. 58–118)*

PLATE TWO

Seeing Gajendra in such an aggrieved position, the unborn Supreme Personality of Godhead, Hari, immediately got down from the back of Garuḍa by His causeless mercy and pulled the King of the elephants, along with the crocodile, out of the water. Then, in the presence of all the demigods, the Lord severed the crocodile's mouth from its body with His disc, thus freeing Gajendra. At once the crocodile assumed a very beautiful form as a Gandharva. In his previous life he had been King Hūhū, the best of the Gandharvas, but Devala Muni cursed him to become a crocodile. Now, having been delivered by the Supreme Personality of Godhead, he regained his original form. Gajendra's good fortune was even greater, for he had been touched directly by the hands of the Supreme Personality of Godhead, and this immediately freed him of all material ignorance and bondage. Thus he received the salvation of *sārūpya-mukti*, by which he achieved the same bodily features as the Lord, being dressed in yellow garments and possessing four hands. *(pp. 120–126)*

PLATE THREE

Gajendra, the King of the elephants, had formerly been a Vaiṣṇava king of the country known as Pāṇḍya, which is in the province of Draviḍa (South India). In his previous life he was known as Indradyumna Mahārāja. Indradyumna had retired from family life and gone to the Malaya Hills, where he had a small cottage for his *āśrama.* He wore matted locks on his head and always engaged in austerities. Once, while observing a vow of silence, he was fully engaged in the worship of the Lord and absorbed in the ecstasy of love of Godhead when the great sage Agastya Muni arrived, surrounded by his disciples. When the *muni* saw that King Indradyumna remained silent and did not follow the etiquette of offering him a reception, he became very angry and spoke this curse against the King: "This King Indradyumna is not at all gentle. Being low and uneducated, he has insulted a *brāhmaṇa.* May he therefore enter the region of darkness and receive the dull, dumb body of an elephant." *(pp. 127–130)*

PLATE FOUR

The demigods and the demons made an armistice between them, arranging to produce nectar by churning the ocean of milk with Mandara Mountain. Thereafter, with great strength, the demons and the demigods, who were all very powerful and who had long, stout arms, uprooted Mandara Mountain. Crying very loudly, they brought it toward the ocean of milk. However, Mount Mandara was solid gold and thus extremely heavy, and because of conveying the great mountain for a long distance, King Indra, Mahārāja Bali and their associates became fatigued. Suddenly, the mountain slipped from their hands, fell down and smashed many demigods and demons. Most of them were killed, and the survivors were frustrated and disheartened, their arms, thighs and shoulders being broken. Therefore the Supreme Personality of Godhead, who knows everything, appeared there on the back of His carrier, Garuḍa. Observing that most of the demons and demigods had been crushed by the falling of the mountain, the Lord glanced over them and brought them back to life. Thus they became free from grief, and they even had no bruises on their bodies. Then the Lord very easily lifted Mount Mandara with one hand and placed it on the back of Garuḍa. *(pp. 233–237)*

PLATE FIVE

Appearing like another great mountain, the Lord manifested Himself on the summit of Mount Mandara and held it with one hand. Then the demigods and the demons worked almost madly for the nectar, encouraged by the Lord, who was above and below the mountain and who had entered the demigods, the demons, the mountain itself, and the great thousand-headed serpent, Vāsuki. The entire ocean became turbulent from the violent churning, and the fish, tortoises and snakes became most agitated. While the ocean was being churned in this way, it first produced a fiercely dangerous poison called *hālahala*. When that uncontrollable poison was forcefully spreading up and down in all directions, all the demigods, along with the Lord Himself, approached Lord Śiva. Feeling unsheltered and afraid, they sought shelter of him. They pleaded, "O greatest of all demigods, O Supersoul of all living entities and cause of happiness and prosperity, we have come to the shelter of your lotus feet. Now please save us from this fiery poison, which is spreading all over the three worlds." When Lord Śiva, who is dedicated to auspicious, benevolent work for humanity, saw that the living entities were extremely disturbed by the poison, he became very compassionate. Thus he took the whole quantity of poison in his palm and drank it. The few drops of poison that scattered from Lord Śiva's hand were drunk by many insects, snakes and plants, who became the first scorpions, cobras, poisonous drugs and other poisonous living entities in the world. *(pp. 252–278)*

PLATE SIX

The goddess of fortune, Ramā, appeared like electricity, surpassing the lightning that might illuminate a marble mountain. Because of her exquisite beauty and her glories, everyone, including the demigods, the demons and the human beings, desired her. They were attracted because she is the source of all opulences, and thus they each worshiped her with their own special presentations: a suitable sitting place from Indra; pure water in golden waterpots from the Ganges and the Yamunā personified; all the herbs needed for installing the Deity from the land personified; milk, yogurt, ghee, urine and cow dung from the cows; everything produced during springtime from spring personified; flower garlands surrounded by bumblebees from Varuṇa; various decorative ornaments from Viśvakarmā; a necklace from Sarasvatī; a lotus flower from Lord Brahmā; and earrings from the inhabitants of Nāgaloka. The great sages performed the bathing ceremony while the Gandharvas chanted all-auspicious Vedic *mantras* and the professional dancers danced and sang. The clouds personified blew conchshells and bugles, beat various drums, and played flutes and stringed instruments. And the great elephants carried big water jugs full of Ganges water and bathed the goddess of fortune, to the accompaniment of Vedic *mantras* chanted by learned *brāhmaṇas.* *(pp. 292–300)*

PLATE SEVEN

While the sons of Kaśyapa, both demons and demigods, were engaged in churning the ocean of milk, a very wonderful male person appeared, carrying a jug filled to the top with nectar. He was as strongly built as a lion; his arms were long, stout and strong; his neck, which was marked with three lines, resembled a conchshell; his eyes were reddish; and his complexion was blackish. He was very young, he was garlanded with flowers, and his entire body was fully decorated with various ornaments. He was dressed in yellow garments, and from his ears hung brightly polished earrings made of pearls. The tips of his hair were anointed with oil, and his chest was very broad. His body had all good features, and he was decorated with bangles. His name was Dhanvantari, a plenary portion of a plenary portion of Lord Viṣṇu. It is he who inaugurated the science of medicine in the universe, and it is he who very quickly cures the diseases of the ever-diseased living entities simply by His fame personified. As one of the demigods, he is permitted to take a share in sacrifices, and only because of him do the demigods achieve a long duration of life. *(pp. 312–314)*

CHAPTER ONE

The Manus, Administrators of the Universe

First of all, let me offer my humble, respectful obeisances unto the lotus feet of my spiritual master, His Divine Grace Śrī Śrīmad Bhaktisiddhānta Sarasvatī Gosvāmī Prabhupāda. Sometime in the year 1935 when His Divine Grace was staying at Rādhā-kuṇḍa, I went to see him from Bombay. At that time, he gave me many important instructions in regard to constructing temples and publishing books. He personally told me that publishing books is more important than constructing temples. Of course, those same instructions remained within my mind for many years. In 1944 I began publishing my *Back to Godhead*, and when I retired from family life in 1958 I began publishing *Śrīmad-Bhāgavatam* in Delhi. When three parts of *Śrīmad-Bhāgavatam* had been published in India, I then started for the United States of America on the thirteenth of August, 1965.

I am continuously trying to publish books, as suggested by my spiritual master. Now, in this year, 1976, I have completed the Seventh Canto of *Śrīmad-Bhāgavatam*, and a summary of the Tenth Canto has already been published as *Kṛṣṇa, the Supreme Personality of Godhead.* Still, the Eighth Canto, Ninth Canto, Tenth Canto, Eleventh Canto and Twelfth Canto are yet to be published. On this occasion, therefore, I am praying to my spiritual master to give me strength to finish this work. I am neither a great scholar nor a great devotee; I am simply a humble servant of my spiritual master, and to the best of my ability I am trying to please him by publishing these books, with the cooperation of my disciples in America. Fortunately, scholars all over the world are appreciating these publications. Let us cooperatively publish more and more volumes of *Śrīmad-Bhāgavatam* just to please His Divine Grace Bhaktisiddhānta Sarasvatī Ṭhākura.

This First Chapter of the Eighth Canto may be summarized as a description of four Manus, namely Svāyambhuva, Svārociṣa, Uttama and

Tāmasa. After hearing descriptions of the dynasty of Svāyambhuva Manu until the end of the Seventh Canto, Mahārāja Parīkṣit desired to know about other Manus. He desired to understand how the Supreme Personality of Godhead descends—not only in the past but at the present and in the future—and how He acts in various pastimes as Manu. Since Parīkṣit Mahārāja was eager to know all this, Śukadeva Gosvāmī gradually described all the Manus, beginning with the six Manus who had appeared in the past.

The first Manu was Svāyambhuva Manu. His two daughters, namely Ākūti and Devahūti, gave birth to two sons, named Yajña and Kapila respectively. Because Śukadeva Gosvāmī had already described the activities of Kapila in the Third Canto, he now described the activities of Yajña. The original Manu, along with his wife, Śatarūpā, went into the forest to practice austerities on the bank of the River Sunandā. They practiced austerities for a hundred years, and then Manu, in a trance, formed prayers to the Supreme Personality of Godhead. Rākṣasas and *asuras* then attempted to devour him, but Yajña, accompanied by his sons the Yāmas and the demigods, killed them. Then Yajña personally took the post of Indra, the King of the heavenly planets.

The second Manu, whose name was Svārociṣa, was the son of Agni, and His sons were headed by Dyumat, Suṣeṇa and Rociṣmat. In the age of this Manu, Rocana became Indra, the ruler of the heavenly planets, and there were many demigods, headed by Tuṣita. There were also many saintly persons, such as Ūrja and Stambha. Among them was Vedaśirā, whose wife, Tuṣitā, gave birth to Vibhu. Vibhu instructed eighty-eight thousand *dṛḍha-vratas*, or saintly persons, on self-control and austerity.

Uttama, the son of Priyavrata, was the third Manu. Among his sons were Pavana, Sṛñjaya and Yajñahotra. During the reign of this Manu, the sons of Vasiṣṭha, headed by Pramada, became the seven saintly persons. The Satyas, Devaśrutas and Bhadras became the demigods, and Satyajit became Indra. From the womb of Sunṛtā, the wife of Dharma, the Lord appeared as Satyasena, and He killed all the Yakṣas and Rākṣasas who were fighting with Satyajit.

Tāmasa, the brother of the third Manu, was the fourth Manu, and he had ten sons, including Pṛthu, Khyāti, Nara and Ketu. During his reign, the Satyakas, Haris, Vīras and others were demigods, the seven great saints were headed by Jyotirdhāma, and Triśikha became Indra.

Harimedhā begot a son named Hari in the womb of his wife Hariṇī. This Hari, an incarnation of God, saved the devotee Gajendra. This incident is described as *gajendra-mokṣaṇa.* At the end of this chapter, Parīkṣit Mahārāja particularly asks about this incident.

TEXT 1

श्रीराजोवाच
स्वायम्भुवस्येह गुरो वंशोऽयं विस्तराच्छ्रुतः ।
यत्र विश्वसृजां सर्गो मनूनन्यान्वदस्व नः ॥ १ ॥

śrī-rājovāca
svāyambhuvasyeha guro
vaṁśo 'yaṁ vistarāc chrutaḥ
yatra viśva-sṛjāṁ sargo
manūn anyān vadasva naḥ

śrī-rājā uvāca—the King (Mahārāja Parīkṣit) said; *svāyambhuvasya*—of the great personality Svāyambhuva Manu; *iha*—in this connection; *guro*—O my spiritual master; *vaṁśaḥ*—dynasty; *ayam*—this; *vistarāt*—extensively; *śrutaḥ*—I have heard (from you); *yatra*—wherein; *viśva-sṛjām*—of the great personalities known as the *prajāpatis,* such as Marīci; *sargaḥ*—creation, involving the birth of many sons and grandsons from the daughters of Manu; *manūn*—Manus; *anyān*—other; *vadasva*—kindly describe; *naḥ*—to us.

TRANSLATION

King Parīkṣit said: O my lord, my spiritual master, now I have fully heard from Your Grace about the dynasty of Svāyambhuva Manu. But there are also other Manus, and I want to hear about their dynasties. Kindly describe them to us.

TEXT 2

मन्वन्तरे हरेर्जन्म कर्माणि च महीयसः ।
गृणन्ति कवयो ब्रह्मंस्तानि नो वद शृण्वताम् ॥ २ ॥

manvantare harer janma
karmāṇi ca mahīyasaḥ
gṛṇanti kavayo brahmaṁs
tāni no vada śṛṇvatām

manvantare—during the change of *manvantaras* (one Manu following another); *hareḥ*—of the Supreme Personality of Godhead; *janma*—appearance; *karmāṇi*—and activities; *ca*—also; *mahīyasaḥ*—of the supremely glorified; *gṛṇanti*—describe; *kavayaḥ*—the great learned persons who have perfect intelligence; *brahman*—O learned *brāhmaṇa* (Śukadeva Gosvāmī); *tāni*—all of them; *naḥ*—to us; *vada*—please describe; *śṛṇvatām*—who are very eager to hear.

TRANSLATION

O learned brāhmaṇa, Śukadeva Gosvāmī, the great learned persons who are completely intelligent describe the activities and appearance of the Supreme Personality of Godhead during the various manvantaras. We are very eager to hear about these narrations. Kindly describe them.

PURPORT

The Supreme Personality of Godhead has different varieties of incarnations, including the *guṇa-avatāras, manvantara-avatāras, līlā-avatāras* and *yuga-avatāras*, all of which are described in the *śāstras*. Without reference to the *śāstras* there can be no question of accepting anyone as an incarnation of the Supreme Personality of Godhead. Therefore, as especially mentioned here, *gṛṇanti kavayaḥ:* the descriptions of various incarnations are accepted by great learned scholars with perfect intelligence. At the present time, especially in India, so many rascals are claiming to be incarnations, and people are being misled. Therefore, the identity of an incarnation should be confirmed by the descriptions of the *śāstras* and by wonderful activities. As described in this verse by the word *mahīyasaḥ*, the activities of an incarnation are not ordinary magic or jugglery, but are wonderful activities. Thus any incarnation of the Supreme Personality of Godhead must be supported by the statements of the *śāstra* and must actually perform wonderful activities. Parīkṣit Mahārāja was eager to hear about the Manus of different ages.

There are fourteen Manus during a day of Brahmā, and the age of each Manu lasts for seventy-one *yugas*. Thus there are thousands of Manus during the life of Brahmā.

TEXT 3

यद्यस्मिन्नन्तरे ब्रह्मन्भगवान्विश्वभावनः ।
कृतवान्कुरुते कर्ता ह्यतीतेऽनागतेऽद्य वा ॥ ३ ॥

yad yasminn antare brahman
bhagavān viśva-bhāvanaḥ
kṛtavān kurute kartā
hy atīte 'nāgate 'dya vā

yat—whatever activities; *yasmin*—in a particular age; *antare*—*manvantara;* *brahman*—O great *brāhmaṇa;* *bhagavān*—the Supreme Personality of Godhead; *viśva-bhāvanaḥ*—who has created this cosmic manifestation; *kṛtavān*—has done; *kurute*—is doing; *kartā*—and will do; *hi*—indeed; *atīte*—in the past; *anāgate*—in the future; *adya*—at the present; *vā*—either.

TRANSLATION

O learned brāhmaṇa, kindly describe to us whatever activities the Supreme Personality of Godhead, who created this cosmic manifestation, has performed in the past manvantaras, is performing at present, and will perform in the future manvantaras.

PURPORT

In *Bhagavad-gītā* the Supreme Personality of Godhead said that both He and the other living entities present on the battlefield had existed in the past, they existed at present, and they would continue to exist in the future. Past, present and future always exist, both for the Supreme Personality of Godhead and for ordinary living entities. *Nityo nityānāṁ cetanaś cetanānām.* Both the Lord and the living entities are eternal and sentient, but the difference is that the Lord is unlimited whereas the living entities are limited. The Supreme Personality of Godhead is the creator of everything, and although the living entities are not created but exist with the Lord eternally, their bodies are created, whereas the

Supreme Lord's body is never created. There is no difference between the Supreme Lord and His body, but the conditioned soul, although eternal, is different from his body.

TEXT 4

श्रीऋषिरुवाच
मनवोऽस्मिन्व्यतीताः षट् कल्पे स्वायम्भुवादयः ।
आद्यस्ते कथितो यत्र देवादीनां च सम्भवः ॥ ४ ॥

śrī-ṛṣir uvāca
manavo 'smin vyatītāḥ ṣaṭ
kalpe svāyambhuvādayaḥ
ādyas te kathito yatra
devādīnāṁ ca sambhavaḥ

śrī-ṛṣiḥ uvāca—the great saint Śukadeva Gosvāmī said; *manavaḥ*—Manus; *asmin*—during this period (one day of Brahmā); *vyatītāḥ*—already past; *ṣaṭ*—six; *kalpe*—in this duration of Brahmā's day; *svāyambhuva*—Svāyambhuva Manu; *ādayaḥ*—and others; *ādyaḥ*—the first one (Svāyambhuva); *te*—unto you; *kathitaḥ*—I have already described; *yatra*—wherein; *deva-ādīnām*—of all the demigods; *ca*—also; *sambhavaḥ*—the appearance.

TRANSLATION

Śukadeva Gosvāmī said: In the present kalpa there have already been six Manus. I have described to you Svāyambhuva Manu and the appearance of many demigods. In this kalpa of Brahmā, Svāyambhuva is the first Manu.

TEXT 5

आकूत्यां देवहूत्यां च दुहित्रोस्तस्य वै मनोः ।
धर्मज्ञानोपदेशार्थं भगवान्पुत्रतां गतः ॥ ५ ॥

ākūtyāṁ devahūtyāṁ ca
duhitros tasya vai manoḥ

dharma-jñānopadeśārthaṁ
bhagavān putratāṁ gataḥ

ākūtyām—from the womb of Ākūti; *devahūtyām ca*—and from the womb of Devahūti; *duhitroḥ*—of the two daughters; *tasya*—of him; *vai*—indeed; *manoḥ*—of Svāyambhuva Manu; *dharma*—religion; *jñāna*—and knowledge; *upadeśa-artham*—for instructing; *bhagavān*—the Supreme Personality of Godhead; *putratām*—sonhood under Ākūti and Devahūti; *gataḥ*—accepted.

TRANSLATION

Svāyambhuva Manu had two daughters, named Ākūti and Devahūti. From their wombs, the Supreme Personality of Godhead appeared as two sons named Yajñamūrti and Kapila respectively. These sons were entrusted with preaching about religion and knowledge.

PURPORT

Devahūti's son was known as Kapila, and Ākūti's son was known as Yajñamūrti. Both of Them taught about religion and philosophical knowledge.

TEXT 6

कृतं पुरा भगवतः कपिलस्यानुवर्णितम् ।
आख्यास्ये भगवान्यज्ञो यच्चकार कुरूद्वह ॥ ६ ॥

kṛtaṁ purā bhagavataḥ
kapilasyānuvarṇitam
ākhyāsye bhagavān yajño
yac cakāra kurūdvaha

kṛtam—already done; *purā*—before; *bhagavataḥ*—of the Supreme Personality of Godhead; *kapilasya*—Kapila, the son of Devahūti; *anuvarṇitam*—fully described; *ākhyāsye*—I shall describe now; *bhagavān*—the Supreme Personality of Godhead; *yajñaḥ*—of the name Yajñapati or Yajñamūrti; *yat*—whatever; *cakāra*—executed; *kuru-udvaha*—O best of the Kurus.

TRANSLATION

O best of the Kurus, I have already described [in the Third Canto] the activities of Kapila, the son of Devahūti. Now I shall describe the activities of Yajñapati, the son of Ākūti.

TEXT 7

विरक्तः कामभोगेषु शतरूपापतिः प्रभुः ।
विसृज्य राज्यं तपसे सभार्यो वनमाविशत् ॥ ७ ॥

viraktaḥ kāma-bhogeṣu
śatarūpā-patiḥ prabhuḥ
visṛjya rājyaṁ tapase
sabhāryo vanam āviśat

viraktaḥ—without attachment; *kāma-bhogeṣu*—in sense gratification (in *gṛhastha* life); *śatarūpā-patiḥ*—the husband of Śatarūpā, namely Svāyambhuva Manu; *prabhuḥ*—who was the master or king of the world; *visṛjya*—after renouncing totally; *rājyam*—his kingdom; *tapase*—for practicing austerities; *sa-bhāryaḥ*—with his wife; *vanam*—the forest; *āviśat*—entered.

TRANSLATION

Svāyambhuva Manu, the husband of Śatarūpā, was by nature not at all attached to enjoyment of the senses. Thus he gave up his kingdom of sense enjoyment and entered the forest with his wife to practice austerities.

PURPORT

As stated in *Bhagavad-gītā* (4.2), *evaṁ paramparā-prāptam imaṁ rājarṣayo viduḥ:* "The supreme science was thus received through the chain of disciplic succession, and the saintly kings understood it in that way." All the Manus were perfect kings. They were *rājarṣis.* In other words, although they held posts as kings of the world, they were as good as great saints. Svāyambhuva Manu, for example, was the emperor of the world, yet he had no desire for sense gratification. This is the meaning of monarchy. The king of the country or the emperor of the empire must be so trained that by nature he renounces sense gratification. It is not that because one becomes king he should unnecessarily spend money for sense gratification. As soon as kings became degraded, spending money for sense gratification, they were lost. Similarly, at the present moment, monarchy having been lost, the people have created democracy, which is also failing. Now, by the laws of nature, the time is coming when dictatorship will put the citizens into more and more difficulty. If the king or dictator individually, or the members of the government collectively, cannot maintain the state or kingdom according to the rules of *Manu-saṁhitā*, certainly their government will not endure.

TEXT 8

सुनन्दायां वर्षशतं पदैकेन भुवं स्पृशन् ।
तप्यमानस्तपो घोरमिदमन्वाह भारत ॥ ८ ॥

sunandāyāṁ varṣa-śataṁ
padaikena bhuvaṁ spṛśan
tapyamānas tapo ghoram
idam anvāha bhārata

sunandāyām—on the bank of the River Sunandā; *varṣa-śatam*—for one hundred years; *pada-ekena*—on one leg; *bhuvam*—the earth; *spṛśan*—touching; *tapyamānaḥ*—he performed austerities; *tapaḥ*—austerities; *ghoram*—very severe; *idam*—the following; *anvāha*—and spoke; *bhārata*—O scion of Bharata.

TRANSLATION

O scion of Bharata, after Svāyambhuva Manu had thus entered the forest with his wife, he stood on one leg on the bank of the River Sunandā, and in this way, with only one leg touching the earth, he performed great austerities for one hundred years. While performing these austerities, he spoke as follows.

PURPORT

Śrīla Viśvanātha Cakravartī Ṭhākura comments that the word *anvāha* means that he chanted or murmured to himself, not that he lectured to anyone.

TEXT 9

श्रीमनुरुवाच
येन चेतयते विश्वं विश्वं चेतयते न यम् ।
यो जागर्ति शयानेऽस्मिन्नायं तं वेद वेद सः ॥ ९ ॥

śrī-manur uvāca
yena cetayate viśvaṁ
viśvaṁ cetayate na yam
yo jāgarti śayāne 'smin
nāyaṁ taṁ veda veda saḥ

śrī-manuḥ uvāca—Svāyambhuva Manu chanted; *yena*—by whom (the Personality of Godhead); *cetayate*—is brought into animation; *viśvam*—the whole universe; *viśvam*—the whole universe (the material world); *cetayate*—animates; *na*—not; *yam*—He whom; *yaḥ*—He who; *jāgarti*—is always awake (watching all activities); *śayāne*—while sleeping; *asmin*—in this body; *na*—not; *ayam*—this living entity; *tam*—Him; *veda*—knows; *veda*—knows; *saḥ*—He.

TRANSLATION

Lord Manu said: The supreme living being has created this material world of animation; it is not that He was created by this material world. When everything is silent, the Supreme Being stays awake as a witness. The living entity does not know Him, but He knows everything.

PURPORT

Here is a distinction between the Supreme Personality of Godhead and the living entities. *Nityo nityānāṁ cetanaś cetanānām.* According to the Vedic version, the Lord is the supreme eternal, the supreme living being. The difference between the Supreme Being and the ordinary living being is that when this material world is annihilated, all the living entities remain silent in oblivion, in a dreaming or unconscious condition, whereas the Supreme Being stays awake as the witness of everything. This material world is created, it stays for some time, and then it is annihilated. Throughout these changes, however, the Supreme Being remains awake. In the material condition of all living entities, there are three stages of dreaming. When the material world is awake and put in working order, this is a kind of dream, a waking dream. When the living entities go to sleep, they dream again. And when unconscious at the time of annihilation, when this material world is unmanifested, they enter another stage of dreaming. At any stage in the material world, therefore, they are all dreaming. In the spiritual world, however, everything is awake.

TEXT 10

आत्मावास्यमिदं विश्वं यत् किञ्चिज्जगत्यां जगत् ।
तेन त्यक्तेन भुञ्जीथा मा गृधः कस्यस्विद्धनम् ॥१०॥

ātmāvāsyam idaṁ viśvaṁ
yat kiñcij jagatyāṁ jagat
tena tyaktena bhuñjīthā
mā gṛdhaḥ kasya svid dhanam

ātma—the Supersoul; *āvāsyam*—living everywhere; *idam*—this universe; *viśvam*—all universes, all places; *yat*—whatever; *kiñcit*—everything that exists; *jagatyām*—in this world, everywhere; *jagat*—everything, animate and inanimate; *tena*—by Him; *tyaktena*—allotted; *bhuñjīthāḥ*—you may enjoy; *mā*—do not; *gṛdhaḥ*—accept; *kasya svit*—of anyone else; *dhanam*—the property.

TRANSLATION

Within this universe, the Supreme Personality of Godhead in His Supersoul feature is present everywhere, wherever there are animate or inanimate beings. Therefore, one should accept only that which is allotted to him; one should not desire to infringe upon the property of others.

PURPORT

Having described the situation of the Supreme Personality of Godhead as transcendental, Svāyambhuva Manu, for the instruction of the sons and grandsons in his dynasty, is now describing all the property of the universe as belonging to the Supreme Personality of Godhead. Manu's instructions are not only for his own sons and grandsons, but for all of human society. The word "man"—or, in Sanskrit, *manuṣya*—has been derived from the name Manu, for all the members of human society are descendants of the original Manu. Manu is also mentioned in *Bhagavad-gītā* (4.1), where the Lord says:

imaṁ vivasvate yogaṁ
proktavān aham avyayam
vivasvān manave prāha
manur ikṣvākave 'bravīt

"I instructed this imperishable science of *yoga* to the sun-god, Vivasvān, and Vivasvān instructed it to Manu, the father of mankind, and Manu in turn instructed it to Ikṣvāku." Svāyambhuva Manu and Vaivasvata Manu have similar duties. Vaivasvata Manu was born of the sun-god, Vivasvān, and his son was Ikṣvāku, the King of the earth. Since Manu is understood to be the original father of humanity, human society should follow his instructions.

Svāyambhuva Manu instructs that whatever exists, not only in the spiritual world but even within this material world, is the property of the Supreme Personality of Godhead, who is present everywhere as the Superconsciousness. As confirmed in *Bhagavad-gītā* (13.3), *kṣetra-jñaṁ cāpi māṁ viddhi sarva-kṣetreṣu bhārata:* in every field—in other words, in every body—the Supreme Lord is existing as the Supersoul. The individual soul is given a body in which to live and act according to the instructions of the Supreme Person, and therefore the Supreme Person also exists within every body. We should not think that we are independent; rather, we should understand that we are allotted a certain portion of the total property of the Supreme Personality of Godhead.

This understanding will lead to perfect communism. Communists think in terms of their own nations, but the spiritual communism instructed here is not only nationwide but universal. Nothing belongs to any nation or any individual person; everything belongs to the Supreme Personality of Godhead. That is the meaning of this verse. *Ātmāvāsyam idaṁ viśvam:* whatever exists within this universe is the property of the

Supreme Personality of Godhead. The modern communistic theory, and also the idea of the United Nations, can be reformed—indeed, rectified—by the understanding that everything belongs to the Supreme Personality of Godhead. The Lord is not a creation of our intelligence; rather, He has created us. *Ātmāvāsyam idaṁ viśvam. Īśāvāsyam idaṁ sarvam.* This universal communism can solve all the problems of the world.

One should learn from the Vedic literature that one's body is also not the property of the individual soul, but is given to the individual soul according to his *karma. Karmaṇā daiva-netreṇa jantur dehopapattaye.* The 8,400,000 different bodily forms are machines given to the individual soul. This is confirmed in *Bhagavad-gītā* (18.61):

īśvaraḥ sarva-bhūtānāṁ
hṛd-deśe 'rjuna tiṣṭhati
bhrāmayan sarva-bhūtāni
yantrārūḍhāni māyayā

"The Supreme Lord is situated in everyone's heart, O Arjuna, and is directing the wanderings of all living entities, who are seated as on a machine, made of the material energy." The Lord, as the Supersoul, sits in everyone's heart and observes the various desires of the individual soul. The Lord is so merciful that He gives the living entity the opportunity to enjoy varieties of desires in suitable bodies, which are nothing but machines (*yantrārūḍhāni māyayā*). These machines are manufactured by the material ingredients of the external energy, and thus the living entity enjoys or suffers according to his desires. This opportunity is given by the Supersoul.

Everything belongs to the Supreme, and therefore one should not usurp another's property. We have a tendency to manufacture many things. Especially nowadays, we are building skyscrapers and developing other material facilities. We should know, however, that the ingredients of the skyscrapers and machines cannot be manufactured by anyone but the Supreme Personality of Godhead. The whole world is nothing but a combination of the five material elements (*tejo-vāri-mṛdāṁ yathā vinimayaḥ*). A skyscraper is a transformation of earth, water and fire. Earth and water are combined and burnt into bricks by fire, and a skyscraper is essentially a tall construction of bricks. Although the bricks may be manufactured by man, the ingredients of the bricks are not. Of course, man, as a manufacturer, may accept a salary from the Supreme Personality of Godhead. That is stated here: *tena tyaktena bhuñjīthāḥ.* One may construct a big skyscraper, but neither the constructor, the merchant nor the worker can claim proprietorship. Proprietorship belongs to the person who has spent for the building. The Supreme Personality of Godhead has manufactured water, earth, air, fire and the sky, and one can use these and take a salary (*tena tyaktena bhuñjīthāḥ*). However, one cannot claim proprietorship. This is perfect communism. Our tendency to construct great buildings should be used only for constructing large and valuable temples in which to install the Deity of the Supreme Personality of Godhead. Then our desire for construction will be fulfilled.

Since all property belongs to the Supreme Personality of Godhead, everything should be offered to the Lord, and we should take only *prasāda* (*tena tyaktena bhuñjīthāḥ*). We should not fight among ourselves to take more than we need. As Nārada said to Mahārāja Yudhiṣṭhira:

yāvad bhriyeta jaṭharaṁ
tāvat svatvaṁ hi dehinām
adhikaṁ yo 'bhimanyeta
sa steno daṇḍam arhati

"One may claim proprietorship to as much wealth as required to maintain body and soul together, but one who desires proprietorship over more than that must be considered a thief, and he deserves to be punished by the laws of nature." (*Bhāg.* 7.14.8) Of course, we need to be maintained in eating, sleeping, mating and defending (*āhāra-nidrā-bhaya-maithuna*), but since the Supreme Lord, the Personality of Godhead, has provided these necessities of life for the birds and bees, why not for mankind? There is no need for economic development; everything is provided. Therefore one should understand that everything belongs to Kṛṣṇa, and with this idea, one may take *prasāda.* However, if one interferes with the allotments of others, he is a thief. We should not accept more than what we actually need. Therefore, if by chance we get an abundance of money, we should always consider that it belongs to the Supreme Personality of Godhead. In Kṛṣṇa consciousness we are getting sufficient money, but we should never think that the money belongs to us; it belongs to the Supreme Personality of Godhead and should be equally distributed to the workers, the devotees. No devotee should claim that any money or property belongs to him. If one thinks that any portion of property of this huge universe belongs to anyone, he is to be considered a thief and is punishable by the laws of nature. *Daivī hy eṣā guṇamayī mama māyā duratyayā:* no one can surpass the vigilance of material nature or hide his intentions from material nature. If human society unlawfully claims that the property of the universe, either partially or wholly, belongs to mankind, all of human society will be cursed as a society of thieves and will be punished by the laws of nature.

TEXT 11

यं पश्यति न पश्यन्तं चक्षुर्यस्य न रिष्यति ।
तं भूतनिलयं देवं सुपर्णमुपधावत ॥११॥

yaṁ paśyati na paśyantaṁ
cakṣur yasya na riṣyati
taṁ bhūta-nilayaṁ devaṁ
suparṇam upadhāvata

yam—He who; *paśyati*—the living entity sees; *na*—not; *paśyantam*—although always seeing; *cakṣuḥ*—eye; *yasya*—whose; *na*—never; *riṣyati*—diminishes; *tam*—Him; *bhūta-nilayam*—the original source of all living entities; *devam*—the Supreme Personality of Godhead; *suparṇam*—who accompanies the living entity as a friend; *upadhāvata*—everyone should worship.

TRANSLATION

Although the Supreme Personality of Godhead constantly watches the activities of the world, no one sees Him. However, one should not think that because no one sees Him, He does not see, for His power to see is never diminished. Therefore, everyone

should worship the Supersoul, who always stays with the individual soul as a friend.

PURPORT

Offering prayers to Kṛṣṇa, Śrīmatī Kuntīdevī, the mother of the Pāṇḍavas, said, *alakṣyaṁ sarva-bhūtānām antar bahir avasthitam:* "Kṛṣṇa, You reside both inside and outside of everything, yet the unintelligent conditioned souls cannot see You." In *Bhagavad-gītā* it is said that one can see the Supreme Personality of Godhead through *jñāna-cakṣuṣaḥ*, eyes of knowledge. He who opens these eyes of knowledge is called a spiritual master. Thus we offer our prayers to the spiritual master with the following *śloka:*

oṁ ajñāna-timirāndhasya
jñānāñjana-śalākayā
cakṣur unmīlitaṁ yena
tasmai śrī-gurave namaḥ

"I offer my respectful obeisances unto my spiritual master, who with the torchlight of knowledge has opened my eyes, which were blinded by the darkness of ignorance." (*Gautamīya Tantra*) The *guru's* task is to open the disciple's eyes of knowledge. When the disciple is awakened from ignorance to knowledge, he can see the Supreme Personality of Godhead everywhere because the Lord actually is everywhere. *Aṇḍāntara-stha-paramāṇu-cayāntara-stham.* The Lord resides within this universe, He resides within the hearts of all living entities, and He resides even within the atom. Because we lack perfect knowledge, we cannot see God, but a little deliberation can help us to see God everywhere. This requires training. With a little deliberation, even the most degraded person can perceive the presence of God. If we take into account whose property is the vast ocean, whose property is the vast land, how the sky exists, how the numberless millions of stars and planets are set in the sky, who has made this universe and whose property it is, we should certainly come to the conclusion that there is a proprietor of everything. When we claim proprietorship over a certain piece of land, whether individually or for our families or nations, we should also consider how we became the proprietors. The land was there before our birth, before we came to the land. How did it become our property? Such deliberation will help us understand that there is a supreme proprietor of everything—the Supreme Personality of Godhead.

The Supreme Godhead is always awake. In the conditioned stage we forget things because we change our bodies, but because the Supreme Personality of Godhead does not change His body, He remembers past, present and future. Kṛṣṇa says in *Bhagavad-gītā* (4.1), *imaṁ vivasvate yogaṁ proktavān aham avyayam:* "I spoke this science of God—*Bhagavad-gītā*—to the sun-god at least forty million years ago." When Arjuna inquired from Kṛṣṇa how He could remember incidents that had taken place so long ago, the Lord answered that Arjuna was also present at that time. Because Arjuna is Kṛṣṇa's friend, wherever Kṛṣṇa goes, Arjuna goes. But the difference is that Kṛṣṇa remembers everything, whereas the living entity like Arjuna, being a minute particle of the Supreme Lord, forgets. Therefore it is said, the Lord's vigilance is never diminished. This is also confirmed in *Bhagavad-gītā* (15.15). *Sarvasya cāhaṁ hṛdi sanniviṣṭo mattaḥ smṛtir jñānam apohanaṁ ca:* the Supreme Personality of Godhead in His Paramātmā feature is always present within the hearts of all living entities, and from Him come memory, knowledge and forgetfulness. This is also indicated in this verse by the word *suparṇam,* which means "friend." In the *Śvetāśvatara Upaniṣad* (4.6) it is therefore said, *dvā suparṇā sayujā sakhāyā samānaṁ vṛkṣaṁ pariṣasvajāte:* two birds are sitting on the same tree as friends. One bird is eating the fruit of the tree, and the other is simply observing. This observing bird is always present as a friend to the eating bird and giving him remembrance of things he wanted to do. Thus if we take into account the Supreme Personality of Godhead in our daily affairs, we can see Him or at least perceive His presence everywhere.

The words *cakṣur yasya na riṣyati* mean that although we cannot see Him, this does not mean that He cannot see us. Nor does He die when the cosmic manifestation is annihilated. The example is given in this connection that the sunshine is present when the sun is present, but when the sun is not present, or when we cannot see the sun, this does not mean that the sun is lost. The sun is there, but we cannot see it. Similarly, although we cannot see the Supreme Personality of Godhead in our present darkness, our lack of knowledge, He is always present, seeing our activities. As the Paramātmā, He is the witness and adviser (*upadraṣṭā* and *anumantā*). Therefore, by following the instructions of the spiritual master and studying authorized literatures, one can understand that God is present before us, seeing everything, although we have no eyes with which to see Him.

TEXT 12

न यस्याद्यन्तौ मध्यं च स्वः परो नान्तरं बहिः ।
विश्वस्यामूनि यद् यस्माद् विश्वं च तदृतं महत् ॥१२॥

na yasyādy-antau madhyaṁ ca
svaḥ paro nāntaraṁ bahiḥ
viśvasyāmūni yad yasmād
viśvaṁ ca tad ṛtaṁ mahat

na—neither; *yasya*—of whom (the Supreme Personality of Godhead); *ādi*—a beginning; *antau*—end; *madhyam*—middle; *ca*—also; *svaḥ*—own; *paraḥ*—others; *na*—nor; *antaram*—inside; *bahiḥ*—outside; *viśvasya*—of the whole cosmic manifestation; *amūni*—all such considerations; *yat*—whose form; *yasmāt*—from He who is the cause of everything; *viśvam*—the whole universe; *ca*—and; *tat*—all of them; *ṛtam*—truth; *mahat*—very, very great.

TRANSLATION

The Supreme Personality of Godhead has no beginning, no end and no middle. Nor does He belong to a particular person or nation. He has no inside or outside. The dualities found within this material world, such as beginning and end, mine and theirs, are all absent from the personality of the Supreme Lord. The universe, which emanates from Him, is another feature of the Lord. Therefore the Supreme Lord is the ultimate truth, and He is complete in greatness.

PURPORT

The Supreme Personality of Godhead, Kṛṣṇa, is described in the *Brahma-saṁhitā* (5.1):

īśvaraḥ paramaḥ kṛṣṇaḥ
sac-cid-ānanda-vigrahaḥ
anādir ādir govindaḥ
sarva-kāraṇa-kāraṇam

"Kṛṣṇa, known as Govinda, is the supreme controller. He has an eternal, blissful, spiritual body. He is the origin of all. He has no other origin, for He is the prime cause of all causes." For the Lord's existence there is no cause, for He is the cause of everything. He is in everything (*mayā tatam idaṁ sarvam*), He is expanded in everything, but He is not everything. He is *acintya-bhedābheda*, simultaneously one and different. That is explained in this verse. In the material condition we have a conception of beginning, end and middle, but for the Supreme Personality of Godhead there are no such things. The universal cosmic manifestation is also the *virāḍ-rūpa* that was shown to Arjuna in *Bhagavad-gītā*. Therefore, since the Lord is present everywhere and all the time, He is the Absolute Truth and the greatest. He is complete in greatness. God is great, and how He is great is explained here.

TEXT 13

स विश्वकायः पुरुहूत ईशः
सत्यः स्वयंज्योतिरजः पुराणः ।
धत्तेऽस्य जन्माद्यजयात्मशक्त्या
तां विद्ययोदस्य निरीह आस्ते ॥१३॥

sa viśva-kāyaḥ puru-hūta īśaḥ
satyaḥ svayaṁ-jyotir ajaḥ purāṇaḥ
dhatte 'sya janmādy-ajayātma-śaktyā
tāṁ vidyayodasya nirīha āste

saḥ—that Supreme Personality of Godhead; *viśva-kāyaḥ*—the total form of the universe (the whole universe is the external body of the Supreme Personality of Godhead); *puru-hūtaḥ*—known by so many names; *īśaḥ*—the supreme controller (with full power); *satyaḥ*—the ultimate truth; *svayam*—personally; *jyotiḥ*—self-effulgent; *ajaḥ*—

unborn, beginningless; *purāṇaḥ*—the oldest; *dhatte*—He performs; *asya*—of this universe; *janma-ādi*—the creation, maintenance and annihilation; *ajayā*—by His external energy; *ātma-śaktyā*—by His personal potency; *tām*—that external material energy; *vidyayā*—by His spiritual potency; *udasya*—giving up; *nirīhaḥ*—without any desire or activity; *āste*—He is existing (untouched by the material energy).

TRANSLATION

The entire cosmic manifestation is the body of the Supreme Personality of Godhead, the Absolute Truth, who has millions of names and unlimited potencies. He is self-effulgent, unborn and changeless. He is the beginning of everything, but He has no beginning. Because He has created this cosmic manifestation by His external energy, the universe appears to be created, maintained and annihilated by Him. Nonetheless, He remains inactive in His spiritual energy and is untouched by the activities of the material energy.

PURPORT

Śrī Caitanya Mahāprabhu says in His *Śikṣāṣṭaka, nāmnām akāri bahudhā nija-sarva-śaktiḥ:* the Supreme Personality of Godhead has many names, which are all nondifferent from the Supreme Person. This is spiritual existence. By chanting the Hare Kṛṣṇa *mahā-mantra*, consisting of names of the Supreme Lord, we find that the name has all the potencies of the person. The Lord's activities are many, and according to His activities He has many names. He appeared as the son of mother Yaśodā, and also as the son of mother Devakī, and therefore He is named Devakī-nandana and Yaśodā-nandana. *Parāsya śaktir vividhaiva śrūyate:* the Lord has a multitude of energies, and therefore He acts in multifarious ways. Yet He has a particular name. The *śāstras* recommend which names we should chant, such as Hare Kṛṣṇa, Hare Kṛṣṇa, Kṛṣṇa Kṛṣṇa, Hare Hare. It is not that we have to search for some name or manufacture one. Rather, we must follow the saintly persons and the *śāstras* in chanting His holy name.

Although the material and spiritual energies both belong to the Lord, He is impossible to understand as long as we are in the material energy. And when we come to the spiritual energy, He is very easy to know. As stated in *Śrīmad-Bhāgavatam* (1.7.23): *māyāṁ vyudasya cic-chaktyā kaivalye sthita ātmani.* Although the external energy belongs to the Lord, when one is in the external energy (*mama māyā duratyayā*) He is very difficult to understand. However, when one comes to the spiritual energy, one can understand Him. Therefore in *Bhagavad-gītā* (18.55) it is said, *bhaktyā mām abhijānāti yāvān yaś cāsmi tattvataḥ:* one who wants to understand the Supreme Personality of Godhead in reality must take to the platform of *bhakti,* or Kṛṣṇa consciousness. This *bhakti* consists of various activities (*śravaṇaṁ kīrtanaṁ viṣṇoḥ smaraṇaṁ pāda-sevanam/ arcanaṁ vandanaṁ dāsyaṁ sakhyam ātma-nivedanam*), and to understand the Lord one must take to this path of devotional service. Even though the people of the world have forgotten God and may say that God is dead, this is not a fact. One can understand God when one takes to the Kṛṣṇa consciousness movement, and thus one can be happy.

TEXT 14

अथाग्रे ऋषयः कर्माणीहन्तेऽकर्महेतवे ।
ईहमानो हि पुरुषः प्रायोऽनीहां प्रपद्यते ॥१४॥

athāgre ṛṣayaḥ karmāṇ-
īhante 'karma-hetave
īhamāno hi puruṣaḥ
prāyo 'nīhāṁ prapadyate

atha—therefore; *agre*—in the beginning; *ṛṣayaḥ*—all learned *ṛṣis,* saintly persons; *karmāṇi*—fruitive activities; *īhante*—execute; *akarma*—freedom from fruitive results; *hetave*—for the purpose of; *īhamānaḥ*—engaging in such activities; *hi*—indeed; *puruṣaḥ*—a person; *prāyaḥ*—almost always; *anīhām*—liberation from *karma; prapadyate*—attains.

TRANSLATION

Therefore, to enable people to reach the stage of activities that are not tinged by fruitive results, great saints first engage people in fruitive activities, for unless one begins by performing activities as recommended in the śāstras, one cannot reach the stage of liberation, or activities that produce no reactions.

PURPORT

In *Bhagavad-gītā* (3.9) Lord Kṛṣṇa advises, *yajñārthāt karmaṇo 'nyatra loko 'yaṁ karma-bandhanaḥ:* "Work done as a sacrifice for Viṣṇu has to be performed, otherwise work binds one to this material world." Generally, everyone is attracted to hard labor for becoming happy in this material world, but although various activities are going on all over the world simply for the sake of happiness, unfortunately only problems are being created from such fruitive activities. Therefore it is advised that active persons engage in activities of Kṛṣṇa consciousness, which are called *yajña,* because then they will gradually come to the platform of devotional service. *Yajña* means Lord Viṣṇu, the *yajña-puruṣa,* the enjoyer of all sacrifices (*bhoktāraṁ yajña-tapasāṁ sarva-loka-maheśvaram*). The Supreme Personality of Godhead is actually the enjoyer, and therefore if we begin our activities for His satisfaction, we will gradually lose our taste for material activities.

Sūta Gosvāmī declared to the great assembly of sages at Naimiṣāraṇya:

ataḥ pumbhir dvija-śreṣṭhā
varṇāśrama-vibhāgaśaḥ
svanuṣṭhitasya dharmasya
saṁsiddhir hari-toṣaṇam

"O best among the twiceborn, it is concluded that the highest perfection one can achieve, by discharging his prescribed duties [*dharma*] according to caste divisions and order of life, is to please the Lord Hari." (*Bhāg.* 1.2.13) According to Vedic principles, everyone must act according to his classification as *brāhmaṇa, kṣatriya, vaiśya, śūdra, brahmacārī, gṛhastha, vānaprastha* or *sannyāsī.* Everyone should progress toward perfection by acting in such a way that Kṛṣṇa will be pleased (*saṁsiddhir hari-toṣaṇam*). One cannot please Kṛṣṇa by sitting idly; one must act according to the directions of the spiritual master for the sake of pleasing the Supreme Personality of Godhead, and then one will gradually come to the stage of pure devotional service. As confirmed in *Śrīmad-Bhāgavatam* (1.5.12):

naiṣkarmyam apy acyuta-bhāva-varjitaṁ
na śobhate jñānam alaṁ nirañjanam

"Knowledge of self-realization, even though freed from all material affinity, does not look well if devoid of a conception of the Infallible [God]." *Jñānīs* recommend that one adopt *naiṣkarmya* by not doing anything but simply meditating and thinking of Brahman, but this is impossible unless one realizes Parabrahman, Kṛṣṇa. If there is no Kṛṣṇa consciousness, any kind of activity, be it philanthropic, political or social, simply causes *karma-bandhana*, bondage to material work.

As long as one is entangled in *karma-bandhana*, one must accept different types of bodies that spoil the human form of facility. Therefore, in *Bhagavad-gītā* (6.3) *karma-yoga* is recommended:

āruruksor muner yogaṁ
karma kāraṇam ucyate
yogārūḍhasya tasyaiva
śamaḥ kāraṇam ucyate

"For one who is a neophyte in the *yoga* system, work is said to be the means; and for one who has already attained to *yoga*, cessation of all material activities is said to be the means." Nonetheless:

karmendriyāṇi saṁyamya
ya āste manasā smaran
indriyārthān vimūḍhātmā
mithyācāraḥ sa ucyate

"One who restrains the senses and organs of action, but whose mind dwells on sense objects, certainly deludes himself and is called a pretender." (Bg. 3.6) One should act for Kṛṣṇa very seriously in order to become fully Kṛṣṇa conscious and should not sit down to imitate such great personalities as Haridāsa Ṭhākura. Śrīla Bhaktisiddhānta Sarasvatī Ṭhākura condemned such imitation. He said:

duṣṭa mana! tumi kisera vaiṣṇava?
pratiṣṭhāra tare, nirjanera ghare,
tava hari-nāma kevala kaitava.

"My dear mind, what kind of devotee are you? Simply for cheap adoration, you sit in a solitary place and pretend to chant the Hare Kṛṣṇa *mahā-mantra*, but this is all cheating." Recently at Māyāpur an African devotee wanted to imitate Haridāsa Ṭhākura, but after fifteen days he became restless and went away. Do not suddenly try to imitate Haridāsa Ṭhākura. Engage yourself in Kṛṣṇa conscious activities, and gradually you will come to the stage of liberation (*muktir hitvānyathā rūpaṁ svarūpeṇa vyavasthitiḥ*).

TEXT 15

ईहते भगवानीशो न हि तत्र विसज्जते ।
आत्मलाभेन पूर्णार्थो नावसीदन्ति येऽनु तम् ॥१५॥

īhate bhagavān īśo
na hi tatra visajjate
ātma-lābhena pūrṇārtho
nāvasīdanti ye 'nu tam

īhate—engages in activities of creation, maintenance and annihilation; *bhagavān*—the Supreme Personality of Godhead, Kṛṣṇa; *īśaḥ*—the supreme controller; *na*—not; *hi*—indeed; *tatra*—in such activities; *visajjate*—He becomes entangled; *ātma-lābhena*—because of His own gain; *pūrṇa-arthaḥ*—who is self-satisfied; *na*—not; *avasīdanti*—are disheartened; *ye*—persons who; *anu*—follow; *tam*—the Supreme Personality of Godhead.

TRANSLATION

The Supreme Personality of Godhead is full in opulence by His own gain, yet He acts as the creator, maintainer and annihilator of this material world. In spite of acting in that way, He is never entangled. Hence devotees who follow in His footsteps are also never entangled.

PURPORT

As stated in *Bhagavad-gītā* (3.9), *yajñārthāt karmaṇo 'nyatra loko 'yaṁ karma-bandhanaḥ:* "Work done as a sacrifice for Viṣṇu has to be performed, otherwise work binds one to this material world." If we do not act in Kṛṣṇa consciousness we shall be entangled, like silkworms in cocoons. The Supreme Personality of Godhead, Kṛṣṇa, appears in order to teach us how to work so that we will not be entangled in this material world. Our real problem is that we are entangled in materialistic activities, and because we are conditioned, our struggle continues through punishment in material existence in one body after another in different forms of life. As the Lord says in *Bhagavad-gītā* (15.7):

mamaivāṁśo jīva-loke
jīva-bhūtaḥ sanātanaḥ
manaḥ ṣaṣṭhānīndriyāṇi
prakṛti-sthāni karṣati

"The living entities in this conditioned world are My eternal, fragmental parts. Due to conditioned life, they are struggling very hard with the six senses, which include the mind." The living entities are actually minute forms who are part and parcel of the Supreme Lord. The Supreme Lord is full in everything, and the small particles of the Lord are also originally qualified like Him, but because of their minute existence, they are infected by material attraction and thus entangled. We must therefore follow the instructions of the Supreme Personality of Godhead, and then, like Kṛṣṇa, who is never entangled by His material activities of creation, maintenance and annihilation, we will have nothing for which to lament (*nāvasīdanti ye 'nu tam*). Kṛṣṇa personally gives instructions in *Bhagavad-gītā*, and anyone who follows these instructions is liberated.

Following Kṛṣṇa's instructions is possible when one is a devotee, for Kṛṣṇa instructs that one should become a devotee. *Man-manā bhava mad-bhakto mad-yājī māṁ namaskuru:* "Always think of Me and become My devotee. Worship Me and offer your homage unto Me." (Bg. 18.65) Always thinking of Kṛṣṇa means chanting the Hare Kṛṣṇa *mantra*, but unless one is an initiated devotee he cannot do this. As soon as one becomes a devotee, he engages in Deity worship (*mad-yājī*). A devotee's business is to offer obeisances to the Lord and the spiritual master constantly. This principle is the recognized way to come to the platform of *bhakti*. As soon as one comes to this platform, he gradually understands the Supreme Personality of Godhead, and simply by understanding Kṛṣṇa one is liberated from material bondage.

TEXT 16

तमीहमानं निरहङ्कृतं बुधं
निराशिषं पूर्णमनन्यचोदितम् ।
नॄञ् शिक्षयन्तं निजवर्त्मसंस्थितं
प्रभुं प्रपद्येऽखिलधर्मभावनम् ॥१६॥

tam īhamānaṁ nirahaṅkṛtaṁ budhaṁ
nirāśiṣaṁ pūrṇam ananya-coditam
nṝñ śikṣayantaṁ nija-vartma-saṁsthitaṁ
prabhuṁ prapadye 'khila-dharma-bhāvanam

tam—unto the same Supreme Personality of Godhead; *īhamānam*—who is acting for our benefit; *nirahaṅkṛtam*—who is without entanglement or desire for gain; *budham*—who is completely in knowledge; *nirāśiṣam*—without desires to enjoy the fruits of His activities; *pūrṇam*—who is full and therefore has no need to fulfill desires; *ananya*—by others; *coditam*—induced or inspired; *nṝn*—all of human society; *śikṣayantam*—to teach (the real path of life); *nija-vartma*—His own personal way of life; *saṁsthitam*—to establish (without deviation); *prabhum*—unto the Supreme Lord; *prapadye*—I request everyone to surrender; *akhila-dharma-bhāvanam*—who is the master of all religious principles or the occupational duties for a human being.

TRANSLATION

The Supreme Personality of Godhead, Kṛṣṇa, works just like an ordinary human being, yet He does not desire to enjoy the fruits of work. He is full in knowledge, free from material desires and diversions, and completely independent. As the supreme teacher of human society, He teaches His own way of activities, and thus He inaugurates the real path of religion. I request everyone to follow Him.

PURPORT

This is the sum and substance of our Kṛṣṇa consciousness movement. We are simply requesting human society to follow in the footsteps of the teacher of *Bhagavad-gītā*. Follow the instructions of *Bhagavad-gītā As It Is*, and your life will be successful. That is the summary of the Kṛṣṇa consciousness movement. The organizer of the Kṛṣṇa consciousness movement is teaching everyone how to follow Lord Rāmacandra, how to follow Lord Kṛṣṇa, and how to follow Śrī Caitanya Mahāprabhu. In this material world, we need a leader for a monarchy or good government. Lord Śrī Rāmacandra, by His practical example, showed how to live for the benefit of all human society. He fought with demons like Rāvaṇa, He carried out the orders of His father, and He remained the faithful husband of mother Sītā. Thus there is no comparison to Lord Rāmacandra's acting as an ideal king. Indeed, people still hanker for *rāma-rājya*, a government conducted like that of Lord Rāmacandra. Similarly, although Lord Kṛṣṇa is the Supreme Personality of Godhead, He taught His disciple and devotee Arjuna how to lead a life ending in going back home, back to Godhead (*tyaktvā dehaṁ punar janma naiti mām eti so 'rjuna*). All teachings—political, economic, social, religious, cultural and philosophical—are to be found in *Bhagavad-gītā*. One only has to follow them strictly. The Supreme Personality of Godhead also comes as Lord Caitanya just to play the part of a pure devotee. Thus the Lord teaches us in different ways just to make our lives successful, and Svāyambhuva Manu requests us to follow Him.

Svāyambhuva Manu is the leader of mankind, and he has given a book called *Manu-saṁhitā* to guide human society. Herein he directs us to follow the Supreme Personality of Godhead in His different incarnations. These incarnations are described in Vedic literature, and Jayadeva Gosvāmī has described ten important incarnations in summary (*keśava dhṛta-mīna-śarīra jaya jagad-īśa hare, keśava dhṛta-nara-hari-rūpa jaya jagad-īśa hare, keśava dhṛta-buddha-śarīra jaya jagad-īśa hare*, etc.). Svāyambhuva Manu instructs us to follow the instructions of God's incarnations, especially Kṛṣṇa's instructions of *Bhagavad-gītā As It Is*.

Appreciating *bhakti-mārga* as instructed by Śrī Caitanya Mahāprabhu, Sārvabhauma Bhaṭṭācārya thus depicted the activities of Śrī Caitanya Mahāprabhu:

vairāgya-vidyā-nija-bhakti-yoga-
śikṣārtham ekaḥ puruṣaḥ purāṇaḥ
śrī-kṛṣṇa-caitanya-śarīra-dhārī
kṛpāmbudhir yas tam ahaṁ prapadye

"Let me take shelter of the Supreme Personality of Godhead, Śrī Kṛṣṇa, who has descended in the form of Lord Caitanya Mahāprabhu to teach us real knowledge, His devotional service, and detachment from whatever does not foster Kṛṣṇa consciousness. He has descended because He is an ocean of transcendental mercy. Let me surrender unto His lotus feet." (*Caitanya-candrodaya-nāṭaka* 6.74) In this age of Kali, people cannot follow the instructions of the Supreme Personality of Godhead, and therefore the Lord Himself takes the part of Śrī Kṛṣṇa Caitanya to teach personally how to become Kṛṣṇa conscious. He asks everyone to follow Him and to become a *guru* to deliver the fallen souls of Kali-yuga.

yāre dekha, tāre kaha 'kṛṣṇa'-upadeśa
āmāra ājñāya guru hañā tāra' ei deśa

"Instruct everyone to follow the orders of Lord Śrī Kṛṣṇa as they are given in *Bhagavad-gītā* and *Śrīmad-Bhāgavatam.* In this way become a spiritual master and try to liberate everyone in this land." (Cc. *Madhya* 7.128) The coherent purpose of Lord Rāmacandra, Lord Kṛṣṇa and Lord Caitanya Mahāprabhu is to teach human society how to be happy by following the instructions of the Supreme Lord.

TEXT 17

श्रीशुक उवाच
इति मन्त्रोपनिषदं व्याहरन्तं समाहितम् ।
दृष्ट्वासुरा यातुधाना जग्धुमभ्यद्रवन् क्षुधा ॥१७॥

śrī-śuka uvāca
iti mantropaniṣadaṁ
vyāharantaṁ samāhitam
dṛṣṭvāsurā yātudhānā
jagdhum abhyadravan kṣudhā

śrī-śukaḥ uvāca—Śrī Śukadeva Gosvāmī said; *iti*—thus; *mantra-upaniṣadam*—the Vedic *mantra* (uttered by Svāyambhuva Manu); *vyāharantam*—taught or chanted; *samāhitam*—concentrated the mind (without being agitated by material conditions); *dṛṣṭvā*—upon seeing (him); *asurāḥ*—the demons; *yātudhānāḥ*—the Rākṣasas; *jagdhum*—desired to devour; *abhyadravan*—running very fast; *kṣudhā*—to satisfy their appetite.

TRANSLATION

Śukadeva Gosvāmī continued: Svāyambhuva Manu was thus in a trance, chanting the mantras of Vedic instruction known as the Upaniṣads. Upon seeing him, the Rākṣasas and asuras, being very hungry, wanted to devour him. Therefore they ran after him with great speed.

TEXT 18

तांस्तथावसितान् वीक्ष्य यज्ञः सर्वगतो हरिः ।
यामैः परिवृतो देवैर्हत्वाशासत् त्रिविष्टपम् ॥१८॥

tāṁs tathāvasitān vīkṣya
yajñaḥ sarva-gato hariḥ
yāmaiḥ parivṛto devair
hatvāśāsat tri-viṣṭapam

tān—the demons and Rākṣasas; *tathā*—in that way; *avasitān*—who were determined to devour Svāyambhuva Manu; *vīkṣya*—upon observing; *yajñaḥ*—Lord Viṣṇu, known as Yajña; *sarva-gataḥ*—who is seated in everyone's heart; *hariḥ*—the Supreme Personality of Godhead; *yāmaiḥ*—with His sons named the Yāmas; *parivṛtaḥ*—surrounded; *devaiḥ*—by the demigods; *hatvā*—after killing (the demons); *aśāsat*—ruled (taking the post of Indra); *tri-viṣṭapam*—the heavenly planets.

TRANSLATION

The Supreme Lord, Viṣṇu, who sits in everyone's heart, appearing as Yajñapati, observed that the Rākṣasas and demons were going to devour Svāyambhuva Manu. Thus the Lord, accompanied by His sons named the Yāmas and by all the other demigods, killed the demons and Rākṣasas. He then took the post of Indra and began to rule the heavenly kingdom.

PURPORT

The various names of the demigods—Lord Brahmā, Lord Śiva, Lord Indra and so on—are not personal names; they are names of different posts. In this regard, we understand that Lord Viṣṇu sometimes becomes Brahmā or Indra when there is no suitable person to occupy these posts.

TEXT 19

स्वारोचिषो द्वितीयस्तु मनुरग्नेः सुतोऽभवत् ।
द्युमत्सुषेणरोचिष्मत्प्रमुखास्तस्य चात्मजाः ॥१९॥

svārociṣo dvitīyas tu
manur agneḥ suto 'bhavat
dyumat-suṣeṇa-rociṣmat
pramukhās tasya cātmajāḥ

svārociṣaḥ—Svārociṣa; *dvitīyaḥ*—the second; *tu*—indeed; *manuḥ*—Manu; *agneḥ*—of Agni; *sutaḥ*—the son; *abhavat*—became; *dyumat*—Dyumat; *suṣeṇa*—Suṣeṇa; *rociṣmat*—Rociṣmat; *pramukhāḥ*—beginning with them; *tasya*—of him (Svārociṣa); *ca*—also; *ātma-jāḥ*—sons.

TRANSLATION

The son of Agni named Svārociṣa became the second Manu. His several sons were headed by Dyumat, Suṣeṇa and Rociṣmat.

PURPORT

manvantaraṁ manur devā
manu-putrāḥ sureśvaraḥ
ṛṣayo 'ṁśāvatāraś ca
hareḥ ṣaḍ vidham ucyate

There are many incarnations of the Supreme Personality of Godhead. Manu, the *manu-putrāḥ* (the sons of Manu), the king of the heavenly planets, and the seven great sages are all partial incarnations of the Supreme Lord. Manu himself, his sons Priyavrata and Uttānapāda, the demigods created by Dakṣa, and the *ṛṣis* like Marīci were all partial incarnations of the Lord during the reign of Svāyambhuva Manu. During that time, the incarnation of the Lord as Yajña took charge of ruling the heavenly planets. The next Manu was Svārociṣa. The Manus and the sages and demigods are further described in the following eleven verses.

TEXT 20

तत्रेन्द्रो रोचनस्त्वासीद् देवाश्च तुषितादयः ।
ऊर्जस्तम्भादयः सप्त ऋषयो ब्रह्मवादिनः ॥२०॥

tatrendro rocanas tv āsīd
devāś ca tuṣitādayaḥ
ūrja-stambhādayaḥ sapta
ṛṣayo brahma-vādinaḥ

tatra—in this *manvantara; indraḥ*—Indra; *rocanaḥ*—Rocana, the son of Yajña; *tu*—but; *āsīt*—became; *devāḥ*—demigods; *ca*—also; *tuṣita-ādayaḥ*—Tuṣita and others; *ūrja*—Ūrja; *stambha*—Stambha; *ādayaḥ*—and others; *sapta*—seven; *ṛṣayaḥ*—great saints; *brahma-vādinaḥ*—all faithful devotees.

TRANSLATION

During the reign of Svārociṣa, the post of Indra was assumed by Rocana, the son of Yajña. Tuṣita and others became the principal demigods, and Ūrja, Stambha and others became the seven saints. All of them were faithful devotees of the Lord.

TEXT 21

ऋषेस्तु वेदशिरसस्तुषिता नाम पत्न्यभूत् ।
तस्यां जज्ञे ततो देवो विभुरित्यभिविश्रुतः ॥२१॥

ṛṣes tu vedaśirasas
tuṣitā nāma patny abhūt
tasyāṁ jajñe tato devo
vibhur ity abhiviśrutaḥ

ṛṣeḥ—of the saintly person; *tu*—indeed; *vedaśirasaḥ*—Vedaśirā; *tuṣitā*—Tuṣitā; *nāma*—named; *patnī*—the wife; *abhūt*—begat; *tasyām*—in her (womb); *jajñe*—took birth; *tataḥ*—thereafter; *devaḥ*—the Lord; *vibhuḥ*—Vibhu; *iti*—thus; *abhiviśrutaḥ*—celebrated as.

TRANSLATION

Vedaśirā was a very celebrated ṛṣi. From the womb of his wife, whose name was Tuṣitā, came the avatāra named Vibhu.

TEXT 22

अष्टाशीतिसहस्राणि मुनयो ये धृतव्रताः ।
अन्वशिक्षन्व्रतं तस्य कौमारब्रह्मचारिणः ॥२२॥

aṣṭāśīti-sahasrāṇi
munayo ye dhṛta-vratāḥ
anvaśikṣan vrataṁ tasya
kaumāra-brahmacāriṇaḥ

aṣṭāśīti—eighty-eight; *sahasrāṇi*—thousand; *munayaḥ*—great saintly persons; *ye*—those who; *dhṛta-vratāḥ*—fixed in vows; *anvaśikṣan*—took instructions; *vratam*—vows; *tasya*—from him (Vibhu); *kaumāra*—who was unmarried; *brahmacāriṇaḥ*—and fixed in the *brahmacārī* stage of life.

TRANSLATION

Vibhu remained a brahmacārī and never married throughout his life. From him, eighty-eight thousand other saintly persons took lessons on self-control, austerity and similar behavior.

TEXT 23

तृतीय उत्तमो नाम प्रियव्रतसुतो मनुः ।
पवनः सृञ्जयो यज्ञहोत्राद्यास्तत्सुता नृप ॥२३॥

tṛtīya uttamo nāma
priyavrata-suto manuḥ

pavanaḥ sṛñjayo yajña-
hotrādyās tat-sutā nṛpa

tṛtīyaḥ—the third; *uttamaḥ*—Uttama; *nāma*—named; *priyavrata*—of King Priyavrata; *sutaḥ*—the son; *manuḥ*—he became the Manu; *pavanaḥ*—Pavana; *sṛñjayaḥ*—Sṛñjaya; *yajñahotra-ādyāḥ*—Yajñahotra and others; *tat-sutāḥ*—the sons of Uttama; *nṛpa*—O King.

TRANSLATION

O King, the third Manu, Uttama, was the son of King Priyavrata. Among the sons of this Manu were Pavana, Sṛñjaya and Yajñahotra.

TEXT 24

वसिष्ठतनयाः सप्त ऋषयः प्रमदादयः ।
सत्या वेदश्रुता भद्रा देवा इन्द्रस्तु सत्यजित् ॥२४॥

vasiṣṭha-tanayāḥ sapta
ṛṣayaḥ pramadādayaḥ
satyā vedaśrutā bhadrā
devā indras tu satyajit

vasiṣṭha-tanayāḥ—the sons of Vasiṣṭha; *sapta*—seven; *ṛṣayaḥ*—the sages; *pramada-ādayaḥ*—headed by Pramada; *satyāḥ*—the Satyas; *vedaśrutāḥ*—Vedaśrutas; *bhadrāḥ*—Bhadras; *devāḥ*—demigods; *indraḥ*—the King of heaven; *tu*—but; *satyajit*—Satyajit.

TRANSLATION

During the reign of the third Manu, Pramada and other sons of Vasiṣṭha became the seven sages. The Satyas, Vedaśrutas and Bhadras became demigods, and Satyajit was selected to be Indra, the King of heaven.

TEXT 25

धर्मस्य सूनृतायां तु भगवान्पुरुषोत्तमः ।
सत्यसेन इति ख्यातो जातः सत्यव्रतैः सह ॥२५॥

dharmasya sūnṛtāyāṁ tu
bhagavān puruṣottamaḥ
satyasena iti khyāto
jātaḥ satyavrataiḥ saha

dharmasya—of the demigod in charge of religion; *sūnṛtāyām*—in the womb of his wife named Sūnṛtā; *tu*—indeed; *bhagavān*—the Supreme Personality of Godhead; *puruṣa-uttamaḥ*—the Supreme Personality of Godhead; *satyasenaḥ*—Satyasena; *iti*—thus; *khyātaḥ*—celebrated; *jātaḥ*—took birth; *satyavrataiḥ*—the Satyavratas; *saha*—with.

TRANSLATION

In this manvantara, the Supreme Personality of Godhead appeared from the womb of Sūnṛtā, who was the wife of Dharma, the demigod in charge of religion. The Lord was celebrated as Satyasena, and He appeared with other demigods, known as the Satyavratas.

TEXT 26

सोऽनृतव्रतदुःशीलानसतो यक्षराक्षसान् ।
भूतद्रुहो भूतगणांश्चावधीत् सत्यजित्सखः ॥२६॥

so 'nṛta-vrata-duḥśīlān
asato yakṣa-rākṣasān
bhūta-druho bhūta-gaṇāṁś
cāvadhīt satyajit-sakhaḥ

saḥ—He (Satyasena); *anṛta-vrata*—who are fond of speaking lies; *duḥśīlān*—misbehaved; *asataḥ*—miscreant; *yakṣa-rākṣasān*—Yakṣas and Rākṣasas; *bhūta-druhaḥ*—who are always against the progress of other living beings; *bhūta-gaṇān*—the ghostly living entities; *ca*—also; *avadhīt*—killed; *satyajit-sakhaḥ*—with His friend Satyajit.

TRANSLATION

Satyasena, along with His friend Satyajit, who was the King of heaven, Indra, killed all the untruthful, impious and misbehaved

Yakṣas, Rākṣasas and ghostly living entities, who gave pains to other living beings.

TEXT 27

चतुर्थ उत्तमभ्राता मनुर्नाम्ना च तामसः ।
पृथुः ख्यातिर्नरः केतुरित्याद्या दश तत्सुताः ॥२७॥

caturtha uttama-bhrātā
manur nāmnā ca tāmasaḥ
pṛthuḥ khyātir naraḥ ketur
ity ādyā daśa tat-sutāḥ

caturtha—the fourth Manu; *uttama-bhrātā*—the brother of Uttama; *manuḥ*—became the Manu; *nāmnā*—celebrated by the name; *ca*—also; *tāmasaḥ*—Tāmasa; *pṛthuḥ*—Pṛthu; *khyātiḥ*—Khyāti; *naraḥ*—Nara; *ketuḥ*—Ketu; *iti*—thus; *ādyāḥ*—headed by; *daśa*—ten; *tat-sutāḥ*—sons of Tāmasa Manu.

TRANSLATION

The brother of the third Manu, Uttama, was celebrated by the name Tāmasa, and he became the fourth Manu. Tāmasa had ten sons, headed by Pṛthu, Khyāti, Nara and Ketu.

TEXT 28

सत्यका हरयो वीरा देवास्त्रिशिख ईश्वरः ।
ज्योतिर्धामादयः सप्त ऋषयस्तामसेऽन्तरे ॥२८॥

satyakā harayo vīrā
devās triśikha īśvaraḥ
jyotirdhāmādayaḥ sapta
ṛṣayas tāmase 'ntare

satyakāḥ—the Satyakas; *harayaḥ*—the Haris; *vīrāḥ*—the Vīras; *devāḥ*—the demigods; *triśikhaḥ*—Triśikha; *īśvaraḥ*—the King of heaven; *jyotirdhāma-ādayaḥ*—headed by the celebrated Jyotirdhāma; *sapta*—seven; *ṛṣayaḥ*—sages; *tāmase*—the reign of Tāmasa Manu; *antare*—within.

TRANSLATION

During the reign of Tāmasa Manu, among the demigods were the Satyakas, Haris and Vīras. The heavenly King, Indra, was Triśikha. The sages in saptarṣi-dhāma were headed by Jyotirdhāma.

TEXT 29

देवा वैधृतयो नाम विधृतेस्तनया नृप ।
नष्टाः कालेन यैर्वेदा विधृताः स्वेन तेजसा ॥२९॥

devā vaidhṛtayo nāma
vidhṛtes tanayā nṛpa
naṣṭāḥ kālena yair vedā
vidhṛtāḥ svena tejasā

devāḥ—the demigods; *vaidhṛtayaḥ*—the Vaidhṛtis; *nāma*—by the name; *vidhṛteḥ*—of Vidhṛti; *tanayāḥ*—who were the sons; *nṛpa*—O King; *naṣṭāḥ*—were lost; *kālena*—by the influence of time; *yaiḥ*—by whom; *vedāḥ*—the *Vedas; vidhṛtāḥ*—were protected; *svena*—by their own; *tejasā*—power.

TRANSLATION

O King, in the Tāmasa manvantara the sons of Vidhṛti, who were known as the Vaidhṛtis, also became demigods. Since in course of time the Vedic authority was lost, these demigods, by their own powers, protected the Vedic authority.

PURPORT

In the Tāmasa *manvantara* there were two kinds of demigods, and one of them was known as the Vaidhṛtis. The duty of the demigods is to protect the authority of the *Vedas.* The word *devatā* refers to one who carries the authority of the *Vedas,* whereas Rākṣasas are those who defy the Vedic authority. If the authority of the *Vedas* is lost, the entire universe becomes chaotic. Therefore, it is the duty of the demigods, as well as kings and aides of governments, to give full protection to the Vedic authority; otherwise human society will be in a chaotic condition in which there cannot be peace or prosperity.

TEXT 30

तत्रापि जज्ञे भगवान्हरिण्यां हरिमेधसः ।
हरिरित्याहृतो येन गजेन्द्रो मोचितो ग्रहात् ॥३०॥

tatrāpi jajñe bhagavān
hariṇyāṁ harimedhasaḥ
harir ity āhṛto yena
gajendro mocito grahāt

tatrāpi—in that period; *jajñe*—appeared; *bhagavān*—the Supreme Personality of Godhead; *hariṇyām*—in the womb of Hariṇī; *harimedhasaḥ*—begotten by Harimedhā; *hariḥ*—Hari; *iti*—thus; *āhṛtaḥ*—called; *yena*—by whom; *gaja-indraḥ*—the King of the elephants; *mocitaḥ*—was freed; *grahāt*—from the mouth of a crocodile.

TRANSLATION

Also in this manvantara, the Supreme Lord, Viṣṇu, took birth from the womb of Hariṇī, the wife of Harimedhā, and He was known as Hari. Hari saved His devotee Gajendra, the King of the elephants, from the mouth of a crocodile.

TEXT 31

श्रीराजोवाच
बादरायण एतत् ते श्रोतुमिच्छामहे वयम् ।
हरिर्यथा गजपतिं ग्राहग्रस्तममूमुचत् ॥३१॥

śrī-rājovāca
bādarāyaṇa etat te
śrotum icchāmahe vayam
harir yathā gaja-patiṁ
grāha-grastam amūmucat

śrī-rājā uvāca—King Parīkṣit said; *bādarāyaṇe*—O son of Bādarāyaṇa (Vyāsadeva); *etat*—this; *te*—from you; *śrotum icchāmahe*—desire to hear; *vayam*—we; *hariḥ*—the Lord Hari; *yathā*—the manner in which; *gaja-patim*—the King of the elephants; *grāha-grastam*—when attacked by the crocodile; *amūmucat*—delivered.

TRANSLATION

King Parīkṣit said: My lord, Bādarāyaṇi, we wish to hear from you in detail how the King of the elephants, when attacked by a crocodile, was delivered by Hari.

TEXT 32

तत्कथासु महत् पुण्यं धन्यं स्वस्त्ययनं शुभम् ।
यत्र यत्रोत्तमश्लोको भगवान्गीयते हरिः ॥३२॥

tat-kathāsu mahat puṇyaṁ
dhanyaṁ svastyayanaṁ śubham
yatra yatrottamaśloko
bhagavān gīyate hariḥ

tat-kathāsu—in those narrations; *mahat*—great; *puṇyam*—pious; *dhanyam*—glorious; *svastyayanam*—auspicious; *śubham*—all good; *yatra*—whenever; *yatra*—wherever; *uttamaślokaḥ*—the Lord, who is known as Uttamaśloka (He who is described by transcendental literature); *bhagavān*—the Supreme Personality of Godhead; *gīyate*—is glorified; *hariḥ*—the Supreme Personality of Godhead.

TRANSLATION

Any literature or narration in which the Supreme Personality of Godhead, Uttamaśloka, is described and glorified is certainly great, pure, glorious, auspicious and all good.

PURPORT

The Kṛṣṇa consciousness movement is spreading all over the world simply by describing Kṛṣṇa. We have published many books, including *Śrī Caitanya-caritāmṛta* in seventeen volumes, four hundred pages each, as well as *Bhagavad-gītā* and *The Nectar of Devotion.* We are also publishing *Śrīmad-Bhāgavatam* in sixty volumes. Wherever a speaker holds discourses from these books and an audience hears him, this will create a good and auspicious situation. Therefore the preaching of Kṛṣṇa consciousness must be done very carefully by the members of the Kṛṣṇa consciousness movement, especially the *sannyāsīs*. This will create an auspicious atmosphere.

TEXT 33

श्रीसूत उवाच
परीक्षितैवं स तु बादरायणिः
प्रायोपविष्टेन कथासु चोदितः ।
उवाच विप्राः प्रतिनन्द्य पार्थिवं
मुदा मुनीनां सदसि स्म शृण्वताम् ॥३३॥

śrī-sūta uvāca
parīkṣitaivaṁ sa tu bādarāyaṇiḥ
prāyopaviṣṭena kathāsu coditaḥ
uvāca viprāḥ pratinandya pārthivaṁ
mudā munīnāṁ sadasi sma śṛṇvatām

śrī-sūtaḥ uvāca—Śrī Sūta Gosvāmī said; *parīkṣitā*—by Mahārāja Parīkṣit; *evam*—thus; *saḥ*—he; *tu*—indeed; *bādarāyaṇiḥ*—Śukadeva Gosvāmī; *prāya-upaviṣṭena*—Parīkṣit Mahārāja, who was awaiting impending death; *kathāsu*—by the words; *coditaḥ*—being encouraged; *uvāca*—spoke; *viprāḥ*—O *brāhmaṇas; pratinandya*—after congratulating; *pārthivam*—Mahārāja Parīkṣit; *mudā*—with great pleasure; *munīnām*—of great sages; *sadasi*—in the assembly; *sma*—indeed; *śṛṇvatām*—who desired to hear.

TRANSLATION

Śrī Sūta Gosvāmī said: O brāhmaṇas, when Parīkṣit Mahārāja, who was awaiting impending death, thus requested Śukadeva Gosvāmī to speak, Śukadeva Gosvāmī, encouraged by the King's words, offered respect to the King and spoke with great pleasure in the assembly of sages, who desired to hear him.

Thus end the Bhaktivedanta purports of the Eighth Canto, First Chapter, of the Śrīmad-Bhāgavatam, *entitled "The Manus, Administrators of the Universe."*

CHAPTER TWO

The Elephant Gajendra's Crisis

The Second, Third and Fourth Chapters of this canto describe how the Lord, during the reign of the fourth Manu, gave protection to the King of the elephants. As described in this Second Chapter, when the King of the elephants, along with his female elephants, was enjoying in the water, a crocodile suddenly attacked him, and the elephant surrendered to the lotus feet of the Personality of Godhead for protection.

In the midst of the ocean of milk, there is a very high and beautiful mountain that has an altitude of ten thousand *yojanas*, or eighty thousand miles. This mountain is known as Trikūṭa. In a valley of Trikūṭa there is a nice garden named Ṛtumat, which was constructed by Varuṇa, and in that area there is a very nice lake. Once the chief of the elephants, along with female elephants, went to enjoy bathing in that lake, and they disturbed the inhabitants of the water. Because of this, the chief crocodile in that water, who was very powerful, immediately attacked the elephant's leg. Thus there ensued a great fight between the elephant and the crocodile. This fight continued for one thousand years. Neither the elephant nor the crocodile died, but since they were in the water, the elephant gradually became weak whereas the power of the crocodile increased more and more. Thus the crocodile became more and more encouraged. Then the elephant, being helpless and seeing that there was no other way for his protection, sought shelter at the lotus feet of the Supreme Personality of Godhead.

TEXT 1

श्रीशुक उवाच

आसीद् गिरिवरो राजंस्त्रिकूट इति विश्रुतः ।
क्षीरोदेनावृतः श्रीमान्योजनायुतमुच्छ्रितः ॥ १ ॥

śrī-śuka uvāca
āsīd girivaro rājaṁs
trikūṭa iti viśrutaḥ

kṣīrodenāvṛtaḥ śrīmān
yojanāyutam ucchritaḥ

śrī-śukaḥ uvāca—Śrī Śukadeva Gosvāmī said; *āsīt*—there was; *giri-varaḥ*—a very big mountain; *rājan*—O King; *tri-kūṭaḥ*—Trikūṭa; *iti*—thus; *viśrutaḥ*—celebrated; *kṣīra-udena*—by the ocean of milk; *āvṛtaḥ*—surrounded; *śrīmān*—very beautiful; *yojana*—a measurement of eight miles; *ayutam*—ten thousand; *ucchritaḥ*—very high.

TRANSLATION

Śukadeva Gosvāmī said: My dear King, there is a very large mountain called Trikūṭa. It is ten thousand yojanas [eighty thousand miles] high. Being surrounded by the ocean of milk, it is very beautifully situated.

TEXTS 2–3

तावता विस्तृतः पर्यक् त्रिभिः शृङ्गैः पयोनिधिम् ।
दिशः खं रोचयन्नास्ते रौप्यायसहिरण्मयैः ॥ २ ॥
अन्यैश्च ककुभः सर्वा रत्नधातुविचित्रितैः ।
नानाद्रुमलतागुल्मैर्निर्घोषैर्निर्झराम्भसाम् ॥ ३ ॥

tāvatā vistṛtaḥ paryak
tribhiḥ śṛṅgaiḥ payo-nidhim
diśaḥ khaṁ rocayann āste
raupyāyasa-hiraṇmayaiḥ

anyaiś ca kakubhaḥ sarvā
ratna-dhātu-vicitritaiḥ
nānā-druma-latā-gulmair
nirghoṣair nirjharāmbhasām

tāvatā—in that way; *vistṛtaḥ*—length and breadth (eighty thousand miles); *paryak*—all around; *tribhiḥ*—with three; *śṛṅgaiḥ*—peaks; *payaḥ-nidhim*—situated on an island in the ocean of milk; *diśaḥ*—all directions; *kham*—the sky; *rocayan*—pleasing; *āste*—standing; *raupya*—made of silver; *ayasa*—iron; *hiraṇmayaiḥ*—and gold; *anyaiḥ*—with other peaks; *ca*—also; *kakubhaḥ*—directions; *sarvāḥ*—all; *ratna*—with jewels; *dhātu*—and minerals; *vicitritaiḥ*—decorated very nicely; *nānā*—with various; *druma-latā*—trees and creepers; *gulmaiḥ*—and shrubs; *nirghoṣaiḥ*—with the sounds of; *nirjhara*—waterfalls; *ambhasām*—of water.

TRANSLATION

The length and breadth of the mountain are of the same measurement [eighty thousand miles]. Its three principal peaks, which are made of iron, silver and gold, beautify all directions and the sky. The mountain also has other peaks, which are full of jewels and minerals and are decorated with nice trees, creepers and shrubs. The sounds of the waterfalls on the mountain create a pleasing vibration. In this way the mountain stands, increasing the beauty of all directions.

TEXT 4

स चावनिज्यमानाङ्घ्रिः समन्तात् पयऊर्मिभिः ।
करोति श्यामलां भूमिं हरिन्मरकताश्मभिः ॥ ४ ॥

sa cāvanijyamānāṅghriḥ
samantāt paya-ūrmibhiḥ
karoti śyāmalāṁ bhūmiṁ
harin-marakatāśmabhiḥ

saḥ—that mountain; *ca*—also; *avanijyamāna-aṅghriḥ*—whose foot is always washed; *samantāt*—all around; *payaḥ-ūrmibhiḥ*—by waves of milk; *karoti*—makes; *śyāmalām*—dark green; *bhūmim*—ground; *harit*—green; *marakata*—with emerald; *aśmabhiḥ*—stones.

TRANSLATION

The ground at the foot of the mountain is always washed by waves of milk that produce emeralds all around in the eight direc-

tions [north, south, east, west and the directions midway between them].

PURPORT

From *Śrīmad-Bhāgavatam* we understand that there are various oceans. Somewhere there is an ocean filled with milk, somewhere an ocean of liquor, an ocean of ghee, an ocean of oil, and an ocean of sweet water. Thus there are different varieties of oceans within this universe. The modern scientists, who have only limited experience, cannot defy these statements; they cannot give us full information about any planet, even the planet on which we live. From this verse, however, we can understand that if the valleys of some mountains are washed with milk, this produces emeralds. No one has the ability to imitate the activities of material nature as conducted by the Supreme Personality of Godhead.

TEXT 5

सिद्धचारणगन्धर्वैर्विद्याधरमहोरगैः ।
किन्नरैरप्सरोभिश्च क्रीडद्भिर्जुष्टकन्दरः ॥ ५ ॥

siddha-cāraṇa-gandharvair
vidyādhara-mahoragaiḥ
kinnarair apsarobhiś ca
krīḍadbhir juṣṭa-kandaraḥ

siddha—by the inhabitants of Siddhaloka; *cāraṇa*—the inhabitants of Cāraṇaloka; *gandharvaiḥ*—the inhabitants of Gandharvaloka; *vidyādhara*—the inhabitants of Vidyādhara-loka; *mahā-uragaiḥ*—the inhabitants of the serpent *loka; kinnaraiḥ*—the Kinnaras; *apsarobhiḥ*—the Apsarās; *ca*—and; *krīḍadbhiḥ*—who were engaged in sporting; *juṣṭa*—enjoyed; *kandaraḥ*—the caves.

TRANSLATION

The inhabitants of the higher planets—the Siddhas, Cāraṇas, Gandharvas, Vidyādharas, serpents, Kinnaras and Apsarās—go to that mountain to sport. Thus all the caves of the mountain are full of these denizens of the heavenly planets.

PURPORT

As ordinary men may play in the salty ocean, the inhabitants of the higher planetary systems go to the ocean of milk. They float in the ocean of milk and also enjoy various sports within the caves of Trikūṭa Mountain.

TEXT 6

यत्र संगीतसन्नादैर्नदद्गुहममर्षया ।
अभिगर्जन्ति हरयः श्लाघिनः परशङ्कया ॥ ६ ॥

yatra saṅgīta-sannādair
nadad-guham amarṣayā
abhigarjanti harayaḥ
ślāghinaḥ para-śaṅkayā

yatra—in that mountain (Trikūṭa); *saṅgīta*—of singing; *sannādaiḥ*—with the vibrations; *nadat*—resounding; *guham*—the caves; *amarṣayā*—because of unbearable anger or envy; *abhigarjanti*—roar; *harayaḥ*—the lions; *ślāghinaḥ*—being very proud of their strength; *para-śaṅkayā*—because of suspecting another lion.

TRANSLATION

Because of the resounding vibrations of the denizens of heaven singing in the caves, the lions there, being very proud of their strength, roar with unbearable envy, thinking that another lion is roaring in that way.

PURPORT

In the higher planetary systems, there are not only different types of human beings, but also animals like lions and elephants. There are trees, and the land is made of emeralds. Such is the creation of the Supreme Personality of Godhead. Śrīla Bhaktivinoda Ṭhākura has sung in this regard, *keśava! tuyā jagata vicitra:* "My Lord Keśava, Your creation is colorful and full of varieties." Geologists, botanists and other so-called scientists speculate about other planetary systems, but being unable to estimate the varieties on other planets, they falsely imagine that all planets but this one are vacant, uninhabited, and full of dust. Although they cannot even estimate the varieties existing throughout the universe, they are very proud of their knowledge, and they are accepted as learned by persons of a similar caliber. As described in *Śrīmad-Bhāgavatam* (2.3.19), *śva-viḍ-varāhoṣṭra-kharaiḥ saṁstutaḥ puruṣaḥ paśuḥ:* materialistic leaders are praised by dogs, hogs, camels and asses, and they themselves are also big animals. One should not be satisfied with the knowledge imparted by a big animal. Rather, one must take knowledge from a perfect person like Śukadeva Gosvāmī. *Mahājano yena gataḥ sa panthāḥ:* our duty is to follow the instructions of the *mahājanas.* There are twelve *mahājanas,* and Śukadeva Gosvāmī is one of them.

svayambhūr nāradaḥ śambhuḥ
kumāraḥ kapilo manuḥ
prahlādo janako bhīṣmo
balir vaiyāsakir vayam
(*Bhāg.* 6.3.20)

Vaiyāsaki is Śukadeva Gosvāmī. Whatever he says we consider to be factual. That is perfect knowledge.

TEXT 7

नानारण्यपशुव्रातसङ्कुलद्रोण्यलङ्कृतः ।
चित्रद्रुमसुरोद्यानकलकण्ठविहङ्गमः ॥ ७ ॥

nānāraṇya-paśu-vrāta-
saṅkula-droṇy-alaṅkṛtaḥ
citra-druma-surodyāna-
kalakaṇṭha-vihaṅgamaḥ

nānā—with varieties of; *araṇya-paśu*—jungle animals; *vrāta*—with a multitude; *saṅkula*—filled; *droṇi*—with valleys; *alaṅkṛtaḥ*—very beautifully decorated; *citra*—with varieties of; *druma*—trees; *sura-udyāna*—in gardens maintained by the demigods; *kalakaṇṭha*—sweetly chirping; *vihaṅgamaḥ*—birds.

TRANSLATION

The valleys beneath Trikūṭa Mountain are beautifully decorated by many varieties of jungle animals, and in the trees, which are maintained in gardens by the demigods, varieties of birds chirp with sweet voices.

TEXT 8

सरित्सरोभिरच्छोदैः पुलिनैर्मणिवालुकैः ।
देवस्त्रीमज्जनामोदसौरभाम्ब्वनिलैर्युतः ॥ ८ ॥

sarit-sarobhir acchodaiḥ
pulinair maṇi-vālukaiḥ
deva-strī-majjanāmoda-
saurabhāmbv-anilair yutaḥ

sarit—with rivers; *sarobhiḥ*—and lakes; *acchodaiḥ*—filled with crystal-clear water; *pulinaiḥ*—beaches; *maṇi*—with small gems; *vālukaiḥ*—resembling grains of sand; *deva-strī*—of the damsels of the demigods; *majjana*—by bathing (in that water); *āmoda*—bodily fragrance; *saurabha*—very fragrant; *ambu*—with the water; *anilaiḥ*—and the air; *yutaḥ*—enriched (the atmosphere of Trikūṭa Mountain).

TRANSLATION

Trikūṭa Mountain has many lakes and rivers, with beaches covered by small gems resembling grains of sand. The water is as clear as crystal, and when the demigod damsels bathe in it, their bodies lend fragrance to the water and the breeze, thus enriching the atmosphere.

PURPORT

Even in the material world, there are many grades of living entities. The human beings on earth generally cover themselves with external fragrances to stop their bad bodily odors, but here we find that because of the bodily fragrance of the demigod damsels, the rivers, the lakes, the breeze and the entire atmosphere of Trikūṭa Mountain also become fragrant. Since the bodies of the damsels in the upper planetary systems are so beautiful, we can just imagine how beautifully formed are the bodies of the Vaikuṇṭha damsels or the damsels in Vṛndāvana, the *gopīs*.

TEXTS 9–13

तस्य द्रोण्यां भगवतो वरुणस्य महात्मनः ।
उद्यानमृतुमन्नाम आक्रीडं सुरयोषिताम् ॥ ९ ॥
सर्वतोऽलङ्कृतं दिव्यैर्नित्यपुष्पफलद्रुमैः ।
मन्दारैः पारिजातैश्च पाटलाशोकचम्पकैः ॥१०॥
चूतैः पियालैः पनसैराम्रैराम्रातकैरपि ।
क्रमुकैर्नारिकेलैश्च खर्जूरैर्बीजपूरकैः ॥११॥
मधुकैः शालतालैश्च तमालैरसनार्जुनैः ।
अरिष्टोडुम्बरप्लक्षैर्वटैः किंशुकचन्दनैः ॥१२॥
पिचुमर्दैः कोविदारैः सरलैः सुरदारुभिः ।
द्राक्षेक्षुरम्भाजम्बुभिर्बदर्यक्षाभयामलैः ॥१३॥

tasya droṇyāṁ bhagavato
varuṇasya mahātmanaḥ
udyānam ṛtuman nāma
ākrīḍaṁ sura-yoṣitām

sarvato 'laṅkṛtaṁ divyair
nitya-puṣpa-phala-drumaiḥ
mandāraiḥ pārijātaiś ca
pāṭalāśoka-campakaiḥ

cūtaiḥ piyālaiḥ panasair
āmrair āmrātakair api
kramukair nārikelaiś ca
kharjūrair bījapūrakaiḥ

madhukaiḥ śāla-tālaiś ca
tamālair asanārjunaiḥ

ariṣṭoḍumbara-plakṣair
vaṭaiḥ kiṁśuka-candanaiḥ

picumardaiḥ kovidāraiḥ
saralaiḥ sura-dārubhiḥ
drākṣekṣu-rambhā-jambubhir
badary-akṣābhayāmalaiḥ

tasya—of that mountain (Trikūṭa); *droṇyām*—in a valley; *bhagavataḥ*—of the great personality; *varuṇasya*—the demigod Varuṇa; *mahā-ātmanaḥ*—who is a great devotee of the Lord; *udyānam*—a garden; *ṛtumat*—Ṛtumat; *nāma*—of the name; *ākrīḍam*—a place of sporting pastimes; *sura-yoṣitām*—of the damsels of the demigods; *sarvataḥ*—everywhere; *alaṅkṛtam*—beautifully decorated; *divyaiḥ*—pertaining to the demigods; *nitya*—always; *puṣpa*—of flowers; *phala*—and fruits; *drumaiḥ*—by trees; *mandāraiḥ*—*mandāra; pārijātaiḥ*—*pārijāta; ca*—also; *pāṭala*—*pāṭala; aśoka*—*aśoka; campakaiḥ*—*campaka; cūtaiḥ*—*cūta* fruits; *piyālaiḥ*—*piyāla* fruits; *panasaiḥ*—*panasa* fruits; *āmraiḥ*—mangoes; *āmrātakaiḥ*—sour fruits called *āmrātaka; api*—also; *kramukaiḥ*—*kramuka* fruits; *nārikelaiḥ*—coconut trees; *ca*—and; *kharjūraiḥ*—date trees; *bījapūrakaiḥ*—pomegranates; *madhukaiḥ*—*madhuka* fruits; *śāla-tālaiḥ*—palm fruits; *ca*—and; *tamālaiḥ*—*tamāla* trees; *asana*—*asana* trees; *arjunaiḥ*—*arjuna* trees; *ariṣṭa*—*ariṣṭa* fruits; *uḍumbara*—big *uḍumbara* trees; *plakṣaiḥ*—*plakṣa* trees; *vaṭaiḥ*—banyan trees; *kiṁśuka*—red flowers with no scent; *candanaiḥ*—sandalwood trees; *picumardaiḥ*—*picumarda* flowers; *kovidāraiḥ*—*kovidāra* fruits; *saralaiḥ*—*sarala* trees; *sura-dārubhiḥ*—*sura-dāru* trees; *drākṣā*—grapes; *ikṣuḥ*—sugarcane; *rambhā*—bananas; *jambubhiḥ*—*jambu* fruits; *badarī*—*badarī* fruits; *akṣa*—*akṣa* fruits; *abhaya*—*abhaya* fruits; *āmalaiḥ*—*āmalakī*, a sour fruit.

TRANSLATION

In a valley of Trikūṭa Mountain there was a garden called Ṛtumat. This garden belonged to the great devotee Varuṇa and was a sporting place for the damsels of the demigods. Flowers and fruits grew there in all seasons. Among them were mandāras,

pārijātas, pāṭalas, aśokas, campakas, cūtas, piyālas, panasas, mangoes, āmrātakas, kramukas, coconut trees, date trees and pomegranates. There were madhukas, palm trees, tamālas, asanas, arjunas, ariṣṭas, uḍumbaras, plakṣas, banyan trees, kiṁśukas and sandalwood trees. There were also picumardas, kovidāras, saralas, sura-dārus, grapes, sugarcane, bananas, jambu, badarīs, akṣas, abhayas and āmalakīs.

TEXTS 14–19

बिल्वैः कपित्थैर्जम्बीरैर्वृतो भल्लातकादिभिः ।
तस्मिन्सरः सुविपुलं लसत्काञ्चनपङ्कजम् ॥१४॥
कुमुदोत्पलकह्लारशतपत्रश्रियोर्जितम् ।
मत्तषट्पदनिर्घुष्टं शकुन्तैश्च कलस्वनैः ॥१५॥
हंसकारण्डवाकीर्णं चक्राह्वैः सारसैरपि ।
जलकुक्कुटकोयष्टिदात्यूहकुलकूजितम् ॥१६॥
मत्स्यकच्छपसञ्चारचलत्पद्मरजःपयः ।
कदम्बवेतसनलनीपवञ्जुलकैर्वृतम् ॥१७॥
कुन्दैः कुरुबकाशोकैः शिरीषैः कूटजेङ्गुदैः ।
कुब्जकैः स्वर्णयूथीभिर्नागपुन्नागजातिभिः ॥१८॥
मल्लिकाशतपत्रैश्च माधवीजालकादिभिः ।
शोभितं तीरजैश्चान्यैर्नित्यर्तुभिरलं द्रुमैः ॥१९॥

bilvaiḥ kapitthair jambīrair
vṛto bhallātakādibhiḥ
tasmin saraḥ suvipulaṁ
lasat-kāñcana-paṅkajam

kumudotpala-kahlāra-
śatapatra-śriyorjitam
matta-ṣaṭ-pada-nirghuṣṭaṁ
śakuntaiś ca kala-svanaiḥ

haṁsa-kāraṇḍavākīrṇaṁ
cakrāhvaiḥ sārasair api
jalakukkuṭa-koyaṣṭi-
dātyūha-kula-kūjitam

matsya-kacchapa-sañcāra-
calat-padma-rajaḥ-payaḥ
kadamba-vetasa-nala-
nīpa-vañjulakair vṛtam

kundaiḥ kurubakāśokaiḥ
śirīṣaiḥ kūṭajeṅgudaiḥ
kubjakaiḥ svarṇa-yūthībhir
nāga-punnāga-jātibhiḥ

mallikā-śatapatraiś ca
mādhavī-jālakādibhiḥ
śobhitaṁ tīra-jaiś cānyair
nityartubhir alaṁ drumaiḥ

bilvaiḥ—*bilva* trees; *kapitthaiḥ*—*kapittha* trees; *jambīraiḥ*—*jambīra* trees; *vṛtaḥ*—surrounded by; *bhallātaka-ādibhiḥ*—*bhallātaka* and other trees; *tasmin*—in that garden; *saraḥ*—a lake; *su-vipulam*—which was very large; *lasat*—shining; *kāñcana*—golden; *paṅka-jam*—filled with lotus flowers; *kumuda*—of *kumuda* flowers; *utpala*—*utpala* flowers; *kahlāra*—*kahlāra* flowers; *śatapatra*—and *śatapatra* flowers; *śriyā*—with the beauty; *ūrjitam*—excellent; *matta*—intoxicated; *ṣaṭ-pada*—bees; *nirghuṣṭam*—hummed; *śakuntaiḥ*—with the chirping of birds; *ca*—and; *kala-svanaiḥ*—whose songs were very melodious; *haṁsa*—swans; *kāraṇḍava*—*kāraṇḍavas; ākīrṇam*—crowded with; *cakrāhvaiḥ*—*cakrāvakas; sārasaiḥ*—cranes; *api*—as well as; *jala-kukkuṭa*—water chickens; *koyaṣṭi*—*koyaṣṭis; dātyūha*—*dātyūhas; kula*—flocks of; *kūjitam*—murmured; *matsya*—of the fish; *kacchapa*—and tortoises; *sañcāra*—because of the movements; *calat*—agitating; *padma*—of the lotuses; *rajaḥ*—by the pollen; *payaḥ*—the water (was decorated); *kadamba*—*kadambas; vetasa*—*vetasas; nala*—*nalas;*

nīpa—nīpas; vañjulakaiḥ—vañjulakas; vṛtam—surrounded by; *kundaiḥ—kundas; kurubaka—kurubakas; aśokaiḥ—aśokas; śirīṣaiḥ—śirīṣas; kūṭaja—kūṭajas; iṅgudaiḥ—iṅgudas; kubjakaiḥ—kubjakas; svarṇa-yūthībhiḥ—svarṇa-yūthīs; nāga—nāgas; punnāga—punnāgas; jātibhiḥ—jātīs; mallikā—mallikās; śatapatraiḥ—śatapatras; ca*—also; *mādhavī—mādhavīs; jālakādibhiḥ—jālakās; śobhitam*—adorned; *tīra-jaiḥ*—growing on the banks; *ca*—and; *anyaiḥ*—others; *nitya-ṛtubhiḥ*—in all seasons; *alam*—abundantly; *drumaiḥ*—with trees (bearing flowers and fruits).

TRANSLATION

In that garden there was a very large lake filled with shining golden lotus flowers and the flowers known as kumuda, kahlāra, utpala and śatapatra, which added excellent beauty to the mountain. There were also bilva, kapittha, jambīra and bhallātaka trees. Intoxicated bumblebees drank honey and hummed with the chirping of the birds, whose songs were very melodious. The lake was crowded with swans, kāraṇḍavas, cakrāvakas, cranes, and flocks of water chickens, dātyūhas, koyaṣṭis and other murmuring birds. Because of the agitating movements of the fish and tortoises, the water was decorated with pollen that had fallen from the lotus flowers. The lake was surrounded by kadamba flowers, vetasa flowers, nalas, nīpas, vañjulakas, kundas, kurubakas, aśokas, śirīṣas, kūṭajas, iṅgudas, kubjakas, svarṇa-yūthīs, nāgas, punnāgas, jātīs, mallikās, śatapatras, jālakās and mādhavī-latās. The banks were also abundantly adorned with varieties of trees that yielded flowers and fruits in all seasons. Thus the entire mountain stood gloriously decorated.

PURPORT

Judging from the exhaustive description of the lakes and rivers on Trikūṭa Mountain, on earth there is no comparison to their superexcellence. On other planets, however, there are many such wonders. For instance, we understand that there are two million different types of trees, and not all of them are exhibited on earth. *Śrīmad-Bhāgavatam* presents the total knowledge of the affairs of the universe. It not only describes this universe, but also takes into account the spiritual world beyond the universe. No one can challenge the *Śrīmad-Bhāgavatam's* descriptions of the material and spiritual worlds. The attempts to go from the earth to the moon have failed, but the people of earth can understand what exists on other planets. There is no need of imagination; one may take actual knowledge from *Śrīmad-Bhāgavatam* and be satisfied.

TEXT 20

तत्रैकदा तद्गिरिकाननाश्रयः
करेणुभिर्वारणयूथपश्चरन् ।
सकण्टकं कीचकवेणुवेत्रवद्
विशालगुल्मं प्ररुजन्वनस्पतीन् ॥२०॥

tatraikadā tad-giri-kānanāśrayaḥ
kareṇubhir vāraṇa-yūtha-paś caran
sakaṇṭakaṁ kīcaka-veṇu-vetravad
viśāla-gulmaṁ prarujan vanaspatīn

tatra—therein; *ekadā*—once upon a time; *tat-giri*—of that mountain (Trikūṭa); *kānana-āśrayaḥ*—who lives in the forest; *kareṇubhiḥ*—accompanied by female elephants; *vāraṇa-yūtha-paḥ*—the leader of the elephants; *caran*—while wandering (toward the lake); *sa-kaṇṭakam*—a place full of thorns; *kīcaka-veṇu-vetra-vat*—with plants and creepers of different names; *viśāla-gulmam*—many thickets; *prarujan*—breaking; *vanaḥ-patīn*—trees and plants.

TRANSLATION

The leader of the elephants who lived in the forest of the mountain Trikūṭa once wandered toward the lake with his female elephants. He broke many plants, creepers, thickets and trees, not caring for their piercing thorns.

TEXT 21

यद्गन्धमात्राद्धरयो गजेन्द्रा
व्याघ्रादयो व्यालमृगाः सखड्गाः ।

महोरगाश्चापि भयाद् द्रवन्ति
सगौरकृष्णाः शरभाश्चमर्यः ॥२१॥

yad-gandha-mātrād dharayo gajendrā
vyāghrādayo vyāla-mṛgāḥ sakhaḍgāḥ
mahoragāś cāpi bhayād dravanti
sagaura-kṛṣṇāḥ sarabhāś camaryaḥ

yat-gandha-mātrāt—simply by the scent of that elephant; *harayaḥ*—lions; *gaja-indrāḥ*—other elephants; *vyāghra-ādayaḥ*—ferocious animals like tigers; *vyāla-mṛgāḥ*—other ferocious animals; *sa-khaḍgāḥ*—rhinoceroses; *mahā-uragāḥ*—big, big serpents; *ca*—also; *api*—indeed; *bhayāt*—because of fear; *dravanti*—running away; *sa*—with; *gaura-kṛṣṇāḥ*—some of them white, some of them black; *sarabhāḥ*—*sarabhas; camaryaḥ*—also *camarīs.*

TRANSLATION

Simply by catching scent of that elephant, all the other elephants, the tigers and the other ferocious animals, such as lions, rhinoceroses, great serpents and black and white sarabhas, fled in fear. The camarī deer also fled.

TEXT 22

वृका वराहा महिषर्क्षशल्या
गोपुच्छशालावृकमर्कटाश्च ।
अन्यत्र क्षुद्रा हरिणाः शशादय-
श्चरन्त्यभीता यदनुग्रहेण ॥२२॥

vṛkā varāhā mahiṣarkṣa-śalyā
gopuccha-śālāvṛka-markaṭāś ca
anyatra kṣudrā hariṇāḥ śaśādayaś
caranty abhītā yad-anugraheṇa

vṛkāḥ—foxes; *varāhāḥ*—boars; *mahiṣa*—buffaloes; *ṛkṣa*—bears; *śalyāḥ*—porcupines; *gopuccha*—a type of deer; *śālāvṛka*—wolves;

markaṭāḥ—monkeys; *ca*—and; *anyatra*—elsewhere; *kṣudrāḥ*—small animals; *hariṇāḥ*—deer; *śaśa-ādayaḥ*—rabbits and others; *caranti*—roaming (in the forest); *abhītāḥ*—without fear; *yat-anugraheṇa*—by the mercy of that elephant.

TRANSLATION

By the mercy of this elephant, animals like the foxes, wolves, buffaloes, bears, boars, gopucchas, porcupines, monkeys, rabbits, the other deer and many other small animals loitered elsewhere in the forest. They were not afraid of him.

PURPORT

All the animals were practically controlled by this elephant, yet although they could move without fear, because of respect they did not stand before him.

TEXTS 23–24

स घर्मतप्तः करिभिः करेणुभि-
र्वृतो मदच्युत्करभैरनुद्रुतः ।
गिरिं गरिम्णा परितः प्रकम्पयन्
निषेव्यमाणोऽलिकुलैर्मदाशनैः ॥२३॥
सरोऽनिलं पङ्कजरेणुरूषितं
जिघ्रन्विदूरान्मदविह्वलेक्षणः ।
वृतः स्वयूथेन तृषार्दितेन तत्
सरोवराभ्यासमथागमद् द्रुतम् ॥२४॥

sa gharma-taptaḥ karibhiḥ kareṇubhir
vṛto madacyut-karabhair anudrutaḥ
giriṁ garimṇā paritaḥ prakampayan
niṣevyamāṇo 'likulair madāśanaiḥ

saro 'nilaṁ paṅkaja-reṇu-rūṣitaṁ
jighran vidūrān mada-vihvalekṣaṇaḥ

vṛtaḥ sva-yūthena tṛṣārditena tat
sarovarābhyāsam athāgamad drutam

saḥ—he (the leader of the elephants); *gharma-taptaḥ*—perspiring; *karibhiḥ*—by other elephants; *kareṇubhiḥ*—as well as female elephants; *vṛtaḥ*—surrounded; *mada-cyut*—liquor dripping from his mouth; *karabhaiḥ*—by small elephants; *anudrutaḥ*—was followed; *girim*—that mountain; *garimṇā*—by the weight of the body; *paritaḥ*—all around; *prakampayan*—causing to tremble; *niṣevyamāṇaḥ*—being served; *ali-kulaiḥ*—by the bumblebees; *mada-aśanaiḥ*—who drank honey; *saraḥ*—from the lake; *anilam*—the breeze; *paṅkaja-reṇu-rūṣitam*—carrying the dust from the lotus flowers; *jighran*—smelling; *vidūrāt*—from a distance; *mada-vihvala*—being intoxicated; *īkṣaṇaḥ*—whose vision; *vṛtaḥ*—surrounded; *sva-yūthena*—by his own associates; *tṛṣā-arditena*—who were afflicted by thirst; *tat*—that; *sarovara-abhyāsam*—to the bank of the lake; *atha*—thus; *agamat*—went; *drutam*—very soon.

TRANSLATION

Surrounded by the herd's other elephants, including females, and followed by the young ones, Gajapati, the leader of the elephants, made Trikūṭa Mountain tremble all around because of the weight of his body. He was perspiring, liquor dripped from his mouth, and his vision was overwhelmed by intoxication. He was being served by bumblebees who drank honey, and from a distance he could smell the dust of the lotus flowers, which was carried from the lake by the breeze. Thus surrounded by his associates, who were afflicted by thirst, he soon arrived at the bank of the lake.

TEXT 25

विगाह्य तस्मिन्नमृताम्बु निर्मलं
हेमारविन्दोत्पलरेणुरूषितम् ।
पपौ निकामं निजपुष्करोद्धृत-
मात्मानमद्भिः स्नपयन्गतक्लमः ॥२५॥

vigāhya tasminn amṛtāmbu nirmalaṁ
hemāravindotpala-reṇu-rūṣitam
papau nikāmaṁ nija-puṣkaroddhṛtam
ātmānam adbhiḥ snapayan gata-klamaḥ

vigāhya—entering; *tasmin*—into the lake; *amṛta-ambu*—water as pure as nectar; *nirmalam*—crystal clear; *hema*—very cold; *aravinda-utpala*—from the lilies and lotuses; *reṇu*—with the dust; *rūṣitam*—which was mixed; *papau*—he drank; *nikāmam*—until fully satisfied; *nija*—own; *puṣkara-uddhṛtam*—drawing with his trunk; *ātmānam*—himself; *adbhiḥ*—with water; *snapayan*—bathing thoroughly; *gata-klamaḥ*—was relieved of all fatigue.

TRANSLATION

The King of the elephants entered the lake, bathed thoroughly and was relieved of his fatigue. Then, with the aid of his trunk, he drank the cold, clear, nectarean water, which was mixed with the dust of lotus flowers and water lilies, until he was fully satisfied.

TEXT 26

स पुष्करेणोद्धृतशीकराम्बुभि-
र्निपाययन्संस्नपयन्यथा गृही ।
घृणी करेणुः करभांश्च दुर्मदो
नाचष्ट कृच्छ्रं कृपणोऽजमायया ॥२६॥

sa puṣkareṇoddhṛta-śīkarāmbubhir
nipāyayan saṁsnapayan yathā gṛhī
ghṛṇī kareṇuḥ karabhāṁś ca durmado
nācaṣṭa kṛcchraṁ kṛpaṇo 'ja-māyayā

saḥ—he (the leader of the elephants); *puṣkareṇa*—with his trunk; *uddhṛta*—by drawing out; *śīkara-ambubhiḥ*—and sprinkling the water; *nipāyayan*—causing them to drink; *saṁsnapayan*—and bathing them; *yathā*—as; *gṛhī*—a householder; *ghṛṇī*—always kind (to the members of his family); *kareṇuḥ*—to his wives, the female elephants;

karabhān—to the children; *ca*—as well as; *durmadaḥ*—who is too attached to the members of his family; *na*—not; *ācaṣṭa*—considered; *kṛcchram*—hardship; *kṛpaṇaḥ*—being without spiritual knowledge; *aja-māyayā*—because of the influence of the external, illusory energy of the Supreme Personality of Godhead.

TRANSLATION

Like a human being who lacks spiritual knowledge and is too attached to the members of his family, the elephant, being illusioned by the external energy of Kṛṣṇa, had his wives and children bathe and drink the water. Indeed, he raised water from the lake with his trunk and sprayed it over them. He did not mind the hard labor involved in this endeavor.

TEXT 27

तं तत्र कश्चिन्नृप दैवचोदितो
ग्राहो बलीयांश्चरणे रुषाग्रहीत् ।
यदृच्छयैवं व्यसनं गतो गजो
यथाबलं सोऽतिबलो विचक्रमे ॥२७॥

taṁ tatra kaścin nṛpa daiva-codito
grāho balīyāṁś caraṇe ruṣāgrahīt
yadṛcchayaivaṁ vyasanaṁ gato gajo
yathā-balaṁ so 'tibalo vicakrame

tam—him (Gajendra); *tatra*—there (in the water); *kaścit*—someone; *nṛpa*—O King; *daiva-coditaḥ*—inspired by providence; *grāhaḥ*—crocodile; *balīyān*—very powerful; *caraṇe*—his foot; *ruṣā*—angrily; *agrahīt*—captured; *yadṛcchayā*—occurring due to providence; *evam*—such; *vyasanam*—a dangerous position; *gataḥ*—having obtained; *gajaḥ*—the elephant; *yathā-balam*—according to his strength; *saḥ*—he; *ati-balaḥ*—with great endeavor; *vicakrame*—tried to get out.

TRANSLATION

By the arrangement of providence, O King, a strong crocodile was angry at the elephant and attacked the elephant's leg in the

water. The elephant was certainly strong, and he tried his best to get free from this danger sent by providence.

TEXT 28

तथातुरं यूथपतिं करेणवो
विकृष्यमाणं तरसा बलीयसा ।
विचुक्रुशुर्दीनधियोऽपरे गजाः
पार्ष्णिग्रहास्तारयितुं न चाशकन् ॥२८॥

tathāturaṁ yūtha-patiṁ kareṇavo
vikṛṣyamāṇaṁ tarasā balīyasā
vicukruśur dīna-dhiyo 'pare gajāḥ
pārṣṇi-grahās tārayituṁ na cāśakan

tathā—then; *āturam*—that grave condition; *yūtha-patim*—the leader of the elephants; *kareṇavaḥ*—his wives; *vikṛṣyamāṇam*—being attacked; *tarasā*—by the strength; *balīyasā*—by the strength (of the crocodile); *vicukruśuḥ*—began to cry; *dīna-dhiyaḥ*—who were less intelligent; *apare*—the other; *gajāḥ*—elephants; *pārṣṇi-grahāḥ*—grasping him from behind; *tārayitum*—to free; *na*—not; *ca*—also; *aśakan*—were able.

TRANSLATION

Thereafter, seeing Gajendra in that grave condition, his wives felt very, very sorry and began to cry. The other elephants wanted to help Gajendra, but because of the crocodile's great strength, they could not rescue him by grasping him from behind.

TEXT 29

नियुध्यतोरेवमिभेन्द्रनक्रयो-
र्विकर्षतोरन्तरतो बहिर्मिथः ।
समाः सहस्रं व्यगमन् महीपते
सप्राणयोश्चित्रममंसतामराः ॥२९॥

niyudhyator evam ibhendra-nakrayor
vikarṣator antarato bahir mithaḥ
samāḥ sahasraṁ vyagaman mahī-pate
saprāṇayoś citram amaṁsatāmarāḥ

niyudhyatoḥ—fighting; *evam*—in this way; *ibha-indra*—of the elephant; *nakrayoḥ*—and the crocodile; *vikarṣatoḥ*—pulling; *antarataḥ*—in the water; *bahiḥ*—outside the water; *mithaḥ*—one another; *samāḥ*—years; *sahasram*—one thousand; *vyagaman*—passed; *mahī-pate*—O King; *sa-prāṇayoḥ*—both alive; *citram*—wonderful; *amaṁsata*—considered; *amarāḥ*—the demigods.

TRANSLATION

O King, the elephant and the crocodile fought in this way, pulling one another in and out of the water, for one thousand years. Upon seeing the fight, the demigods were very surprised.

TEXT 30

ततो गजेन्द्रस्य मनोबलौजसां
कालेन दीर्घेण महानभूद् व्ययः ।
विकृष्यमाणस्य जलेऽवसीदतो
विपर्ययोऽभूत् सकलं जलौकसः ॥३०॥

tato gajendrasya mano-balaujasāṁ
kālena dīrgheṇa mahān abhūd vyayaḥ
vikṛṣyamāṇasya jale 'vasīdato
viparyayo 'bhūt sakalaṁ jalaukasaḥ

tataḥ—thereafter; *gaja-indrasya*—of the King of the elephants; *manaḥ*—of the strength of enthusiasm; *bala*—the physical strength; *ojasām*—and the strength of the senses; *kālena*—because of years of fighting; *dīrgheṇa*—prolonged; *mahān*—great; *abhūt*—became; *vyayaḥ*—the expenditure; *vikṛṣyamāṇasya*—who was being pulled (by the crocodile); *jale*—into the water (a foreign place); *avasīdataḥ*—reduced (mental, physical and sensory strength); *viparyayaḥ*—the opposite; *abhūt*—became; *sakalam*—all of them; *jala-okasaḥ*—the crocodile, whose home is the water.

TRANSLATION

Thereafter, because of being pulled into the water and fighting for many long years, the elephant became diminished in his mental, physical and sensual strength. The crocodile, on the contrary, being an animal of the water, increased in enthusiasm, physical strength and sensual power.

PURPORT

In the fighting between the elephant and the crocodile, the difference was that although the elephant was extremely powerful, he was in a foreign place, in the water. During one thousand years of fighting, he could not get any food, and under the circumstances his bodily strength diminished, and because his bodily strength diminished, his mind also became weak and his senses less powerful. The crocodile, however, being an animal of the water, had no difficulties. He was getting food and was therefore getting mental strength and sensual encouragement. Thus while the elephant became reduced in strength, the crocodile became more and more powerful. Now, from this we may take the lesson that in our fight with *māyā* we should not be in a position in which our strength, enthusiasm and senses will be unable to fight vigorously. Our Kṛṣṇa consciousness movement has actually declared war against the illusory energy, in which all the living entities are rotting in a false understanding of civilization. The soldiers in this Kṛṣṇa consciousness movement must always possess physical strength, enthusiasm and sensual power. To keep themselves fit, they must therefore place themselves in a normal condition of life. What constitutes a normal condition will not be the same for everyone, and therefore there are divisions of *varṇāśrama*—*brāhmaṇa, kṣatriya, vaiśya, śūdra, brahmacarya, gṛhastha, vānaprastha* and *sannyāsa*. Especially in this age, Kali-yuga, it is advised that no one take *sannyāsa*.

aśvamedhaṁ gavālambhaṁ
sannyāsaṁ pala-paitṛkam

devareṇa sutotpattiṁ
kalau pañca vivarjayet
(*Brahma-vaivarta Purāṇa*)

From this we can understand that in this age the *sannyāsa-āśrama* is forbidden because people are not strong. Śrī Caitanya Mahāprabhu showed us an example in taking *sannyāsa* at the age of twenty-four years, but even Sārvabhauma Bhaṭṭācārya advised Śrī Caitanya Mahāprabhu to be extremely careful because He had taken *sannyāsa* at an early age. For preaching we give young boys *sannyāsa*, but actually it is being experienced that they are not fit for *sannyāsa*. There is no harm, however, if one thinks that he is unfit for *sannyāsa;* if he is very much agitated sexually, he should go to the *āśrama* where sex is allowed, namely the *gṛhastha-āśrama*. That one has been found to be very weak in one place does not mean that he should stop fighting the crocodile of *māyā*. One should take shelter of the lotus feet of Kṛṣṇa, as we shall see Gajendra do, and at the same time one can be a *gṛhastha* if he is satisfied with sexual indulgence. There is no need to give up the fight. Śrī Caitanya Mahāprabhu therefore recommended, *sthāne sthitāḥ śruti-gatāṁ tanu-vāṅ-manobhiḥ*. One may stay in whichever *āśrama* is suitable for him; it is not essential that one take *sannyāsa*. If one is sexually agitated, he can enter the *gṛhastha-āśrama*. But one must continue fighting. For one who is not in a transcendental position, to take *sannyāsa* artificially is not a very great credit. If *sannyāsa* is not suitable, one may enter the *gṛhastha-āśrama* and fight *māyā* with great strength. But one should not give up the fighting and go away.

TEXT 31

इत्थं गजेन्द्रः स यदाप संकटं
प्राणस्य देही विवशो यदृच्छया ।
अपारयन्नात्मविमोक्षणे चिरं
दध्याविमां बुद्धिमथाभ्यपद्यत ॥३१॥

itthaṁ gajendraḥ sa yadāpa saṅkaṭaṁ
prāṇasya dehī vivaśo yadṛcchayā

apārayann ātma-vimokṣaṇe ciraṁ
dadhyāv imāṁ buddhim athābhyapadyata

ittham—in this way; *gaja-indraḥ*—the King of the elephants; *saḥ*—he; *yadā*—when; *āpa*—obtained; *saṅkaṭam*—such a dangerous position; *prāṇasya*—of life; *dehī*—who is embodied; *vivaśaḥ*—circumstantially helpless; *yadṛcchayā*—by the will of providence; *apārayan*—being unable; *ātma-vimokṣaṇe*—to save himself; *ciram*—for a long time; *dadhyau*—began to think seriously; *imām*—this; *buddhim*—decision; *atha*—thereupon; *abhyapadyata*—reached.

TRANSLATION

When the King of the elephants saw that he was under the clutches of the crocodile by the will of providence and, being embodied and circumstantially helpless, could not save himself from danger, he was extremely afraid of being killed. He consequently thought for a long time and finally reached the following decision.

PURPORT

Everyone in the material world is engaged in a struggle for existence. Everyone tries to save himself from danger, but when one is unable to save himself, if he is pious, he then takes shelter of the lotus feet of the Supreme Personality of Godhead. This is confirmed in *Bhagavad-gītā* (7.16):

catur-vidhā bhajante māṁ
janāḥ sukṛtino 'rjuna
ārto jijñāsur arthārthī
jñānī ca bharatarṣabha

Four kinds of pious men—namely, one who is in danger, one who is in need of money, one who is searching for knowledge and one who is inquisitive—begin to take shelter of the Supreme Personality of Godhead in order to be saved or to advance. The King of the elephants, in his condition of danger, decided to seek shelter of the lotus feet of the Lord. After considerable thought, he intelligently arrived at this correct decision. Such a decision is not reached by a sinful man. Therefore in

Bhagavad-gītā it is said that those who are pious (*sukṛtī*) can decide that in a dangerous or awkward condition one should seek shelter of the lotus feet of Kṛṣṇa.

TEXT 32

न मामिमे ज्ञातय आतुरं गजाः
कुतः करिण्यः प्रभवन्ति मोचितुम् ।
ग्राहेण पाशेन विधातुरावृतो-
ऽप्यहं च तं यामि परं परायणम् ॥३२॥

na māṁ ime jñātaya āturaṁ gajāḥ
kutaḥ kariṇyaḥ prabhavanti mocitum
grāheṇa pāśena vidhātur āvṛto
'py ahaṁ ca taṁ yāmi paraṁ parāyaṇam

na—not; *mām*—me; *ime*—all these; *jñātayaḥ*—friends and relatives (the other elephants); *āturam*—in my distress; *gajāḥ*—the elephant; *kutaḥ*—how; *kariṇyaḥ*—my wives; *prabhavanti*—are able; *mocitum*—to deliver (from this dangerous position); *grāheṇa*—by the crocodile; *pāśena*—by the network of ropes; *vidhātuḥ*—of providence; *āvṛtaḥ*—captured; *api*—although (I am in such a position); *aham*—I; *ca*—also; *tam*—that (Supreme Personality of Godhead); *yāmi*—take shelter of; *param*—who is transcendental; *parāyaṇam*—and who is the shelter of even the exalted demigods like Brahmā and Śiva.

TRANSLATION

The other elephants, who are my friends and relatives, could not rescue me from this danger. What then to speak of my wives? They cannot do anything. It is by the will of providence that I have been attacked by this crocodile, and therefore I shall seek shelter of the Supreme Personality of Godhead, who is always the shelter of everyone, even of great personalities.

PURPORT

This material world is described as *padaṁ padaṁ yad vipadām*, which means that at every step there is danger. A fool wrongly thinks that he is happy in this material world, but in fact he is not, for one who thinks that way is only illusioned. At every step, at every moment, there is danger. In modern civilization one thinks that if he has a nice home and a nice car his life is perfect. In the Western countries, especially in America, it is very nice to possess a good car, but as soon as one is on the road, there is danger because at any moment an accident may take place and one will be killed. The record actually shows that so many people die in such accidents. Therefore if we actually think that this material world is a very happy place, this is our ignorance. Real knowledge is that this material world is full of danger. We may struggle for existence as far as our intelligence allows and may try to take care of ourselves, but unless the Supreme Personality of Godhead, Kṛṣṇa, ultimately saves us from danger, our attempts will be useless. Therefore Prahlāda Mahārāja says:

bālasya neha śaraṇaṁ pitarau nṛsiṁha
nārtasya cāgadam udanvati majjato nauḥ
taptasya tat-pratividhir ya ihāñjaseṣṭas
tāvad vibho tanu-bhṛtāṁ tvad-upekṣitānām
(*Bhāg.* 7.9.19)

We may invent so many ways to be happy or to counteract the dangers of this material world, but unless our attempts are sanctioned by the Supreme Personality of Godhead, they will never make us happy. Those who try to be happy without taking shelter of the Supreme Personality of Godhead are *mūḍhas*, rascals. *Na māṁ duṣkṛtino mūḍhāḥ prapadyante narādhamāḥ.* Those who are the lowest of men refuse to take to Kṛṣṇa consciousness because they think that they will be able to protect themselves without Kṛṣṇa's care. This is their mistake. The decision of the King of the elephants, Gajendra, was correct. In such a dangerous position, he sought shelter of the Supreme Personality of Godhead.

TEXT 33

यः कश्चनेशो बलिनोऽन्तकोरगात्
प्रचण्डवेगादभिधावतो भृशम् ।
भीतं प्रपन्नं परिपाति यद्भया-
न्मृत्युः प्रधावत्यरणं तमीमहि ॥३३॥

yaḥ kaścaneśo balino 'ntakoragāt
pracaṇḍa-vegād abhidhāvato bhṛśam
bhītaṁ prapannaṁ paripāti yad-bhayān
mṛtyuḥ pradhāvaty araṇaṁ tam īmahi

yaḥ—He who (the Supreme Personality of Godhead); *kaścana*—someone; *īśaḥ*—the supreme controller; *balinaḥ*—very powerful; *antaka-uragāt*—from the great serpent of time, which brings death; *pracaṇḍa-vegāt*—whose force is fearful; *abhidhāvataḥ*—who is chasing; *bhṛśam*—endlessly (every hour and every minute); *bhītam*—one who is afraid of death; *prapannam*—who is surrendered (to the Supreme Personality of Godhead); *paripāti*—He protects; *yat-bhayāt*—from fear of the Lord; *mṛtyuḥ*—death itself; *pradhāvati*—runs away; *araṇam*—the actual shelter of everyone; *tam*—unto Him; *īmahi*—I surrender or take shelter.

TRANSLATION

The Supreme Personality of Godhead is certainly not known to everyone, but He is very powerful and influential. Therefore, although the serpent of eternal time, which is fearful in force, endlessly chases everyone, ready to swallow him, if one who fears this serpent seeks shelter of the Lord, the Lord gives him protection, for even death runs away in fear of the Lord. I therefore surrender unto Him, the great and powerful supreme authority who is the actual shelter of everyone.

PURPORT

One who is intelligent understands that there is a great and supreme authority above everything. That great authority appears in different incarnations to save the innocent from disturbances. As confirmed in *Bhagavad-gītā* (4.8), *paritrāṇāya sādhūnāṁ vināśāya ca duṣkṛtām:* the Lord appears in His various incarnations for two purposes—to annihilate the *duṣkṛtī,* the sinful, and to protect His devotees. The King of the elephants decided to surrender unto Him. This is intelligent. One must know that great Supreme Personality of Godhead and surrender unto Him. The Lord comes personally to instruct us how to be happy, and only fools and rascals do not see by intelligence this supreme authority, the Supreme Person. In the *śruti-mantra* it is said:

bhīṣāsmād vātaḥ pavate
bhīṣodeti sūryaḥ
bhīṣāsmād agniś candraś ca
mṛtyur dhāvati pañcamaḥ
(*Taittirīya Upaniṣad* 2.8)

It is out of fear of the Supreme Personality of Godhead that the wind is blowing, that the sun is distributing heat and light, and that death is chasing everyone. Thus there is a supreme controller, as confirmed in *Bhagavad-gītā* (9.10): *mayādhyakṣeṇa prakṛtiḥ sūyate sacarācaram.* This material manifestation is working so well because of the supreme controller. Any intelligent person, therefore, can understand that there is a supreme controller. Furthermore, the supreme controller Himself appears as Lord Kṛṣṇa, as Lord Caitanya Mahāprabhu and as Lord Rāmacandra to give us instructions and to show us by example how to surrender unto the Supreme Personality of Godhead. Yet those who are *duṣkṛtī*, the lowest of men, do not surrender (*na māṁ duṣkṛtino mūḍhāḥ prapadyante narādhamāḥ*).

In *Bhagavad-gītā* the Lord clearly says, *mṛtyuḥ sarva-haraś cāham:* "I am all-devouring death." Thus *mṛtyu,* or death, is the representative who takes everything away from the living entity who has accepted a material body. No one can say, "I do not fear death." This is a false proposition. Everyone fears death. However, one who seeks shelter of the Supreme Personality of Godhead can be saved from death. One may argue, "Does the devotee not die?" The answer is that a devotee certainly must give up his body, for the body is material. The difference is, however, that for one who surrenders to Kṛṣṇa fully and who is protected by Kṛṣṇa, the present body is his last; he will not again receive a material body to be subjected to death. This is assured in *Bhagavad-gītā* (4.9). *Tyaktvā dehaṁ punar janma naiti mām eti so 'rjuna:* a devotee, after giving up his body, does not accept a material body, but returns home, back to Godhead. We are always in danger because at any moment death can take place. It is not that only Gajendra, the King of the elephants, was afraid of death. Everyone should fear death because everyone is caught by the crocodile of eternal time and may die at any moment. The best course, therefore, is to seek shelter of Kṛṣṇa, the Supreme Personality of Godhead, and be saved from the struggle for existence in this material world, in which one repeatedly takes birth and dies. To reach this understanding is the ultimate goal of life.

Thus end the Bhaktivedanta purports of the Eighth Canto, Second Chapter, of the Śrīmad-Bhāgavatam, *entitled "The Elephant Gajendra's Crisis."*

CHAPTER THREE

Gajendra's Prayers of Surrender

In this chapter, the prayers by Gajendra, the King of the elephants, are described. It appears that the King of the elephants was formerly a human being known as Indradyumna and that he learned a prayer to the Supreme Lord. Fortunately he remembered that prayer and began to chant it to himself. First he offered his respectful obeisances to the Supreme Personality of Godhead, and because of his awkward position in having been attacked by the crocodile, he expressed his inability to recite prayers nicely. Nonetheless, he tried to chant the *mantra* and expressed himself in appropriate words as follows.

"The Supreme Personality of Godhead is the cause of all causes, the original person from whom everything has emanated. He is the root cause of this cosmic manifestation, and the entire cosmos rests in Him, yet He is transcendental, for He does everything in relation to the material world through His external energy. He is eternally situated in the spiritual world—in Vaikuṇṭha or Goloka Vṛndāvana—where He engages in His eternal pastimes. The material world is a product of His external energy, or material nature, which works under His direction. It is thus that creation, maintenance and annihilation take place. The Lord exists at all times. This is extremely difficult for a nondevotee to understand. Although the transcendental Supreme Personality of Godhead is perceivable by everyone, only the pure devotees perceive His presence and activities. The Supreme Personality of Godhead is completely free from material birth, death, old age and disease. Indeed, if anyone in this material world takes shelter of Him, he also becomes situated in that transcendental position. For the satisfaction of the devotee (*paritrāṇāya sādhūnām*), the Lord appears and exhibits His activities. His appearance, disappearance and other pastimes are not at all material. One who knows this secret can enter the kingdom of God. In the Lord, all opposing elements are adjusted. The Lord is situated in everyone's heart. He is the controller of everything, He is the witness of all activities, and He is the original source of all living entities. Indeed, all living entities are parts of

Him, for He is the origin of Mahā-Viṣṇu, who is the source of the living entities within this material world. The Lord can observe the activities of our senses, which can work and achieve material results because of His mercy. Although He is the original source of everything, He is untouched by any of His by-products. In this way He is like a gold mine, which is the source of gold in ornaments and yet is different from the ornaments themselves. The Lord is worshiped by the method prescribed in the *Pañcarātras.* He is the source of our knowledge, and He can give us liberation. Therefore it is our duty to understand Him according to the instructions of devotees, in particular the spiritual master. Although for us the mode of goodness is covered, by following the instructions of saintly persons and the spiritual master we can be freed from material clutches.

"The self-effulgent material form of the Supreme Personality of Godhead is adored by nondevotees, His impersonal form is adored by those advanced in spiritual knowledge, and His feature as the localized Supersoul is appreciated by *yogīs.* But His original form as a person is understood only by devotees. That Supreme Personality of Godhead is competent to dissipate the darkness of the conditioned soul through His instructions in *Bhagavad-gītā.* He is the ocean of transcendental qualities and can be understood only by liberated persons freed from the bodily concept of life. By His causeless mercy, the Lord can rescue the conditioned soul from the material clutches and enable him to return home, back to Godhead, to become His personal associate. Nonetheless, a pure devotee does not aspire to go back to Godhead; he is simply satisfied with executing his service in this material world. A pure devotee does not ask anything from the Supreme Personality of Godhead. His only prayer is to be freed from the material conception of life and to be engaged in the Lord's transcendental loving service."

In this way the King of the elephants, Gajendra, offered prayers directly to the Supreme Personality of Godhead, without mistaking Him for one of the demigods. None of the demigods came to see him, not even Brahmā or Śiva. Rather, the Supreme Personality of Godhead, Nārāyaṇa, seated on Garuḍa, personally appeared before him. Gajendra, by lifting his trunk, offered obeisances to the Lord, and the Lord immediately pulled him from the water along with the crocodile who had captured his leg. Then the Lord killed the crocodile and thus rescued Gajendra.

TEXT 1

श्रीबादरायणिरुवाच
एवं व्यवसितो बुद्ध्या समाधाय मनो हृदि ।
जजाप परमं जाप्यं प्राग्जन्मन्यनुशिक्षितम् ॥ १ ॥

śrī-bādarāyaṇir uvāca
evaṁ vyavasito buddhyā
samādhāya mano hṛdi
jajāpa paramaṁ jāpyaṁ
prāg-janmany anuśikṣitam

śrī-bādarāyaṇiḥ uvāca—Śrī Śukadeva Gosvāmī said; *evam*—thus; *vyavasitaḥ*—fixed; *buddhyā*—by intelligence; *samādhāya*—for concentration; *manaḥ*—the mind; *hṛdi*—in consciousness or in the heart; *jajāpa*—he chanted; *paramam*—a supreme; *jāpyam*—*mantra* he had learned from great devotees; *prāk-janmani*—in his previous birth; *anuśikṣitam*—practiced.

TRANSLATION

Śrī Śukadeva Gosvāmī continued: Thereafter, the King of the elephants, Gajendra, fixed his mind in his heart with perfect intelligence and chanted a mantra which he had learned in his previous birth as Indradyumna and which he remembered by the grace of Kṛṣṇa.

PURPORT

Such remembrance is described in *Bhagavad-gītā* (6.43–44):

tatra taṁ buddhi-saṁyogaṁ
labhate paurva-dehikam
yatate ca tato bhūyaḥ
saṁsiddhau kuru-nandana

pūrvābhyāsena tenaiva
hriyate hy avaśo 'pi saḥ

In these verses it is assured that even if a person engaged in devotional service falls down, he is not degraded, but is placed in a position in which he will in due course of time remember the Supreme Personality of Godhead. As explained later, Gajendra was formerly King Indradyumna, and somehow or other in his next life he became King of the elephants. Now Gajendra was in danger, and although he was in a body other than that of a human being, he remembered the *stotra* he had chanted in his previous life. *Yatate ca tato bhūyaḥ saṁsiddhau kuru-nandana.* To enable one to achieve perfection, Kṛṣṇa gives one the chance to remember Him again. This is proved here, for although the King of the elephants, Gajendra, was put in danger, this was a chance for him to remember his previous devotional activities so that he could immediately be rescued by the Supreme Personality of Godhead.

It is imperative, therefore, that all devotees in Kṛṣṇa consciousness practice chanting some *mantra.* Certainly one should chant the Hare Kṛṣṇa *mantra,* which is the *mahā-mantra,* or great *mantra,* and also one should practice chanting *cintāmaṇi-prakara-sadmasu* or the Nṛsiṁha *strotra* (*ito nṛsiṁhaḥ parato nṛsiṁho yato yato yāmi tato nṛsiṁhaḥ*). Every devotee should practice in order to chant some *mantra* perfectly so that even though he may be imperfect in spiritual consciousness in this life, in his next life he will not forget Kṛṣṇa consciousness, even if he becomes an animal. Of course, a devotee should try to perfect his Kṛṣṇa consciousness in this life, for simply by understanding Kṛṣṇa and His instructions, after giving up this body one can return home, back to Godhead. Even if there is some falldown, practice of Kṛṣṇa consciousness never goes in vain. For example, Ajāmila, in his boyhood, practiced chanting the name of Nārāyaṇa under the direction of his father, but later, in his youth, he fell down and became a drunkard, woman-hunter, rogue and thief. Nonetheless, because of chanting the name of Nārāyaṇa for the purpose of calling his son, whom he had named Nārāyaṇa, he became advanced, even though he was involved in sinful activities. Therefore, we should not forget the chanting of the Hare Kṛṣṇa *mantra* under any circumstances. It will help us in the greatest danger, as we find in the life of Gajendra.

TEXT 2

श्रीगजेन्द्र उवाच

ॐ नमो भगवते तस्मै यत एतच्चिदात्मकम् ।
पुरुषायादिबीजाय परेशायाभिधीमहि ॥ २ ॥

śrī-gajendra uvāca
oṁ namo bhagavate tasmai
yata etac cid-ātmakam
puruṣāyādi-bījāya
pareśāyābhidhīmahi

śrī-gajendraḥ uvāca—Gajendra, the King of elephants, said; *oṁ*—O my Lord; *namaḥ*—I offer my respectful obeisances unto You; *bhagavate*—unto the Supreme Personality of Godhead; *tasmai*—unto Him; *yataḥ*—from whom; *etat*—this body and the material manifestation; *cit-ātmakam*—is moving due to consciousness (the spirit soul); *puruṣāya*—unto the Supreme Person; *ādi-bījāya*—who is the origin or root cause of everything; *para-īśāya*—who is supreme, transcendental and worshipable for such exalted persons as Brahmā and Śiva; *abhidhīmahi*—let me meditate upon Him.

TRANSLATION

The King of the elephants, Gajendra, said: I offer my respectful obeisances unto the Supreme Person, Vāsudeva [oṁ namo bhagavate vāsudevāya]. Because of Him this material body acts due to the presence of spirit, and He is therefore the root cause of everyone. He is worshipable for such exalted persons as Brahmā and Śiva, and He has entered the heart of every living being. Let me meditate upon Him.

PURPORT

In this verse the words *etac cid-ātmakam* are very important. The material body certainly consists only of material elements, but when one awakens to Kṛṣṇa conscious understanding, the body is no longer material but spiritual. The material body is meant for sense enjoyment, whereas the spiritual body engages in the transcendental loving service of the Lord. Therefore, a devotee who engages in the service of the Supreme Lord and who constantly thinks of Him should never be considered to have a material body. It is therefore enjoined, *guruṣu nara-matiḥ:* one should stop thinking of the spiritual master as an ordinary human being with a material body. *Arcye viṣṇau śilā-dhīḥ:* everyone knows that the Deity in the temple is made of stone, but to think that the Deity is merely stone is an offense. Similarly, to think that the body of the spiritual master consists of material ingredients is offensive. Atheists think that devotees foolishly worship a stone statue as God and an ordinary man as the *guru*. The fact is, however, that by the grace of Kṛṣṇa's omnipotence, the so-called stone statue of the Deity is directly the Supreme Personality of Godhead, and the body of the spiritual master is directly spiritual. A pure devotee who is engaged in unalloyed devotional service should be understood to be situated on the transcendental platform (*sa guṇān samatītyaitān brahma-bhūyāya kalpate*). Let us therefore offer our obeisances unto the Supreme Personality of Godhead, by whose mercy so-called material things also become spiritual when they are engaged in spiritual activity.

Oṁkāra (*praṇava*) is the symbolic sound representation of the Supreme Personality of Godhead. *Oṁ tat sad iti nirdeśo brahmaṇas tri-vidhaḥ smṛtaḥ:* the three words *oṁ tat sat* immediately invoke the Supreme Person. Therefore Kṛṣṇa says that He is *oṁkāra* in all the Vedic *mantras* (*praṇavaḥ sarva-vedeṣu*). The Vedic *mantras* are pronounced beginning with *oṁkāra* to indicate immediately the Supreme Personality of Godhead. *Śrīmad-Bhāgavatam*, for example, begins with the words *oṁ namo bhagavate vāsudevāya*. There is no difference between the Supreme Personality of Godhead, Vāsudeva, and *oṁkāra* (*praṇava*). We should be careful to understand that *oṁkāra* does not indicate anything *nirākāra*, or formless. Indeed, this verse immediately says, *oṁ namo bhagavate*. Bhagavān is a person. Thus *oṁkāra* is the representation of the Supreme Person. *Oṁkāra* is not meant to be impersonal, as the Māyāvādī philosophers consider it to be. This is distinctly expressed here by the word *puruṣāya*. The supreme truth addressed by *oṁkāra* is *puruṣa*, the Supreme Person; He is not impersonal. Unless He is a person, how can He control the great, stalwart controllers of this universe? Lord Viṣṇu, Lord Brahmā and Lord Śiva are the supreme controllers of this universe, but Lord Viṣṇu is offered obeisances even by Lord Śiva and Lord Brahmā. Therefore this verse uses the word *pareśāya*, which indicates that the Supreme Personality of Godhead is worshiped by exalted demigods. *Pareśāya* means *parameśvara*. Lord Brahmā and Lord Śiva are *īśvaras*, great controllers, but Lord Viṣṇu is *parameśvara*, the supreme controller.

TEXT 3

यस्मिन्निदं यतश्चेदं येनेदं य इदं स्वयम् ।
योऽस्मात् परस्माच्च परस्तं प्रपद्ये स्वयम्भुवम् ॥ ३ ॥

yasminn idaṁ yataś cedaṁ
yenedaṁ ya idaṁ svayam
yo 'smāt parasmāc ca paras
taṁ prapadye svayambhuvam

yasmin—the basic platform on which; *idam*—the universe rests; *yataḥ*—the ingredients from which; *ca*—and; *idam*—the cosmic manifestation is produced; *yena*—by whom; *idam*—this cosmic manifestation is created and maintained; *yaḥ*—He who; *idam*—this material world; *svayam*—is Himself; *yaḥ*—He who; *asmāt*—from the effect (this material world); *parasmāt*—from the cause; *ca*—and; *paraḥ*—transcendental or different; *tam*—unto Him; *prapadye*—I surrender; *svayambhuvam*—unto the supreme self-sufficient.

TRANSLATION

The Supreme Godhead is the supreme platform on which everything rests, the ingredient by which everything has been produced, and the person who has created and is the only cause of this cosmic manifestation. Nonetheless, He is different from the cause and the result. I surrender unto Him, the Supreme Personality of Godhead, who is self-sufficient in everything.

PURPORT

In *Bhagavad-gītā* (9.4) the Lord says, *mayā tatam idaṁ sarvaṁ jagad avyakta-mūrtinā:* "I am the Supreme Personality of Godhead, but everything rests upon My energy, just as an earthen pot rests on the earth." The place where an earthen pot rests is also earth. Then again, the earthen pot is manufactured by a potter, whose body is a product of earth. The potter's wheel with which the pot is made is an expansion of earth, and the ingredients from which the pot are made are also earth. As confirmed in the *śruti-mantra, yato vā imāni bhūtāni jāyante. yena jātāni jīvanti. yat prayanty abhisaṁviśanti.* The original cause of everything is the Supreme Personality of Godhead, and after being annihilated, everything enters into Him (*prakṛtiṁ yānti māmikām*). Thus the Supreme Lord, the Personality of Godhead—Lord Rāmacandra or Lord Kṛṣṇa—is the original cause of everything.

īśvaraḥ paramaḥ kṛṣṇaḥ
sac-cid-ānanda-vigrahaḥ
anādir ādir govindaḥ
sarva-kāraṇa-kāraṇam

"Kṛṣṇa, who is known as Govinda, is the supreme controller. He has an eternal, blissful, spiritual body. He is the origin of all. He has no other origin, for He is the prime cause of all causes." (*Brahma-saṁhitā* 5.1) The Lord is the cause for everything, but there is no cause for Him. *Sarvaṁ khalv idaṁ brahma. Mat-sthāni sarva-bhūtāni na cāhaṁ teṣv avasthitaḥ.* Although He is everything, His personality is different from the cosmic manifestation.

TEXT 4

यः स्वात्मनीदं निजमाययार्पितं
क्वचिद् विभातं क्व च तत् तिरोहितम् ।
अविद्धदृक् साक्ष्युभयं तदीक्षते
स आत्ममूलोऽवतु मां परात्परः ॥ ४ ॥

yaḥ svātmanīdaṁ nija-māyayārpitaṁ
kvacid vibhātaṁ kva ca tat tirohitam
aviddha-dṛk sākṣy ubhayaṁ tad īkṣate
sa ātma-mūlo 'vatu māṁ parāt-paraḥ

yaḥ—the Supreme Personality of Godhead who; *sva-ātmani*—in Him; *idam*—this cosmic manifestation; *nija-māyayā*—by His own potency; *arpitam*—invested; *kvacit*—sometimes, at the beginning of a *kalpa; vibhātam*—it is manifested; *kva ca*—sometimes, during dissolution; *tat*—that(manifestation); *tirohitam*—not visible; *aviddha-dṛk*—He sees everything (in all these circumstances); *sākṣī*—the witness; *ubhayam*—both (manifestation and annihilation); *tat īkṣate*—sees everything, without loss of sight; *saḥ*—that Supreme Personality of Godhead; *ātma-mūlaḥ*—self-sufficient, having no other cause; *avatu*—please give protection; *mām*—unto me; *parāt-paraḥ*—He is transcendental to transcendental, or above all transcendence.

TRANSLATION

The Supreme Personality of Godhead, by expanding His own energy, keeps this cosmic manifestation visible and again sometimes renders it invisible. He is both the supreme cause and the supreme result, the observer and the witness, in all circumstances. Thus He is transcendental to everything. May that Supreme Personality of Godhead give me protection.

PURPORT

The Supreme Personality of Godhead has multipotencies (*parāsya śaktir vividhaiva śrūyate*). Therefore, as soon as He likes, He uses one of His potencies, and by that expansion He creates this cosmic manifestation. Again, when the cosmic manifestation is annihilated, it rests in Him. Nonetheless, He is infallibly the supreme observer. Under any circumstances, the Supreme Lord is changeless. He is simply a witness and is aloof from all creation and annihilation.

TEXT 5

कालेन पञ्चत्वमितेषु कृत्स्नशो
लोकेषु पालेषु च सर्वहेतुषु ।
तमस्तदासीद् गहनं गभीरं
यस्तस्य पारेऽभिविराजते विभुः ॥ ५ ॥

kālena pañcatvam iteṣu kṛtsnaśo
lokeṣu pāleṣu ca sarva-hetuṣu
tamas tadāsīd gahanaṁ gabhīraṁ
yas tasya pāre 'bhivirājate vibhuḥ

kālena—in due course of time (after millions and millions of years); *pañcatvam*—when everything illusory is annihilated; *iteṣu*—all transformations; *kṛtsnaśaḥ*—with everything within this cosmic manifestation; *lokeṣu*—all the planets, or everything that exists; *pāleṣu*—maintainers like Lord Brahmā; *ca*—also; *sarva-hetuṣu*—all causative existences; *tamaḥ*—great darkness; *tadā*—then; *āsīt*—was; *gahanam*—very dense; *gabhīram*—very deep; *yaḥ*—the Supreme Personality of Godhead who; *tasya*—this dark situation; *pāre*—over and above; *abhivirājate*—exists or shines; *vibhuḥ*—the Supreme.

TRANSLATION

In due course of time, when all the causative and effective manifestations of the universe, including the planets and their directors and maintainers, are annihilated, there is a situation of dense darkness. Above this darkness, however, is the Supreme Personality of Godhead. I take shelter of His lotus feet.

PURPORT

From the Vedic *mantras* we understand that the Supreme Personality of Godhead is above everything. He is supreme, above all the demigods, including Lord Brahmā and Lord Śiva. He is the supreme controller. When everything disappears by the influence of His energy, the cosmic situation is one of dense darkness. The Supreme Lord, however, is the sunshine, as confirmed in the Vedic *mantras: āditya-varṇaṁ tamasaḥ parastāt.* In our daily experience, when we on earth are in the darkness of night, the sun is always luminous somewhere in the sky. Similarly, the Supreme Personality of Godhead, the supreme sun, always remains luminous, even when the entire cosmic manifestation is annihilated in due course of time.

TEXT 6

न यस्य देवा ऋषयः पदं विदु-
जन्तुः पुनः कोऽर्हति गन्तुमीरितुम् ।
यथा नटस्याकृतिभिर्विचेष्टतो
दुरत्ययानुक्रमणः स मावतु ॥ ६ ॥

na yasya devā ṛṣayaḥ padaṁ vidur
jantuḥ punaḥ ko 'rhati gantum īritum
yathā naṭasyākṛtibhir viceṣṭato
duratyayānukramaṇaḥ sa māvatu

na—neither; *yasya*—He of whom; *devāḥ*—the demigods; *ṛṣayaḥ*—great sages; *padam*—position; *viduḥ*—can understand; *jantuḥ*—unintelligent living beings like animals; *punaḥ*—again; *kaḥ*—who; *arhati*—is able; *gantum*—to enter into the knowledge; *īritum*—or to express by words; *yathā*—as; *naṭasya*—of the artist; *ākṛtibhiḥ*—by bodily features; *viceṣṭataḥ*—dancing in different ways; *duratyaya*—very difficult; *anukramaṇaḥ*—His movements; *saḥ*—that Supreme Personality of Godhead; *mā*—unto me; *avatu*—may give His protection.

TRANSLATION

An artist onstage, being covered by attractive dresses and dancing with different movements, is not understood by his audience; similarly, the activities and features of the supreme artist cannot be understood even by the demigods or great sages, and certainly not by those who are unintelligent like animals. Neither the demigods and sages nor the unintelligent can understand the features of the Lord, nor can they express in words His actual position. May that Supreme Personality of Godhead give me protection.

PURPORT

A similar understanding was expressed by Kuntīdevī. The Supreme Lord exists everywhere, within and without. He even exists within the heart. *Sarvasya cāhaṁ hṛdi sanniviṣṭo. Īśvaraḥ sarva-bhūtānāṁ hṛd-deśe 'rjuna tiṣṭhati.* Thus it is indicated that one can find the Supreme Lord within one's heart. There are many, many *yogīs* trying to find Him. *Dhyānāvasthita-tad-gatena manasā paśyanti yaṁ yoginaḥ.* Nonetheless, even great *yogīs*, demigods, saints and sages have been unable to understand the bodily features of that great artist, nor could they understand the meaning of His movements. What then is to be said of ordinary speculators like the so-called philosophers of this material world? For them He is impossible to understand. Therefore we must accept the statements given by the Supreme when He kindly incarnates to instruct us. We must simply accept the word of Lord Rāmacandra, Lord Kṛṣṇa and Lord Śrī Caitanya Mahāprabhu and follow in Their footsteps. Then it may be possible for us to know the purpose of Their incarnations.

janma karma ca me divyam
evaṁ yo vetti tattvataḥ
tyaktvā dehaṁ punar janma
naiti mām eti so 'rjuna
(Bg. 4.9)

If by the Lord's grace one can understand Him, one will immediately be delivered, even within his material body. The material body will no longer have any function, and whatever activities take place with the body will be activities of Kṛṣṇa consciousness. In this way one may give up his body and return home, back to Godhead.

TEXT 7

दिदृक्षवो यस्य पदं सुमङ्गलं
विमुक्तसङ्गा मुनयः सुसाधवः ।
चरन्त्यलोकव्रतमव्रणं वने
भूतात्मभूताः सुहृदः स मे गतिः ॥ ७ ॥

didṛkṣavo yasya padaṁ sumaṅgalaṁ
vimukta-saṅgā munayaḥ susādhavaḥ
caranty aloka-vratam avraṇaṁ vane
bhūtātma-bhūtāḥ suhṛdaḥ sa me gatiḥ

didṛkṣavaḥ—those who desire to see (the Supreme Personality of Godhead); *yasya*—of Him; *padam*—the lotus feet; *su-maṅgalam*—all-auspicious; *vimukta-saṅgāḥ*—persons who are completely disinfected of material conditions; *munayaḥ*—great sages; *su-sādhavaḥ*—those who are highly elevated in spiritual consciousness; *caranti*—practice; *aloka-vratam*—vows of *brahmacarya, vānaprastha* or *sannyāsa; avraṇam*—without any fault; *vane*—in the forest; *bhūta-ātma-bhūtāḥ*—those who are equal to all living entities; *suhṛdaḥ*—those who are friends to everyone; *saḥ*—that same Supreme Personality of Godhead; *me*—my; *gatiḥ*—destination.

TRANSLATION

Renunciants and great sages who see all living beings equally, who are friendly to everyone and who flawlessly practice in the forest the vows of brahmacarya, vānaprastha and sannyāsa desire to see the all-auspicious lotus feet of the Supreme Personality of Godhead. May that same Supreme Personality of Godhead be my destination.

PURPORT

This verse describes the qualifications for devotees or persons highly elevated in spiritual consciousness. Devotees are always equal to everyone, seeing no distinction between lower and higher classes. *Paṇḍitāḥ sama-darśinaḥ.* They look upon everyone as a spirit soul who is part and parcel of the Supreme Lord. Thus they are competent to search for the Supreme Personality of Godhead. Understanding that the Supreme Personality of Godhead is the friend of everyone (*suhṛdaṁ sarva-bhūtānām*), they act as friends of everyone on behalf of the Supreme Lord. Making no distinction between one nation and another or one community and another, they preach Kṛṣṇa consciousness, the teachings of *Bhagavad-gītā*, everywhere. Thus they are competent to see the lotus feet of the Lord. Such preachers in Kṛṣṇa consciousness are called *paramahaṁsas.* As indicated by the word *vimukta-saṅga,* they have nothing to do with material conditions. One must take shelter of such a devotee in order to see the Supreme Personality of Godhead.

TEXTS 8–9

न विद्यते यस्य च जन्म कर्म वा
न नामरूपे गुणदोष एव वा ।
तथापि लोकाप्ययसंभवाय यः
स्वमायया तान्यनुकालमृच्छति ॥ ८ ॥
तस्मै नमः परेशाय ब्रह्मणेऽनन्तशक्तये ।
अरूपायोरुरूपाय नम आश्चर्यकर्मणे ॥ ९ ॥

na vidyate yasya ca janma karma vā
na nāma-rūpe guṇa-doṣa eva vā
tathāpi lokāpyaya-sambhavāya yaḥ
sva-māyayā tāny anukālam ṛcchati

tasmai namaḥ pareśāya
brahmaṇe 'nanta-śaktaye
arūpāyoru-rūpāya
nama āścarya-karmaṇe

na—not; *vidyate*—there is; *yasya*—of whom (the Supreme Personality of Godhead); *ca*—also; *janma*—birth; *karma*—activities; *vā*—or; *na*—nor; *nāma-rūpe*—any material name or material form; *guṇa*—qualities; *doṣaḥ*—fault; *eva*—certainly; *vā*—either; *tathāpi*—still; *loka*—of this cosmic manifestation; *apyaya*—who is the destruction; *sambhavāya*—and creation; *yaḥ*—He who; *sva-māyayā*—by His own potency; *tāni*—activities; *anukālam*—eternally; *ṛcchati*—accepts; *tasmai*—unto Him; *namaḥ*—I offer my obeisances; *para*—transcendental; *īśāya*—who is the supreme controller; *brahmaṇe*—who is the Supreme Brahman (Parabrahman); *ananta-śaktaye*—with unlimited potency; *arūpāya*—possessing no material form; *uru-rūpāya*—possessing various forms as incarnations; *namaḥ*—I offer my obeisances; *āścarya-karmaṇe*—whose activities are wonderful.

TRANSLATION

The Supreme Personality of Godhead has no material birth, activities, name, form, qualities or faults. To fulfill the purpose for which this material world is created and destroyed, He comes in the form of a human being like Lord Rāma or Lord Kṛṣṇa by His original internal potency. He has immense potency, and in various forms, all free from material contamination, He acts wonderfully. He is therefore the Supreme Brahman. I offer my respects to Him.

PURPORT

In the *Viṣṇu Purāṇa* it is said, *guṇāṁś ca doṣāṁś ca mune vyatīta samasta-kalyāṇa-guṇātmako hi.* The Supreme Personality of Godhead has no material form, qualities or faults. He is spiritual and is the only reservoir of all spiritual qualities. As stated in *Bhagavad-gītā* (4.8) by the Supreme Personality of Godhead, *paritrāṇāya sādhūnāṁ vināśāya ca duṣkṛtām.* The Lord's activities of saving the devotees and annihilating the demons are transcendental. Anyone annihilated by the Supreme Personality of Godhead gets the same result as a devotee who is protected by the Lord; both of them are transcendentally promoted. The only difference is that a devotee goes directly to the spiritual planets and becomes an associate of the Supreme Lord, whereas demons are promoted to *brahmaloka,* the impersonal effulgence of the Lord. Both of them, however, are transcendentally promoted. The Lord's killing or annihilating of the demons is not exactly like the killing of this material world. Although He appears to act within the modes of material nature, He is *nirguṇa,* above the modes of nature. His name is not material; otherwise how could one get liberation by chanting Hare Kṛṣṇa, Hare Rāma? The names of the Lord like Rāma and Kṛṣṇa are nondifferent from the person Rāma and Kṛṣṇa. Thus by chanting the Hare Kṛṣṇa *mantra* one constantly associates with Rāma and Kṛṣṇa, the Supreme Personality of Godhead, and therefore becomes liberated. A practical example is Ajāmila, who always remained transcendental to his activities simply by chanting the name Nārāyaṇa. If this was true of Ajāmila, what is to be said of the Supreme Lord? When the Lord comes to this material world, He does not become a product of matter. This is confirmed throughout *Bhagavad-gītā* (*janma-karma ca me divyam, avajānanti māṁ mūḍhāḥ mānuṣīṁ tanum āśritam*). Therefore, when the Supreme Personality of Godhead—Rāma or Kṛṣṇa—descends to act transcendentally for our benefit, we should not consider Him an ordinary human being. When the Lord comes, He does so on the basis of His spiritual potency (*sambhavāmy ātma-māyayā*). Because He is not forced to come by the material energy, He is always transcendental. One should not consider the Supreme Lord an ordinary human being. Material names and forms are contaminated, but spiritual name and spiritual form are transcendental.

TEXT 10

नम आत्मप्रदीपाय साक्षिणे परमात्मने ।
नमो गिरां विदूराय मनसश्चेतसामपि ॥१०॥

nama ātma-pradīpāya
sākṣiṇe paramātmane
namo girāṁ vidūrāya
manasaś cetasām api

namaḥ—I offer my respectful obeisances; *ātma-pradīpāya*—unto He who is self-effulgent or who gives enlightenment to the living entities; *sākṣiṇe*—who is situated in everyone's heart as a witness; *parama-ātmane*—unto the Supreme Soul, the Supersoul; *namaḥ*—I offer my respectful obeisances; *girām*—by words; *vidūrāya*—who is impossible to reach; *manasaḥ*—by the mind; *cetasām*—or by consciousness; *api*—even.

TRANSLATION

I offer my respectful obeisances unto the Supreme Personality of Godhead, the self-effulgent Supersoul, who is the witness in everyone's heart, who enlightens the individual soul and who cannot be reached by exercises of the mind, words or consciousness.

PURPORT

The Supreme Personality of Godhead, Kṛṣṇa, cannot be understood by the individual soul through mental, physical or intellectual exercises. It is by the grace of the Supreme Personality of Godhead that the individual soul is enlightened. Therefore, the Lord is described here as *ātma-pradīpa.* The Lord is like the sun, which illuminates everything and cannot be illuminated by anyone. Therefore, if one is serious about understanding the Supreme, one must receive enlightenment from Him, as instructed in *Bhagavad-gītā.* One cannot understand the Supreme Personality of Godhead by one's mental, physical or intellectual powers.

TEXT 11

सत्त्वेन प्रतिलभ्याय नैष्कर्म्येण विपश्चिता ।
नमः कैवल्यनाथाय निर्वाणसुखसंविदे ॥११॥

sattvena pratilabhyāya
naiṣkarmyeṇa vipaścitā

namaḥ kaivalya-nāthāya
nirvāṇa-sukha-saṁvide

sattvena—by pure devotional service; *prati-labhyāya*—unto the Supreme Personality of Godhead, who is achieved by such devotional activities; *naiṣkarmyeṇa*—by transcendental activities; *vipaścitā*—by persons who are sufficiently learned; *namaḥ*—I offer my respectful obeisances; *kaivalya-nāthāya*—unto the master of the transcendental world; *nirvāṇa*—for one completely freed from material activities; *sukha*—of happiness; *saṁvide*—who is the bestower.

TRANSLATION

The Supreme Personality of Godhead is realized by pure devotees who act in the transcendental existence of bhakti-yoga. He is the bestower of uncontaminated happiness and is the master of the transcendental world. Therefore I offer my respect unto Him.

PURPORT

As stated in *Bhagavad-gītā*, the Supreme Personality of Godhead can be understood only by devotional service. *Bhaktyā mām abhijānāti yāvān yaś cāsmi tattvataḥ.* If one wants to know the Supreme Personality of Godhead in truth, one must take to the activities of devotional service. These activities are called *sattva* or *śuddha-sattva.* In the material world, activities of goodness, which are symptomatic of a pure *brāhmaṇa*, are appreciated. But the activities of devotional service are *śuddha-sattva;* in other words, they are on the transcendental platform. Only by devotional service can one understand the Supreme.

Devotional service is called *naiṣkarmya.* Mere negation of material activity will not endure. *Naiṣkarmyam apy acyuta-bhāva-varjitam.* Unless one performs activities with reference to Kṛṣṇa consciousness, cessation of material activities will not be helpful. In hopes of achieving *naiṣkarmya*, freedom from material action, many highly elevated *sannyāsīs* stopped their activities, yet they failed and returned to the material platform to act as materialistic persons. But once one is engaged in the spiritual activities of *bhakti-yoga*, one does not fall down. Our Kṛṣṇa consciousness movement is therefore an attempt to engage everyone always in spiritual activity, by which one becomes transcendental to material actions. The spiritual activities of *bhakti-mārga—śravaṇaṁ kīrtanaṁ viṣṇoḥ smaraṇaṁ pāda-sevanam*—lead one to understand the Supreme Personality of Godhead. Therefore, as stated here, *sattvena pratilabhyāya naiṣkarmyeṇa vipaścitā:* "The Supreme Personality of Godhead is realized by pure devotees who act in the transcendental existence of *bhakti-yoga.*"

The *Gopāla-tāpanī Upaniṣad* (15) says, *bhaktir asya bhajanaṁ tad ihāmutropādhi-nairāsyenaivāmuṣmin manasaḥ kalpanam etad eva ca naiṣkarmyam.* This is a definition of *naiṣkarmya.* One acts in *naiṣkarmya* when he fully engages in Kṛṣṇa conscious activities without material desires to enjoy, either here or in the upper planetary systems, in the present life or in a future life (*iha-amutra*). *Anyābhilāṣitā-śūnyam.* When one is freed from all contamination and he acts in devotional service under the direction of the spiritual master, one is on the platform of *naiṣkarma.* By such transcendental devotional service, the Lord is served. I offer my respectful obeisances unto Him.

TEXT 12

नमः शान्ताय घोराय मूढाय गुणधर्मिणे ।
निर्विशेषाय साम्याय नमो ज्ञानघनाय च ॥१२॥

namaḥ śāntāya ghorāya
mūḍhāya guṇa-dharmiṇe
nirviśeṣāya sāmyāya
namo jñāna-ghanāya ca

namaḥ—all obeisances; *śāntāya*—unto He who is above all material qualities and completely peaceful, or unto Vāsudeva, the Supersoul in every living entity; *ghorāya*—unto the fierce forms of the Lord like Jāmadagnya and Nṛsiṁhadeva; *mūḍhāya*—the form of the Lord as an animal, such as the boar; *guṇa-dharmiṇe*—who accepts different qualities within the material world; *nirviśeṣāya*—who is without material qualities, being fully spiritual; *sāmyāya*—Lord Buddha, the form of *nirvāṇa,* wherein the material qualities stop; *namaḥ*—I offer my respectful obeisances; *jñāna-ghanāya*—who is knowledge or the impersonal Brahman; *ca*—also.

TRANSLATION

I offer my respectful obeisances to Lord Vāsudeva, who is all-pervading, to the Lord's fierce form as Lord Nṛsiṁhadeva, to the Lord's form as an animal [Lord Varāhadeva], to Lord Dattātreya, who preached impersonalism, to Lord Buddha, and to all the other incarnations. I offer my respectful obeisances unto the Lord, who has no material qualities but who accepts the three qualities goodness, passion and ignorance within this material world. I also offer my respectful obeisances unto the impersonal Brahman effulgence.

PURPORT

In the previous verses it has been described that although the Supreme Personality of Godhead has no material form, He accepts innumerable forms to favor His devotees and kill the demons. As stated in *Śrīmad-Bhāgavatam*, there are so many incarnations of the Supreme Personality of Godhead that they are like the waves of a river. The waves of a river flow incessantly, and no one can count how many waves there are. Similarly, no one can calculate when and how the different incarnations of the Lord appear according to the necessities of time, place and candidates. The Lord appears perpetually. As Kṛṣṇa says in *Bhagavad-gītā* (4.7):

yadā yadā hi dharmasya
glānir bhavati bhārata
abhyutthānam adharmasya
tadātmānaṁ sṛjāmy aham

"Whenever and wherever there is a decline in religious practice, O descendant of Bharata, and a predominant rise of irreligion—at that time I descend Myself." In the material world there is always the possibility of deviation from Kṛṣṇa consciousness, and therefore Kṛṣṇa and His devotees always act in various forms to curb such godlessness.

Even impersonalists who stress the knowledge feature of the Supreme Personality of Godhead want to merge in the effulgence of the Lord. Therefore, here the word *jñāna-ghanāya* indicates that for atheists who disbelieve in the form and existence of the Lord, all these various incarnations appear. Since the Lord comes to teach in so many forms, no one can say that there is no God. The word *jñāna-ghanāya* is especially used here to refer to those whose knowledge has become solidified by dint of their searching for the Lord through speculative philosophical understanding. Superficial knowledge is useless for understanding the Supreme Personality of Godhead, but when one's knowledge becomes extremely intense and deep, one understands Vāsudeva (*vāsudevaḥ sarvam iti sa mahātmā sudurlabhaḥ*). A *jñānī* attains this stage after many, many births. Therefore the word *jñāna-ghanāya* is used here. The word *śantāya* indicates that Lord Vāsudeva is situated in everyone's heart but does not act with the living entity. Impersonalist *jñānīs* realize Vāsudeva when they are fully mature in knowledge (*vāsudevaḥ sarvam iti sa mahātmā sudurlabhaḥ*).

TEXT 13

क्षेत्रज्ञाय नमस्तुभ्यं सर्वाध्यक्षाय साक्षिणे ।
पुरुषायात्ममूलाय मूलप्रकृतये नमः ॥१३॥

kṣetra-jñāya namas tubhyaṁ
sarvādhyakṣāya sākṣiṇe
puruṣāyātma-mūlāya
mūla-prakṛtaye namaḥ

kṣetra-jñāya—unto the one who knows everything of the external body; *namaḥ*—I offer my respectful obeisances; *tubhyam*—unto You; *sarva*—everything; *adhyakṣāya*—who are superintending, managing; *sākṣiṇe*—who are the witness, Paramātmā, or *antaryāmī; puruṣāya*—the Supreme Person; *ātma-mūlāya*—who are the original source of everything; *mūla-prakṛtaye*—unto the *puruṣa-avatāra*, the origin of *prakṛti* and *pradhāna; namaḥ*—I offer my respectful obeisances.

TRANSLATION

I beg to offer my respectful obeisances unto You, who are the Supersoul, the superintendent of everything, and the witness of all that occurs. You are the Supreme Person, the origin of material nature and of the total material energy. You are also the owner of the material body. Therefore, You are the supreme complete. I offer my respectful obeisances unto You.

PURPORT

In *Bhagavad-gītā* (13.3) the Lord says, *kṣetra-jñaṁ cāpi māṁ viddhi sarva-kṣetreṣu bhārata:* "O scion of Bharata, you should understand that I am also the knower in all bodies." Every one of us is thinking, "I am this body" or "This is my body," but actually the truth is different. Our bodies are given to us by the supreme proprietor. The living entity, who is also *kṣetra-jña*, or the knower of the body, is not the body's only proprietor; the actual proprietor of the body is the Supreme Personality of Godhead, who is the supreme *kṣetra-jña*. For example, we may rent and occupy a house, but actually the owner of the house is the landlord. Similarly, we may be allotted a certain type of body as a facility with which to enjoy this material world, but the actual proprietor of the body is the Supreme Personality of Godhead. He is called *sarvādhyakṣa* because everything in the material world works under His supervision. This is confirmed in *Bhagavad-gītā* (9.10), wherein the Lord says, *mayādhyakṣeṇa prakṛtiḥ sūyate sacarācaram:* "This material nature, working under My direction, O son of Kuntī, is producing all moving and unmoving beings." From *prakṛti*, or material nature, come so many varieties of living entities, including aquatics, plants, trees, insects, birds, animals, human beings and demigods. *Prakṛti* is the mother, and the Supreme Personality of Godhead is the father (*ahaṁ bīja-pradaḥ pitā*).

Prakṛti can give us material bodies, but as spirit souls we are parts and parcels of the Supreme Personality of Godhead. This is confirmed in *Bhagavad-gītā* (15.7): *mamaivāṁśo jīva-loke jīva-bhūtaḥ sanātanaḥ.* The living entity, being part and parcel of God, is not a product of this material world. Therefore the Lord is described in this verse as *ātma-mūla*, the original source of everything. He is the seed of all existences (*bījaṁ māṁ sarva-bhūtānām*). In *Bhagavad-gītā* (14.4) the Lord says:

sarva-yoniṣu kaunteya
mūrtayaḥ sambhavanti yāḥ
tāsāṁ brahma mahad yonir
ahaṁ bīja-pradaḥ pitā

"It should be understood that all living entities, in all species of life, O son of Kuntī, are made possible by birth in this material nature, and that I am the seed-giving father." Plants, trees, insects, aquatics, demigods, beasts, birds and all other living entities are sons or parts and parcels of the Supreme Lord, but because they are struggling with different mentalities, they have been given different types of bodies (*manaḥ ṣaṣṭhānīndriyāṇi prakṛti-sthāni karṣati*). Thus they have become sons of *prakṛti*, or material nature, which is impregnated by the Supreme Personality of Godhead. Every living entity in this material world is struggling for existence, and the only salvation or relief from the cycle of birth and death in the evolutionary process is full surrender. This is indicated by the word *namaḥ*, "I offer my respectful obeisances unto You."

TEXT 14

सर्वेन्द्रियगुणद्रष्ट्रे सर्वप्रत्ययहेतवे ।
असताच्छाययोक्ताय सदाभासाय ते नमः ॥१४॥

sarvendriya-guṇa-draṣṭre
sarva-pratyaya-hetave
asatā cchāyayoktāya
sad-ābhāsāya te namaḥ

sarva-indriya-guṇa-draṣṭre—unto the seer of all objectives pursued by the senses; *sarva-pratyaya-hetave*—who is the solution to all doubts (and without whose help one cannot solve all doubts and inabilities); *asatā*—with the manifestation of unreality or illusion; *chāyayā*—because of the resemblance; *uktāya*—called; *sat*—of reality; *ābhāsāya*—unto the reflection; *te*—unto You; *namaḥ*—I offer my respectful obeisances.

TRANSLATION

My Lord, You are the observer of all the objectives of the senses. Without Your mercy, there is no possibility of solving the problem of doubts. The material world is just like a shadow resembling You. Indeed, one accepts this material world as real because it gives a glimpse of Your existence.

PURPORT

To paraphrase this verse: "The objectives of sensual activities are actually observed by You. Without Your direction, the living entity cannot take even a step forward. As confirmed in *Bhagavad-gītā* (15.15), *sarvasya cāhaṁ hṛdi sanniviṣṭo mattaḥ smṛtir jñānam apohanaṁ ca.* You are situated in everyone's heart, and only from You come remembrance and forgetfulness. *Chāyeva yasya bhuvanāni bibharti durgā.* The living entity under the clutches of *māyā* wants to enjoy this material world, but unless You give him directions and remind him, he cannot make progress in pursuing his shadowy objective in life. The conditioned soul wrongly progresses toward the wrong objective, life after life, and he is reminded of that objective by You. In one life the conditioned soul desires to progress toward a certain objective, but after his body changes, he forgets everything. Nonetheless, my Lord, because he wanted to enjoy something of this world, You remind him of this in his next birth. *Mattaḥ smṛtir jñānam apohanaṁ ca.* Because the conditioned soul wants to forget You, by Your grace You give him opportunities, life after life, by which he can almost perpetually forget You. Therefore You are eternally the director of the conditioned souls. It is because You are the original cause of everything that everything appears real. The ultimate reality is Your Lordship, the Supreme Personality of Godhead. I offer my respectful obeisances unto You."

The word *sarva-pratyaya-hetave* is explained by Śrīla Viśvanātha Cakravartī Ṭhākura, who says that a result gives one a glimpse of its cause. For example, since an earthen pot is the result of the actions of a potter, by seeing the earthen pot one can guess at the existence of the potter. Similarly, this material world resembles the spiritual world, and any intelligent person can guess how it is acting. As explained in *Bhagavad-gītā*, *mayādhyakṣeṇa prakṛtiḥ sūyate sa-carācaram.* The activities of the material world suggest that behind them is the superintendence of the Lord.

TEXT 15

नमो नमस्तेऽखिलकारणाय
निष्कारणायाद्भुतकारणाय ।
सर्वागमाम्नायमहार्णवाय
नमोऽपवर्गाय परायणाय ॥१५॥

namo namas te 'khila-kāraṇāya
niṣkāraṇāyādbhuta-kāraṇāya

sarvāgamāmnāya-mahārṇavāya
namo 'pavargāya parāyaṇāya

namaḥ—I offer my respectful obeisances; *namaḥ*—again I offer my respectful obeisances; *te*—unto You; *akhila-kāraṇāya*—unto the supreme cause of everything; *niṣkāraṇāya*—unto You who are causeless; *adbhuta-kāraṇāya*—the wonderful cause of everything; *sarva*—all; *āgama-āmnāya*—unto the source of the *paramparā* system of all Vedic knowledge; *mahā-arṇavāya*—the great ocean of knowledge, or the great ocean wherein all the rivers of knowledge merge; *namaḥ*—I offer my obeisances; *apavargāya*—unto You who can give deliverance or liberation; *para-ayaṇāya*—the shelter of all transcendentalists.

TRANSLATION

My Lord, You are the cause of all causes, but You Yourself have no cause. Therefore You are the wonderful cause of everything. I offer my respectful obeisances unto You, who are the shelter of the Vedic knowledge contained in the śāstras like the Pañcarātras and Vedānta-sūtra, which are Your representations, and who are the source of the paramparā system. Because it is You who can give liberation, You are the only shelter for all transcendentalists. Let me offer my respectful obeisances unto You.

PURPORT

The Supreme Personality of Godhead is described herein as the wonderful cause. He is wonderful in the sense that although there may be unlimited emanations from the Supreme Personality of Godhead (*janmādy asya yataḥ*), He always remains complete (*pūrṇasya pūrṇam ādāya pūrṇam evāvaśiṣyate*). In our experience in the material world, if we have a bank balance of one million dollars, as we withdraw money from the bank the balance gradually diminishes until it becomes nil. However, the Supreme Lord, the Personality of Godhead, is so complete that although innumerable Personalities of Godhead expand from Him, He remains the same Supreme Personality of Godhead. *Pūrṇasya pūrṇam ādāya pūrṇam evāvaśiṣyate.* Therefore He is the wonderful cause. *Govindam ādi-puruṣaṁ tam ahaṁ bhajāmi.*

īśvaraḥ paramaḥ kṛṣṇaḥ
sac-cid-ānanda-vigrahaḥ
anādir ādir govindaḥ
sarva-kāraṇa-kāraṇam

"Kṛṣṇa, who is known as Govinda, is the supreme controller. He has an eternal, blissful, spiritual body. He is the origin of all. He has no other origin, for He is the prime cause of all causes." (*Brahma-saṁhitā* 5.1)

Even in this material world, we can understand that the sun has existed for millions of years and has given off heat and light since its creation, yet the sun still retains its power and never changes. What then is to be said of the supreme cause, *paraṁ brahma,* Kṛṣṇa? Everything emanates from Him perpetually, yet He maintains His original form (*sac-cid-ānanda-vigrahaḥ*). Kṛṣṇa personally says in *Bhagavad-gītā* (10.8), *mattaḥ sarvaṁ pravartate:* "Everything emanates from Me." Everything emanates from Kṛṣṇa eternally, yet He is the same Kṛṣṇa and does not change. Therefore He is the shelter of all transcendentalists who are eager to get free from material bondage.

Everyone must take shelter of Kṛṣṇa. It is therefore advised:

akāmaḥ sarva-kāmo vā
mokṣa-kāma udāra-dhīḥ
tīvreṇa bhakti-yogena
yajeta puruṣaṁ param

"Whether one desires everything or nothing or desires to merge into the existence of the Lord, he is intelligent only if he worships Lord Kṛṣṇa, the Supreme Personality of Godhead, by rendering transcendental loving service." (*Bhāg.* 2.3.10) *Paraṁ brahma,* the Supreme Lord, and *paraṁ dhāma,* the supreme repose, is Kṛṣṇa. Therefore anyone who desires anything—whether he be a *karmī,* a *jñānī* or a *yogī*—should try to perceive the Supreme Personality of Godhead very seriously, and all of his desires will be fulfilled. The Lord says, *ye yathā māṁ prapadyante tāṁs tathaiva bhajāmy aham:* "As the living entities surrender unto Me, I reward them accordingly." Even the *karmī* who wants everything for his enjoyment can get it from Kṛṣṇa. For Kṛṣṇa, supplying what he wants is not at all difficult. Actually, however, one should worship Kṛṣṇa, the Supreme Personality of Godhead, for the sake of getting liberation.

Vedaiś ca sarvair aham eva vedyaḥ. By studying the Vedic literature, one should understand Kṛṣṇa. As confirmed here, *sarvāgamāmnāya-mahārṇavāya.* He is the ocean, and all Vedic knowledge flows toward Him. Therefore, intelligent transcendentalists take shelter of the Supreme Personality of Godhead (*sarva-dharmān parityajya mām ekaṁ śaraṇaṁ vraja*). This is the ultimate goal.

TEXT 16

गुणारणिच्छन्नचिदुष्मपाय
तत्क्षोभविस्फूर्जितमानसाय ।
नैष्कर्म्यभावेन विवर्जितागम-
स्वयंप्रकाशाय नमस्करोमि ॥१६॥

guṇāraṇi-cchanna-cid-uṣmapāya
tat-kṣobha-visphūrjita-mānasāya
naiṣkarmya-bhāvena vivarjitāgama-
svayaṁ-prakāśāya namas karomi

guṇa—by the three *guṇas,* the modes of material nature (*sattva, rajas* and *tamas*); *araṇi*—by *araṇi* wood; *channa*—covered; *cit*—of knowledge; *uṣmapāya*—unto He whose fire; *tat-kṣobha*—of the agitation of the modes of material nature; *visphūrjita*—outside; *mānasāya*—unto He whose mind; *naiṣkarmya-bhāvena*—because of the stage of spiritual understanding; *vivarjita*—in those who give up; *āgama*—Vedic principles; *svayam*—personally; *prakāśāya*—unto He who is manifest; *namaḥ karomi*—I offer my respectful obeisances.

TRANSLATION

My Lord, as the fire in araṇi wood is covered, You and Your unlimited knowledge are covered by the material modes of nature. Your mind, however, is not attentive to the activities of the modes of nature. Those who are advanced in spiritual knowledge are not subject to the regulative principles directed in the Vedic

literatures. Because such advanced souls are transcendental, You personally appear in their pure minds. Therefore I offer my respectful obeisances unto You.

PURPORT

In *Bhagavad-gītā* (10.11) it is said:

teṣām evānukampārtham
aham ajñāna-jaṁ tamaḥ
nāśayāmy ātma-bhāva-stho
jñāna-dīpena bhāsvatā

For a devotee who has taken the lotus feet of the Lord within his heart, the Lord gives spiritual enlightenment, known as *jñāna-dīpa*, by special mercy from within. This *jñāna-dīpa* is compared to the fire hidden within *araṇi* wood. To perform fire sacrifices, great sages previously did not ignite a fire directly; the fire would be invoked from *araṇi* wood. Similarly, all living entities are covered by the modes of material nature, and the fire of knowledge can be ignited only by the Supreme Personality of Godhead when one takes Him within one's heart. *Sa vai manaḥ kṛṣṇa-padāravindayoḥ.* If one takes seriously the lotus feet of Kṛṣṇa, who is seated within one's heart, the Lord eradicates all ignorance. By the torch of knowledge, one immediately understands everything properly by the special mercy of the Supreme Lord and becomes self-realized. In other words, although a devotee may externally not be very well educated, because of his devotional service the Supreme Personality of Godhead gives him enlightenment from within. If the Lord gives enlightenment from within, how can one be in ignorance? Therefore the allegation of the Māyāvādīs that the devotional path is for the unintelligent or uneducated is untrue.

yasyāsti bhaktir bhagavaty akiñcanā
sarvair guṇais tatra samāsate surāḥ
(*Bhāg.* 5.18.12)

If one becomes an unalloyed devotee of the Supreme Lord, he automatically manifests all good qualities. Such a devotee is above the instructions of the *Vedas.* He is a *paramahaṁsa.* Even without going through the Vedic literature, a devotee becomes pure and enlightened by the mercy of the Lord. "Therefore, my Lord," the devotee says, "I offer my respectful obeisances unto You."

TEXT 17

मादृक्प्रपन्नपशुपाशविमोक्षणाय
मुक्ताय भूरिकरुणाय नमोऽलयाय ।
स्वांशेन सर्वतनुभृन्मनसि प्रतीत-
प्रत्यग्दृशे भगवते बृहते नमस्ते ॥१७॥

mādṛk prapanna-paśu-pāśa-vimokṣaṇāya
muktāya bhūri-karuṇāya namo 'layāya
svāṁśena sarva-tanu-bhṛn-manasi pratīta-
pratyag-dṛśe bhagavate bṛhate namas te

mādṛk—like me; *prapanna*—surrendered; *paśu*—an animal; *pāśa*—from entanglement; *vimokṣaṇāya*—unto He who releases; *muktāya*—unto the Supreme, who is untouched by the contamination of material nature; *bhūri-karuṇāya*—who are unlimitedly merciful; *namaḥ*—I offer my respectful obeisances; *alayāya*—who are never inattentive or idle (for the purpose of my deliverance); *sva-aṁśena*—by Your partial feature as Paramātmā; *sarva*—of all; *tanu-bhṛt*—the living entities embodied in material nature; *manasi*—in the mind; *pratīta*—who are acknowledged; *pratyak-dṛśe*—as the direct observer (of all activities); *bhagavate*—unto the Supreme Personality of Godhead; *bṛhate*—who are unlimited; *namaḥ*—I offer my respectful obeisances; *te*—unto You.

TRANSLATION

Since an animal such as I has surrendered unto You, who are supremely liberated, certainly You will release me from this dangerous position. Indeed, being extremely merciful, You incessantly try to deliver me. By your partial feature as Paramātmā, You are situated in the hearts of all embodied beings. You are celebrated as direct transcendental knowledge, and You are unlimited.

I offer my respectful obeisances unto You, the Supreme Personality of Godhead.

PURPORT

The words *bṛhate namas te* have been explained by Śrīla Viśvanātha Cakravartī Ṭhākura: *bṛhate śrī-kṛṣṇāya.* The Supreme Personality of Godhead is Kṛṣṇa. There are many *tattvas*, such as *viṣṇu-tattva, jīva-tattva* and *śakti-tattva*, but above everything is the *viṣṇu-tattva*, which is all-pervading. This all-pervading feature of the Supreme Personality of Godhead is explained in *Bhagavad-gītā* (10.42), wherein the Lord says:

athavā bahunaitena
kiṁ jñātena tavārjuna
viṣṭabhyāham idaṁ kṛtsnam
ekāṁśena sthito jagat

"But what need is there, Arjuna, for all this detailed knowledge? With a single fragment of Myself I pervade and support this entire universe." Thus Kṛṣṇa says that the entire material world is maintained by His partial representation as Paramātmā. The Lord enters every universe as Garbhodakaśāyī Viṣṇu and then expands Himself as Kṣīrodakaśāyī Viṣṇu to enter the hearts of all living entities and even enter the atoms. *Aṇḍāntara-stha-paramāṇu-cayāntara-stham.* Every universe is full of atoms, and the Lord is not only within the universe but also within the atoms. Thus within every atom the Supreme Lord exists in His Viṣṇu feature as Paramātmā, but all the *viṣṇu-tattvas* emanate from Kṛṣṇa. As confirmed in *Bhagavad-gītā* (10.2), *aham ādir hi devānām:* Kṛṣṇa is the *ādi*, or beginning, of the *devas* of this material world—Brahmā, Viṣṇu and Maheśvara. Therefore He is described here as *bhagavate bṛhate.* Everyone is *bhagavān*—everyone possesses opulence—but Kṛṣṇa is *bṛhān bhagavān*, the possessor of unlimited opulence. *Īśvaraḥ paramaḥ kṛṣṇaḥ.* Kṛṣṇa is the origin of everyone. *Ahaṁ sarvasya prabhavaḥ.* Even Brahmā, Viṣṇu and Maheśvara come from Kṛṣṇa. *Mattaḥ parataraṁ nānyat kiñcid asti dhanañjaya:* there is no personality superior to Kṛṣṇa. Therefore Viśvanātha Cakravartī Ṭhākura says that *bhagavate bṛhate* means "unto Śrī Kṛṣṇa."

In this material world, everyone is a *paśu,* an animal, because of the bodily conception of life.

yasyātma-buddhiḥ kuṇape tri-dhātuke
sva-dhīḥ kalatrādiṣu bhauma ijya-dhīḥ
yat tīrtha-buddhiḥ salile na karhicij
janeṣv abhijñeṣu sa eva go-kharaḥ

"A human being who identifies the body made of three elements as the self, who considers the by-products of the body to be his kinsmen, who considers the land of his birth to be worshipable, and who goes to a place of pilgrimage simply to bathe rather than to meet men of transcendental knowledge there is to be considered like a cow or an ass." (*Bhāg.* 10.84.13) Practically everyone, therefore, is a *paśu,* an animal, and everyone is attacked by the crocodile of material existence. Not only the King of the elephants but every one of us is being attacked by the crocodile and is suffering the consequences.

Only Kṛṣṇa can deliver us from this material existence. Indeed, He is always trying to deliver us. *Īśvaraḥ sarva-bhūtānāṁ hṛd-deśe 'rjuna tiṣṭhati.* He is within our hearts and is not at all inattentive. His only aim is to deliver us from material life. It is not that He becomes attentive to us only when we offer prayers to Him. Even before we offer our prayers, He incessantly tries to deliver us. He is never lazy in regard to our deliverance. Therefore this verse says, *bhūri-karuṇāya namo 'layāya.* It is the causeless mercy of the Supreme Lord that He always tries to bring us back home, back to Godhead. God is liberated, and He tries to make us liberated, but although He is constantly trying, we refuse to accept His instructions (*sarva-dharmān parityajya mām ekaṁ śaraṇaṁ vraja*). Nonetheless, He has not become angry. Therefore He is described here as *bhūri-karuṇāya,* unlimitedly merciful in delivering us from this miserable material condition of life and taking us back home, back to Godhead.

TEXT 18

आत्मात्मजाप्तगृहवित्तजनेषु सक्तै-
दुर्ष्प्रापणाय गुणसङ्गविवर्जिताय ।

मुक्तात्मभिः स्वहृदये परिभाविताय
ज्ञानात्मने भगवते नम ईश्वराय ॥१८॥

ātmātma-jāpta-gṛha-vitta-janeṣu saktair
duṣprāpaṇāya guṇa-saṅga-vivarjitāya
muktātmabhiḥ sva-hṛdaye paribhāvitāya
jñānātmane bhagavate nama īśvarāya

ātma—the mind and body; *ātma-ja*—sons and daughters; *āpta*—friends and relatives; *gṛha*—home, community, society and nation; *vitta*—wealth; *janeṣu*—to various servants and assistants; *saktaiḥ*—by those who are too attached; *duṣprāpaṇāya*—unto You, who are very difficult to achieve; *guṇa-saṅga*—by the three modes of material nature; *vivarjitāya*—who are not contaminated; *mukta-ātmabhiḥ*—by persons who are already liberated; *sva-hṛdaye*—within the core of the heart; *paribhāvitāya*—unto You, who are always meditated upon; *jñāna-ātmane*—the reservoir of all enlightenment; *bhagavate*—unto the Supreme Personality of Godhead; *namaḥ*—I offer my respectful obeisances; *īśvarāya*—unto the supreme controller.

TRANSLATION

My Lord, those who are completely freed from material contamination always meditate upon You within the cores of their hearts. You are extremely difficult to attain for those like me who are too attached to mental concoction, home, relatives, friends, money, servants and assistants. You are the Supreme Personality of Godhead, uncontaminated by the modes of nature. You are the reservoir of all enlightenment, the supreme controller. I therefore offer my respectful obeisances unto You.

PURPORT

Although the Supreme Personality of Godhead comes into the material world, He is unaffected by the modes of material nature. This is confirmed in *Īśopaniṣad. Apāpa-viddham:* He is not contaminated. This same fact is described here. *Guṇa-saṅga-vivarjitāya.* Although the

Supreme Personality of Godhead appears as an incarnation within this material world, He is unaffected by the modes of material nature. As stated in *Bhagavad-gītā* (9.11), *avajānanti māṁ mūḍhā mānuṣīṁ tanum āśritam:* foolish men with insufficient knowledge deride the Personality of Godhead because He appears just like a human being. Therefore the Supreme Personality of Godhead can be understood only by the *muktātmā*, the liberated soul. *Muktātmabhiḥ sva-hṛdaye paribhāvitāya:* only the liberated person can constantly think of Kṛṣṇa. Such a person is the greatest of all *yogīs.*

yoginām api sarveṣāṁ
mad-gatenāntarātmanā
śraddhāvān bhajate yo māṁ
sa me yuktatamo mataḥ

"Of all *yogīs*, he who always abides in Me with great faith, worshiping Me in transcendental loving service, is most intimately united with Me in *yoga* and is the highest of all." (Bg. 6.47)

TEXT 19

यं धर्मकामार्थविमुक्तिकामा
भजन्त इष्टां गतिमाप्नुवन्ति ।
किं चाशिषो रात्यपि देहमव्ययं
करोतु मेऽदभ्रदयो विमोक्षणम् ॥१९॥

yaṁ dharma-kāmārtha-vimukti-kāmā
bhajanta iṣṭāṁ gatim āpnuvanti
kiṁ cāśiṣo rāty api deham avyayaṁ
karotu me 'dabhra-dayo vimokṣaṇam

yam—the Supreme Personality of Godhead who; *dharma-kāma-artha-vimukti-kāmāḥ*—persons who desire the four principles of religion, economic development, sense gratification and salvation; *bhajantaḥ*—by worshiping; *iṣṭām*—the objective; *gatim*—destination; *āpnuvanti*—can achieve; *kim*—what to speak of; *ca*—also; *āśiṣaḥ*—

other benedictions; *rāti*—He bestows; *api*—even; *deham*—a body; *avyayam*—spiritual; *karotu*—may He bestow benediction; *me*—unto me; *adabhra-dayaḥ*—the Supreme Personality of Godhead, who is unlimitedly merciful; *vimokṣaṇam*—liberation from the present danger and from the material world.

TRANSLATION

After worshiping the Supreme Personality of Godhead, those who are interested in the four principles of religion, economic development, sense gratification and liberation obtain from Him what they desire. What then is to be said of other benedictions? Indeed, sometimes the Lord gives a spiritual body to such ambitious worshipers. May that Supreme Personality of Godhead, who is unlimitedly merciful, bestow upon me the benediction of liberation from this present danger and from the materialistic way of life.

PURPORT

Some men within this material world are *akāmī*, free from material desire, some are ambitious to get more and more material profit, and some desire fulfillment in religious life, economic development, sense gratification and finally liberation.

akāmaḥ sarva-kāmo vā
mokṣa-kāma udāra-dhīḥ
tīvreṇa bhakti-yogena
yajeta puruṣaṁ param
(*Bhāg.* 2.3.10)

It is recommended that whatever one's position—whether one demands no material profit, all material profit or ultimately liberation—one should offer his obedient devotional service to the Lord, and one will get what he desires. Kṛṣṇa is so kind. *Ye yathā māṁ prapadyante tāṁs tathaiva bhajāmy aham.* The Lord reciprocates. Whatever even an ordinary living entity wants, Kṛṣṇa gives. Kṛṣṇa is situated in everyone's heart, and He gives that which is desired by the living entity.

īśvaraḥ sarva-bhūtānāṁ
hṛd-deśe 'rjuna tiṣṭhati
bhrāmayan sarva-bhūtāni
yantrārūḍhāni māyayā

"The Supreme Lord is situated in everyone's heart, O Arjuna, and is directing the wanderings of all living entities, who are seated as on a machine, made of the material energy." (Bg. 18.61) The Lord gives everyone an opportunity to fulfill his ambitions. Even such a devotee as Dhruva Mahārāja wanted the material benediction of a kingdom greater than that of his father, and although he received a spiritual body, he also got the kingdom, for the Supreme Personality of Godhead does not disappoint anyone who takes shelter of His lotus feet. Therefore, since Gajendra, King of the elephants, had surrendered to the Supreme Personality of Godhead to get free from the present danger and, indirectly, from the present danger of materialistic life, why should the Supreme Personality of Godhead not fulfill his desire?

TEXTS 20–21

एकान्तिनो यस्य न कञ्चनार्थं
वाञ्छन्ति ये वै भगवत्प्रपन्नाः ।
अत्यद्भुतं तच्चरितं सुमङ्गलं
गायन्त आनन्दसमुद्रमग्नाः ॥२०॥
तमक्षरं ब्रह्म परं परेश-
मव्यक्तमाध्यात्मिकयोगगम्यम् ।
अतीन्द्रियं सूक्ष्ममिवातिदूर-
मनन्तमाद्यं परिपूर्णमीडे ॥२१॥

ekāntino yasya na kañcanārthaṁ
vāñchanti ye vai bhagavat-prapannāḥ
aty-adbhutaṁ tac-caritaṁ sumaṅgalaṁ
gāyanta ānanda-samudra-magnāḥ

tam akṣaraṁ brahma paraṁ pareśam
avyaktam ādhyātmika-yoga-gamyam
atīndriyaṁ sūkṣmam ivātidūram
anantam ādyaṁ paripūrṇam īḍe

ekāntinaḥ—unalloyed devotees (who have no desire other than Kṛṣṇa consciousness); *yasya*—the Lord, of whom; *na*—not; *kañcana*—some; *artham*—benediction; *vāñchanti*—desire; *ye*—those devotees who; *vai*—indeed; *bhagavat-prapannāḥ*—fully surrendered unto the lotus feet of the Lord; *ati-adbhutam*—which are wonderful; *tat-caritam*—the activities of the Lord; *su-maṅgalam*—and very auspicious (to hear); *gāyantaḥ*—by chanting and hearing; *ānanda*—of transcendental bliss; *samudra*—in the ocean; *magnāḥ*—who are immersed; *tam*—unto Him; *akṣaram*—eternally existing; *brahma*—the Supreme; *param*—transcendental; *para-īśam*—the Lord of the supreme personalities; *avyaktam*—invisible or not able to be realized by the mind and senses; *ādhyātmika*—transcendental; *yoga*—by *bhakti-yoga,* devotional service; *gamyam*—obtainable (*bhaktyā mām abhijānāti*); *ati-indriyam*—beyond the perception of material senses; *sūkṣmam*—minute; *iva*—like; *ati-dūram*—very far away; *anantam*—unlimited; *ādyam*—the original cause of everything; *paripūrṇam*—completely full; *īḍe*—I offer my obeisances.

TRANSLATION

Unalloyed devotees, who have no desire other than to serve the Lord, worship Him in full surrender and always hear and chant about His activities, which are most wonderful and auspicious. Thus they always merge in an ocean of transcendental bliss. Such devotees never ask the Lord for any benediction. I, however, am in danger. Thus I pray to that Supreme Personality of Godhead, who is eternally existing, who is invisible, who is the Lord of all great personalities, such as Brahmā, and who is available only by transcendental bhakti-yoga. Being extremely subtle, He is beyond the reach of my senses and transcendental to all external realization. He is unlimited, He is the original cause, and He is completely full in everything. I offer my obeisances unto Him.

PURPORT

anyābhilāṣitā-śūnyaṁ
jñāna-karmādy-anāvṛtam
ānukūlyena kṛṣṇānu-
śīlanaṁ bhaktir uttamā
(*Bhakti-rasāmṛta-sindhu* 1.1.11)

"One should render transcendental loving service to the Supreme Lord Kṛṣṇa favorably and without desire for material profit or gain through fruitive activities or philosophical speculation. That is called pure devotional service." Unalloyed devotees have nothing to ask from the Supreme Personality of Godhead, but Gajendra, the King of the elephants, was circumstantially asking for an immediate benediction because he had no other way to be rescued. Sometimes, when there is no alternative, a pure devotee, being fully dependent on the mercy of the Supreme Lord, prays for some benediction. But in such a prayer there is also regret. One who always hears and chants about the transcendental pastimes of the Lord is always situated on a platform on which he has nothing to ask in terms of material benefits. Unless one is a completely pure devotee, one cannot enjoy the transcendental bliss derived from chanting and dancing in the ecstasy of the *saṅkīrtana* movement. Such ecstasy is not possible for an ordinary devotee. Lord Śrī Caitanya Mahāprabhu showed us how one can enjoy transcendental bliss simply by chanting, hearing and dancing in ecstasy. This is *bhakti-yoga.* Therefore the King of the elephants, Gajendra, said, *ādhyātmika-yoga-gamyam,* indicating that unless one is situated on this transcendental platform, one cannot approach the Supreme Lord. The benediction of being able to approach the Lord can be achieved after many, many births, yet Śrī Caitanya Mahāprabhu has awarded this benediction to everyone, even to the fallen souls who have no heritage of anything in spiritual life. That is actually being seen in the Kṛṣṇa consciousness movement. Therefore the path of *bhakti-yoga* is the spotless process by which to approach the Supreme Personality of Godhead. *Bhaktyāham ekayā grāhyaḥ:* only through devotional service can one approach the Supreme Lord. The Lord says in *Bhagavad-gītā* (7.1):

mayy āsakta-manāḥ pārtha
yogaṁ yuñjan mad-āśrayaḥ

asaṁśayaṁ samagraṁ māṁ
yathā jñāsyasi tac chṛṇu

"Now hear, O son of Pṛthā [Arjuna], how by practicing *yoga* in full consciousness of Me, with mind attached to Me, you can know Me in full, free from doubt." Simply by being attached to Kṛṣṇa consciousness and by thinking of the lotus feet of Kṛṣṇa constantly, one can fully understand the Supreme Personality of Godhead, without a doubt.

TEXTS 22–24

यस्य ब्रह्मादयो देवा वेदा लोकाश्चराचराः ।
नामरूपविभेदेन फल्ग्व्या च कलया कृताः ॥२२॥
यथार्चिषोऽग्नेः सवितुर्गभस्तयो
निर्यान्ति संयान्त्यसकृत् स्वरोचिषः ।
तथा यतोऽयं गुणसम्प्रवाहो
बुद्धिर्मनः खानि शरीरसर्गाः ॥२३॥
स वै न देवासुरमर्त्यतिर्यङ्
न स्त्री न षण्ढो न पुमान् न जन्तुः ।
नायं गुणः कर्म न सन्न चासन्
निषेधशेषो जयतादशेषः ॥२४॥

yasya brahmādayo devā
vedā lokāś carācarāḥ
nāma-rūpa-vibhedena
phalgvyā ca kalayā kṛtāḥ

yathārciṣo 'gneḥ savitur gabhastayo
niryānti saṁyānty asakṛt sva-rociṣaḥ
tathā yato 'yaṁ guṇa-sampravāho
buddhir manaḥ khāni śarīra-sargāḥ

sa vai na devāsura-martya-tiryaṅ
na strī na ṣaṇḍho na pumān na jantuḥ

nāyaṁ guṇaḥ karma na san na cāsan
niṣedha-śeṣo jayatād aśeṣaḥ

yasya—of the Supreme Personality of Godhead who; *brahma-ādayaḥ*—the great demigods, headed by Lord Brahmā; *devāḥ*—and other demigods; *vedāḥ*—the Vedic knowledge; *lokāḥ*—different personalities; *cara-acarāḥ*—the moving and the nonmoving (like trees and plants); *nāma-rūpa*—of different names and different forms; *vibhedena*—by such divisions; *phalgvyā*—who are less important; *ca*—also; *kalayā*—by the parts; *kṛtāḥ*—created; *yathā*—as; *arciṣaḥ*—the sparks; *agneḥ*—of fire; *savituḥ*—from the sun; *gabhastayaḥ*—the shining particles; *niryānti*—emanate from; *saṁyānti*—and enter into; *asakṛt*—again and again; *sva-rociṣaḥ*—as parts and parcels; *tathā*—similarly; *yataḥ*—the Personality of Godhead from whom; *ayam*—this; *guṇa-sampravāhaḥ*—continuous manifestation of the different modes of nature; *buddhiḥ manaḥ*—the intelligence and mind; *khāni*—the senses; *śarīra*—of the body (gross and subtle); *sargāḥ*—the divisions; *saḥ*—that Supreme Personality of Godhead; *vai*—indeed; *na*—is not; *deva*—demigod; *asura*—demon; *martya*—human being; *tiryak*—bird or beast; *na*—neither; *strī*—woman; *na*—nor; *ṣaṇḍaḥ*—neuter; *na*—neither; *pumān*—man; *na*—nor; *jantuḥ*—living being or animal; *na ayam*—nor is He; *guṇaḥ*—material quality; *karma*—fruitive activity; *na*—is not; *sat*—manifestation; *na*—nor; *ca*—also; *asat*—nonmanifestation; *niṣedha*—of the discrimination of *neti neti* ("not this, not this"); *śeṣaḥ*—He is the end; *jayatāt*—all glories unto Him; *aśeṣaḥ*—who is unlimited.

TRANSLATION

The Supreme Personality of Godhead creates His minor parts and parcels, the jīva-tattva, beginning with Lord Brahmā, the demigods and the expansions of Vedic knowledge [Sāma, Ṛg, Yajur and Atharva] and including all other living entities, moving and nonmoving, with their different names and characteristics. As the sparks of a fire or the shining rays of the sun emanate from their source and merge into it again and again, the mind, the intelligence, the senses, the gross and subtle material bodies, and the continuous transformations of the different modes of nature all

emanate from the Lord and again merge into Him. He is neither demigod nor demon, neither human nor bird or beast. He is not woman, man, or neuter, nor is He an animal. He is not a material quality, a fruitive activity, a manifestation or nonmanifestation. He is the last word in the discrimination of "not this, not this," and He is unlimited. All glories to the Supreme Personality of Godhead!

PURPORT

This is a summary description of the Supreme Personality of Godhead's unlimited potency. That supreme one is acting in different phases by manifesting His parts and parcels, which are all simultaneously differently situated by His different potencies (*parāsya śaktir vividhaiva śrūyate*). Each and every potency is acting quite naturally (*svābhāvikī jñāna-bala-kriyā ca*). Therefore the Lord is unlimited. *Na tat-samaś cābhyadhikaś ca dṛśyate:* nothing is equal to Him, nor is anything greater than Him. Although He manifests Himself in so many ways, personally He has nothing to do (*na tasya kāryaṁ karaṇaṁ ca vidyate*), for everything is done by expansions of His unlimited energies.

TEXT 25

जिजीविषे नाहमिहामुया कि-
मन्तर्बहिश्चावृतयेभयोन्या ।
इच्छामि कालेन न यस्य विप्लव-
स्तस्यात्मलोकावरणस्य मोक्षम् ॥२५॥

jijīviṣe nāham ihāmuyā kim
antar bahiś cāvṛtayebha-yonyā
icchāmi kālena na yasya viplavas
tasyātma-lokāvaraṇasya mokṣam

jijīviṣe—wish to live long; *na*—not; *aham*—I; *iha*—in this life; *amuyā*—or in the next life (I do not wish to live upon being saved from this dangerous position); *kim*—what is the value; *antaḥ*—internally; *bahiḥ*—externally; *ca*—and; *āvṛtayā*—covered by ignorance; *ibha-yonyā*—in this birth as an elephant; *icchāmi*—I desire; *kālena*—

because of the influence of time; *na*—there is not; *yasya*—of which; *viplavaḥ*—annihilation; *tasya*—that; *ātma-loka-āvaraṇasya*—from the covering of self-realization; *mokṣam*—liberation.

TRANSLATION

I do not wish to live anymore after I am released from the attack of the crocodile. What is the use of an elephant's body covered externally and internally by ignorance? I simply desire eternal liberation from the covering of ignorance. That covering is not destroyed by the influence of time.

PURPORT

In this material world, every living entity is covered by the darkness of ignorance. Therefore the *Vedas* enjoin that one should approach the Supreme Lord through the spiritual master, who is described and offered prayers in the *Gautamīya-tantra* as follows:

oṁ ajñāna-timirāndhasya
jñānāñjana-śalākayā
cakṣur unmīlitaṁ yena
tasmai śrī-gurave namaḥ

"I offer my respectful obeisances unto my spiritual master, who with the torchlight of knowledge has opened my eyes, which were blinded by the darkness of ignorance." Although one may struggle for existence in this material world, to live forever is impossible. One must understand, however, that this struggle for existence is due to ignorance, for otherwise every living being is an eternal part of the Supreme Lord. There is no need to live as an elephant or man, American or Indian; one should desire only to achieve liberation from the cycle of birth and death. Because of ignorance, we consider every life offered by nature to be happy and pleasing, but in the degraded life within this material world, from the life of Lord Brahmā down to that of an ant, no one can actually be happy. We are making so many plans to live happily, but there cannot be any happiness in this material world, however we may try to make a permanent settlement in this life or that.

TEXT 26

सोऽहं विश्वसृजं विश्वमविश्वं विश्ववेदसम् ।
विश्वात्मानमजं ब्रह्म प्रणतोऽस्मि परं पदम् ॥२६॥

so 'haṁ viśva-sṛjaṁ viśvam
aviśvaṁ viśva-vedasam
viśvātmānam ajaṁ brahma
praṇato 'smi paraṁ padam

saḥ—that; *aham*—I (the person desiring release from material life); *viśva-sṛjam*—unto He who has created this cosmic manifestation; *viśvam*—who is Himself the whole cosmic presentation; *aviśvam*—although He is transcendental to the cosmic manifestation; *viśva-vedasam*—who is the knower or ingredient of this universal manifestation; *viśva-ātmānam*—the soul of the universe; *ajam*—who is never born, eternally existing; *brahma*—the Supreme; *praṇataḥ asmi*—I offer my respectful obeisances; *param*—who is transcendental; *padam*—the shelter.

TRANSLATION

Now, fully desiring release from material life, I offer my respectful obeisances unto that Supreme Person who is the creator of the universe, who is Himself the form of the universe and who is nonetheless transcendental to this cosmic manifestation. He is the supreme knower of everything in this world, the Supersoul of the universe. He is the unborn, supremely situated Lord. I offer my respectful obeisances unto Him.

PURPORT

Sometimes when *bhakti-yoga*, Kṛṣṇa consciousness, is preached to the common man, people argue, "Where is Kṛṣṇa? Where is God? Can you show Him to us?" In this verse the answer is given that if we are sufficiently intelligent, we must know that there is someone who has created the entire cosmic manifestation, who has supplied and has become the ingredients for this cosmic manifestation, who is eternally existing, but who is not within the cosmic manifestation. Simply on the basis of this suggestion, one can offer respectful obeisances unto the Supreme Lord. This is the beginning of devotional life.

TEXT 27

योगरन्धितकर्माणो हृदि योगविभाविते ।
योगिनो यं प्रपश्यन्ति योगेशं तं नतोऽस्म्यहम् ॥२७॥

yoga-randhita-karmāṇo
hṛdi yoga-vibhāvite
yogino yaṁ prapaśyanti
yogeśaṁ taṁ nato 'smy aham

yoga-randhita-karmāṇaḥ—persons whose reactions to fruitive activities have been burnt up by *bhakti-yoga; hṛdi*—within the core of the heart; *yoga-vibhāvite*—completely purified and clean; *yoginaḥ*—mystics who are competent; *yam*—unto the Personality of Godhead who; *prapaśyanti*—directly see; *yoga-īśam*—unto that Supreme Personality of Godhead, the master of all mystic *yoga; tam*—unto Him; *nataḥ asmi*—offering obeisances; *aham*—I.

TRANSLATION

I offer my respectful obeisances unto the Supreme, the Supersoul, the master of all mystic yoga, who is seen in the core of the heart by perfect mystics when they are completely purified and freed from the reactions of fruitive activity by practicing bhakti-yoga.

PURPORT

The King of the elephants, Gajendra, simply accepted that there must be someone who has created this cosmic manifestation and has supplied its ingredients. This should be admitted by everyone, even the most determined atheists. Why, then, do the nondevotees and atheists not admit this? The reason is that they are polluted by the reactions of their fruitive activities. One must be freed from all the dirt accumulated within the heart due to fruitive activities performed one after another. One must wash off this dirt by practicing *bhakti-yoga. Yoga-randhita-*

karmāṇaḥ. As long as one is covered by material nature's modes of ignorance and passion, there is no possibility of understanding the Supreme Lord. *Tadā rajas-tamo-bhāvāḥ kāma-lobhādayaś ca ye.* When one is freed from the modes of ignorance and passion, one becomes free from the lowest qualities—*kāma* and *lobha,* lust and greed.

Nowadays there are so many *yoga* schools to encourage people in developing their lusty desires and greed through the practice of *yoga.* People are therefore very much fond of so-called *yoga* practice. The actual practice of *yoga,* however, is described here. As authoritatively stated in the *Śrīmad-Bhāgavatam* (12.13.1), *dhyānāvasthita-tad-gatena manasā paśyanti yaṁ yoginaḥ:* a *yogī* is one who always meditates on the lotus feet of the Supreme Personality of Godhead. This is also confirmed in the *Brahma-saṁhitā* (5.38):

premāñjana-cchurita-bhakti-vilocanena
santaḥ sadaiva hṛdayeṣu vilokayanti
yaṁ śyāmasundaram acintya-guṇa-svarūpaṁ
govindam ādi-puruṣaṁ tam ahaṁ bhajāmi

"I worship Govinda, the primeval Lord, who is Śyāmasundara, Kṛṣṇa Himself, with inconceivable innumerable attributes, whom the pure devotees see in their heart of hearts with the eye of devotion tinged with the salve of love." The *bhakti-yogī* constantly sees Śyāmasundara—beautiful Lord Kṛṣṇa with His blackish bodily hue. Because the King of the elephants, Gajendra, thought himself an ordinary animal, he thought himself unfit to see the Lord. In his humility, he thought that he could not practice *yoga.* In other words, how can those who are like animals in the bodily concept of life, and who have no purity of consciousness, practice *yoga?* In the present day, people who have no control over their senses, who have no understanding of philosophy and who do not follow religious principles or rules and regulations are nonetheless pretending to be *yogīs.* This is the greatest anomaly in the practice of mystic *yoga.*

TEXT 28

नमो नमस्तुभ्यमसह्यवेग-
शक्तित्रयायाखिलधीगुणाय ।

प्रपन्नपालाय दुरन्तशक्तये
कदिन्द्रियाणामनवाप्यवर्त्मने ॥२८॥

namo namas tubhyam asahya-vega-
śakti-trayāyākhila-dhī-guṇāya
prapanna-pālāya duranta-śaktaye
kad-indriyāṇām anavāpya-vartmane

namaḥ—I offer my respectful obeisances; *namaḥ*—again I offer my respectful obeisances; *tubhyam*—unto You; *asahya*—formidable; *vega*—forces; *śakti-trayāya*—unto the Supreme Person, who has threefold potencies; *akhila*—of the universe; *dhī*—for the intelligence; *guṇāya*—who appears as the sense objects; *prapanna-pālāya*—unto the Supreme, who gives shelter to the surrendered; *duranta-śaktaye*—who possesses energies very difficult to overcome; *kat-indriyāṇām*—by persons unable to control their senses; *anavāpya*—who is unattainable; *vartmane*—on the path.

TRANSLATION

My Lord, You are the controller of formidable strength in three kinds of energy. You appear as the reservoir of all sense pleasure and the protector of the surrendered souls. You possess unlimited energy, but You are unapproachable by those who are unable to control their senses. I offer my respectful obeisances unto You again and again.

PURPORT

Attachment, greed and lust are three formidable forces that prevent one from concentrating upon the lotus feet of the Supreme Personality of Godhead. These forces act because the Supreme Lord does not like to be realized by nondevotees and atheists. However, when one surrenders unto the lotus feet of the Lord, these impediments are withdrawn, and one can realize the Supreme Personality of Godhead. Therefore the Lord is the protector of the surrendered soul. One cannot become a devotee until one surrenders unto the Lord's lotus feet. Then the Lord gives one the intelligence from within by which one can return home, back to Godhead.

TEXT 29

नायं वेद स्वमात्मानं यच्छक्त्याहंधिया हतम् ।
तं दुरत्ययमाहात्म्यं भगवन्तमितोऽस्म्यहम् ॥२९॥

nāyaṁ veda svam ātmānaṁ
yac-chaktyāhaṁ-dhiyā hatam
taṁ duratyaya-māhātmyaṁ
bhagavantam ito 'smy aham

na—not; *ayam*—people in general; *veda*—know; *svam*—own; *ātmānam*—identity; *yat-śaktyā*—by whose influence; *aham*—I am independent; *dhiyā*—by this intelligence; *hatam*—defeated or covered; *tam*—unto Him; *duratyaya*—difficult to understand; *māhātmyam*—whose glories; *bhagavantam*—of the Supreme Personality of Godhead; *itaḥ*—taking shelter; *asmi aham*—I am.

TRANSLATION

I offer my respectful obeisances unto the Supreme Personality of Godhead, by whose illusory energy the jīva, who is part and parcel of God, forgets his real identity because of the bodily concept of life. I take shelter of the Supreme Personality of Godhead, whose glories are difficult to understand.

PURPORT

As stated in *Bhagavad-gītā,* every living entity—regardless of whether he be human, demigod, animal, bird, bee or whatever—is part and parcel of the Supreme Personality of Godhead. The Lord and the living entity are intimately related like father and son. Unfortunately, because of material contact, the living entity forgets this and wants to enjoy the material world independently, according to his own plan. This illusion (*māyā*) is very difficult to surmount. *Māyā* covers the living entity because of his willingness to forget the Supreme Personality of Godhead and make his own plan to enjoy this material world. As long as this contamination continues, the conditioned soul will be unable to understand his real identity and will perpetually continue under illusion, life after life. *Ato gṛha-kṣetra-sutāpta-vittair janasya moho 'yam ahaṁ mameti*

(*Bhāg.* 5.5.8). As long as the living entity is not enlightened so that he may understand his real position, he will be attracted to materialistic life, to house, country or field, to society, sons, family, community, bank balance and so on. Covered by all this, he will continue to think, "I am this body, and everything related to this body is mine." This materialistic conception of life is extremely difficult to surmount, but one who surrenders to the Supreme Personality of Godhead, as did Gajendra, the King of the elephants, comes to enlightenment on the Brahman platform.

brahma-bhūtaḥ prasannātmā
na śocati na kāṅkṣati
samaḥ sarveṣu bhūteṣu
mad-bhaktiṁ labhate parām

"One who is transcendentally situated at once realizes the Supreme Brahman and becomes fully joyful. He never laments nor desires to have anything; he is equally disposed toward all living entities. In that state he attains pure devotional service unto Me." (Bg. 18.54) Since a devotee is completely on the Brahman platform, he is not jealous of any other living entity (*samaḥ sarveṣu bhūteṣu*).

TEXT 30

श्रीशुक उवाच
एवं गजेन्द्रमुपवर्णितनिर्विशेषं
ब्रह्मादयो विविधलिङ्गभिदाभिमानाः ।
नैते यदोपससृपुर्निखिलात्मकत्वात्
तत्राखिलामरमयो हरिराविरासीत् ॥३०॥

śrī-śuka uvāca
evaṁ gajendram upavarṇita-nirviśeṣaṁ
brahmādayo vividha-liṅga-bhidābhimānāḥ
naite yadopasasṛpur nikhilātmakatvāt
tatrākhilāmara-mayo harir āvirāsīt

śrī-śukaḥ uvāca—Śrī Śukadeva Gosvāmī said; *evam*—in this way; *gajendram*—unto the King of the elephants, Gajendra; *upavarṇita*—

whose description; *nirviśeṣam*—not directed to any particular person (but to the Supreme, although he did not know who the Supreme is); *brahmā-ādayaḥ*—the demigods, beginning with Brahmā, Śiva, Indra and Candra; *vividha*—varieties; *liṅga-bhidā*—with separate forms; *abhimānāḥ*—considering themselves separate authorities; *na*—not; *ete*—all of them; *yadā*—when; *upasasṛpuḥ*—approached; *nikhila-ātmakatvāt*—because the Supreme Personality of Godhead is the Supersoul of everyone; *tatra*—there; *akhila*—of the universe; *amara-mayaḥ*—consisting of the demigods (who are only external parts of the body); *hariḥ*—the Supreme Personality of Godhead, who can take away everything; *āvirāsīt*—appeared (before the elephant).

TRANSLATION

Śrī Śukadeva Gosvāmī continued: When the King of the elephants was describing the supreme authority, without mentioning any particular person, he did not invoke the demigods, headed by Lord Brahmā, Lord Śiva, Indra and Candra. Thus none of them approached him. However, because Lord Hari is the Supersoul, Puruṣottama, the Personality of Godhead, He appeared before Gajendra.

PURPORT

From the description of Gajendra, he apparently was aiming at the supreme authority although he did not know who the supreme authority is. He conjectured, "There is a supreme authority who is above everything." Under the circumstances, the Lord's various expansions, such as Lord Brahmā, Lord Śiva, Candra and Indra, all thought, "Gajendra is not asking our help. He is asking the help of the Supreme, who is above all of us." As Gajendra has described, the Supreme Lord has various parts and parcels, including the demigods, human beings and animals, all covered by separate forms. Although the demigods are in charge of maintaining different aspects of the universe, Gajendra thought that they were unable to rescue him. *Hariṁ vinā naiva mṛtiṁ taranti:* no one can rescue anyone from the dangers of birth, death, old age and disease. It is only the Supreme Personality of Godhead who can rescue one from the dangers of material existence. Therefore an intelligent person, to get free from this dangerous existence, approaches the Supreme Personality of Godhead, not any demigod. As confirmed in *Bhagavad-gītā* (7.20), *kāmais tais tair hṛta-jñānāḥ prapadyante 'nya-devatāḥ:* those who are unintelligent approach the various demigods for temporary material benefits. Actually, however, these demigods cannot rescue the living entity from the dangers of material existence. Like other living entities, the demigods are merely external parts of the Supreme Personality of Godhead's transcendental body. As stated in the Vedic *mantras, sa ātmā aṅgāny anyā devatāḥ.* Within the body is the *ātmā*, the soul, whereas the various parts of the body like the hands and legs are external. Similarly, the *ātmā* of the entire cosmic manifestation is Nārāyaṇa, Lord Viṣṇu, and all the demigods, human beings and other living entities are parts of His body.

It may also be concluded that since a tree lives on the strength of its root and when the root is nourished with water all the parts of the tree are nourished, one should worship the Supreme Personality of Godhead, who is the original root of everything. Although the Supreme Personality of Godhead is very difficult to approach, He is very near to us because He lives within our hearts. As soon as the Lord understands that one is seeking His favor by fully surrendering, naturally He immediately takes action. Therefore although the demigods did not come to the aid of Gajendra, the Supreme Personality of Godhead immediately appeared before him because of his fervent prayer. This does not mean that the demigods were angry with Gajendra, for actually when Lord Viṣṇu is worshiped, all the other demigods are also worshiped. *Yasmin tuṣṭe jagat tuṣṭam:* if the Supreme Personality of Godhead is satisfied, everyone is satisfied.

yathā taror mūla-niṣecanena
tṛpyanti tat-skandha-bhujopaśākhāḥ
prāṇopahārāc ca yathendriyāṇāṁ
tathaiva sarvārhaṇam acyutejyā

"As pouring water on the root of a tree energizes the trunk, branches, twigs and everything else, and as supplying food to the stomach enlivens the senses and limbs of the body, so simply worshiping the Supreme Personality of Godhead through devotional service automatically satisfies the demigods, who are parts of that Supreme Personality." (*Bhāg.* 4.31.14) When the Supreme Personality of Godhead is worshiped, all the demigods are satisfied.

TEXT 31

तं तद्वदार्तमुपलभ्य जगन्निवासः
स्तोत्रं निशम्य दिविजैः सह संस्तुवद्भिः ।
छन्दोमयेन गरुडेन समुह्यमान-
श्चक्रायुधोऽभ्यगमदाशु यतो गजेन्द्रः ॥३१॥

taṁ tadvad ārtam upalabhya jagan-nivāsaḥ
stotraṁ niśamya divijaiḥ saha saṁstuvadbhiḥ
chandomayena garuḍena samuhyamānaś
cakrāyudho 'bhyagamad āśu yato gajendraḥ

tam—unto him (Gajendra); *tadvat*—in that way; *ārtam*—who was very depressed (because of being attacked by the crocodile); *upalabhya*—understanding; *jagat-nivāsaḥ*—the Lord, who exists everywhere; *stotram*—the prayer; *niśamya*—hearing; *divijaiḥ*—the denizens of the heavenly planets; *saha*—with; *saṁstuvadbhiḥ*—who were offering their prayers also; *chandomayena*—with the speed He desired; *garuḍena*—by Garuḍa; *samuhyamānaḥ*—being carried; *cakra*—carrying His disc; *āyudhaḥ*—and other weapons, like the club; *abhyagamat*—arrived; *āśu*—immediately; *yataḥ*—where; *gajendraḥ*—the King of the elephants, Gajendra, was situated.

TRANSLATION

After understanding the awkward condition of Gajendra, who had offered his prayers, the Supreme Personality of Godhead, Hari, who lives everywhere, appeared with the demigods, who were offering prayers to Him. Carrying His disc and other weapons, He appeared there on the back of His carrier, Garuḍa, with great speed, according to His desire. Thus He appeared before Gajendra.

PURPORT

Śrīla Viśvanātha Cakravartī Ṭhākura specifically hints that since Gajendra was in such a difficult position and was praying for the mercy of the Supreme Personality of Godhead, the demigods, who could have immediately gone to his rescue, hesitated to go there. Since they considered Gajendra's prayer to be directed toward the Lord, they felt offended, and this in itself was offensive. Consequently, when the Lord went there, they also went and offered prayers to the Lord so that their offense might be excused.

TEXT 32

सोऽन्तःसरस्युरुबलेन गृहीत आर्तो
दृष्ट्वा गरुत्मति हरिं ख उपात्तचक्रम् ।
उत्क्षिप्य साम्बुजकरं गिरमाह कृच्छ्रा-
न्नारायणाखिलगुरो भगवन् नमस्ते ॥३२॥

so 'ntaḥ-sarasy urubalena gṛhīta ārto
dṛṣṭvā garutmati hariṁ kha upātta-cakram
utkṣipya sāmbuja-karaṁ giram āha kṛcchrān
nārāyaṇākhila-guro bhagavan namas te

saḥ—he (Gajendra); *antaḥ-sarasi*—in the water; *uru-balena*—with great force; *gṛhītaḥ*—who had been captured by the crocodile; *ārtaḥ*—and severely suffering; *dṛṣṭvā*—upon seeing; *garutmati*—on the back of Garuḍa; *harim*—the Lord; *khe*—in the sky; *upātta-cakram*—wielding His disc; *utkṣipya*—raising; *sa-ambuja-karam*—his trunk, along with a lotus flower; *giram āha*—uttered the words; *kṛcchrāt*—with great difficulty (because of his precarious position); *nārāyaṇa*—O my Lord Nārāyaṇa; *akhila-guro*—O universal Lord; *bhagavan*—O Supreme Personality of Godhead; *namaḥ te*—I offer my respectful obeisances unto You.

TRANSLATION

Gajendra had been forcefully captured by the crocodile in the water and was feeling acute pain, but when he saw that Nārāyaṇa, wielding His disc, was coming in the sky on the back of Garuḍa, he immediately took a lotus flower in his trunk, and with great difficulty due to his painful condition, he uttered the following words: "O my Lord, Nārāyaṇa, master of the universe, O Supreme Personality of Godhead, I offer my respectful obeisances unto You."

PURPORT

The King of the elephants was so very eager to see the Supreme Personality of Godhead that when he saw the Lord coming in the sky, with great pain and in a feeble voice he offered respect to the Lord. A devotee does not consider a dangerous position to be dangerous, for in such a dangerous position he can fervently pray to the Lord in great ecstasy. Thus a devotee regards danger as a good opportunity. *Tat te 'nukampāṁ susamīkṣamāṇah.* When a devotee is in great danger, he sees that danger to be the great mercy of the Lord because it is an opportunity to think of the Lord very sincerely and with undiverted attention. *Tat te 'nukampāṁ susamīkṣamāno bhuñjāna evātma-kṛtaṁ vipākam* (*Bhāg.* 10.14.8). He does not accuse the Supreme Personality of Godhead for having let His devotee fall into such a dangerous condition. Rather, he considers that dangerous condition to be due to his past misdeeds and takes it as an opportunity to pray to the Lord and offer thanks for having been given such an opportunity. When a devotee lives in this way, his salvation—his going back home, back to Godhead—is guaranteed. We can see this to be true from the example of Gajendra, who anxiously prayed to the Lord and thus received an immediate chance to return home, back to Godhead.

TEXT 33

तं वीक्ष्य पीडितमजः सहसावतीर्य
सग्राहमाशु सरसः कृपयोज्जहार ।
ग्राहाद् विपाटितमुखादरिणा गजेन्द्रं
संपश्यतां हरिरमूमुचदुच्छ्रियाणाम् ॥३३॥

taṁ vīkṣya pīḍitam ajaḥ sahasāvatīrya
sa-grāham āśu sarasaḥ kṛpayojjahāra
grāhād vipāṭita-mukhād ariṇā gajendraṁ
sampaśyatāṁ harir amūm ucad ucchriyāṇām

tam—him (Gajendra); *vīkṣya*—after seeing (in that condition); *pīḍitam*—who was very aggrieved; *ajaḥ*—the unborn, the Supreme Personality of Godhead; *sahasā*—all of a sudden; *avatīrya*—getting down (from the back of Garuḍa); *sa-grāham*—with the crocodile; *āśu*—

immediately; *sarasaḥ*—from the water; *kṛpayā*—out of great mercy; *ujjahāra*—took out; *grāhāt*—from the crocodile; *vipāṭita*—separated; *mukhāt*—from the mouth; *ariṇā*—with the disc; *gajendram*—Gajendra; *sampaśyatām*—who were looking on; *hariḥ*—the Supreme Personality of Godhead; *amūm*—him (Gajendra); *ucat*—saved; *ucchriyāṇām*—in the presence of all the demigods.

TRANSLATION

Thereafter, seeing Gajendra in such an aggrieved position, the unborn Supreme Personality of Godhead, Hari, immediately got down from the back of Garuḍa by His causeless mercy and pulled the King of the elephants, along with the crocodile, out of the water. Then, in the presence of all the demigods, who were looking on, the Lord severed the crocodile's mouth from its body with His disc. In this way He saved Gajendra, the King of the elephants.

Thus end the Bhaktivedanta purports of the Eighth Canto, Third Chapter, of the Śrīmad-Bhāgavatam, *entitled "Gajendra's Prayers of Surrender."*

CHAPTER FOUR

Gajendra Returns to the Spiritual World

This Fourth Chapter describes the previous birth of Gajendra and the crocodile. It tells how the crocodile became a Gandharva and how Gajendra became an associate of the Supreme Personality of Godhead.

There was a king on the Gandharva planet whose name was Hūhū. Once this King Hūhū was enjoying with women in the water, and while enjoying he pulled the leg of Devala Ṛṣi, who was also taking a bath in the water. Upon this, the sage became very angry and immediately cursed him to become a crocodile. King Hūhū was very sorry when cursed in that way, and he begged pardon from the sage, who in compassion gave him the benediction that he would be freed when Gajendra was delivered by the Personality of Godhead. Thus the crocodile was delivered when killed by Nārāyaṇa.

When Gajendra, by the mercy of the Lord, became one of the Lord's associates in Vaikuṇṭha, he got four hands. This achievement is called *sārūpya-mukti*, or the liberation of receiving a spiritual body exactly like that of Nārāyaṇa. Gajendra, in his previous birth, had been a great devotee of Lord Viṣṇu. His name was Indradyumna, and he was the King of the Tāmila country. Following the Vedic principles, this King retired from family life and constructed a small cottage in the Malayācala Hills, where he always worshiped the Supreme Personality of Godhead in silence. Agastya Ṛṣi, along with many disciples, once approached King Indradyumna's *āśrama*, but because the King was meditating on the Supreme Personality of Godhead, he could not receive Agastya Ṛṣi properly. Thus the *ṛṣi* became very angry and cursed the King to become a dull elephant. In accordance with this curse, the King was born as an elephant, and he forgot all about his previous activities in devotional service. Nonetheless, in his birth as an elephant, when he was dangerously attacked by the crocodile, he remembered his past life in devotional service and remembered a prayer he had learned in that life. Because of this prayer, he again received the mercy of the Lord. Thus he was immediately delivered, and he became one of the Lord's four-handed associates.

Śukadeva Gosvāmī ends this chapter by describing the good fortune of the elephant. Śukadeva Gosvāmī says that by hearing the narration of Gajendra's deliverance, one can also get the opportunity to be delivered. Śukadeva Gosvāmī vividly describes this, and thus the chapter ends.

TEXT 1

श्रीशुक उवाच
तदा देवर्षिगन्धर्वा ब्रह्मेशानपुरोगमाः ।
मुमुचुः कुसुमासारं शंसन्तः कर्म तद्धरेः ॥ १ ॥

śrī-śuka uvāca
tadā devarṣi-gandharvā
brahmeśāna-purogamāḥ
mumucuḥ kusumāsāraṁ
śaṁsantaḥ karma tad dhareḥ

śrī-śukaḥ uvāca—Śrī Śukadeva Gosvāmī said; *tadā*—at that time (when Gajendra was delivered); *deva-ṛṣi-gandharvāḥ*—the demigods, sages and Gandharvas; *brahma-īśāna-purogamāḥ*—headed by Lord Brahmā and Lord Śiva; *mumucuḥ*—showered; *kusuma-āsāram*—a covering of flowers; *śaṁsantaḥ*—while praising; *karma*—transcendental activity; *tat*—that (*gajendra-mokṣaṇa*); *hareḥ*—of the Supreme Personality of Godhead.

TRANSLATION

Śrī Śukadeva Gosvāmī said: When the Lord delivered Gajendra, King of the elephants, all the demigods, sages and Gandharvas, headed by Brahmā and Śiva, praised this activity of the Supreme Personality of Godhead and showered flowers upon both the Lord and Gajendra.

PURPORT

It is evident from this chapter that great sages like Devala Ṛṣi, Nārada Muni and Agastya Muni will sometimes curse someone. The curse of such a personality, however, is in fact a benediction. Both the crocodile, who had been a Gandharva in his previous life, and Gajendra, who had been a king named Indradyumna, were cursed, but both of them benefited. Indradyumna, in his birth as an elephant, attained salvation and became a personal associate of the Lord in Vaikuṇṭha, and the crocodile regained his status as a Gandharva. We find evidence in many places that the curse of a great saint or devotee is not a curse but a benediction.

TEXT 2

नेदुर्दुन्दुभयो दिव्या गन्धर्वा ननृतुर्जगुः ।
ऋषयश्चारणाः सिद्धास्तुष्टुवुः पुरुषोत्तमम् ॥ २ ॥

nedur dundubhayo divyā
gandharvā nanṛtur jaguḥ
ṛṣayaś cāraṇāḥ siddhās
tuṣṭuvuḥ puruṣottamam

neduḥ—vibrated; *dundubhayaḥ*—kettledrums; *divyāḥ*—in the sky of the higher planetary system; *gandharvāḥ*—residents of Gandharvaloka; *nanṛtuḥ*—danced; *jaguḥ*—and sang; *ṛṣayaḥ*—all the saintly sages; *cāraṇāḥ*—the inhabitants of the Cāraṇa planet; *siddhāḥ*—the inhabitants of the Siddha planet; *tuṣṭuvuḥ*—offered prayers; *puruṣa-uttamam*—to the Supreme Personality of Godhead, Puruṣottama, the best of males.

TRANSLATION

There was a beating of kettledrums in the heavenly planets, the inhabitants of Gandharvaloka began to dance and sing, while great sages and the inhabitants of Cāraṇaloka and Siddhaloka offered prayers to the Supreme Personality of Godhead, Puruṣottama.

TEXTS 3–4

योऽसौ ग्राहः स वै सद्यः परमाश्चर्यरूपधृक् ।
मुक्तो देवलशापेन हूहूर्गन्धर्वसत्तमः ॥ ३ ॥

प्रणम्य शिरसाधीशमुत्तमश्लोकमव्ययम् ।
अगायत यशोधाम कीर्तन्यगुणसत्कथम् ॥ ४ ॥

yo 'sau grāhaḥ sa vai sadyaḥ
paramāścarya-rūpa-dhṛk
mukto devala-śāpena
hūhūr gandharva-sattamaḥ

praṇamya śirasādhīśam
uttama-ślokam avyayam
agāyata yaśo-dhāma
kīrtanya-guṇa-sat-katham

yaḥ—he who; *asau*—that; *grāhaḥ*—became a crocodile; *saḥ*—he; *vai*—indeed; *sadyaḥ*—immediately; *parama*—very nice; *āścarya*—wonderful; *rūpa-dhṛk*—possessing the form (of his original Gandharva position); *muktaḥ*—was delivered; *devala-śāpena*—by the cursing of Devala Ṛṣi; *hūhūḥ*—whose name was formerly Hūhū; *gandharva-sattamaḥ*—the best of Gandharvaloka; *praṇamya*—offering his obeisances; *śirasā*—by the head; *adhīśam*—unto the supreme master; *uttama-ślokam*—who is worshiped by the choicest verses; *avyayam*—who is the supreme eternal; *agāyata*—he began to chant; *yaśaḥ-dhāma*—the glories of the Lord; *kīrtanya-guṇa-sat-katham*—whose transcendental pastimes and qualities are glorious.

TRANSLATION

The best of the Gandharvas, King Hūhū, having been cursed by Devala Muni, had become a crocodile. Now, having been delivered by the Supreme Personality of Godhead, he assumed a very beautiful form as a Gandharva. Understanding by whose mercy this had happened, he immediately offered his respectful obeisances with his head and began chanting prayers just suitable for the transcendental Lord, the supreme eternal, who is worshiped by the choicest verses.

PURPORT

The story of how the Gandharva had become a crocodile will be described later. The curse by which the Gandharva took this position was actually a blessing, not a curse. One should not be displeased when a saintly person curses someone, for his curse, indirectly, is a blessing. The Gandharva had the mentality of an inhabitant of the celestial planetary system, and for him to become an associate of the Supreme Lord would have taken millions of long years. However, because he was cursed by Devala Ṛṣi, he became a crocodile and in only one life was fortunate enough to see the Supreme Personality of Godhead face to face and be promoted to the spiritual world to become one of the Lord's associates. Similarly, Gajendra was also delivered by the Supreme Personality of Godhead when he was freed from the curse of Agastya Muni.

TEXT 5

सोऽनुकम्पित ईशेन परिक्रम्य प्रणम्य तम् ।
लोकस्य पश्यतो लोकं स्वमगान्मुक्तकिल्बिषः ॥ ५ ॥

so 'nukampita īśena
parikramya praṇamya tam
lokasya paśyato lokaṁ
svam agān mukta-kilbiṣaḥ

saḥ—he (King Hūhū); *anukampitaḥ*—being favored; *īśena*—by the Supreme Lord; *parikramya*—circumambulating; *praṇamya*—offering his obeisances; *tam*—unto Him; *lokasya*—all the demigods and men; *paśyataḥ*—while seeing; *lokam*—to the planet; *svam*—his own; *agāt*—went back; *mukta*—being delivered; *kilbiṣaḥ*—from the reactions of his sin.

TRANSLATION

Having been favored by the causeless mercy of the Supreme Personality of Godhead and having regained his original form, King Hūhū circumambulated the Lord and offered his obeisances. Then, in the presence of all the demigods, headed by Brahmā, he returned to Gandharvaloka. He had been freed of all sinful reactions.

TEXT 6

गजेन्द्रो भगवत्स्पर्शाद् विमुक्तोऽज्ञानबन्धनात् ।
प्राप्तो भगवतो रूपं पीतवासाश्चतुर्भुजः ॥ ६ ॥

gajendro bhagavat-sparśād
vimukto 'jñāna-bandhanāt
prāpto bhagavato rūpaṁ
pīta-vāsāś catur-bhujaḥ

gajendraḥ—the King of the elephants, Gajendra; *bhagavat-sparśāt*—because of being touched by the hand of the Supreme Personality of Godhead; *vimuktaḥ*—was immediately freed; *ajñāna-bandhanāt*—from all kinds of ignorance, especially the bodily concept of life; *prāptaḥ*—achieved; *bhagavataḥ*—of the Supreme Personality of Godhead; *rūpam*—the same bodily features; *pīta-vāsāḥ*—wearing yellow garments; *catuḥ-bhujaḥ*—and four-handed, with conchshell, disc, club and lotus.

TRANSLATION

Because Gajendra, King of the elephants, had been touched directly by the hands of the Supreme Personality of Godhead, he was immediately freed of all material ignorance and bondage. Thus he received the salvation of sārūpya-mukti, in which he achieved the same bodily features as the Lord, being dressed in yellow garments and possessing four hands.

PURPORT

If one is favored by the Supreme Personality of Godhead by having his gross body touched by the Lord, his body turns into a spiritual body, and he can go back home, back to Godhead. Gajendra assumed a spiritual body when his body was touched by the Lord. Similarly, Dhruva Mahārāja assumed his spiritual body in this way. *Arcanā-paddhati*, daily worship of the Deity, provides an opportunity to touch the body of the Supreme Personality of Godhead, and thus it enables one to be fortunate enough to get a spiritual body and go back to Godhead. Not only by touching the body of the Supreme Lord, but simply by hearing about His pastimes, chanting His glories, touching His feet and offering worship—in other words, by serving the Lord somehow or other—one is purified of material contamination. This is the result of touching the Supreme Lord. One who is a pure devotee (*anyābhilāṣitā-śūnyam*), who acts according to the *śāstra* and the words of the Supreme Personality of Godhead, certainly becomes purified. Like Gajendra, he assumes a spiritual body and returns home, back to Godhead.

TEXT 7

स वै पूर्वमभूद् राजा पाण्ड्यो द्रविडसत्तमः ।
इन्द्रद्युम्न इति ख्यातो विष्णुव्रतपरायणः ॥ ७ ॥

sa vai pūrvam abhūd rājā
pāṇḍyo draviḍa-sattamaḥ
indradyumna iti khyāto
viṣṇu-vrata-parāyaṇaḥ

saḥ—this elephant (Gajendra); *vai*—indeed; *pūrvam*—formerly; *abhūt*—was; *rājā*—a king; *pāṇḍyaḥ*—of the country known as Pāṇḍya; *draviḍa-sat-tamaḥ*—the best of those born in Draviḍa-deśa, South India; *indradyumnaḥ*—by the name Mahārāja Indradyumna; *iti*—thus; *khyātaḥ*—celebrated; *viṣṇu-vrata-parāyaṇaḥ*—who was a first-class Vaiṣṇava, always engaged in the service of the Lord.

TRANSLATION

This Gajendra had formerly been a Vaiṣṇava and the king of the country known as Pāṇḍya, which is in the province of Draviḍa [South India]. In his previous life, he was known as Indradyumna Mahārāja.

TEXT 8

स एकदाराधनकाल आत्मवान्
गृहीतमौनव्रत ईश्वरं हरिम् ।
जटाधरस्तापस आप्लुतोऽच्युतं
समर्चयामास कुलाचलाश्रमः ॥ ८ ॥

sa ekadārādhana-kāla ātmavān
gṛhīta-mauna-vrata īśvaraṁ harim

jaṭā-dharas tāpasa āpluto 'cyutaṁ
samarcayām āsa kulācalāśramaḥ

saḥ—that Indradyumna Mahārāja; *ekadā*—once upon a time; *ārādhana-kāle*—at the time of worshiping the Deity; *ātmavān*—engaged in devotional service in meditation with great attention; *gṛhīta*—taken; *mauna-vrataḥ*—the vow of silence (not talking with anyone); *īśvaram*—the supreme controller; *harim*—the Personality of Godhead; *jaṭā-dharaḥ*—with matted locks; *tāpasaḥ*—always engaged in austerity; *āplutaḥ*—always merged in love for the Supreme Personality of Godhead; *acyutam*—the infallible Lord; *samarcayām āsa*—was worshiping; *kulācala-āśramaḥ*—he made his *āśrama* in Kulācala (the Malaya Hills).

TRANSLATION

Indradyumna Mahārāja retired from family life and went to the Malaya Hills, where he had a small cottage for his āśrama. He wore matted locks on his head and always engaged in austerities. Once, while observing a vow of silence, he was fully engaged in the worship of the Lord and absorbed in the ecstasy of love of Godhead.

TEXT 9

यदृच्छया तत्र महायशा मुनिः
समागमच्छिष्यगणैः परिश्रितः ।
तं वीक्ष्य तूष्णीमकृतार्हणादिकं
रहस्युपासीनमृषिश्चुकोप ह ॥ ९ ॥

yadṛcchayā tatra mahā-yaśā muniḥ
samāgamac chiṣya-gaṇaiḥ pariśritaḥ
taṁ vīkṣya tūṣṇīm akṛtārhaṇādikaṁ
rahasy upāsīnam ṛṣiś cukopa ha

yadṛcchayā—out of his own will (without being invited); *tatra*—there; *mahā-yaśāḥ*—very celebrated, well-known; *muniḥ*—Agastya Muni; *samāgamat*—arrived; *śiṣya-gaṇaiḥ*—by his disciples;

pariśritaḥ—surrounded; *tam*—him; *vīkṣya*—seeing; *tūṣṇīm*—silent; *akṛta-arhaṇa-ādikam*—without offering a respectful reception; *rahasi*—in a secluded place; *upāsīnam*—sitting in meditation; *ṛṣiḥ*—the great sage; *cukopa*—became very angry; *ha*—it so happened.

TRANSLATION

While Indradyumna Mahārāja was engaged in ecstatic meditation, worshiping the Supreme Personality of Godhead, the great sage Agastya Muni arrived there, surrounded by his disciples. When the Muni saw that Mahārāja Indradyumna, who was sitting in a secluded place, remained silent and did not follow the etiquette of offering him a reception, he was very angry.

TEXT 10

तस्मा इमं शापमदादसाधु-
रयं दुरात्माकृतबुद्धिरद्य ।
विप्रावमन्ता विशतां तमिस्रं
यथा गजः स्तब्धमतिः स एव ॥१०॥

tasmā imaṁ śāpam adād asādhur
ayaṁ durātmākṛta-buddhir adya
viprāvamantā viśatāṁ tamisraṁ
yathā gajaḥ stabdha-matiḥ sa eva

tasmai—unto Mahārāja Indradyumna; *imam*—this; *śāpam*—curse; *adāt*—he gave; *asādhuḥ*—not at all gentle; *ayam*—this; *durātmā*—degraded soul; *akṛta*—without education; *buddhiḥ*—his intelligence; *adya*—now; *vipra*—of a *brāhmaṇa; avamantā*—insulter; *viśatām*—let him enter; *tamisram*—darkness; *yathā*—as; *gajaḥ*—an elephant; *stabdha-matiḥ*—possessing blunt intelligence; *saḥ*—he; *eva*—indeed.

TRANSLATION

Agastya Muni then spoke this curse against the King: This King Indradyumna is not at all gentle. Being low and uneducated, he has

insulted a brāhmaṇa. May he therefore enter the region of darkness and receive the dull, dumb body of an elephant.

PURPORT

An elephant is very strong, it has a very big body, and it can work very hard and eat a large quantity of food, but its intelligence is not at all commensurate with its size and strength. Thus in spite of so much bodily strength, the elephant works as a menial servant for a human being. Agastya Muni thought it wise to curse the King to become an elephant because the powerful King did not receive Agastya Muni as one is obliged to receive a *brāhmaṇa.* Yet although Agastya Muni cursed Mahārāja Indradyumna to become an elephant, the curse was indirectly a benediction, for by undergoing one life as an elephant, Indradyumna Mahārāja ended the reactions for all the sins of his previous life. Immediately after the expiry of the elephant's life, he was promoted to Vaikuṇṭhaloka to become a personal associate of the Supreme Personality of Godhead, Nārāyaṇa, in a body exactly like that of the Lord. This is called *sārūpya-mukti.*

TEXTS 11–12

श्रीशुक उवाच

एवं शप्त्वा गतोऽगस्त्यो भगवान् नृप सानुगः ।
इन्द्रद्युम्नोऽपि राजर्षिर्दिष्टं तदुपधारयन् ॥११॥
आपन्नः कौञ्जरीं योनिमात्मस्मृतिविनाशिनीम् ।
हर्यर्चनानुभावेन यद्गजत्वेऽप्यनुस्मृतिः ॥१२॥

śrī-śuka uvāca
evaṁ śaptvā gato 'gastyo
bhagavān nṛpa sānugaḥ
indradyumno 'pi rājarṣir
diṣṭaṁ tad upadhārayan

āpannaḥ kauñjarīṁ yonim
ātma-smṛti-vināśinīm
hary-arcanānubhāvena
yad-gajatve 'py anusmṛtiḥ

śrī-śukaḥ uvāca—Śrī Śukadeva Gosvāmī said; *evam*—thus; *śaptvā*—after cursing; *gataḥ*—left that place; *agastyaḥ*—Agastya Muni; *bhagavān*—so powerful; *nṛpa*—O King; *sa-anugaḥ*—with his associates; *indradyumnaḥ*—King Indradyumna; *api*—also; *rājarṣiḥ*—although he was a *rājarṣi; diṣṭam*—because of past deeds; *tat*—that curse; *upadhārayan*—considering; *āpannaḥ*—got; *kauñjarīm*—of an elephant; *yonim*—the species; *ātma-smṛti*—remembrance of one's identity; *vināśinīm*—which destroys; *hari*—the Supreme Personality of Godhead; *arcana-anubhāvena*—because of worshiping; *yat*—that; *gajatve*—in the body of an elephant; *api*—although; *anusmṛtiḥ*—the opportunity to remember his past devotional service.

TRANSLATION

Śukadeva Gosvāmī continued: My dear King, after Agastya Muni had thus cursed King Indradyumna, the Muni left that place along with his disciples. Since the King was a devotee, he accepted Agastya Muni's curse as welcome because it was the desire of the Supreme Personality of Godhead. Therefore, although in his next life he got the body of an elephant, because of devotional service he remembered how to worship and offer prayers to the Lord.

PURPORT

This is the unique position of a devotee of the Supreme Personality of Godhead. Although the King was cursed, he welcomed the curse because a devotee is always aware that nothing can happen without the desire of the Supreme Lord. Although the King was not at fault, Agastya Muni cursed him, and when this happened the King considered it to be due to his past misdeeds. *Tat te 'nukampāṁ susamīkṣamāṇaḥ* (*Bhāg.* 10.14.8). This is a practical example of how a devotee thinks. He regards any reverses in life as blessings of the Supreme Personality of Godhead. Therefore, instead of being agitated by such reverses, he continues his activities of devotional service, and Kṛṣṇa takes care of him and enables him to be promoted to the spiritual world, back to Godhead. If a devotee has to suffer the reactions of his past misdeeds, the Supreme Lord arranges for him to be given only a token of these reactions, and very soon he is freed from all the reactions of material contamination. One should therefore adhere to devotional service, and the Lord Himself will very soon see to one's promotion to the spiritual world. A devotee should not be disturbed by unfortunate circumstances, but must continue his regular program, depending on the Lord for everything. The word *upadhārayan,* "considering," is very significant in this verse. This word indicates that a devotee knows what is what; he understands what is happening in material, conditional life.

TEXT 13

एवं विमोक्ष्य गजयूथपमब्जनाभ-
स्तेनापि पार्षदगतिं गमितेन युक्तः ।
गन्धर्वसिद्धविबुधैरुपगीयमान-
कर्माद्भुतं स्वभवनं गरुडासनोऽगात् ॥१३॥

evaṁ vimokṣya gaja-yūtha-pam abja-nābhas
tenāpi pārṣada-gatiṁ gamitena yuktaḥ
gandharva-siddha-vibudhair upagīyamāna-
karmādbhutaṁ sva-bhavanaṁ garuḍāsano 'gāt

evam—thus; *vimokṣya*—delivering; *gaja-yūtha-pam*—the King of the elephants, Gajendra; *abja-nābhaḥ*—the Supreme Personality of Godhead, from whose navel sprouts a lotus flower; *tena*—by him (Gajendra); *api*—also; *pārṣada-gatim*—the position of the Lord's associate; *gamitena*—who had already gotten; *yuktaḥ*—accompanied; *gandharva*—by the denizens of Gandharvaloka; *siddha*—the denizens of Siddhaloka; *vibudhaiḥ*—and by all great learned sages; *upagīyamāna*—were being glorified; *karma*—whose transcendental activities; *adbhutam*—all-wonderful; *sva-bhavanam*—to His own abode; *garuḍa-āsanaḥ*—sitting on the back of Garuḍa; *agāt*—returned.

TRANSLATION

Upon delivering the King of the elephants from the clutches of the crocodile, and from material existence, which resembles a crocodile, the Lord awarded him the status of sārūpya-mukti. In the presence of the Gandharvas, the Siddhas and the other demigods,

who were praising the Lord for His wonderful transcendental activities, the Lord, sitting on the back of His carrier, Garuḍa, returned to His all-wonderful abode and took Gajendra with Him.

PURPORT

In this verse the word *vimokṣya* is significant. For a devotee, *mokṣa* or *mukti*—salvation—means getting the position of the Lord's associate. The impersonalists are satisfied to get the liberation of merging in the Brahman effulgence, but for a devotee, *mukti* (liberation) means not to merge in the effulgence of the Lord, but to be directly promoted to the Vaikuṇṭha planets and to become an associate of the Lord. In this regard, there is a relevant verse in *Śrīmad-Bhāgavatam* (10.14.8):

tat te 'nukampāṁ susamīkṣamāṇo
bhuñjāna evātma-kṛtaṁ vipākam
hṛd-vāg-vapurbhir vidadhan namas te
jīveta yo mukti-pade sa dāya-bhāk

"One who seeks Your compassion and thus tolerates all kinds of adverse conditions due to the *karma* of his past deeds, who engages always in Your devotional service with his mind, words and body, and who always offers obeisances unto You, is certainly a bona fide candidate for liberation." A devotee who tolerates everything in this material world and patiently executes his devotional service can become *mukti-pade sa dāya-bhāk*, a bona fide candidate for liberation. The word *dāya-bhāk* refers to a hereditary right to the Lord's mercy. A devotee must simply engage in devotional service, not caring about material situations. Then he automatically becomes a rightful candidate for promotion to Vaikuṇṭhaloka. The devotee who renders unalloyed service to the Lord gets the right to be promoted to Vaikuṇṭhaloka, just as a son inherits the property of his father.

When a devotee gets liberation, he becomes free from material contamination and engages as a servant of the Lord. This is explained in *Śrīmad-Bhāgavatam* (2.10.6): *muktir hitvānyathā rūpaṁ svarūpeṇa vyavasthitiḥ.* The word *svarūpa* refers to *sārūpya-mukti*—going back home, back to Godhead, and remaining the Lord's eternal associate, having regained a spiritual body exactly resembling that of the Lord, with four hands, holding the *śaṅkha, cakra, gadā* and *padma.* The difference between the *mukti* of the impersonalist and that of the devotee is that the devotee is immediately appointed an eternal servant of the Lord, whereas the impersonalist, although merging in the effulgence of the *brahmajyoti,* is still insecure and therefore generally falls again to this material world. *Āruhya kṛcchreṇa paraṁ padaṁ tataḥ patanty adho 'nādṛta-yuṣmad-aṅghrayaḥ* (*Bhāg.* 10.2.32). Although the impersonalist rises to the Brahman effulgence and enters into that effulgence, he has no engagement in the service of the Lord, and therefore he is again attracted to materialistic philanthropic activities. Thus he comes down to open hospitals and educational institutions, feed poor men and perform similar materialistic activities, which the impersonalist thinks are more precious than serving the Supreme Personality of Godhead. *Anādṛta-yuṣmad-aṅghrayaḥ.* The impersonalists do not think that the service of the Lord is more valuable than serving the poor man or starting a school or hospital. Although they say *brahma satyaṁ jagan mithyā*—"Brahman is real, and the material world is false"—they are nonetheless very eager to serve the false material world and neglect the service of the lotus feet of the Supreme Personality of Godhead.

TEXT 14

एतन्महाराज तवेरितो मया
कृष्णानुभावो गजराजमोक्षणम् ।
स्वर्ग्यं यशस्यं कलिकल्मषापहं
दुःस्वप्ननाशं कुरुवर्य शृण्वताम् ॥१४॥

etan mahā-rāja taverito mayā
kṛṣṇānubhāvo gaja-rāja-mokṣaṇam
svargyaṁ yaśasyaṁ kali-kalmaṣāpahaṁ
duḥsvapna-nāśaṁ kuru-varya śṛṇvatām

etat—this; *mahā-rāja*—O King Parīkṣit; *tava*—unto you; *īritaḥ*—described; *mayā*—by me; *kṛṣṇa-anubhāvaḥ*—the unlimited potency of Lord Kṛṣṇa (by which He can deliver a devotee); *gaja-rāja-mokṣaṇam*—delivering the King of the elephants; *svargyam*—giving elevation to higher planetary systems; *yaśasyam*—increasing one's reputation as a devotee; *kali-kalmaṣa-apaham*—diminishing the contamination of the Kali-yuga; *duḥsvapna-nāśam*—counteracting the causes of bad dreams; *kuru-varya*—O best among the Kurus; *śṛṇvatām*—of persons who hear this narration.

TRANSLATION

My dear King Parīkṣit, I have now described the wonderful power of Kṛṣṇa, as displayed when the Lord delivered the King of the elephants. O best of the Kuru dynasty, those who hear this narration become fit to be promoted to the higher planetary systems. Simply because of hearing this narration, they gain a reputation as devotees, they are unaffected by the contamination of Kali-yuga, and they never see bad dreams.

TEXT 15

यथानुकीर्तयन्त्येतच्छ्रेयस्कामा द्विजातयः ।
शुचयः प्रातरुत्थाय दुःस्वप्नाद्युपशान्तये ॥१५॥

yathānukīrtayanty etac
chreyas-kāmā dvijātayaḥ
śucayaḥ prātar utthāya
duḥsvapnādy-upaśāntaye

yathā—without deviation; *anukīrtayanti*—they chant; *etat*—this narration of the deliverance of Gajendra; *śreyaḥ-kāmāḥ*—persons who desire their own auspiciousness; *dvi-jātayaḥ*—the twiceborn (*brāhmaṇas, kṣatriyas* and *vaiśyas*); *śucayaḥ*—especially the *brāhmaṇas,* who are always clean; *prātaḥ*—in the morning; *utthāya*—after getting up from sleep; *duḥsvapna-ādi*—beginning with sleeping badly at night; *upaśāntaye*—to counteract all troublesome positions.

TRANSLATION

Therefore, after getting up from bed in the morning, those who desire their own welfare—especially the brāhmaṇas, kṣatriyas, vaiśyas and in particular the brāhmaṇa Vaiṣṇavas—should chant

this narration as it is, without deviation, to counteract the troubles of bad dreams.

PURPORT

Every verse in the Vedic literature, especially in the *Śrīmad-Bhāgavatam* and *Bhagavad-gītā*, is a Vedic *mantra*. Here the words *yathānukīrtayanti* are used to recommend that this literature be presented as it is. Unscrupulous persons, however, deviate from the actual narration and interpret the text in their own way with grammatical jugglery. Such deviations are to be avoided. This is a Vedic injunction supported by Śukadeva Gosvāmī, one of the *mahājanas*, or authorities. He says, *yathānukīrtayanti:* one should recite the *mantra* as it is, without deviation, for then one will be eligible to rise to the platform of all good fortune. Śukadeva Gosvāmī especially recommends that those who are *brāhmaṇas* (*śucayaḥ*) recite all these *mantras* after rising from bed in the morning.

Because of sinful activities, at night we have bad dreams, which are very troublesome. Indeed, Mahārāja Yudhiṣṭhira was obliged to see hell because of a slight deviation from devotional service to the Lord. Therefore, *duḥsvapna*—bad dreams—occur because of sinful activities. A devotee sometimes accepts a sinful person as his disciple, and to counteract the sinful reactions he accepts from the disciple, he has to see a bad dream. Nonetheless, the spiritual master is so kind that in spite of having bad dreams due to the sinful disciple, he accepts this troublesome business for the deliverance of the victims of Kali-yuga. After initiation, therefore, a disciple should be extremely careful not to commit again any sinful act that might cause difficulties for himself and the spiritual master. Before the Deity, before the fire, before the spiritual master and before the Vaiṣṇavas, the honest disciple promises to refrain from all sinful activity. Therefore he must not again commit sinful acts and thus create a troublesome situation.

TEXT 16

इदमाह हरिः प्रीतो गजेन्द्रं कुरुसत्तम ।
शृण्वतां सर्वभूतानां सर्वभूतमयो विभुः ॥१६॥

idam āha hariḥ prīto
gajendraṁ kuru-sattama
śṛṇvatāṁ sarva-bhūtānāṁ
sarva-bhūta-mayo vibhuḥ

idam—this; *āha*—said; *hariḥ*—the Supreme Personality of Godhead; *prītaḥ*—being pleased; *gajendram*—unto Gajendra; *kuru-sat-tama*—O best of the Kuru dynasty; *śṛṇvatām*—hearing; *sarva-bhūtānām*—in the presence of everyone; *sarva-bhūta-mayaḥ*—all-pervading Personality of Godhead; *vibhuḥ*—the great.

TRANSLATION

O best of the Kuru dynasty, the Supreme Personality of Godhead, the Supersoul of everyone, being thus pleased, addressed Gajendra in the presence of everyone there. He spoke the following blessings.

TEXTS 17–24

श्रीभगवानुवाच

ये मां त्वां च सरश्चेदं गिरिकन्दरकाननम् ।
वेत्रकीचकवेणूनां गुल्मानि सुरपादपान् ॥१७॥
शृङ्गाणीमानि धिष्ण्यानि ब्रह्मणो मे शिवस्य च ।
क्षीरोदं मे प्रियं धाम श्वेतद्वीपं च भास्वरम् ॥१८॥
श्रीवत्सं कौस्तुभं मालां गदां कौमोदकीं मम ।
सुदर्शनं पाञ्चजन्यं सुपर्णं पतगेश्वरम् ॥१९॥
शेषं च मत्कलां सूक्ष्मां श्रियं देवीं मदाश्रयाम् ।
ब्रह्माणं नारदमृषिं भवं प्रह्लादमेव च ॥२०॥
मत्स्यकूर्मवराहाद्यैरवतारैः कृतानि मे ।
कर्माण्यनन्तपुण्यानि सूर्यं सोमं हुताशनम् ॥२१॥
प्रणवं सत्यमव्यक्तं गोविप्रान् धर्ममव्ययम् ।
दाक्षायणीर्धर्मपत्नीः सोमकश्यपयोरपि ॥२२॥

गङ्गां सरस्वतीं नन्दां कालिन्दीं सितवारणम् ।
ध्रुवं ब्रह्मऋषीन्सप्त पुण्यश्लोकांश्च मानवान् ॥२३॥
उत्थायापररात्रान्ते प्रयताः सुसमाहिताः ।
स्मरन्ति मम रूपाणि मुच्यन्ते तेंऽहसोऽखिलात् ॥२४॥

śrī-bhagavān uvāca
ye māṁ tvāṁ ca saraś cedaṁ
giri-kandara-kānanam
vetra-kīcaka-veṇūnāṁ
gulmāni sura-pādapān

śṛṅgāṇīmāni dhiṣṇyāni
brahmaṇo me śivasya ca
kṣīrodaṁ me priyaṁ dhāma
śveta-dvīpaṁ ca bhāsvaram

śrīvatsaṁ kaustubhaṁ mālāṁ
gadāṁ kaumodakīṁ mama
sudarśanaṁ pāñcajanyaṁ
suparṇaṁ patageśvaram

śeṣaṁ ca mat-kalāṁ sūkṣmāṁ
śriyaṁ devīṁ mad-āśrayām
brahmāṇaṁ nāradam ṛṣiṁ
bhavaṁ prahrādam eva ca

matsya-kūrma-varāhādyair
avatāraiḥ kṛtāni me
karmāṇy ananta-puṇyāni
sūryaṁ somaṁ hutāśanam

praṇavaṁ satyam avyaktaṁ
go-viprān dharmam avyayam
dākṣāyaṇīr dharma-patnīḥ
soma-kaśyapayor api

gaṅgāṁ sarasvatīṁ nandāṁ
kālindīṁ sita-vāraṇam
dhruvaṁ brahma-ṛṣīn sapta
puṇya-ślokāṁś ca mānavān

utthāyāpara-rātrānte
prayatāḥ susamāhitāḥ
smaranti mama rūpāṇi
mucyante te 'ṁhaso 'khilāt

śrī-bhagavān uvāca—the Supreme Personality of Godhead said; *ye*—those who; *mām*—Me; *tvām*—you; *ca*—also; *saraḥ*—lake; *ca*—also; *idam*—this; *giri*—hill (Trikūṭa Mountain); *kandara*—caves; *kānanam*—gardens; *vetra*—of cane; *kīcaka*—hollow bamboo; *veṇūnām*—and of another kind of bamboo; *gulmāni*—clusters; *sura-pādapān*—celestial trees; *śṛṅgāṇi*—the peaks; *imāni*—these; *dhiṣṇyāni*—abodes; *brahmaṇaḥ*—of Lord Brahmā; *me*—of Me; *śivasya*—of Lord Śiva; *ca*—also; *kṣīra-udam*—the ocean of milk; *me*—My; *priyam*—very dear; *dhāma*—place; *śveta-dvīpam*—known as the white island; *ca*—also; *bhāsvaram*—always brilliant with spiritual rays; *śrīvatsam*—the mark named Śrīvatsa; *kaustubham*—the Kaustubha gem; *mālām*—garland; *gadām*—club; *kaumodakīm*—known as Kaumodakī; *mama*—My; *sudarśanam*—Sudarśana disc; *pāñca-janyam*—conchshell named Pāñcajanya; *suparṇam*—Garuḍa; *pataga-īśvaram*—the king of all birds; *śeṣam*—the resting place Śeṣa Nāga; *ca*—and; *mat-kalām*—My expanded part; *sūkṣmām*—very subtle; *śriyam devīm*—the goddess of fortune; *mat-āśrayām*—all dependent upon Me; *brahmāṇam*—Lord Brahmā; *nāradam ṛṣim*—the great saint Nārada Muni; *bhavam*—Lord Śiva; *prahrādam eva ca*—as well as Prahlāda; *matsya*—the Matsya incarnation; *kūrma*—the Kūrma incarnation; *varāha*—the boar incarnation; *ādyaiḥ*—and so on; *avatāraiḥ*—by different incarnations; *kṛtāni*—done; *me*—My; *karmāṇi*—activities; *ananta*—unlimited; *puṇyāni*—auspicious, pious; *sūryam*—the sun-god; *somam*—the moon-god; *hutāśanam*—the fire-god; *praṇavam*—the *oṁkāra mantra; satyam*—the Absolute Truth; *avyaktam*—the total material energy; *go-viprān*—the cows and *brāhmaṇas; dharmam*—

devotional service; *avyayam*—never ending; *dākṣāyaṇīḥ*—the daughters of Dakṣa; *dharma-patnīḥ*—bona fide wives; *soma*—of the moon-god; *kaśyapayoḥ*—and of the great *ṛṣi* Kaśyapa; *api*—also; *gaṅgām*—the River Ganges; *sarasvatīm*—the River Sarasvatī; *nandām*—the River Nandā; *kālindīm*—the River Yamunā; *sita-vāraṇam*—the elephant Airāvata; *dhruvam*—Dhruva Mahārāja; *brahma-ṛṣīn*—great *ṛṣis; sapta*—seven; *puṇya-ślokān*—extremely pious; *ca*—and; *mānavān*—human beings; *utthāya*—getting up; *apara-rātra-ante*—at the end of the night; *prayatāḥ*—being very careful; *su-samāhitāḥ*—with concentrated minds; *smaranti*—remember; *mama*—My; *rūpāṇi*—forms; *mucyante*—are delivered; *te*—such persons; *aṁhasaḥ*—from sinful reactions; *akhilāt*—of all kinds.

TRANSLATION

The Supreme Personality of Godhead said: Freed from all sinful reactions are those who rise from bed at the end of night, early in the morning, and fully concentrate their minds with great attention upon My form; your form; this lake; this mountain; the caves; the gardens; the cane plants; the bamboo plants; the celestial trees; the residential quarters of Me, Lord Brahmā and Lord Śiva; the three peaks of Trikūṭa Mountain, made of gold, silver and iron; My very pleasing abode [the ocean of milk]; the white island, Śvetadvīpa, which is always brilliant with spiritual rays; My mark of Śrīvatsa; the Kaustubha gem; My Vaijayantī garland; My club, Kaumodakī; My Sudarśana disc and Pāñcajanya conchshell; My bearer, Garuḍa, the king of the birds; My bed, Śeṣa Nāga; My expansion of energy the goddess of fortune; Lord Brahmā; Nārada Muni; Lord Śiva; Prahlāda; My incarnations like Matsya, Kūrma and Varāha; My unlimited all-auspicious activities, which yield piety to he who hears them; the sun; the moon; fire; the mantra oṁkāra; the Absolute Truth; the total material energy; the cows and brāhmaṇas; devotional service; the wives of Soma and Kaśyapa, who are all daughters of King Dakṣa; the Rivers Ganges, Sarasvatī, Nandā and Yamunā [Kālindī]; the elephant Airāvata; Dhruva Mahārāja; the seven ṛṣis; and the pious human beings.

TEXT 25

ये मां स्तुवन्त्यनेनाङ्ग प्रतिबुध्य निशात्यये ।
तेषां प्राणात्यये चाहं ददामि विपुलां गतिम् ॥२५॥

ye māṁ stuvanty anenāṅga
pratibudhya niśātyaye
teṣāṁ prāṇātyaye cāhaṁ
dadāmi vipulāṁ gatim

ye—those who; *mām*—unto Me; *stuvanti*—offer prayers; *anena*—in this way; *aṅga*—O King; *pratibudhya*—getting up; *niśa-atyaye*—at the end of night; *teṣām*—for them; *prāṇa-atyaye*—at the time of death; *ca*—also; *aham*—I; *dadāmi*—give; *vipulām*—the eternal, unlimited; *gatim*—transferral to the spiritual world.

TRANSLATION

My dear devotee, unto those who rise from bed at the end of night and offer Me the prayers offered by you, I give an eternal residence in the spiritual world at the end of their lives.

TEXT 26

श्रीशुक उवाच

इत्यादिश्य हृषीकेशः प्राध्माय जलजोत्तमम् ।
हर्षयन्विबुधानीकमारुरोह खगाधिपम् ॥२६॥

śrī-śuka uvāca
ity ādiśya hṛṣīkeśaḥ
prādhmāya jalajottamam
harṣayan vibudhānīkam
āruroha khagādhipam

śrī-śukaḥ uvāca—Śrī Śukadeva Gosvāmī said; *iti*—thus; *ādiśya*—advising; *hṛṣīkeśaḥ*—the Supreme Personality of Godhead, known as Hṛṣīkeśa; *prādhmāya*—blowing; *jala-ja-uttamam*—the conchshell, the best of the aquatics; *harṣayan*—pleasing; *vibudha-anīkam*—the host of demigods, headed by Lord Brahmā and Lord Śiva; *āruroha*—got up; *khaga-adhipam*—on the back of Garuḍa.

TRANSLATION

Śrī Śukadeva Gosvāmī continued: After giving this instruction, the Lord, who is known as Hṛṣīkeśa, bugled with His Pāñcajanya conchshell, in this way pleasing all the demigods, headed by Lord Brahmā. Then He mounted the back of His carrier, Garuḍa.

Thus end the Bhaktivedanta purports of the Eighth Canto, Fourth Chapter, of the Śrīmad-Bhāgavatam, *entitled "Gajendra Returns to the Spiritual World."*

CHAPTER FIVE

The Demigods Appeal to the Lord for Protection

This chapter describes the fifth and sixth Manus, and it also describes the prayers of the demigods and the curse of Durvāsā Muni.

The brother of Tāmasa, the fourth Manu, who has previously been described, was the fifth Manu, Raivata. The sons of Raivata included Arjuna, Bali and Vindhya. During the reign of this Manu, Indra, the King of heaven, was known as Vibhu. Among the demigods were the Bhūtarayas, and among the seven *ṛṣis* were Hiraṇyaromā, Vedaśirā and Ūrdhvabāhu. The *ṛṣi* known as Śubhra, by his wife, Vikuṇṭhā, gave birth to the Supreme Personality of Godhead, Vaikuṇṭha. This Supreme Personality of Godhead manifested a Vaikuṇṭha planet at the request of Ramādevī. His power and activities are mentioned in the Third Canto.

The sixth Manu was Cākṣuṣa, the son of Cakṣu Manu. Among the sons of the sixth Manu were Pūru, Pūruṣa and Sudyumna. During the reign of this Manu, Mantradruma was Indra, the King of the heavenly planets. Among the demigods were the Āpyas, and among the seven *ṛṣis* were Haviṣmān and Vīraka. The wife of Vairāja, whose name was Devasambhūti, gave birth to Ajita, an incarnation of the Supreme Personality of Godhead. This Ajita, taking the shape of a tortoise and holding the mountain known as Mandara on His back, churned the ocean and produced nectar for the demigods.

Mahārāja Parīkṣit was very eager to hear about the churning of the ocean, and therefore Śukadeva Gosvāmī began to explain to him how the demigods, having been cursed by Durvāsā Muni, were defeated in battle by the *asuras*. When the demigods were deprived of their heavenly kingdom, they went to the assembly house of Lord Brahmā and informed Lord Brahmā of what had happened. Then Brahmā, along with all the demigods, went to the shore of the ocean of milk and offered prayers to Kṣīrodakaśāyī Viṣṇu.

TEXT 1

श्रीशुक उवाच
राजन्नुदितमेतत् ते हरेः कर्माघनाशनम् ।
गजेन्द्रमोक्षणं पुण्यं रैवतं त्वन्तरं शृणु ॥ १ ॥

śrī-śuka uvāca
rājann uditam etat te
hareḥ karmāgha-nāśanam
gajendra-mokṣaṇaṁ puṇyaṁ
raivataṁ tv antaraṁ śṛṇu

śrī-śukaḥ uvāca—Śrī Śukadeva Gosvāmī said; *rājan*—O King; *uditam*—already described; *etat*—this; *te*—unto you; *hareḥ*—of the Lord; *karma*—activity; *agha-nāśanam*—by hearing which one can be freed from all misfortune; *gajendra-mokṣaṇam*—deliverance of Gajendra, the King of the elephants; *puṇyam*—very pious to hear and describe; *raivatam*—about Raivata Manu; *tu*—but; *antaram*—in this millennium; *śṛṇu*—kindly hear from me.

TRANSLATION

Śukadeva Gosvāmī continued: O King, I have described to you the pastime of Gajendra-mokṣaṇa, which is most pious to hear. By hearing of such activities of the Lord, one can be freed from all sinful reactions. Now please listen as I describe Raivata Manu.

TEXT 2

पञ्चमो रैवतो नाम मनुस्तामससोदरः ।
बलिविन्ध्यादयस्तस्य सुता हार्जुनपूर्वकाः ॥ २ ॥

pañcamo raivato nāma
manus tāmasa-sodaraḥ
bali-vindhyādayas tasya
sutā hārjuna-pūrvakāḥ

pañcamaḥ—the fifth; *raivataḥ*—Raivata; *nāma*—by the name; *manuḥ*—Manu; *tāmasa-sodaraḥ*—the brother of Tāmasa Manu; *bali*—

Bali; *vindhya*—Vindhya; *ādayaḥ*—and so on; *tasya*—his; *sutāḥ*—sons; *ha*—certainly; *arjuna*—Arjuna; *pūrvakāḥ*—heading all the sons.

TRANSLATION

The brother of Tāmasa Manu was the fifth Manu, named Raivata. His sons were headed by Arjuna, Bali and Vindhya.

TEXT 3

विभुरिन्द्रः सुरगणा राजन्भूतरयादयः ।
हिरण्यरोमा वेदशिरा ऊर्ध्वबाह्वादयो द्विजाः ॥ ३ ॥

vibhur indraḥ sura-gaṇā
rājan bhūtarayādayaḥ
hiraṇyaromā vedaśirā
ūrdhvabāhv-ādayo dvijāḥ

vibhuḥ—Vibhu; *indraḥ*—the King of heaven; *sura-gaṇāḥ*—the demigods; *rājan*—O King; *bhūtaraya-ādayaḥ*—headed by the Bhūtarayas; *hiraṇyaromā*—Hiraṇyaromā; *vedaśirā*—Vedaśirā; *ūrdhvabāhu*—Ūrdhvabāhu; *ādayaḥ*—and others; *dvijāḥ*—the *brāhmaṇas* or *ṛṣis* who occupied the seven planets.

TRANSLATION

O King, in the millennium of Raivata Manu the King of heaven was known as Vibhu, among the demigods were the Bhūtarayas, and among the seven brāhmaṇas who occupied the seven planets were Hiraṇyaromā, Vedaśirā and Ūrdhvabāhu.

TEXT 4

पत्नी विकुण्ठा शुभ्रस्य वैकुण्ठैः सुरसत्तमैः ।
तयोः स्वकलया जज्ञे वैकुण्ठो भगवान्स्वयम् ॥ ४ ॥

patnī vikuṇṭhā śubhrasya
vaikuṇṭhaiḥ sura-sattamaiḥ

tayoḥ sva-kalayā jajñe
vaikuṇṭho bhagavān svayam

patnī—the wife; *vikuṇṭhā*—named Vikuṇṭhā; *śubhrasya*—of Śubhra; *vaikuṇṭhaiḥ*—with the Vaikuṇṭhas; *sura-sat-tamaiḥ*—demigods; *tayoḥ*—by Vikuṇṭhā and Śubhra; *sva-kalayā*—with plenary expansions; *jajñe*—appeared; *vaikuṇṭhaḥ*—the Lord; *bhagavān*—the Supreme Personality of Godhead; *svayam*—personally.

TRANSLATION

From the combination of Śubhra and his wife, Vikuṇṭhā, there appeared the Supreme Personality of Godhead, Vaikuṇṭha, along with demigods who were His personal plenary expansions.

TEXT 5

वैकुण्ठः कल्पितो येन लोको लोकनमस्कृतः ।
रमया प्रार्थ्यमानेन देव्या तत्प्रियकाम्यया ॥ ५ ॥

vaikuṇṭhaḥ kalpito yena
loko loka-namaskṛtaḥ
ramayā prārthyamānena
devyā tat-priya-kāmyayā

vaikuṇṭhaḥ—a Vaikuṇṭha planet; *kalpitaḥ*—was constructed; *yena*—by whom; *lokaḥ*—planet; *loka-namaskṛtaḥ*—worshiped by all people; *ramayā*—by Ramā, the goddess of fortune; *prārthyamānena*—being so requested; *devyā*—by the goddess; *tat*—her; *priya-kāmyayā*—just to please.

TRANSLATION

Just to please the goddess of fortune, the Supreme Personality of Godhead, Vaikuṇṭha, at her request, created another Vaikuṇṭha planet, which is worshiped by everyone.

PURPORT

Śrīla Viśvanātha Cakravartī Ṭhākura remarks here that this Vaikuṇṭha planet, like *Śrīmad-Bhāgavatam*, appears and is said to be born or created, but both *Śrīmad-Bhāgavatam* and Vaikuṇṭha eternally exist beyond the material universes, which are enveloped by eight kinds of coverings. As described in the Second Canto, Lord Brahmā saw Vaikuṇṭha before the creation of the universe. Vīrarāghava Ācārya mentions that this Vaikuṇṭha is within the universe. It is situated above the mountain known as Lokāloka. This planet is worshiped by everyone.

TEXT 6

तस्यानुभावः कथितो गुणाश्च परमोदयाः ।
भौमान्रेणून्स विममे यो विष्णोर्वर्णयेद् गुणान् ॥ ६ ॥

tasyānubhāvaḥ kathito
guṇāś ca paramodayāḥ
bhaumān reṇūn sa vimame
yo viṣṇor varṇayed guṇān

tasya—of the Supreme Personality of Godhead appearing as Vaikuṇṭha; *anubhāvaḥ*—great activities; *kathitaḥ*—were explained; *guṇāḥ*—transcendental qualities; *ca*—also; *parama-udayāḥ*—greatly glorious; *bhaumān*—earthly; *reṇūn*—particles; *saḥ*—someone; *vimame*—can count; *yaḥ*—such a person; *viṣṇoḥ*—of Lord Viṣṇu; *varṇayet*—can count; *guṇān*—the transcendental qualities.

TRANSLATION

Although the great activities and transcendental qualities of the Supreme Personality of Godhead's various incarnations are wonderfully described, sometimes we are unable to understand them. Yet everything is possible for Lord Viṣṇu. If one could count the atoms of the universe, then he could count the qualities of the Supreme Personality of Godhead. But no one can count the atoms of the universe, nor can anyone count the transcendental qualities of the Lord.

PURPORT

The Lord's glorious activities referred to in this connection took place after His personal bodyguards Jaya and Vijaya became Daityas, having been cursed by the great sages Sanaka, Sanātana, Sanat-kumāra and Sanandana. Jaya, as Hiraṇyākṣa, had to fight with Varāhadeva, and that same Varāhadeva is mentioned in regard to the Raivata millennium. The fighting, however, took place during the reign of the first Manu, Svāyambhuva. Therefore according to some authorities there are two Varāhas. According to others, however, Varāha appeared during the regime of Svāyambhuva Manu and stayed in the water until that of Raivata Manu. Some may doubt that this could be possible, but the answer is that everything is possible. If one could count the atoms within the universe, one could count the qualities of Lord Viṣṇu. But the atoms of the universe are impossible for anyone to count, and similarly no one can count the transcendental qualities of the Lord.

TEXT 7

षष्ठश्च चक्षुषः पुत्रश्चाक्षुषो नाम वै मनुः ।
पूरुपूरुषसुद्युम्नप्रमुखाश्चाक्षुषात्मजाः ॥ ७ ॥

ṣaṣṭhaś ca cakṣuṣaḥ putraś
cākṣuṣo nāma vai manuḥ
pūru-pūruṣa-sudyumna-
pramukhāś cākṣuṣātmajāḥ

ṣaṣṭhaḥ—the sixth; *ca*—and; *cakṣuṣaḥ*—of Cakṣu; *putraḥ*—the son; *cākṣuṣaḥ*—Cākṣuṣa; *nāma*—named; *vai*—indeed; *manuḥ*—Manu; *pūru*—Pūru; *pūruṣa*—Pūruṣa; *sudyumna*—Sudyumna; *pramukhāḥ*—headed by; *cākṣuṣa-ātma-jāḥ*—the sons of Cākṣuṣa.

TRANSLATION

The son of Cakṣu known as Cākṣuṣa was the sixth Manu. He had many sons, headed by Pūru, Pūruṣa and Sudyumna.

TEXT 8

इन्द्रो मन्त्रद्रुमस्तत्र देवा आप्यादयो गणाः ।
मुनयस्तत्र वै राजन्हविष्मद्वीरकादयः ॥ ८ ॥

indro mantradrumas tatra
devā āpyādayo gaṇāḥ
munayas tatra vai rājan
haviṣmad-vīrakādayaḥ

indraḥ—the King of heaven; *mantradrumaḥ*—known as Mantradruma; *tatra*—in that sixth *manvantara; devāḥ*—the demigods; *āpya-ādayaḥ*—the Āpyas and others; *gaṇāḥ*—that assembly; *munayaḥ*—the seven sages; *tatra*—there; *vai*—indeed; *rājan*—O King; *haviṣmat*—of the name Haviṣmān; *vīraka-ādayaḥ*—Vīraka and others.

TRANSLATION

During the reign of Cākṣuṣa Manu, the King of heaven was known as Mantradruma. Among the demigods were the Āpyas, and among the great sages were Haviṣmān and Vīraka.

TEXT 9

तत्रापि देवसम्भूत्यां वैराजस्याभवत् सुतः ।
अजितो नाम भगवानंशेन जगतः पतिः ॥ ९ ॥

tatrāpi devasambhūtyāṁ
vairājasyābhavat sutaḥ
ajito nāma bhagavān
aṁśena jagataḥ patiḥ

tatra api—again in that sixth *manvantara; devasambhūtyām*—by Devasambhūti; *vairājasya*—by her husband, Vairāja; *abhavat*—there was; *sutaḥ*—a son; *ajitaḥ nāma*—by the name Ajita; *bhagavān*—the Supreme Personality of Godhead; *aṁśena*—partially; *jagataḥ patiḥ*—the master of the universe.

TRANSLATION

In this sixth manvantara millennium, Lord Viṣṇu, the master of the universe, appeared in His partial expansion. He was begotten by Vairāja in the womb of his wife, Devasambhūti, and His name was Ajita.

TEXT 10

पयोधिं येन निर्मथ्य सुराणां साधिता सुधा ।
भ्रममाणोऽम्भसि धृतः कूर्मरूपेण मन्दरः ॥१०॥

payodhiṁ yena nirmathya
surāṇāṁ sādhitā sudhā
bhramamāṇo 'mbhasi dhṛtaḥ
kūrma-rūpeṇa mandaraḥ

payodhim—the ocean of milk; *yena*—by whom; *nirmathya*—by churning; *surāṇām*—of the demigods; *sādhitā*—produced; *sudhā*—nectar; *bhramamāṇaḥ*—moving here and there; *ambhasi*—within the water; *dhṛtaḥ*—was staying; *kūrma-rūpeṇa*—in the form of a tortoise; *mandaraḥ*—the mountain known as Mandara.

TRANSLATION

By churning the ocean of milk, Ajita produced nectar for the demigods. In the form of a tortoise, He moved here and there, carrying on His back the great mountain known as Mandara.

TEXTS 11–12

श्रीराजोवाच

यथा भगवता ब्रह्मन्मथितः क्षीरसागरः ।
यदर्थं वा यतश्चाद्रिं दधाराम्बुचरात्मना ॥११॥
यथामृतं सुरैः प्राप्तं किञ्चान्यदभवत् ततः ।
एतद् भगवतः कर्म वदस्व परमाद्भुतम् ॥१२॥

śrī-rājovāca
yathā bhagavatā brahman
mathitaḥ kṣīra-sāgaraḥ
yad-arthaṁ vā yataś cādriṁ
dadhārāmbucarātmanā

yathāmṛtaṁ suraiḥ prāptaṁ
kiṁ cānyad abhavat tataḥ

etad bhagavataḥ karma
vadasva paramādbhutam

śrī-rājā uvāca—King Parīkṣit inquired; *yathā*—as; *bhagavatā*—by the Supreme Personality of Godhead; *brahman*—O learned *brāhmaṇa; mathitaḥ*—churned; *kṣīra-sāgaraḥ*—the ocean of milk; *yat-artham*—what was the purpose; *vā*—either; *yataḥ*—wherefrom, for what reason; *ca*—and; *adrim*—the mountain (Mandara); *dadhāra*—was staying; *ambucara-ātmanā*—in the form of a tortoise; *yathā*—as; *amṛtam*—nectar; *suraiḥ*—by the demigods; *prāptam*—was achieved; *kim*—what; *ca*—and; *anyat*—other; *abhavat*—became; *tataḥ*—thereafter; *etat*—all these; *bhagavataḥ*—of the Supreme Personality of Godhead; *karma*—pastimes, activities; *vadasva*—kindly describe; *parama-adbhutam*—because they are so wonderful.

TRANSLATION

King Parīkṣit inquired: O great brāhmaṇa, Śukadeva Gosvāmī, why and how did Lord Viṣṇu churn the ocean of milk? For what reason did He stay in the water as a tortoise and hold up Mandara Mountain? How did the demigods obtain the nectar, and what other things were produced from the churning of the ocean? Kindly describe all these wonderful activities of the Lord.

TEXT 13

त्वया सङ्कथ्यमानेन महिम्ना सात्वतां पतेः ।
नातितृप्यति मे चित्तं सुचिरं तापतापितम् ॥१३॥

tvayā saṅkathyamānena
mahimnā sātvatāṁ pateḥ
nātitṛpyati me cittaṁ
suciraṁ tāpa-tāpitam

tvayā—by Your Holiness; *saṅkathyamānena*—being described; *mahimnā*—by all the glories; *sātvatām pateḥ*—of the Supreme Personality of Godhead, the master of the devotees; *na*—not; *ati-tṛpyati*—is sufficiently satisfied; *me*—my; *cittam*—heart; *suciram*—for such a long time; *tāpa*—by miseries; *tāpitam*—being distressed.

TRANSLATION

My heart, which is disturbed by the three miserable conditions of material life, is not yet sated with hearing you describe the glorious activities of the Lord, the Supreme Personality of Godhead, who is the master of the devotees.

TEXT 14

श्रीसूत उवाच
सम्पृष्टो भगवानेवं द्वैपायनसुतो द्विजाः ।
अभिनन्द्य हरेर्वीर्यमभ्याचष्टुं प्रचक्रमे ॥१४॥

śrī-sūta uvāca
sampṛṣṭo bhagavān evaṁ
dvaipāyana-suto dvijāḥ
abhinandya harer vīryam
abhyācaṣṭuṁ pracakrame

śrī-sūtaḥ uvāca—Śrī Sūta Gosvāmī said; *sampṛṣṭaḥ*—being questioned; *bhagavān*—Śukadeva Gosvāmī; *evam*—thus; *dvaipāyana-sutaḥ*—the son of Vyāsadeva; *dvi-jāḥ*—O *brāhmaṇas* assembled here; *abhinandya*—congratulating Mahārāja Parīkṣit; *hareḥ vīryam*—the glories of the Supreme Personality of Godhead; *abhyācaṣṭum*—to describe; *pracakrame*—endeavored.

TRANSLATION

Śrī Sūta Gosvāmī said: O learned brāhmaṇas assembled here at Naimiṣāraṇya, when Śukadeva Gosvāmī, the son of Dvaipāyana, was thus questioned by the King, he congratulated the King and then endeavored to describe further the glories of the Supreme Personality of Godhead.

TEXTS 15–16

श्रीशुक उवाच
यदा युद्धेऽसुरैर्देवा बध्यमानाः शितायुधैः ।
गतासवो निपतिता नोत्तिष्ठेरन्स्म भूरिशः ॥१५॥

यदा दुर्वासः शापेन सेन्द्रा लोकास्त्रयो नृप ।
निःश्रीकाश्चाभवंस्तत्र नेशुरिज्यादयः क्रियाः ॥१६॥

śrī-śuka uvāca
yadā yuddhe 'surair devā
badhyamānāḥ śitāyudhaiḥ
gatāsavo nipatitā
nottiṣṭheran sma bhūriśaḥ

yadā durvāsaḥ śāpena
sendrā lokās trayo nṛpa
niḥśrīkāś cābhavaṁs tatra
neśur ijyādayaḥ kriyāḥ

śrī-śukaḥ uvāca—Śrī Śukadeva Gosvāmī said; *yadā*—when; *yuddhe*—in the fighting; *asuraiḥ*—by the demons; *devāḥ*—the demigods; *badhyamānāḥ*—beseiged; *śita-āyudhaiḥ*—by serpent weapons; *gata-āsavaḥ*—almost dead; *nipatitāḥ*—some of them having fallen; *na*—not; *uttiṣṭheran*—got up again; *sma*—so became; *bhūriśaḥ*—the majority of them; *yadā*—when; *durvāsaḥ*—of Durvāsā Muni; *śāpena*—with the curse; *sa-indrāḥ*—with Indra; *lokāḥ trayaḥ*—the three worlds; *nṛpa*—O King; *niḥśrīkāḥ*—without any material opulence; *ca*—also; *abhavan*—became; *tatra*—at that time; *neśuḥ*—could not be performed; *ijya-ādayaḥ*—sacrifices; *kriyāḥ*—ritualistic ceremonies.

TRANSLATION

Śukadeva Gosvāmī said: When the asuras, with their serpent weapons, severely attacked the demigods in a fight, many of the demigods fell and lost their lives. Indeed, they could not be revived. At that time, O King, the demigods had been cursed by Durvāsā Muni, the three worlds were poverty-stricken, and therefore ritualistic ceremonies could not be performed. The effects of this were very serious.

PURPORT

It is described that while Durvāsā Muni was passing on the road, he saw Indra on the back of his elephant and was pleased to offer Indra a garland from his own neck. Indra, however, being too puffed up, took the garland, and without respect for Durvāsā Muni, he placed it on the trunk of his carrier elephant. The elephant, being an animal, could not understand the value of the garland, and thus the elephant threw the garland between its legs and smashed it. Seeing this insulting behavior, Durvāsā Muni immediately cursed Indra to be poverty-stricken, bereft of all material opulence. Thus the demigods, afflicted on one side by the fighting demons and on the other by the curse of Durvāsā Muni, lost all the material opulences in the three worlds.

To be extremely opulent in materialistic advancement is sometimes very risky. The materially opulent person does not care about anyone, and thus he commits offenses to great personalities, such as devotees and great saints. This is the way of material opulence. As described by Śukadeva Gosvāmī, *dhana-durmadāndha:* too much wealth makes one blind. This happens even to Indra in his heavenly kingdom, and what to speak of others in this material world? When one is materially opulent, he should learn to be sober and well-behaved toward Vaiṣṇavas and saintly persons; otherwise he will fall down.

TEXTS 17–18

निशाम्यैतत् सुरगणा महेन्द्रवरुणादयः ।
नाध्यगच्छन्स्वयं मन्त्रैर्मन्त्रयन्तो विनिश्चितम् ॥१७॥
ततो ब्रह्मसभां जग्मुर्मेरोर्मूर्धनि सर्वशः ।
सर्वं विज्ञापयांचक्रुः प्रणताः परमेष्ठिने ॥१८॥

niśāmyaitat sura-gaṇā
mahendra-varuṇādayaḥ
nādhyagacchan svayaṁ mantrair
mantrayanto viniścitam

tato brahma-sabhāṁ jagmur
meror mūrdhani sarvaśaḥ
sarvaṁ vijñāpayāṁ cakruḥ
praṇatāḥ parameṣṭhine

niśāmya—hearing; *etat*—this incident; *sura-gaṇāḥ*—all the demigods; *mahā-indra*—King Indra; *varuṇa-ādayaḥ*—Varuṇa and other demigods; *na*—not; *adhyagacchan*—reached; *svayam*—personally; *mantraiḥ*—by deliberation; *mantrayantaḥ*—discussing; *viniścitam*—a real conclusion; *tataḥ*—thereupon; *brahma-sabhām*—to the assembly of Lord Brahmā; *jagmuḥ*—they went; *meroḥ*—of Sumeru Mountain; *mūrdhani*—on the top; *sarvaśaḥ*—all of them; *sarvam*—everything; *vijñāpayām cakruḥ*—they informed; *praṇatāḥ*—offered obeisances; *parameṣṭhine*—unto Lord Brahmā.

TRANSLATION

Lord Indra, Varuṇa and the other demigods, seeing their lives in such a state, consulted among themselves, but they could not find any solution. Then all the demigods assembled and went together to the peak of Sumeru Mountain. There, in the assembly of Lord Brahmā, they fell down to offer Lord Brahmā their obeisances, and then they informed him of all the incidents that had taken place.

TEXTS 19–20

स विलोक्येन्द्रवाय्वादीन् निःसत्त्वान्विगतप्रभान् ।
लोकानमङ्गलप्रायानसुरानयथा विभुः ॥१९॥
समाहितेन मनसा संस्मरन्पुरुषं परम् ।
उवाचोत्फुल्लवदनो देवान्स भगवान्परः ॥२०॥

sa vilokyendra-vāyv-ādīn
niḥsattvān vigata-prabhān
lokān amaṅgala-prāyān
asurān ayathā vibhuḥ

samāhitena manasā
saṁsmaran puruṣaṁ param
uvācotphulla-vadano
devān sa bhagavān paraḥ

saḥ—Lord Brahmā; *vilokya*—looking over; *indra-vāyu-ādīn*—all the demigods, headed by Lord Indra and Vāyu; *niḥsattvān*—bereft of all spiritual potency; *vigata-prabhān*—bereft of all effulgence; *lokān*—all the three worlds; *amaṅgala-prāyān*—merged into misfortune; *asurān*—all the demons; *ayathāḥ*—flourishing; *vibhuḥ*—Lord Brahmā, the supreme within this material world; *samāhitena*—by full adjustment; *manasā*—of the mind; *saṁsmaran*—remembering again and again; *puruṣam*—the Supreme Person; *param*—transcendental; *uvāca*—said; *utphulla-vadanaḥ*—bright-faced; *devān*—unto the demigods; *saḥ*—he; *bhagavān*—the most powerful; *paraḥ*—of the demigods.

TRANSLATION

Upon seeing that the demigods were bereft of all influence and strength and that the three worlds were consequently devoid of auspiciousness, and upon seeing that the demigods were in an awkward position whereas all the demons were flourishing, Lord Brahmā, who is above all the demigods and who is most powerful, concentrated his mind on the Supreme Personality of Godhead. Thus being encouraged, he became bright-faced and spoke to the demigods as follows.

PURPORT

After hearing from the demigods the real situation, Lord Brahmā was very much concerned because the demons were unnecessarily so powerful. When demons become powerful, the entire world is placed in an awkward position because demons are simply interested in their own sense gratification and not in the welfare of the world. Demigods or devotees, however, are concerned with the welfare of all living beings. Śrīla Rūpa Gosvāmī, for example, left his ministership and went to Vṛndāvana for the benefit of the entire world (*lokānāṁ hita-kāriṇau*). This is the nature of a saintly person or demigod. Even impersonalists think of the welfare of all people. Thus Brahmā was very much concerned at seeing the demons in power.

TEXT 21

अहं भवो यूयमथोऽसुरादयो
मनुष्यतिर्यग्द्रुमघर्मजातयः ।

यस्यावतारांशकलाविसर्जिता
व्रजाम सर्वे शरणं तमव्ययम् ॥२१॥

ahaṁ bhavo yūyam atho 'surādayo
manuṣya-tiryag-druma-gharma-jātayaḥ
yasyāvatārāṁśa-kalā-visarjitā
vrajāma sarve śaraṇaṁ tam avyayam

aham—I; *bhavaḥ*—Lord Śiva; *yūyam*—all of you demigods; *atho*—as well as; *asura-ādayaḥ*—demons and others; *manuṣya*—the human beings; *tiryak*—the animals; *druma*—the trees and plants; *gharma-jātayaḥ*—as well as the insects and germs born of perspiration; *yasya*—of whom (the Supreme Personality of Godhead); *avatāra*—of the *puruṣa* incarnation; *aṁśa*—of His part and parcel, the *guṇa-avatāra,* Brahmā; *kalā*—of Brahmā's sons; *visarjitāḥ*—produced by the generation; *vrajāma*—we shall go; *sarve*—all of us; *śaraṇam*—unto the shelter; *tam*—unto the Supreme; *avyayam*—the inexhaustible.

TRANSLATION

Lord Brahmā said: I, Lord Śiva, all of you demigods, the demons, the living entities born of perspiration, the living beings born of eggs, the trees and plants sprouting from the earth, and the living entities born from embryos—all come from the Supreme Lord, from His incarnation of rajo-guṇa [Lord Brahmā, the guṇa-avatāra] and from the great sages [ṛṣis] who are part of me. Let us therefore go to the Supreme Lord and take shelter of His lotus feet.

PURPORT

Some creatures are born from embryos, some from perspiration, and some from seeds. In this way, all living entities emanate from the *guṇa-avatāra* of the Supreme Personality of Godhead. Ultimately, the Supreme Personality of Godhead is the shelter of all living entities.

TEXT 22

न यस्य वध्यो न च रक्षणीयो
नोपेक्षणीयादरणीयपक्षः ।

तथापि सर्गस्थितिसंयमार्थं
धत्ते रजःसत्त्वतमांसि काले ॥२२॥

na yasya vadhyo na ca rakṣaṇīyo
nopekṣaṇīyādaraṇīya-pakṣaḥ
tathāpi sarga-sthiti-saṁyamārthaṁ
dhatte rajaḥ-sattva-tamāṁsi kāle

na—not; *yasya*—by whom (the Lord); *vadhyaḥ*—anyone is to be killed; *na*—nor; *ca*—also; *rakṣaṇīyaḥ*—anyone is to be protected; *na*—nor; *upekṣaṇīya*—to be neglected; *ādaraṇīya*—to be worshiped; *pakṣaḥ*—part; *tathāpi*—still; *sarga*—creation; *sthiti*—maintenance; *saṁyama*—and annihilation; *artham*—for the sake of; *dhatte*—He accepts; *rajaḥ*—passion; *sattva*—goodness; *tamāṁsi*—and ignorance; *kāle*—in due course of time.

TRANSLATION

For the Supreme Personality of Godhead there is no one to be killed, no one to be protected, no one to be neglected and no one to be worshiped. Nonetheless, for the sake of creation, maintenance and annihilation according to time, He accepts different forms as incarnations either in the mode of goodness, the mode of passion or the mode of ignorance.

PURPORT

This verse explains that the Supreme Personality of Godhead is equal to everyone. This is confirmed by the Lord Himself in *Bhagavad-gītā* (9.29):

samo 'haṁ sarva-bhūteṣu
na me dveṣyo 'sti na priyaḥ
ye bhajanti tu māṁ bhaktyā
mayi te teṣu cāpy aham

"I envy no one, nor am I partial to anyone. I am equal to all. But whoever renders service unto Me in devotion is a friend, is in Me, and I am also a friend to him." Although the Lord is impartial, He gives special attention to His devotees. Therefore the Lord says in *Bhagavad-gītā* (4.8):

paritrāṇāya sādhūnāṁ
vināśāya ca duṣkṛtām
dharma-saṁsthāpanārthāya
sambhavāmi yuge yuge

"To deliver the pious and to annihilate the miscreants, as well as to reestablish the principles of religion, I advent Myself millennium after millennium." The Lord has nothing to do with anyone's protection or destruction, but for the creation, maintenance and annihilation of this material world He apparently has to act either in goodness, in passion or in darkness. Actually, however, He is unaffected by these modes of material nature. He is the Supreme Lord of everyone. As a king sometimes punishes or rewards someone to maintain law and order, the Supreme Personality of Godhead, although having nothing to do with the activities of this material world, sometimes appears as various incarnations according to the time, place and object.

TEXT 23

अयं च तस्य स्थितिपालनक्षणः
सत्त्वं जुषाणस्य भवाय देहिनाम् ।
तस्माद् व्रजामः शरणं जगद्गुरुं
स्वानां स नो धास्यति शं सुरप्रियः ॥२३॥

ayaṁ ca tasya sthiti-pālana-kṣaṇaḥ
sattvaṁ juṣāṇasya bhavāya dehinām
tasmād vrajāmaḥ śaraṇaṁ jagad-guruṁ
svānāṁ sa no dhāsyati śaṁ sura-priyaḥ

ayam—this period; *ca*—also; *tasya*—of the Supreme Personality of Godhead; *sthiti-pālana-kṣaṇaḥ*—the time for maintenance, or for establishing His rule; *sattvam*—the mode of goodness; *juṣāṇasya*—accepting (now, without waiting); *bhavāya*—for the increased development or establishment; *dehinām*—of all living entities who accept material bodies; *tasmāt*—therefore; *vrajāmaḥ*—let us take; *śaraṇam*—shelter; *jagat-gurum*—at the lotus feet of the Supreme Personality of Godhead, who is the universal teacher; *svānām*—His own persons;

saḥ—He (the Supreme Personality of Godhead); *naḥ*—unto us; *dhāsyati*—will give; *śam*—the good fortune we need; *sura-priyaḥ*—because He is naturally very dear to the devotees.

TRANSLATION

Now is the time to invoke the mode of goodness of the living entities who have accepted material bodies. The mode of goodness is meant to establish the Supreme Lord's rule, which will maintain the existence of the creation. Therefore, this is the opportune moment to take shelter of the Supreme Personality of Godhead. Because He is naturally very kind and dear to the demigods, He will certainly bestow good fortune upon us.

PURPORT

The material world is conducted by the three modes of nature, namely *sattva-guṇa, rajo-guṇa* and *tamo-guṇa.* By *rajo-guṇa* everything material is created, by *sattva-guṇa* everything material is maintained properly, and by *tamo-guṇa,* when the creation is improperly situated, everything is destroyed.

From this verse we can understand the situation of Kali-yuga, through which we are now passing. Just before the beginning of Kali-yuga—or, in other words, at the end of Dvāpara-yuga—Lord Śrī Kṛṣṇa appeared and left His instructions in the form of *Bhagavad-gītā,* in which He asked all living entities to surrender unto Him. Since the beginning of Kali-yuga, however, people have practically been unable to surrender to the lotus feet of Kṛṣṇa, and therefore, after some five thousand years, Kṛṣṇa came again as Śrī Caitanya Mahāprabhu just to teach the entire world how to surrender unto Him, unto Śrī Kṛṣṇa, and thus be purified.

Surrendering unto the lotus feet of Kṛṣṇa means achieving complete purification. Kṛṣṇa says in *Bhagavad-gītā* (18.66):

sarva-dharmān parityajya
mām ekaṁ śaraṇaṁ vraja
ahaṁ tvāṁ sarva-pāpebhyo
mokṣayiṣyāmi mā śucaḥ

"Abandon all varieties of religion and just surrender unto Me. I shall deliver you from all sinful reaction. Do not fear." Thus as soon as one surrenders unto the lotus feet of Kṛṣṇa, one certainly becomes free from all contamination.

Kali-yuga is full of contamination. This is described in the *Śrīmad-Bhāgavatam* (12.3.51):

kaler doṣa-nidhe rājann
asti hy eko mahān guṇaḥ
kīrtanād eva kṛṣṇasya
mukta-saṅgaḥ paraṁ vrajet

This age of Kali is full of unlimited faults. Indeed, it is just like an ocean of faults (*doṣa-nidhi*). But there is one chance, one opportunity. *Kīrtanād eva kṛṣṇasya mukta-saṅgaḥ paraṁ vrajet:* simply by chanting the Hare Kṛṣṇa *mantra,* one can be freed from the contamination of Kali-yuga and, in his original spiritual body, can return home, back to Godhead. This is the opportunity of Kali-yuga.

When Kṛṣṇa appeared, He gave His orders, and when Kṛṣṇa Himself appeared as a devotee, as Śrī Caitanya Mahāprabhu, He showed us the path by which to cross the ocean of Kali-yuga. That is the path of the Hare Kṛṣṇa movement. When Śrī Caitanya Mahāprabhu appeared, He ushered in the era for the *saṅkīrtana* movement. It is also said that for ten thousand years this era will continue. This means that simply by accepting the *saṅkīrtana* movement and chanting the Hare Kṛṣṇa *mahā-mantra,* the fallen souls of this Kali-yuga will be delivered. After the Battle of Kurukṣetra, at which *Bhagavad-gītā* was spoken, Kali-yuga continues for 432,000 years, of which only 5,000 years have passed. Thus there is still a balance of 427,000 years to come. Of these 427,000 years, the 10,000 years of the *saṅkīrtana* movement inaugurated by Śrī Caitanya Mahāprabhu 500 years ago provide the opportunity for the fallen souls of Kali-yuga to take to the Kṛṣṇa consciousness movement, chant the Hare Kṛṣṇa *mahā-mantra* and thus be delivered from the clutches of material existence and return home, back to Godhead.

Chanting of the Hare Kṛṣṇa *mahā-mantra* is potent always, but it is especially potent in this age of Kali. Therefore Śukadeva Gosvāmī, while instructing Mahārāja Parīkṣit, stressed this chanting of the Hare Kṛṣṇa *mantra.*

kaler doṣa-nidhe rājann
asti hy eko mahān guṇaḥ
kīrtanād eva kṛṣṇasya
mukta-saṅgaḥ paraṁ vrajet

"My dear King, although Kali-yuga is full of faults, there is still one good quality about this age. It is that simply by chanting the Hare Kṛṣṇa *mahā-mantra,* one can become free from material bondage and be promoted to the transcendental kingdom." (*Bhāg.* 12.3.51) Those who have accepted the task of spreading the Hare Kṛṣṇa *mahā-mantra* in full Kṛṣṇa consciousness should take this opportunity to deliver people very easily from the clutches of material existence. Our duty, therefore, is to follow the instructions of Śrī Caitanya Mahāprabhu and preach the Kṛṣṇa consciousness movement all over the world very sincerely. This is the best welfare activity for the peace and prosperity of human society.

Śrī Caitanya Mahāprabhu's movement consists of spreading *kṛṣṇa-saṅkīrtana. Paraṁ vijayate śrī-kṛṣṇa-saṅkīrtanam:* "All glories to the Śrī Kṛṣṇa *saṅkīrtana!*" Why is it so glorious? This has also been explained by Śrī Caitanya Mahāprabhu. *Ceto-darpaṇa-mārjanam:* by the chanting of the Hare Kṛṣṇa *mahā-mantra,* one's heart is cleansed. The whole difficulty is that in this age of Kali there is no *sattva-guṇa* and no clearance of the heart, and therefore people are making the mistake of identifying with their bodies. Even the big philosophers and scientists with whom we deal are practically all under the impression that they are their bodies. The other day we were discussing a prominent philosopher, Thomas Huxley, who was proud of being an Englishman. This means that he was in the bodily conception of life. Everywhere we find this same misunderstanding. As soon as one is in the bodily conception of life, one is nothing but an animal like a cat or a dog (*sa eva go-kharaḥ*). Thus the most dangerous of the dirty things within our hearts is this misidentification of the body as the self. Under the influence of this misunderstanding, one thinks, "I am this body. I am an Englishman. I am an Indian. I am an American. I am Hindu. I am Muslim." This misconception is the strongest impediment, and it must be removed. That is the instruction of *Bhagavad-gītā* and of Śrī Caitanya Mahāprabhu. Indeed, *Bhagavad-gītā* begins with this instruction:

dehino 'smin yathā dehe
kaumāraṁ yauvanaṁ jarā
tathā dehāntara-prāptir
dhīras tatra na muhyati

"As the embodied soul continually passes, in this body, from boyhood to youth to old age, the soul similarly passes into another body at death. The self-realized soul is not bewildered by such a change." (Bg. 2.13) Although the soul is within the body, nevertheless, because of misunderstanding and animal propensities one accepts the body as the self. Caitanya Mahāprabhu therefore says, *ceto-darpaṇa-mārjanam.* To cleanse the core of the heart, which is full of misunderstanding, is possible only through *śrī-kṛṣṇa-saṅkīrtana.* The leaders of the Kṛṣṇa consciousness movement should very seriously take this opportunity to be kind to the fallen souls by delivering them from the misunderstanding of materialistic life.

One cannot be happy in any way within this material world. As stated in *Bhagavad-gītā* (8.16):

ābrahma-bhuvanāl lokāḥ
punar āvartino 'rjuna

"From the highest planet in this material world down to the lowest, all are places of misery wherein repeated birth and death take place." Therefore, not to speak of going to the moon, even if one is promoted to the highest planetary system, Brahmaloka, there cannot be any happiness in this material world. If one actually wants happiness, one must go to the spiritual world. The material world is characterized by a struggle for existence, and survival of the fittest is a well-known principle, but the poor souls of this material world do not know what is survival and who is fit. Survival does not mean that one should die; survival means that one should not die, but should enjoy an everlastingly blissful life of knowledge. This is survival. The Kṛṣṇa consciousness movement is meant to make every person fit for survival. Indeed, it is meant to stop the struggle for existence. The *Śrīmad-Bhāgavatam* and *Bhagavad-gītā* give definite directions on how to stop the struggle for existence and how to survive in eternal life. The *saṅkīrtana* movement, therefore, is a great opportunity. Simply by hearing *Bhagavad-gītā* and chanting the Hare Kṛṣṇa *mahā-mantra*, one becomes completely purified. Thus the struggle for existence ceases, and one goes back home, back to Godhead.

TEXT 24

श्रीशुक उवाच
इत्याभाष्य सुरान्वेधाः सह देवैररिन्दम ।
अजितस्य पदं साक्षाज्जगाम तमसः परम् ॥२४॥

śrī-śuka uvāca
ity ābhāṣya surān vedhāḥ
saha devair arindama
ajitasya padaṁ sākṣāj
jagāma tamasaḥ param

śrī-śukaḥ uvāca—Śrī Śukadeva Gosvāmī said; *iti*—thus; *ābhāṣya*—talking; *surān*—unto the demigods; *vedhāḥ*—Lord Brahmā, who is the head of this universe and who gives everyone good sense in Vedic knowledge; *saha*—with; *devaiḥ*—the demigods; *arim-dama*—O Mahārāja Parīkṣit, subduer of all kinds of enemies (such as the senses); *ajitasya*—of the Supreme Personality of Godhead; *padam*—to the place; *sākṣāt*—directly; *jagāma*—went; *tamasaḥ*—the world of darkness; *param*—transcendental to, beyond.

TRANSLATION

O Mahārāja Parīkṣit, subduer of all enemies, after Lord Brahmā finished speaking to the demigods, he took them with him to the abode of the Supreme Personality of Godhead, which is beyond this material world. The Lord's abode is on an island called Śvetadvīpa, which is situated in the ocean of milk.

PURPORT

Mahārāja Parīkṣit is addressed here as *arindama*, "subduer of all enemies." Not only do we have enemies outside of our bodies, but within our bodies there are many enemies, such as lusty desires, anger and greed. Mahārāja Parīkṣit is specifically addressed as *arindama* because in his political life he was able to subdue all kinds of enemies, and even though he was a young king, as soon as he heard that he was going to die within seven days, he immediately left his kingdom. He did not follow the dictates of enemies within his body, such as lust, greed and anger. He was not at all angry with the *muni's* son who had cursed him. Rather, he accepted the curse and prepared for his death in the association of Śukadeva Gosvāmī. Death is inevitable; no one can surpass the force of death. Therefore Mahārāja Parīkṣit, while fully alive, wanted to hear *Śrīmad-Bhāgavatam.* He is consequently addressed here as *arindama.*

Another word, *sura-priya,* is also significant. Although Kṛṣṇa, the Supreme Personality of Godhead, is equal toward everyone, He is especially inclined toward His devotees (*ye bhajanti tu māṁ bhaktyā mayi te teṣu cāpy aham*). The devotees are all demigods. There are two kinds of men within this world. One is called the *deva,* and the other is called the *asura.* The *Padma Purāṇa* states:

dvau bhūta-sargau loke 'smin
daiva āsura eva ca
viṣṇu-bhaktaḥ smṛto daiva
āsuras tad-viparyayaḥ

Anyone who is a devotee of Lord Kṛṣṇa is called a *deva,* and others, even though they may be devotees of demigods, are called *asuras.* Rāvaṇa, for example, was a great devotee of Lord Śiva, but he is described as an *asura.* Similarly, Hiraṇyakaśipu is described as a great devotee of Lord Brahmā, yet he was also an *asura.* Therefore, only the devotee of Lord Viṣṇu is called *sura,* not *asura.* Lord Kṛṣṇa is very much pleased with His devotees, even if they are not on the topmost stage of devotional service. Even on the lower stages of devotional service one is transcendental, and if one continues with devotional life, he continues to be a *deva* or *sura.* If one continues in this way, Kṛṣṇa will always be pleased with him and will give him all instructions so that he may very easily return home, back to Godhead.

Concerning *ajitasya padam*, the abode of the Supreme Personality of Godhead in the milk ocean of this material world, Śrīla Viśvanātha Cakravartī Ṭhākura says: *padaṁ kṣīrodadhi-stha-śvetadvīpaṁ tamasaḥ prakṛteḥ param.* The island known as Śvetadvīpa, which is in the ocean of milk, is transcendental. It has nothing to do with this material world. A city government may have a rest house where the governor and important government officers stay. Such a rest house is not an ordinary house. Similarly, although Śvetadvīpa, which is in the ocean of milk, is in this material world, it is *paraṁ padam*, transcendental.

TEXT 25

तत्रादृष्टस्वरूपाय श्रुतपूर्वाय वै प्रभुः ।
स्तुतिमब्रूत दैवीभिर्गीर्भिस्त्ववहितेन्द्रियः ॥२५॥

tatrādṛṣṭa-svarūpāya
śruta-pūrvāya vai prabhuḥ
stutim abrūta daivībhir
gīrbhis tv avahitendriyaḥ

tatra—there (at the Lord's abode known as Śvetadvīpa); *adṛṣṭa-svarūpāya*—unto the Supreme Personality of Godhead, who was not seen even by Lord Brahmā; *śruta-pūrvāya*—but who was heard about from the *Vedas; vai*—indeed; *prabhuḥ*—Lord Brahmā; *stutim*—prayers derived from Vedic literature; *abrūta*—performed; *daivībhiḥ*—by prayers mentioned in the Vedic literature or offered by persons strictly following Vedic principles; *gīrbhiḥ*—by such sound vibrations or songs; *tu*—then; *avahita-indriyaḥ*—fixed in mind, without deviation.

TRANSLATION

There [at Śvetadvīpa], Lord Brahmā offered prayers to the Supreme Personality of Godhead, even though he had never seen the Supreme Lord. Simply because Lord Brahmā had heard about the Supreme Personality of Godhead from Vedic literature, with a fixed mind he offered the Lord prayers as written or approved by Vedic literature.

PURPORT

It is said that when Brahmā and the other demigods go to see the Supreme Personality of Godhead in Śvetadvīpa, they cannot directly see Him, but their prayers are heard by the Lord, and the needful action is taken. This we have seen in many instances. The word *śruta-pūrvāya* is significant. We get experience by directly seeing or by hearing. If it is not possible to see someone directly, we can hear about him from authentic sources. Sometimes people ask whether we can show them God. This is ludicrous. It is not necessary for one to see God before he can accept God. Our sensory perception is always incomplete. Therefore, even if we see God, we may not be able to understand Him. When Kṛṣṇa was on earth, many, many people saw Him but could not understand that He is the Supreme Personality of Godhead. *Avajānanti māṁ mūḍhā mānuṣīṁ tanum āśritam.* Even though the rascals and fools saw Kṛṣṇa personally, they could not understand that He is the Supreme Personality of Godhead. Even upon seeing God personally, one who is unfortunate cannot understand Him. Therefore we have to hear about God, Kṛṣṇa, from the authentic Vedic literature and from persons who understand the Vedic version properly. Even though Brahmā had not seen the Supreme Personality of Godhead before, he was confident that the Lord was there in Śvetadvīpa. Thus he took the opportunity to go there and offer prayers to the Lord.

These prayers were not ordinary concocted prayers. Prayers must be approved by Vedic literature, as indicated in this verse by the words *daivībhir gīrbhiḥ.* In our Kṛṣṇa consciousness movement we do not allow any song that has not been approved or sung by bona fide devotees. We cannot allow cinema songs to be sung in the temple. We generally sing two songs. One is *śrī-kṛṣṇa-caitanya prabhu nityānanda śrī-advaita gadādhara śrīvāsādi-gaura-bhakta-vṛnda.* This is bona fide. It is always mentioned in the *Caitanya-caritāmṛta,* and it is accepted by the *ācāryas.* The other, of course, is the *mahā-mantra*—Hare Kṛṣṇa, Hare Kṛṣṇa, Kṛṣṇa Kṛṣṇa, Hare Hare/ Hare Rāma, Hare Rāma, Rāma Rāma, Hare Hare. We may also sing the songs of Narottama dāsa Ṭhākura, Bhaktivinoda Ṭhākura and Locana dāsa Ṭhākura, but these two songs—"*śrī-kṛṣṇa-caitanya*" and the Hare Kṛṣṇa *mahā-mantra*—are sufficient to please the Supreme Personality of Godhead, although we cannot see

Him. Seeing the Lord is not as important as appreciating Him from the authentic literature or the authentic statements of authorized persons.

TEXT 26

श्रीब्रह्मोवाच
अविक्रियं सत्यमनन्तमाद्यं
गुहाशयं निष्कलमप्रतर्क्यम् ।
मनोऽग्रयानं वचसानिरुक्तं
नमामहे देववरं वरेण्यम् ॥२६॥

śrī-brahmovāca
avikriyaṁ satyam anantam ādyaṁ
guhā-śayaṁ niṣkalam apratarkyam
mano-'grayānaṁ vacasāniruktaṁ
namāmahe deva-varaṁ vareṇyam

śrī-brahmā uvāca—Lord Brahmā said; *avikriyam*—unto the Personality of Godhead, who never changes (as opposed to material existence); *satyam*—the eternal supreme truth; *anantam*—unlimited; *ādyam*—the original cause of all causes; *guhā-śayam*—present in everyone's heart; *niṣkalam*—without any decrease in potency; *apratarkyam*—inconceivable, not within the jurisdiction of material arguments; *manaḥ-agrayānam*—more quick than the mind, inconceivable to mental speculation; *vacasā*—by jugglery of words; *aniruktam*—indescribable; *namāmahe*—all of us demigods offer our respectful obeisances; *deva-varam*—unto the Supreme Lord, who is not equalled or surpassed by anyone; *vareṇyam*—the supreme worshipable, who is worshiped by the Gāyatrī *mantra.*

TRANSLATION

Lord Brahmā said: O Supreme Lord, O changeless, unlimited supreme truth. You are the origin of everything. Being all-pervading, You are in everyone's heart and also in the atom. You have no material qualities. Indeed, You are inconceivable. The mind cannot catch You by speculation, and words fail to describe

You. You are the supreme master of everyone, and therefore You are worshipable for everyone. We offer our respectful obeisances unto You.

PURPORT

The Supreme Personality of Godhead is not anything of material creation. Everything material must change from one form to another—for example, from earth to earthen pot and from earthen pot to earth again. All our creations are temporary, impermanent. The Supreme Personality of Godhead, however, is eternal, and similarly the living entities, who are parts of Him, are also eternal (*mamaivāṁśo jīva-loke jīva-bhūtaḥ sanātanaḥ*). The Supreme Personality of Godhead is *sanātana*, eternal, and the individual living entities are also eternal. The difference is that Kṛṣṇa, or God, is the supreme eternal, whereas the individual souls are minute, fragmental eternals. As stated in *Bhagavad-gītā* (13.3), *kṣetrajñaṁ cāpi māṁ viddhi sarva-kṣetreṣu bhārata*. Although the Lord is a living being and the individual souls are living beings, the Supreme Lord, unlike the individual souls, is *vibhu*, all-pervading, and *ananta*, unlimited. The Lord is the cause of everything. The living entities are innumerable, but the Lord is one. No one is greater than Him, and no one is equal to Him. Thus the Lord is the supreme worshipable object, as understood from the Vedic *mantras* (*na tat-samaś cābhyadhikaś ca dṛśyate*). The Lord is supreme because no one can evaluate Him by mental speculation or jugglery of words. The Lord can travel more quickly than the mind. In the *śruti-mantras* of *Īśopaniṣad* it is said:

anejad ekaṁ manaso javīyo
nainad devā āpnuvan pūrvam arṣat
tad dhāvato 'nyān atyeti tiṣṭhat
tasminn apo mātariśvā dadhāti

"Although fixed in His abode, the Personality of Godhead is swifter than the mind and can overcome all others running. The powerful demigods cannot approach Him. Although in one place, He controls those who supply the air and rain. He surpasses all in excellence." (*Īśopaniṣad* 4) Thus the Supreme is never to be equaled by the subordinate living entities.

Because the Lord is situated in everyone's heart and the individual living entity is not, never should the individual living entity be equated with the Supreme Lord. In *Bhagavad-gītā* (15.15) the Lord says, *sarvasya cāhaṁ hṛdi sanniviṣṭaḥ:* "I am situated in everyone's heart." This does not mean, however, that everyone is equal to the Lord. In the *śruti-mantras* it is also said, *hṛdi hy ayam ātmā pratiṣṭhitaḥ.* In the beginning of *Śrīmad-Bhāgavatam* it is said, *satyaṁ paraṁ dhīmahi.* The Vedic *mantras* say, *satyaṁ jñānam anantam* and *niṣkalaṁ niṣkriyaṁ śāntaṁ niravadyam.* God is supreme. Although naturally He does not do anything, He is doing everything. As the Lord says in *Bhagavad-gītā:*

mayā tatam idaṁ sarvaṁ
jagad avyakta-mūrtinā
mat-sthāni sarva-bhūtāni
na cāhaṁ teṣv avasthitaḥ

"By Me, in My unmanifested form, this entire universe is pervaded. All beings are in Me, but I am not in them." (Bg. 9.4)

mayādhyakṣeṇa prakṛtiḥ
sūyate sacarācaram
hetunānena kaunteya
jagad viparivartate

"This material nature, working under My direction, O son of Kuntī, is producing all moving and unmoving beings. By its rule this manifestation is created and annihilated again and again." (Bg. 9.10) Thus although the Lord is silent in His abode, He is doing everything through His different energies (*parāsya śaktir vividhaiva śrūyate*) .

All the Vedic *mantras,* or *śruti-mantras,* are included in this verse spoken by Lord Brahmā, for Brahmā and his followers, the Brahma-sampradāya, understand the Supreme Personality of Godhead through the *paramparā* system. We have to gain understanding through the words of our predecessors. There are twelve *mahājanas,* or authorities, of whom Brahmā is one.

svayambhūr nāradaḥ śambhuḥ
kumāraḥ kapilo manuḥ

prahlādo janako bhīṣmo
balir vaiyāsakir vayam
(*Bhāg.* 6.3.20)

We belong to the disciplic succession of Brahmā, and therefore we are known as the Brahma-sampradāya. As the demigods follow Lord Brahmā to understand the Supreme Personality of Godhead, we also have to follow the authorities of the *paramparā* system to understand the Lord.

TEXT 27

विपश्चितं प्राणमनोधियात्मना-
मर्थेन्द्रियाभासमनिद्रमव्रणम् ।
छायातपौ यत्र न गृध्रपक्षौ
तमक्षरं खं त्रियुगं व्रजामहे ॥२७॥

vipaścitaṁ prāṇa-mano-dhiyātmanām
arthendriyābhāsam anidram avraṇam
chāyātapau yatra na gṛdhra-pakṣau
tam akṣaraṁ khaṁ tri-yugaṁ vrajāmahe

vipaścitam—unto the omniscient; *prāṇa*—how the living force is working; *manaḥ*—how the mind is working; *dhiya*—how the intelligence is working; *ātmanām*—of all living entities; *artha*—the objects of the senses; *indriya*—the senses; *ābhāsam*—knowledge; *anidram*—always awake and free from ignorance; *avraṇam*—without a material body subject to pains and pleasures; *chāyā-ātapau*—the shelter for all who are suffering from ignorance; *yatra*—wherein; *na*—not; *gṛdhra-pakṣau*—partiality toward any living being; *tam*—unto Him; *akṣaram*—infallible; *kham*—all-pervading like the sky; *tri-yugam*—appearing with six opulences in three *yugas* (Satya, Tretā and Dvāpara); *vrajāmahe*—I take shelter.

TRANSLATION

The Supreme Personality of Godhead directly and indirectly knows how everything, including the living force, mind and

intelligence, is working under His control. He is the illuminator of everything and has no ignorance. He does not have a material body subject to the reactions of previous activities, and He is free from the ignorance of partiality and materialistic education. I therefore take shelter of the lotus feet of the Supreme Lord, who is eternal, all-pervading and as great as the sky and who appears with six opulences in three yugas [Satya, Tretā and Dvāpara].

PURPORT

In the beginning of *Śrīmad-Bhāgavatam* the Supreme Personality of Godhead is described in this way: *janmādy asya yato 'nvayād itaratаś cārtheṣv abhijñaḥ.* The Lord is the origin of all emanations, and He directly and indirectly knows everything about all the activities within His creation. Therefore the Lord is addressed here as *vipaścitam,* one who is full of all knowledge or who knows everything. The Lord is the Supreme Soul, and He knows everything about the living entities and their senses.

The word *anidram,* meaning "always awake and free from ignorance," is very important in this verse. As stated in *Bhagavad-gītā* (15.15), *mattaḥ smṛtir jñānam apohanaṁ ca:* it is the Lord who gives intelligence to everyone and who causes everyone to forget. There are millions and millions of living entities, and the Lord gives them directions. Therefore He has no time to sleep, and He is never in ignorance of our activities. The Lord is the witness of everything; He sees what we are doing at every moment. The Lord is not covered by a body resulting from *karma.* Our bodies are formed as a result of our past deeds (*karmaṇā daiva-netreṇa*), but the Supreme Personality of Godhead does not have a material body, and therefore He has no *avidyā,* ignorance. He does not sleep, but is always alert and awake.

The Supreme Lord is described as *tri-yuga* because although He appeared variously in Satya-yuga, Tretā-yuga and Dvāpara-yuga, when He appeared in Kali-yuga He never declared Himself the Supreme Personality of Godhead.

kṛṣṇa-varṇaṁ tviṣākṛṣṇaṁ
sāṅgopāṅgāstra-pārṣadam

The Lord appears in Kali-yuga as a devotee. Thus although He is Kṛṣṇa, He chants the Hare Kṛṣṇa *mantra* like a devotee. Still, *Śrīmad-Bhāgavatam* (11.5.32) recommends:

yajñaiḥ saṅkīrtana-prāyair
yajanti hi sumedhasaḥ

Śrī Caitanya Mahāprabhu, whose complexion is not black like that of Kṛṣṇa but is golden (*tviṣākṛṣṇam*), is the Supreme Personality of Godhead. He is accompanied by associates like Nityānanda, Advaita, Gadādhara and Śrīvāsa. Those who are sufficiently intelligent worship this Supreme Personality of Godhead by performing *saṅkīrtana-yajña.* In this incarnation, the Supreme Lord declares Himself not to be the Supreme Lord, and therefore He is known as Tri-yuga.

TEXT 28

अजस्य चक्रं त्वजयेर्यमाणं
मनोमयं पञ्चदशारमाशु ।
त्रिनाभि विद्युच्चलमष्टनेमि
यदक्षमाहुस्तमृतं प्रपद्ये ॥२८॥

ajasya cakraṁ tv ajayeryamāṇaṁ
manomayaṁ pañcadaśāram āśu
tri-nābhi vidyuc-calam aṣṭa-nemi
yad-akṣam āhus tam ṛtaṁ prapadye

ajasya—of the living being; *cakram*—the wheel (the cycle of birth and death in this material world); *tu*—but; *ajayā*—by the external energy of the Supreme Lord; *īryamāṇam*—going around with great force; *manaḥ-mayam*—which is nothing but a mental creation depending chiefly on the mind; *pañcadaśa*—fifteen; *aram*—possessing spokes; *āśu*—very quick; *tri-nābhi*—having three naves (the three modes of material nature); *vidyut*—like electricity; *calam*—moving; *aṣṭa-nemi*—made of eight fellies (the eight external energies of the Lord—*bhūmir āpo 'nalo vāyuḥ*, etc.); *yat*—who; *akṣam*—the hub; *āhuḥ*—they say;

tam—unto Him; *ṛtam*—the fact; *prapadye*—let us offer our respectful obeisances.

TRANSLATION

In the cycle of material activities, the material body resembles the wheel of a mental chariot. The ten senses [five for working and five for gathering knowledge] and the five life airs within the body form the fifteen spokes of the chariot's wheel. The three modes of nature [goodness, passion and ignorance] are its center of activities, and the eight ingredients of nature [earth, water, fire, air, sky, mind, intelligence and false ego] comprise the rim of the wheel. The external, material energy moves this wheel like electrical energy. Thus the wheel revolves very quickly around its hub or central support, the Supreme Personality of Godhead, who is the Supersoul and the ultimate truth. We offer our respectful obeisances unto Him.

PURPORT

The cycle of repeated birth and death is figuratively described herein. As stated in *Bhagavad-gītā* (7.5):

apareyam itas tv anyāṁ
prakṛtiṁ viddhi me parām
jīva-bhūtāṁ mahā-bāho
yayedaṁ dhāryate jagat

The entire world is going on because the living entity, who is part and parcel of the Supreme Lord, is utilizing the material energy. Under the clutches of the material energy, the *jīvātmā* is revolving on the wheel of birth and death under the direction of the Supreme Personality of Godhead. The central point is the Supersoul. As explained in *Bhagavad-gītā* (18.61):

īśvaraḥ sarva-bhūtānāṁ
hṛd-deśe 'rjuna tiṣṭhati
bhrāmayan sarva-bhūtāni
yantrārūḍhāni māyayā

"The Supreme Lord is situated in everyone's heart, O Arjuna, and is directing the wanderings of all living entities, who are seated as on a machine, made of the material energy." The material body of the living entity is a result of the conditioned soul's activities, and because the supporter is the Supersoul, the Supersoul is the true reality. Every one of us, therefore, should offer respectful obeisances to this central reality. One should not be misguided by the activities of this material world and forget the central point, the Absolute Truth. That is the instruction given here by Lord Brahmā.

TEXT 29

य एकवर्णं तमसः परं त-
दलोकमव्यक्तमनन्तपारम् ।
आसाञ्चकारोपसुपर्णमेन-
मुपासते योगरथेन धीराः ॥२९॥

ya eka-varṇaṁ tamasaḥ paraṁ tad
alokam avyaktam ananta-pāram
āsāṁ cakāropasuparṇam enam
upāsate yoga-rathena dhīrāḥ

yaḥ—the Supreme Personality of Godhead who; *eka-varṇam*—absolute, situated in pure goodness; *tamasaḥ*—to the darkness of the material world; *param*—transcendental; *tat*—that; *alokam*—who cannot be seen; *avyaktam*—not manifested; *ananta-pāram*—unlimited, beyond the measurement of material time and space; *āsām cakāra*—situated; *upa-suparṇam*—on the back of Garuḍa; *enam*—Him; *upāsate*—worship; *yoga-rathena*—by the vehicle of mystic *yoga; dhīrāḥ*—persons who are sober, undisturbed by material agitation.

TRANSLATION

The Supreme Personality of Godhead is situated in pure goodness [śuddha-sattva], and therefore He is eka-varṇa—the oṁkāra [praṇava]. Because the Lord is beyond the cosmic manifestation, which is considered to be darkness, He is not visible to material

eyes. Nonetheless, He is not separated from us by time or space, but is present everywhere. Seated on His carrier, Garuḍa, He is worshiped by means of mystical yogic power by those who have achieved freedom from agitation. Let us all offer our respectful obeisances unto Him.

PURPORT

Sattvaṁ viśuddhaṁ vasudeva-śabditam (*Bhāg.* 4.3.23). In this material world, the three modes of material nature—goodness, passion and ignorance—prevail. Among these three, goodness is the platform of knowledge, and passion brings about a mixture of knowledge and ignorance, but the mode of ignorance is full of darkness. Therefore the Supreme Personality of Godhead is beyond darkness and passion. He is on the platform where goodness or knowledge is not disturbed by passion and ignorance. This is called the *vasudeva* platform. It is on this platform of *vasudeva* that Vāsudeva, or Kṛṣṇa, can appear. Thus Kṛṣṇa appeared on this planet as the son of Vasudeva. Because the Lord is situated beyond the three modes of material nature, He is unseen by those who are dominated by these three modes. One must therefore become *dhīra*, or undisturbed by the modes of material nature. The process of *yoga* may be practiced by one who is free from the agitation of these modes. Therefore *yoga* is defined in this way: *yoga indriya-saṁyamaḥ.* As previously explained, we are disturbed by the *indriyas*, or senses. Moreover, we are agitated by the three modes of material nature, which are imposed upon us by the external energy. In conditional life, the living entity moves turbulently in the whirlpool of birth and death, but when one is situated on the transcendental platform of *viśuddha-sattva*, pure goodness, he can see the Supreme Personality of Godhead, who sits on the back of Garuḍa. Lord Brahmā offers his respectful obeisances unto that Supreme Lord.

TEXT 30

न यस्य कश्चातितितर्ति मायां
यया जनो मुह्यति वेद नार्थम् ।
तं निर्जितात्मात्मगुणं परेशं
नमाम भूतेषु समं चरन्तम् ॥३०॥

na yasya kaścātititarti māyāṁ
yayā jano muhyati veda nārtham
taṁ nirjitātmātma-guṇaṁ pareśaṁ
namāma bhūteṣu samaṁ carantam

na—not; *yasya*—of whom (the Supreme Personality of Godhead); *kaśca*—anyone; *atititarti*—is able to overcome; *māyām*—the illusory energy; *yayā*—by whom (by the illusory energy); *janaḥ*—people in general; *muhyati*—become bewildered; *veda*—understand; *na*—not; *artham*—the aim of life; *tam*—unto Him (the Supreme Personality of Godhead); *nirjita*—completely controlling; *ātmā*—the living entities; *ātma-guṇam*—and His external energy; *para-īśam*—the Lord, who is transcendentally situated; *namāma*—we offer our respectful obeisances; *bhūteṣu*—unto all living beings; *samam*—equally situated, or equipoised; *carantam*—controlling or ruling them.

TRANSLATION

No one can overcome the Supreme Personality of Godhead's illusory energy [māyā], which is so strong that it bewilders everyone, making one lose the sense to understand the aim of life. That same māyā, however, is subdued by the Supreme Personality of Godhead, who rules everyone and who is equally disposed toward all living entities. Let us offer our obeisances unto Him.

PURPORT

The prowess of the Supreme Personality of Godhead, Viṣṇu, certainly controls all living entities, so much so that the living entities have forgotten the aim of life. *Na te viduḥ svārtha-gatiṁ hi viṣṇum:* the living entities have forgotten that the aim of life is to go back home, back to Godhead. The external energy of the Supreme Personality of Godhead gives all conditioned souls what appears to be an opportunity to be happy within this material world, but that is *māyā;* in other words, it is a dream that is never to be fulfilled. Thus every living being is illusioned by the external energy of the Supreme Lord. That illusory energy is undoubtedly very strong, but she is fully under the control of the transcendental person who is described in this verse as *pareśam,* the transcendental Lord. The Lord is not a part of the material creation, but is beyond the creation. Therefore, not only does He control the conditioned souls through His external energy, but He also controls the external energy itself. *Bhagavad-gītā* clearly says that the strong material energy controls everyone and that getting out of her control is extremely difficult. That controlling energy belongs to the Supreme Personality of Godhead and works under His control. The living entities, however, being subdued by the material energy, have forgotten the Supreme Personality of Godhead.

TEXT 31

इमे वयं यत्प्रिययैव तन्वा
सत्त्वेन सृष्टा बहिरन्तराविः ।
गतिं न सूक्ष्मामृषयश्च विद्महे
कुतोऽसुराद्या इतरप्रधानाः ॥३१॥

ime vayaṁ yat-priyayaiva tanvā
sattvena sṛṣṭā bahir-antar-āviḥ
gatiṁ na sūkṣmām ṛṣayaś ca vidmahe
kuto 'surādyā itara-pradhānāḥ

ime—these; *vayam*—we (the demigods); *yat*—to whom; *priyayā*—appearing very near and dear; *eva*—certainly; *tanvā*—the material body; *sattvena*—by the mode of goodness; *sṛṣṭāḥ*—created; *bahiḥ-antaḥ-āviḥ*—although fully aware, internally and externally; *gatim*—destination; *na*—not; *sūkṣmām*—very subtle; *ṛṣayaḥ*—great saintly persons; *ca*—also; *vidmahe*—understand; *kutaḥ*—how; *asura-ādyāḥ*—the demons and atheists; *itara*—who are insignificant in their identities; *pradhānāḥ*—although they are leaders of their own societies.

TRANSLATION

Since our bodies are made of sattva-guṇa, we, the demigods, are internally and externally situated in goodness. All the great saints are also situated in that way. Therefore, if even we cannot understand the Supreme Personality of Godhead, what is to be said of those who are most insignificant in their bodily constitutions, being situated in the modes of passion and ignorance? How can

they understand the Lord? Let us offer our respectful obeisances unto Him.

PURPORT

Atheists and demons cannot understand the Supreme Personality of Godhead, although He is situated within everyone. For them the Lord finally appears in the form of death, as confirmed in *Bhagavad-gītā* (*mṛtyuḥ sarva-haraś cāham*). Atheists think that they are independent, and therefore they do not care about the supremacy of the Lord, yet the Lord asserts His supremacy when He overcomes them as death. At the time of death, their attempts to use their so-called scientific knowledge and philosophical speculation to deny the supremacy of the Lord cannot work. Hiraṇyakaśipu, for example, was an exalted representative of the atheistic class of men. He always challenged the existence of God, and thus he became inimical even toward his own son. Everyone was afraid of Hiraṇyakaśipu's atheistic principles. Nonetheless, when Lord Nṛsiṁhadeva appeared in order to kill him, Hiraṇyakaśipu's atheistic principles could not save him. Lord Nṛsiṁhadeva killed Hiraṇyakaśipu and took away all his power, influence and pride. Atheistic men, however, never understand how everything they create is annihilated. The Supersoul is situated within them, but because of the predominance of the modes of passion and ignorance, they cannot understand the supremacy of the Lord. Even the demigods, the devotees, who are transcendentally situated or situated on the platform of goodness, are not fully aware of the qualities and position of the Lord. How then can the demons and atheists understand the Supreme Personality of Godhead? It is not possible. Therefore, to gain this understanding, the demigods, headed by Lord Brahmā, offered their respectful obeisances to the Lord.

TEXT 32

पादौ महीयं स्वकृतैव यस्य
चतुर्विधो यत्र हि भूतसर्गः ।
स वै महापूरुष आत्मतन्त्रः
प्रसीदतां ब्रह्म महाविभूतिः ॥३२॥

pādau mahīyaṁ sva-kṛtaiva yasya
catur-vidho yatra hi bhūta-sargaḥ
sa vai mahā-pūruṣa ātma-tantraḥ
prasīdatāṁ brahma mahā-vibhūtiḥ

pādau—His lotus feet; *mahī*—the earth; *iyam*—this; *sva-kṛta*—created by Himself; *eva*—indeed; *yasya*—of whom; *catuḥ-vidhaḥ*—of four kinds of living entities; *yatra*—wherein; *hi*—indeed; *bhūta-sargaḥ*—material creation; *saḥ*—He; *vai*—indeed; *mahā-pūruṣaḥ*—the Supreme Person; *ātma-tantraḥ*—self-sufficient; *prasīdatām*—may He be merciful to us; *brahma*—the greatest; *mahā-vibhūtiḥ*—with unlimited potency.

TRANSLATION

On this earth there are four kinds of living entities, who are all created by Him. The material creation rests on His lotus feet. He is the great Supreme Person, full of opulence and power. May He be pleased with us.

PURPORT

The word *mahī* refers to the five material elements—earth, water, air, fire and sky—which rest upon the lotus feet of the Supreme Personality of Godhead. *Mahat-padaṁ puṇya-yaśo murāreḥ.* The *mahat-tattva,* the total material energy, rests on His lotus feet, for the cosmic manifestation is but another opulence of the Lord. In this cosmic manifestation there are four kinds of living entities—*jarāyu-ja* (those born from embryos), *aṇḍa-ja* (those born from eggs), *sveda-ja* (those born from perspiration), and *udbhij-ja* (those born from seeds). Everything is generated from the Lord, as confirmed in the *Vedānta-sūtra* (*janmādy asya yataḥ*). No one is independent, but the Supreme Soul is completely independent. *Janmādy asya yato 'nvayād itarataś cārtheṣv abhijñaḥ sva-rāṭ.* The word *sva-rāṭ* means "independent." We are dependent, whereas the Supreme Lord is completely independent. Therefore the Supreme Lord is the greatest of all. Even Lord Brahmā, who created the cosmic manifestation, is but another opulence of the Supreme Personality of Godhead. The material creation is activated by the Lord, and therefore the Lord is not a part of the material creation. The Lord exists in His original, spiritual position. The universal form of the Lord, *vairāja-mūrti,* is another feature of the Supreme Personality of Godhead.

TEXT 33

अम्भस्तु यद्रेत उदारवीर्यं
सिध्यन्ति जीवन्त्युत वर्धमानाः ।
लोका यतोऽथाखिललोकपालाः
प्रसीदतां नः स महाविभूतिः ॥३३॥

ambhas tu yad-reta udāra-vīryaṁ
sidhyanti jīvanty uta vardhamānāḥ
lokā yato 'thākhila-loka-pālāḥ
prasīdatāṁ naḥ sa mahā-vibhūtiḥ

ambhaḥ—the masses of water seen on this planet or on others; *tu*—but; *yat-retaḥ*—His semen; *udāra-vīryam*—so powerful; *sidhyanti*—are generated; *jīvanti*—live; *uta*—indeed; *vardhamānāḥ*—flourish; *lokāḥ*—all the three worlds; *yataḥ*—from which; *atha*—also; *akhila-loka-pālāḥ*—all the demigods throughout the universe; *prasīdatām*—may be pleased; *naḥ*—upon us; *saḥ*—He; *mahā-vibhūtiḥ*—a person with unlimited potency.

TRANSLATION

The entire cosmic manifestation has emerged from water, and it is because of water that all living entities endure, live and develop. This water is nothing but the semen of the Supreme Personality of Godhead. Therefore, may the Supreme Personality of Godhead, who has such great potency, be pleased with us.

PURPORT

Despite the theories of so-called scientists, the vast quantities of water on this planet and on other planets are not created by a mixture of hydrogen and oxygen. Rather, the water is sometimes explained to be the perspiration and sometimes the semen of the Supreme Personality of Godhead. It is from water that all living entities emerge, and because of water they live and grow. If there were no water, all life would cease. Water is the source of life for everyone. Therefore, by the grace of the Supreme Personality of Godhead, we have so much water all over the world.

TEXT 34

सोमं मनो यस्य समामनन्ति
दिवौकसां यो बलमन्ध आयुः ।
ईशो नगानां प्रजनः प्रजानां
प्रसीदतां नः स महाविभूतिः ॥३४॥

somaṁ mano yasya samāmananti
divaukasāṁ yo balam andha āyuḥ
īśo nagānāṁ prajanaḥ prajānāṁ
prasīdatāṁ naḥ sa mahā-vibhūtiḥ

somam—the moon; *manaḥ*—the mind; *yasya*—of whom (of the Supreme Personality of Godhead); *samāmananti*—they say; *divaukasām*—of the denizens of the upper planetary systems; *yaḥ*—who; *balam*—the strength; *andhaḥ*—the food grains; *āyuḥ*—the duration of life; *īśaḥ*—the Supreme Lord; *nagānām*—of the trees; *prajanaḥ*—the source of breeding; *prajānām*—of all living entities; *prasīdatām*—may He be pleased; *naḥ*—upon us; *saḥ*—that Supreme Personality of Godhead; *mahā-vibhūtiḥ*—the source of all opulences.

TRANSLATION

Soma, the moon, is the source of food grains, strength and longevity for all the demigods. He is also the master of all vegetation and the source of generation for all living entities. As stated by learned scholars, the moon is the mind of the Supreme Personality of Godhead. May that Supreme Personality of Godhead, the source of all opulences, be pleased with us.

PURPORT

Soma, the predominating deity of the moon, is the source of food grains and therefore the source of strength even for the celestial beings, the demigods. He is the vital force for all vegetation. Unfortunately, modern so-called scientists, who do not fully understand the moon, describe the moon as being full of deserts. Since the moon is the source for our vegetation, how can the moon be a desert? The moonshine is the vital force for all vegetation, and therefore we cannot possibly accept that the moon is a desert.

TEXT 35

अग्निर्मुखं यस्य तु जातवेदा
जातः क्रियाकाण्डनिमित्तजन्मा ।
अन्तःसमुद्रेऽनुपचन्स्वधातून्
प्रसीदतां नः स महाविभूतिः ॥३५॥

agnir mukhaṁ yasya tu jāta-vedā
jātaḥ kriyā-kāṇḍa-nimitta-janmā
antaḥ-samudre 'nupacan sva-dhātūn
prasīdatāṁ naḥ sa mahā-vibhūtiḥ

agniḥ—fire; *mukham*—the mouth through which the Supreme Personality of Godhead eats; *yasya*—of whom; *tu*—but; *jāta-vedāḥ*—the producer of wealth or of all necessities of life; *jātaḥ*—produced; *kriyā-kāṇḍa*—ritualistic ceremonies; *nimitta*—for the sake of; *janmā*—formed for this reason; *antaḥ-samudre*—within the depths of the ocean; *anupacan*—always digesting; *sva-dhātūn*—all elements; *prasīdatām*—may be pleased; *naḥ*—upon us; *saḥ*—He; *mahā-vibhūtiḥ*—the supremely powerful.

TRANSLATION

Fire, which is born for the sake of accepting oblations in ritualistic ceremonies, is the mouth of the Supreme Personality of Godhead. Fire exists within the depths of the ocean to produce wealth, and fire is also present in the abdomen to digest food and produce various secretions for the maintenance of the body. May that supremely powerful Personality of Godhead be pleased with us.

TEXT 36

यच्चक्षुरासीत् तरणिर्देवयानं
त्रयीमयो ब्रह्मण एष धिष्ण्यम् ।
द्वारं च मुक्तेरमृतं च मृत्युः
प्रसीदतां नः स महाविभूतिः ॥३६॥

yac-cakṣur āsīt taraṇir deva-yānaṁ
trayīmayo brahmaṇa eṣa dhiṣṇyam
dvāraṁ ca mukter amṛtaṁ ca mṛtyuḥ
prasīdatāṁ naḥ sa mahā-vibhūtiḥ

yat—that which; *cakṣuḥ*—eye; *āsīt*—became; *taraṇiḥ*—the sun-god; *deva-yānam*—the predominating deity for the path of deliverance for the demigods; *trayī-mayaḥ*—for the sake of guidance in *karma-kāṇḍa* Vedic knowledge; *brahmaṇaḥ*—of the supreme truth; *eṣaḥ*—this; *dhiṣṇyam*—the place for realization; *dvāram ca*—as well as the gateway; *mukteḥ*—for liberation; *amṛtam*—the path of eternal life; *ca*—as well as; *mṛtyuḥ*—the cause of death; *prasīdatām*—may He be pleased; *naḥ*—upon us; *saḥ*—that Supreme Personality of Godhead; *mahā-vibhūtiḥ*—the all-powerful.

TRANSLATION

The sun-god marks the path of liberation, which is called arcirādi-vartma. He is the chief source for understanding of the Vedas, he is the abode where the Absolute Truth can be worshiped, He is the gateway to liberation, and he is the source of eternal life as well as the cause of death. The sun-god is the eye of the Lord. May that Supreme Lord, who is supremely opulent, be pleased with us.

PURPORT

The sun-god is considered to be the chief of the demigods. He is also considered to be the demigod who watches the northern side of the universe. He gives help for understanding the *Vedas*. As confirmed in *Brahma-saṁhitā* (5.52):

yac-cakṣur eṣa savitā sakala-grahāṇāṁ
rājā samasta-sura-mūrtir aśeṣa-tejāḥ
yasyājñayā bhramati sambhṛta-kāla-cakro
govindam ādi-puruṣaṁ tam ahaṁ bhajāmi

"The sun, full of infinite effulgence, is the king of all the planets and the image of the good soul. The sun is like the eye of the Supreme Lord. I adore the primeval Lord Govinda, in pursuance of whose order the sun performs his journey, mounting the wheel of time." The sun is actually the eye of the Lord. In the Vedic *mantras* it is said that unless the Supreme Personality of Godhead sees, no one can see. Unless there is sunlight, no living entity on any planet can see. Therefore the sun is considered to be the eye of the Supreme Lord. That is confirmed here by the words *yac-cakṣur āsīt* and in the *Brahma-saṁhitā* by the words *yac-cakṣur eṣa savitā.* The word *savitā* means the sun-god.

TEXT 37

प्राणादभूद् यस्य चराचराणां
प्राणः सहो बलमोजश्च वायुः ।
अन्वास्म सम्राजमिवानुगा वयं
प्रसीदतां नः स महाविभूतिः ॥३७॥

prāṇād abhūd yasya carācarāṇāṁ
prāṇaḥ saho balam ojaś ca vāyuḥ
anvāsma samrājam ivānugā vayaṁ
prasīdatāṁ naḥ sa mahā-vibhūtiḥ

prāṇāt—from the vital force; *abhūt*—generated; *yasya*—of whom; *cara-acarāṇām*—of all living entities, moving and nonmoving; *prāṇaḥ*—the vital force; *sahaḥ*—the basic principle of life; *balam*—strength; *ojaḥ*—the vital force; *ca*—and; *vāyuḥ*—the air; *anvāsma*—follow; *samrājam*—an emperor; *iva*—like; *anugāḥ*—followers; *vayam*—all of us; *prasīdatām*—may be pleased; *naḥ*—upon us; *saḥ*—He; *mahā-vibhūtiḥ*—the supremely powerful.

TRANSLATION

All living entities, moving and nonmoving, receive their vital force, their bodily strength and their very lives from the air. All of us follow the air for our vital force, exactly as servants follow an emperor. The vital force of air is generated from the original vital force of the Supreme Personality of Godhead. May that Supreme Lord be pleased with us.

TEXT 38

श्रोत्राद् दिशो यस्य हृदश्च खानि
प्रजज्ञिरे खं पुरुषस्य नाभ्याः ।
प्राणेन्द्रियात्मासुशरीरकेतः
प्रसीदतां नः स महाविभूतिः ॥३८॥

śrotrād diśo yasya hṛdaś ca khāni
prajajñire khaṁ puruṣasya nābhyāḥ
prāṇendriyātmāsu-śarīra-ketaḥ
prasīdatāṁ naḥ sa mahā-vibhūtiḥ

śrotrāt—from the ears; *diśaḥ*—different directions; *yasya*—of whom; *hṛdaḥ*—from the heart; *ca*—also; *khāni*—the holes of the body; *prajajñire*—generated; *kham*—the sky; *puruṣasya*—of the Supreme Person; *nābhyāḥ*—from the navel; *prāṇa*—of the life force; *indriya*—senses; *ātmā*—mind; *asu*—vital force; *śarīra*—and body; *ketaḥ*—the shelter; *prasīdatām*—may be pleased; *naḥ*—upon us; *saḥ*—He; *mahā-vibhūtiḥ*—the supremely powerful.

TRANSLATION

May the supremely powerful Personality of Godhead be pleased with us. The different directions are generated from His ears, the holes of the body come from His heart, and the vital force, the senses, the mind, the air within the body, and the ether, which is the shelter of the body, come from His navel.

TEXT 39

बलान्महेन्द्रस्त्रिदशाः प्रसादा-
न्मन्योर्गिरीशो धिषणाद्ु विरिञ्चः ।
खेभ्यस्तुछन्दांस्यृषयो मेढ्रतः कः
प्रसीदतां नः स महाविभूतिः ॥३९॥

balān mahendras tri-daśāḥ prasādān
manyor girīśo dhiṣaṇād viriñcaḥ
khebhyas tu chandāṁsy ṛṣayo meḍhrataḥ kaḥ
prasīdatāṁ naḥ sa mahā-vibhūtiḥ

balāt—by His strength; *mahā-indraḥ*—King Indra became possible; *tri-daśāḥ*—as well as the demigods; *prasādāt*—by satisfaction; *manyoḥ*—by anger; *giri-īśaḥ*—Lord Śiva; *dhiṣaṇāt*—from sober intelligence; *viriñcaḥ*—Lord Brahmā; *khebhyaḥ*—from the bodily holes; *tu*—as well as; *chandāṁsi*—Vedic *mantras; ṛṣayaḥ*—great saintly persons; *meḍhrataḥ*—from the genitals; *kaḥ*—the *prajāpatis; prasīdatām*—may be pleased; *naḥ*—upon us; *saḥ*—He; *mahā-vibhūtiḥ*—the Supreme Personality of Godhead, who has extraordinary power.

TRANSLATION

Mahendra, the King of Heaven, was generated from the prowess of the Lord, the demigods were generated from the mercy of the Lord, Lord Śiva was generated from the anger of the Lord, and Lord Brahmā from His sober intelligence. The Vedic mantras were generated from the bodily holes of the Lord, and the great saints and prajāpatis were generated from His genitals. May that supremely powerful Lord be pleased with us.

TEXT 40

श्रीर्वक्षसः पितरश्छाययासन्
धर्मः स्तनादितरः पृष्ठतोऽभूत् ।

द्यौर्यस्य शीर्ष्णोऽप्सरसो विहारात्
प्रसीदतां नः स महाविभूतिः ॥४०॥

śrīr vakṣasaḥ pitaraś chāyayāsan
dharmaḥ stanād itaraḥ pṛṣṭhato 'bhūt
dyaur yasya śīrṣṇo 'psaraso vihārāt
prasīdatāṁ naḥ sa mahā-vibhūtiḥ

śrīḥ—the goddess of fortune; *vakṣasaḥ*—from His chest; *pitaraḥ*—the inhabitants of Pitṛloka; *chāyayā*—from His shadow; *āsan*—became possible; *dharmaḥ*—the principle of religion; *stanāt*—from His bosom; *itaraḥ*—irreligion (the opposite of *dharma*); *pṛṣṭhataḥ*—from the back; *abhūt*—became possible; *dyauḥ*—the heavenly planets; *yasya*—of whom; *śīrṣṇaḥ*—from the top of the head; *apsarasaḥ*—the inhabitants of Apsaroloka; *vihārāt*—by His sense enjoyment; *prasīdatām*—kindly be pleased; *naḥ*—upon us; *saḥ*—He (the Supreme Personality of Godhead); *mahā-vibhūtiḥ*—the greatest in all prowess.

TRANSLATION

The goddess of fortune was generated from His chest, the inhabitants of Pitṛloka from His shadow, religion from His bosom, and irreligion [the opposite of religion] from His back. The heavenly planets were generated from the top of His head, and the Apsarās from His sense enjoyment. May that supremely powerful Personality of Godhead be pleased with us.

TEXT 41

विप्रो मुखाद् ब्रह्म च यस्य गुह्यं
राजन्य आसीद् भुजयोर्बलं च ।
ऊर्वोर्विडोजोऽङ्घ्रिरवेदशूद्रौ
प्रसीदतां नः स महाविभूतिः ॥४१॥

vipro mukhād brahma ca yasya guhyaṁ
rājanya āsīd bhujayor balaṁ ca
ūrvor viḍ ojo 'ṅghrir aveda-śūdrau
prasīdatāṁ naḥ sa mahā-vibhūtiḥ

viprah—the *brāhmaṇas; mukhāt*—from His mouth; *brahma*—the Vedic literatures; *ca*—also; *yasya*—of whom; *guhyam*—from His confidential knowledge; *rājanyaḥ*—the *kṣatriyas; āsīt*—became possible; *bhujayoḥ*—from His arms; *balam ca*—as well as bodily strength; *ūrvoḥ*—from the thighs; *viṭ*—*vaiśyas; ojaḥ*—and their expert productive knowledge; *aṅghriḥ*—from His feet; *aveda*—those who are beyond the jurisdiction of Vedic knowledge; *śūdrau*—the worker class; *prasīdatām*—may be pleased; *naḥ*—upon us; *saḥ*—He; *mahā-vibhūtiḥ*—the supremely powerful Personality of Godhead.

TRANSLATION

The brāhmaṇas and Vedic knowledge come from the mouth of the Supreme Personality of Godhead, the kṣatriyas and bodily strength come from His arms, the vaiśyas and their expert knowledge in productivity and wealth come from His thighs, and the śūdras, who are outside of Vedic knowledge, come from His feet. May that Supreme Personality of Godhead, who is full in prowess, be pleased with us.

TEXT 42

लोभोऽधरात् प्रीतिरुपर्यभूद् द्युति-
नस्तः पशव्यः स्पर्शेन कामः ।
भ्रुवोर्यमः पक्ष्मभवस्तु कालः
प्रसीदतां नः स महाविभूतिः ॥४२॥

lobho 'dharāt prītir upary abhūd dyutir
nastaḥ paśavyaḥ sparśena kāmaḥ
bhruvor yamaḥ pakṣma-bhavas tu kālaḥ
prasīdatāṁ naḥ sa mahā-vibhūtiḥ

lobhaḥ—greed; *adharāt*—from the lower lip; *prītiḥ*—affection; *upari*—from the upper lip; *abhūt*—became possible; *dyutiḥ*—bodily luster; *nastaḥ*—from the nose; *paśavyaḥ*—fit for the animals; *sparśena*—by the touch; *kāmaḥ*—lusty desires; *bhruvoḥ*—from the eyebrows; *yamaḥ*—Yamarāja became possible; *pakṣma-bhavaḥ*—from the eyelashes; *tu*—but; *kālaḥ*—eternal time, which brings death;

prasīdatām—be pleased; *naḥ*—upon us; *saḥ*—He; *mahā-vibhūtiḥ*—the Supreme Personality of Godhead, who has great prowess.

TRANSLATION

Greed is generated from His lower lip, affection from His upper lip, bodily luster from His nose, animalistic lusty desires from His sense of touch, Yamarāja from His eyebrows, and eternal time from His eyelashes. May that Supreme Lord be pleased with us.

TEXT 43

द्रव्यं वयः कर्म गुणान्विशेषं
यद्योगमायाविहितान्वदन्ति ।
यद् दुर्विभाव्यं प्रबुधापबाधं
प्रसीदतां नः स महाविभूतिः ॥४३॥

dravyaṁ vayaḥ karma guṇān viśeṣaṁ
yad-yogamāyā-vihitān vadanti
yad durvibhāvyaṁ prabudhāpabādhaṁ
prasīdatāṁ naḥ sa mahā-vibhūtiḥ

dravyam—the five elements of the material world; *vayaḥ*—time; *karma*—fruitive activities; *guṇān*—the three modes of material nature; *viśeṣam*—the varieties caused by combinations of the twenty-three elements; *yat*—that which; *yoga-māyā*—by the Lord's creative potency; *vihitān*—all done; *vadanti*—all learned men say; *yat durvibhāvyam*—which is actually extremely difficult to understand; *prabudha-apabādham*—rejected by the learned, by those who are fully aware; *prasīdatām*—may be pleased; *naḥ*—upon us; *saḥ*—He; *mahā-vibhūtiḥ*—the controller of everything.

TRANSLATION

All learned men say that the five elements, eternal time, fruitive activity, the three modes of material nature, and the varieties produced by these modes are all creations of yogamāyā. This material world is therefore extremely difficult to understand, but those

who are highly learned have rejected it. May the Supreme Personality of Godhead, who is the controller of everything, be pleased with us.

PURPORT

The word *durvibhāvyam* is very important in this verse. No one can understand how everything is happening in this material world by the arrangement of the Supreme Personality of Godhead through His material energies. As stated in *Bhagavad-gītā* (9.10), *mayādhyakṣeṇa prakṛtiḥ sūyate sacarācaram:* everything is actually happening under the direction of the Supreme Personality of Godhead. This much we can learn, but how it is happening is extremely difficult to understand. We cannot even understand how the affairs within our body are systematically taking place. The body is a small universe, and since we cannot understand how things are happening in this small universe, how can we understand the affairs of the bigger universe? Actually this universe is very difficult to understand, yet learned sages have advised, as Kṛṣṇa has also advised, that this material world is *duḥkhālayam aśāśvatam;* in other words, it is a place of misery and temporality. One must give up this world and go back home, back to the Personality of Godhead. Materialists may argue, "If this material world and its affairs are impossible to understand, how can we reject it?" The answer is provided by the word *prabudhāpabādham.* We have to reject this material world because it is rejected by those who are learned in Vedic wisdom. Even though we cannot understand what this material world is, we should be ready to reject it in accordance with the advice of learned persons, especially the advice of Kṛṣṇa. Kṛṣṇa says:

mām upetya punar janma
duḥkhālayam aśāśvatam
nāpnuvanti mahātmānaḥ
saṁsiddhiṁ paramāṁ gatāḥ

"After attaining Me, the great souls, who are *yogīs* in devotion, never return to this temporary world, which is full of miseries, because they have attained the highest perfection." (Bg. 8.15) One has to return home, back to Godhead, for this is the highest perfection of life. To go back to Godhead means to reject this material world. Although we cannot understand the functions of this material world and whether it is good for us or bad for us, in accordance with the advice of the supreme authority we must reject it and go back home, back to Godhead.

TEXT 44

नमोऽस्तु तस्मा उपशान्तशक्तये
स्वाराज्यलाभप्रतिपूरितात्मने ।
गुणेषु मायारचितेषु वृत्तिभि-
र्न सज्जमानाय नभस्वदूतये ॥४४॥

namo 'stu tasmā upaśānta-śaktaye
svārājya-lābha-pratipūritātmane
guṇeṣu māyā-raciteṣu vṛttibhir
na sajjamānāya nabhasvad-ūtaye

namaḥ—our respectful obeisances; *astu*—let there be; *tasmai*—unto Him; *upaśānta-śaktaye*—who does not endeavor to achieve anything else, who is free from restlessness; *svārājya*—completely independent; *lābha*—of all gains; *pratipūrita*—fully achieved; *ātmane*—unto the Supreme Personality of Godhead; *guṇeṣu*—of the material world, which is moving because of the three modes of nature; *māyā-raciteṣu*—things created by the external energy; *vṛttibhiḥ*—by such activities of the senses; *na sajjamānāya*—one who does not become attached, or one who is above material pains and pleasures; *nabhasvat*—the air; *ūtaye*—unto the Lord, who has created this material world as His pastime.

TRANSLATION

Let us offer our respectful obeisances unto the Supreme Personality of Godhead, who is completely silent, free from endeavor, and completely satisfied by His own achievements. He is not attached to the activities of the material world through His senses. Indeed, in performing His pastimes in this material world, He is just like the unattached air.

PURPORT

We can simply understand that behind the activities of material nature is the Supreme Lord, by whose indications everything takes place, although we cannot see Him. Even without seeing Him, we should offer Him our respectful obeisances. We should know that He is complete. Everything is done systematically by His energies (*parāsya śaktir vividhaiva śrūyate*), and therefore He has nothing to do (*na tasya kāryaṁ karaṇaṁ ca vidyate*). As indicated here by the word *upaśānta-śaktaye*, His different energies act, but although He sets these energies in action, He Himself has nothing to do. He is not attached to anything, for He is the Supreme Personality of Godhead. Therefore, let us offer our respectful obeisances unto Him.

TEXT 45

स त्वं नो दर्शयात्मानमस्मत्करणगोचरम् ।
प्रपन्नानां दिदृक्षूणां सस्मितं ते मुखाम्बुजम् ॥४५॥

sa tvaṁ no darśayātmānam
asmat-karaṇa-gocaram
prapannānāṁ didṛkṣūṇāṁ
sasmitaṁ te mukhāmbujam

saḥ—He (the Supreme Personality of Godhead); *tvam*—You are my Lord; *naḥ*—to us; *darśaya*—be visible; *ātmānam*—in Your original form; *asmat-karaṇa-gocaram*—appreciable by our direct senses, especially by our eyes; *prapannānām*—we are all surrendered unto You; *didṛkṣūṇām*—yet we wish to see You; *sasmitam*—smiling; *te*—Your; *mukha-ambujam*—lotuslike face.

TRANSLATION

O Supreme Personality of Godhead, we are surrendered unto You, yet we wish to see You. Please make Your original form and smiling lotus face visible to our eyes and appreciable to our other senses.

PURPORT

The devotees are always eager to see the Supreme Personality of Godhead in His original form, with His smiling lotuslike face. They are not interested in experiencing the impersonal form. The Lord has both impersonal and personal features. The impersonalists have no idea of the personal feature of the Lord, but Lord Brahmā and the members of his disciplic succession want to see the Lord in His personal form. Without a personal form there can be no question of a smiling face, which is clearly indicated here by the words *sasmitam te mukhāmbujam.* Those who are in the Vaiṣṇava *sampradāya* of Brahmā always want to see the Supreme Personality of Godhead. They are eager to realize the Lord's personal feature, not the impersonal feature. As clearly stated here, *asmat-karaṇa-gocaram:* the personal feature of the Lord can be directly perceived by our senses.

TEXT 46

तैस्तैः स्वेच्छाभूतै रूपैः काले काले स्वयं विभो ।
कर्म दुर्विषहं यन्नो भगवांस्तत् करोति हि ॥४६॥

tais taiḥ svecchā-bhūtai rūpaiḥ
kāle kāle svayaṁ vibho
karma durviṣahaṁ yan no
bhagavāṁs tat karoti hi

taiḥ—by such appearances; *taiḥ*—by such incarnations; *sva-icchā-bhūtaiḥ*—all appearing by Your personal sweet will; *rūpaiḥ*—by factual forms; *kāle kāle*—in different millenniums; *svayam*—personally; *vibho*—O Supreme; *karma*—activities; *durviṣaham*—uncommon (unable to be enacted by anyone else); *yat*—that which; *naḥ*—unto us; *bhagavān*—the Supreme Personality of Godhead; *tat*—that; *karoti*—executes; *hi*—indeed.

TRANSLATION

O Lord, O Supreme Personality of Godhead, by Your sweet will You appear in various incarnations, millennium after millennium, and act wonderfully, performing uncommon activities that would be impossible for us.

PURPORT

The Lord says in *Bhagavad-gītā* (4.7):

yadā yadā hi dharmasya
glānir bhavati bhārata
abhyutthānam adharmasya
tadātmānaṁ sṛjāmy aham

"Whenever and wherever there is a decline in religious practice, O descendant of Bharata, and a predominant rise of irreligion—at that time I descend Myself." Thus it is not imagination but a fact that the Supreme Personality of Godhead, by His sweet will, appears in different incarnations, such as Matsya, Kūrma, Varāha, Nṛsiṁha, Vāmana, Paraśurāma, Rāmacandra, Balarāma, Buddha and many other forms. Devotees are always eager to see one of the Lord's innumerable forms. It is said that just as no one can count how many waves there are in the sea, no one can count the forms of the Lord. This does not mean, however, that anyone can claim to be a form of the Lord and be acceptable as an incarnation. The incarnation of the Supreme Personality of Godhead must be accepted in terms of the descriptions found in the *śāstras*. Lord Brahmā is eager to see the incarnation of the Lord, or the original source of all incarnations; he is not eager to see an imposter. The incarnation's activities are proof of His identity. All the incarnations described in the *śāstras* act wonderfully (*keśava dhṛta-mīna-śarīra jaya jagadīśa hare*). It is only by the personal sweet will of the Supreme Personality of Godhead that He appears and disappears, and only fortunate devotees can expect to see Him face to face.

TEXT 47

क्लेशभूर्यल्पसाराणि कर्माणि विफलानि वा ।
देहिनां विषयार्तानां न तथैवार्पितं त्वयि ॥४७॥

kleśa-bhūry-alpa-sārāṇi
karmāṇi viphalāni vā
dehināṁ viṣayārtānāṁ
na tathaivārpitaṁ tvayi

kleśa—hardship; *bhūri*—very much; *alpa*—very little; *sārāṇi*—good result; *karmāṇi*—activities; *viphalāni*—frustration; *vā*—either;

dehinām—of persons; *viṣaya-artānām*—who are eager to enjoy the material world; *na*—not; *tathā*—like that; *eva*—indeed; *arpitam*—dedicated; *tvayi*—unto Your Lordship.

TRANSLATION

Karmīs are always anxious to accumulate wealth for their sense gratification, but for that purpose they must work very hard. Yet even though they work hard, the results are not satisfying. Indeed, sometimes their work results only in frustration. But devotees who have dedicated their lives to the service of the Lord can achieve substantial results without working very hard. These results exceed the devotee's expectations.

PURPORT

We can practically see how the devotees who have dedicated their lives for the service of the Lord in the Kṛṣṇa consciousness movement are getting immense opportunities for the service of the Supreme Personality of Godhead without working very hard. The Kṛṣṇa consciousness movement actually started with only forty rupees, but now it has more than forty crores worth of property, and all this opulence has been achieved within eight or ten years. No *karmī* can expect to improve his business so swiftly, and besides that, whatever a *karmī* acquires is temporary and sometimes frustrating. In Kṛṣṇa consciousness, however, everything is encouraging and improving. The Kṛṣṇa consciousness movement is not very popular with the *karmīs* because this movement recommends that one refrain from illicit sex, meat-eating, gambling and intoxication. These are restrictions that *karmīs* very much dislike. Nonetheless, in the presence of so many enemies, this movement is progressing, going forward without impediments. If the devotees continue to spread this movement, dedicating life and soul to the lotus feet of Kṛṣṇa, no one will be able to check it. The movement will go forward without limits. Chant Hare Kṛṣṇa!

TEXT 48

नावमः कर्मकल्पोऽपि विफलायेश्वरार्पितः ।
कल्पते पुरुषस्यैष स ह्यात्मा दयितो हितः ॥४८॥

nāvamaḥ karma-kalpo 'pi
viphalāyeśvarārpitaḥ
kalpate puruṣasyaiva
sa hy ātmā dayito hitaḥ

na—not; *avamaḥ*—very little, or insignificant; *karma*—activities; *kalpaḥ*—rightly executed; *api*—even; *viphalāya*—go in vain; *īśvara-arpitaḥ*—because of being dedicated to the Supreme Personality of Godhead; *kalpate*—it is so accepted; *puruṣasya*—of all persons; *eva*—indeed; *saḥ*—the Supreme Personality of Godhead; *hi*—certainly; *ātmā*—the Supersoul, the supreme father; *dayitaḥ*—extremely dear; *hitaḥ*—beneficial.

TRANSLATION

Activities dedicated to the Supreme Personality of Godhead, even if performed in small measure, never go in vain. The Supreme Personality of Godhead, being the supreme father, is naturally very dear and always ready to act for the good of the living entities.

PURPORT

In *Bhagavad-gītā* (2.40), the Lord says *svalpam apy asya dharmasya trāyate mahato bhayāt:* this *dharma*, devotional service, is so important that even if performed to a very small, almost negligible extent, it can give one the supreme result. There are many instances in the history of the world in which even a slight service rendered to the Lord has saved a living entity from the greatest danger. Ajāmila, for example, was saved by the Supreme Personality of Godhead from the greatest danger, that of going to hell. He was saved simply because he chanted the name Nārāyaṇa at the end of his life. When Ajāmila chanted this holy name of the Lord, Nārāyaṇa, he did not chant knowingly; actually he was calling his youngest son, whose name was Nārāyaṇa. Nonetheless, Lord Nārāyaṇa took this chanting seriously, and thus Ajāmila achieved the result of *ante nārāyaṇa-smṛtiḥ*, remembering Nārāyaṇa at the end of life. If one somehow or other remembers the holy name of Nārāyaṇa, Kṛṣṇa or Rāma at the end of life, he immediately achieves the transcendental result of going back home, back to Godhead.

The Supreme Personality of Godhead is actually the only object of our love. As long as we are in this material world we have so many desires to fulfill, but when we come in touch with the Supreme Personality of Godhead, we immediately become perfect and fully satisfied, just as a child is fully satisfied when he comes to the lap of his mother. Dhruva Mahārāja went to the forest to achieve some material result by austerity and penance, but when he actually saw the Supreme Personality of Godhead he said, "I do not want any material benediction. I am completely satisfied." Even if one wants some material benefit from serving the Supreme Personality of Godhead, this can be achieved extremely easily, without hard labor. Therefore the *śāstra* recommends:

akāmaḥ sarva-kāmo vā
mokṣa-kāma udāra-dhīḥ
tīvreṇa bhakti-yogena
yajeta puruṣaṁ param

"Whether one desires everything or nothing or desires to merge into the existence of the Lord, he is intelligent only if he worships Lord Kṛṣṇa, the Supreme Personality of Godhead, by rendering transcendental loving service." (*Bhāg.* 2.3.10) Even if one has material desires, one can undoubtedly achieve what he wants by rendering service to the Lord.

TEXT 49

यथा हि स्कन्धशाखानां तरोर्मूलावसेचनम् ।
एवमाराधनं विष्णोः सर्वेषामात्मनश्च हि ॥४९॥

yathā hi skandha-śākhānāṁ
taror mūlāvasecanam
evam ārādhanaṁ viṣṇoḥ
sarveṣām ātmanaś ca hi

yathā—as; *hi*—indeed; *skandha*—of the trunk; *śākhānām*—and of the branches; *taroḥ*—of a tree; *mūla*—the root; *avasecanam*—watering; *evam*—in this way; *ārādhanam*—worship; *viṣṇoḥ*—of Lord Viṣṇu; *sarveṣām*—of everyone; *ātmanaḥ*—of the Supersoul; *ca*—also; *hi*—indeed.

TRANSLATION

When one pours water on the root of a tree, the trunk and branches of the tree are automatically pleased. Similarly, when one becomes a devotee of Lord Viṣṇu, everyone is served, for the Lord is the Supersoul of everyone.

PURPORT

As stated in the *Padma Purāṇa:*

ārādhanānāṁ sarveṣāṁ
viṣṇor ārādhanaṁ param
tasmāt parataraṁ devi
tadīyānāṁ samarcanam

"Of all types of worship, worship of Lord Viṣṇu is best, and better than the worship of Lord Viṣṇu is the worship of His devotee, the Vaiṣṇava." There are many demigods worshiped by people who are attached to material desires (*kāmais tais tair hṛta-jñānāḥ prapadyante 'nya-devatāḥ*). Because people are embarrassed by so many material desires, they worship Lord Śiva, Lord Brahmā, the goddess Kālī, Durgā, Gaṇeśa and Sūrya to achieve different results. However, one can achieve all these results simultaneously just by worshiping Lord Viṣṇu. As stated elsewhere in the *Bhāgavatam* (4.31.14):

yathā taror mūla-niṣecanena
tṛpyanti tat-skandha-bhujopaśākhāḥ
prāṇopahārāc ca yathendriyāṇāṁ
tathaiva sarvārhaṇam acyutejyā

"Just by pouring water on the root of a tree, one nourishes its trunk and all of its branches, fruits and flowers, and just by supplying food to the stomach, one satisfies all the limbs of the body. Similarly, by worshiping Lord Viṣṇu one can satisfy everyone." Kṛṣṇa consciousness is not a sectarian religious movement. Rather, it is meant for all-embracing welfare activities for the world. One can enter this movement without discrimination in terms of caste, creed, religion or nationality. If one is trained to worship the Supreme Personality of Godhead, Kṛṣṇa, who is the origin of *viṣṇu-tattva*, one can become fully satisfied and perfect in all respects.

TEXT 50

नमस्तुभ्यमनन्ताय दुर्वितर्क्यात्मकर्मणे ।
निर्गुणाय गुणेशाय सत्त्वस्थाय च साम्प्रतम् ॥५०॥

namas tubhyam anantāya
durvitarkyātma-karmaṇe
nirguṇāya guṇeśāya
sattva-sthāya ca sāmpratam

namaḥ—all obeisances; *tubhyam*—unto You, my Lord; *anantāya*—who are everlasting, transcending the three phases of time (past, present and future); *durvitarkya-ātma-karmaṇe*—unto You, who perform inconceivable activities; *nirguṇāya*—which are all transcendental, free from the inebriety of material qualities; *guṇa-īśāya*—unto You, who control the three modes of material nature; *sattva-sthāya*—who are in favor of the material quality of goodness; *ca*—also; *sāmpratam*—at present.

TRANSLATION

My Lord, all obeisances unto You, who are eternal, beyond time's limits of past, present and future. You are inconceivable in Your activities, You are the master of the three modes of material nature, and, being transcendental to all material qualities, You are free from material contamination. You are the controller of all three of the modes of nature, but at the present You are in favor of the quality of goodness. Let us offer our respectful obeisances unto You.

PURPORT

The Supreme Personality of Godhead controls the material activities manifested by the three modes of material nature. As stated in *Bhagavad-gītā, nirguṇaṁ guṇa-bhoktṛ ca:* the Supreme Personality of Godhead is always transcendental to the material qualities (*sattva-guṇa, rajo-guṇa* and *tamo-guṇa*), but nonetheless He is their controller. The

Lord manifests Himself in three features—as Brahmā, Viṣṇu and Maheśvara—to control these three qualities. He personally takes charge of *sattva-guṇa* as Lord Viṣṇu, and He entrusts the charge of *rajo-guṇa* and *tamo-guṇa* to Lord Brahmā and Lord Śiva. Ultimately, however, He is the controller of all three *guṇas*. Lord Brahmā, expressing his appreciation, said that because Lord Viṣṇu had now taken charge of the activities of goodness, there was every hope that the demigods would be successful in fulfilling their desires. The demigods were harassed by the demons, who were infested with *tamo-guṇa*. However, as Lord Brahmā has previously described, since the time of *sattva-guṇa* had now arrived, the demigods could naturally expect to fulfill their desires. The demigods are supposedly well advanced in knowledge, yet they could not understand the knowledge of the Supreme Personality of Godhead. Therefore the Lord is addressed here as *anantāya*. Although Lord Brahmā knows past, present and future, he is unable to understand the unlimited knowledge of the Supreme Personality of Godhead.

Thus end the Bhaktivedanta purports of the Eighth Canto, Fifth Chapter, of the Śrīmad-Bhāgavatam, *entitled "The Demigods Appeal to the Lord for Protection."*

CHAPTER SIX

The Demigods and Demons Declare a Truce

This chapter describes how the Lord appeared before the demigods when they offered Him their prayers. Following the advice of the Supreme Personality of Godhead, the demigods executed a truce with the demons for the purpose of churning nectar from the sea.

Because of the prayers offered by the demigods in the previous chapter, Lord Kṣīrodakaśāyī Viṣṇu was pleased with the demigods, and thus He appeared before them. The demigods were almost blinded by His transcendental bodily effulgence. At first, therefore, they could not even see any part of His body. After some time, however, when Brahmā could see the Lord, he, along with Lord Śiva, began to offer the Lord prayers.

Lord Brahmā said: "The Supreme Personality of Godhead, being beyond birth and death, is eternal. He has no material qualities. Yet He is the ocean of unlimited auspicious qualities. He is subtler than the most subtle, He is invisible, and His form is inconceivable. He is worshipable for all the demigods. Innumerable universes exist within His form, and therefore He is never separated from these universes by time, space or circumstances. He is the chief and the *pradhāna.* Although He is the beginning, the middle and the end of the material creation, the idea of pantheism conceived by Māyāvādī philosophers has no validity. The Supreme Personality of Godhead controls the entire material manifestation through His subordinate agent, the external energy. Because of His inconceivable transcendental position, He is always the master of the material energy. The Supreme Personality of Godhead, in His various forms, is always present even within this material world, but the material qualities cannot touch Him. One can understand His position only by His instructions, as given in *Bhagavad-gītā.*" As stated in *Bhagavad-gītā* (10.10), *dadāmi buddhi-yogaṁ tam. Buddhi-yoga* means *bhakti-yoga.* Only through the process of *bhakti-yoga* can one understand the Supreme Lord.

When offered prayers by Lord Śiva and Lord Brahmā, the Supreme Personality of Godhead was pleased. Thus He gave appropriate instructions to all the demigods. The Supreme Personality of Godhead, who is known as Ajita, unconquerable, advised the demigods to make a peace proposal to the demons, so that after formulating a truce, the demigods and demons could churn the ocean of milk. The rope would be the biggest serpent, known as Vāsuki, and the churning rod would be Mandara Mountain. Poison would also be produced from the churning, but it would be taken by Lord Śiva, and so there would be no need to fear it. Many other attractive things would be generated by the churning, but the Lord warned the demigods not to be captivated by such things. Nor should the demigods be angry if there were some disturbances. After advising the demigods in this way, the Lord disappeared from the scene.

Following the instructions of the Supreme Personality of Godhead, the demigods established a peace with Mahārāja Bali, the King of the demons. Then both the demons and the demigods started for the ocean, taking Mandara Mountain with them. Because of the great heaviness of the mountain, the demigods and demons became fatigued, and some of them actually died. Then the Supreme Personality of Godhead, Viṣṇu, appeared there on the back of His carrier, Garuḍa, and by His mercy He brought these demigods and demons back to life. The Lord then lifted the mountain with one of His hands and placed it on the back of Garuḍa. The Lord sat on the mountain and was carried to the spot of the churning by Garuḍa, who placed the mountain in the middle of the sea. Then the Lord asked Garuḍa to leave that place because as long as Garuḍa was present, Vāsuki could not come there.

TEXT 1

श्रीशुक उवाच

एवं स्तुतः सुरगणैर्भगवान् हरिरीश्वरः ।
तेषामाविरभूद् राजन्सहस्रार्कोदयद्युतिः ॥ १ ॥

śrī-śuka uvāca
evaṁ stutaḥ sura-gaṇair
bhagavān harir īśvaraḥ

teṣām āvirabhūd rājan
sahasrārkodaya-dyutiḥ

śrī-śukaḥ uvāca—Śrī Śukadeva Gosvāmī said; *evam*—in this way; *stutaḥ*—being worshiped by prayers; *sura-gaṇaiḥ*—by the demigods; *bhagavān*—the Supreme Personality of Godhead; *hariḥ*—the vanquisher of all inauspiciousness; *īśvaraḥ*—the supreme controller; *teṣām*—in front of Lord Brahmā and all the demigods; *āvirabhūt*—appeared there; *rājan*—O King (Parīkṣit); *sahasra*—of thousands; *arka*—of suns; *udaya*—like the rising; *dyutiḥ*—His effulgence.

TRANSLATION

Śrī Śukadeva Gosvāmī said: O King Parīkṣit, the Supreme Personality of Godhead, Hari, being thus worshiped with prayers by the demigods and Lord Brahmā, appeared before them. His bodily effulgence resembled the simultaneous rising of thousands of suns.

TEXT 2

तेनैव सहसा सर्वे देवाः प्रतिहतेक्षणाः ।
नापश्यन्खं दिशः क्षौणीमात्मानं च कुतो विभुम् ॥२॥

tenaiva sahasā sarve
devāḥ pratihatekṣaṇāḥ
nāpaśyan khaṁ diśaḥ kṣauṇīm
ātmānaṁ ca kuto vibhum

tena eva—because of this; *sahasā*—all of a sudden; *sarve*—all; *devāḥ*—the demigods; *pratihata-īkṣaṇāḥ*—their vision being blocked; *na*—not; *apaśyan*—could see; *kham*—the sky; *diśaḥ*—the directions; *kṣauṇīm*—land; *ātmānam ca*—also themselves; *kutaḥ*—and where is the question of seeing; *vibhum*—the Supreme Lord.

TRANSLATION

The vision of all the demigods was blocked by the Lord's effulgence. Thus they could see neither the sky, the directions, the

land, nor even themselves, what to speak of seeing the Lord, who was present before them.

TEXTS 3–7

विरिञ्चो भगवान्दृष्ट्वा सह शर्वेण तां तनुम् ।
स्वच्छां मरकतश्यामां कञ्जगर्भारुणेक्षणाम् ॥ ३ ॥
तप्तहेमावदातेन लसत्कौशेयवाससा ।
प्रसन्नचारुसर्वाङ्गीं सुमुखीं सुन्दरभ्रुवम् ॥ ४ ॥
महामणिकिरीटेन केयूराभ्यां च भूषिताम् ।
कर्णाभरणनिर्भातकपोलश्रीमुखाम्बुजाम् ॥ ५ ॥
काञ्चीकलापवलयहारनूपुरशोभिताम् ।
कौस्तुभाभरणां लक्ष्मीं बिभ्रतीं वनमालिनीम् ॥ ६ ॥
सुदर्शनादिभिः स्वास्त्रैर्मूर्तिमद्भिरुपासिताम् ।
तुष्टाव देवप्रवरः सशर्वः पुरुषं परम् ।
सर्वामरगणैः साकं सर्वाङ्गैरवनिं गतैः ॥ ७ ॥

viriñco bhagavān dṛṣṭvā
saha śarveṇa tāṁ tanum
svacchāṁ marakata-śyāmāṁ
kañja-garbhāruṇekṣaṇām

tapta-hemāvadātena
lasat-kauśeya-vāsasā
prasanna-cāru-sarvāṅgīṁ
sumukhīṁ sundara-bhruvam

mahā-maṇi-kirīṭena
keyūrābhyāṁ ca bhūṣitām
karṇābharaṇa-nirbhāta-
kapola-śrī-mukhāmbujām

kāñcīkalāpa-valaya-
hāra-nūpura-śobhitām

kaustubhābharaṇāṁ lakṣmīṁ
bibhratīṁ vana-mālinīm

sudarśanādibhiḥ svāstrair
mūrtimadbhir upāsitām
tuṣṭāva deva-pravaraḥ
saśarvaḥ puruṣaṁ param
sarvāmara-gaṇaiḥ sākaṁ
sarvāṅgair avaniṁ gataiḥ

viriñcaḥ—Lord Brahmā; *bhagavān*—who is also addressed as *bhagavān* because of his powerful position; *dṛṣṭvā*—by seeing; *saha*—with; *śarveṇa*—Lord Śiva; *tām*—unto the Supreme Lord; *tanum*—His transcendental form; *svacchām*—without material contamination; *marakata-śyāmām*—with a bodily luster like the light of a blue gem; *kañja-garbha-aruṇa-īkṣaṇām*—with pinkish eyes like the womb of a lotus flower; *tapta-hema-avadātena*—with a luster like that of molten gold; *lasat*—shining; *kauśeya-vāsasā*—dressed in yellow silk garments; *prasanna-cāru-sarva-aṅgīm*—all the parts of whose body were graceful and very beautiful; *su-mukhīm*—with a smiling face; *sundara-bhruvam*—whose eyebrows were very beautifully situated; *mahā-maṇi-kirīṭena*—with a helmet bedecked with valuable jewels; *keyūrābhyām ca bhūṣitām*—decorated with all kinds of ornaments; *karṇa-ābharaṇa-nirbhāta*—illuminated by the rays of the jewels on His ears; *kapola*—with cheeks; *śrī-mukha-ambujām*—whose beautiful lotuslike face; *kāñcī-kalāpa-valaya*—ornaments like the belt on the waist and bangles on the hands; *hāra-nūpura*—with a necklace on the chest and ankle bells on the legs; *śobhitām*—all beautifully set; *kaustubha-ābharaṇām*—whose chest was decorated with the Kaustubha gem; *lakṣmīm*—the goddess of fortune; *bibhratīm*—moving; *vana-mālinīm*—with flower garlands; *sudarśana-ādibhiḥ*—bearing the Sudarśana *cakra* and others; *sva-astraiḥ*—with His weapons; *mūrtimadbhiḥ*—in His original form; *upāsitām*—being worshiped; *tuṣṭāva*—satisfied; *deva-pravaraḥ*—the chief of the demigods; *sa-śarvaḥ*—with Lord Śiva; *puruṣam param*—the Supreme Personality; *sarva-amara-gaṇaiḥ*—accompanied by all the demigods; *sākam*—with; *sarva-aṅgaiḥ*—with all the parts of the body; *avanim*—on the ground; *gataiḥ*—prostrated.

TRANSLATION

Lord Brahmā, along with Lord Śiva, saw the crystal-clear personal beauty of the Supreme Personality of Godhead, whose blackish body resembles a marakata gem, whose eyes are reddish like the depths of a lotus, who is dressed with garments that are yellow like molten gold, and whose entire body is attractively decorated. They saw His beautiful, smiling, lotuslike face, crowned by a helmet bedecked with valuable jewels. The Lord has attractive eyebrows, and His cheeks are adorned with earrings. Lord Brahmā and Lord Śiva saw the belt on the Lord's waist, the bangles on His arms, the necklace on His chest, and the ankle bells on His legs. The Lord is bedecked with flower garlands, His neck is decorated with the Kaustubha gem, and He carries with Him the goddess of fortune and His personal weapons, like His disc and club. When Lord Brahmā, along with Lord Śiva and the other demigods, thus saw the form of the Lord, they all immediately fell to the ground, offering their obeisances.

TEXT 8

श्रीब्रह्मोवाच
अजातजन्मस्थितिसंयमाया-
गुणाय निर्वाणसुखार्णवाय ।
अणोरणिम्नेऽपरिगण्यधाम्ने
महानुभावाय नमो नमस्ते ॥ ८ ॥

śrī-brahmovāca
ajāta-janma-sthiti-saṁyamāyā-
guṇāya nirvāṇa-sukhārṇavāya
aṇor aṇimne 'pariganya-dhāmne
mahānubhāvāya namo namas te

śrī-brahmā uvāca—Lord Brahmā said; *ajāta-janma-sthiti-saṁyamāya*—unto the Supreme Personality of Godhead, who is never born but whose appearance in different incarnations never ceases; *aguṇāya*—never affected by the material modes of nature (*sattva-guṇa, rajo-guṇa* and *tamo-guṇa*); *nirvāṇa-sukha-arṇavāya*—unto the ocean of eternal bliss, beyond material existence; *aṇoḥ aṇimne*—smaller than the atom; *apariganya-dhāmne*—whose bodily features are never to be conceived by material speculation; *mahā-anubhāvāya*—whose existence is inconceivable; *namaḥ*—offering our obeisances; *namaḥ*—again offering our obeisances; *te*—unto You.

TRANSLATION

Lord Brahmā said: Although You are never born, Your appearance and disappearance as an incarnation never cease. You are always free from the material qualities, and You are the shelter of transcendental bliss resembling an ocean. Eternally existing in Your transcendental form, You are the supreme subtle of the most extremely subtle. We therefore offer our respectful obeisances unto You, the Supreme, whose existence is inconceivable.

PURPORT

The Lord says in *Bhagavad-gītā* (4.6):

ajo 'pi sann avyayātmā
bhūtānām īśvaro 'pi san
prakṛtiṁ svām adhiṣṭhāya
sambhavāmy ātma-māyayā

"Although I am unborn and My transcendental body never deteriorates, and although I am the Lord of all sentient beings, I still appear in every millennium in My original transcendental form." In the following verse in *Bhagavad-gītā* (4.7), the Lord says:

yadā yadā hi dharmasya
glānir bhavati bhārata
abhyutthānam adharmasya
tadātmānaṁ sṛjāmy aham

"Whenever and wherever there is a decline in religious practice, O descendant of Bharata, and a predominant rise of irreligion—at that time I descend Myself." Thus although the Supreme Lord is unborn, there is no cessation to His appearance in different forms as incarnations like Lord Kṛṣṇa and Lord Rāma. Since His incarnations are eternal, the various activities performed by these incarnations are also eternal. The Supreme Personality of Godhead does not appear because He is forced to do so by *karma* like ordinary living entities who are forced to accept a certain type of body. It is to be understood that the Lord's body and activities are all transcendental, being free from the contamination of the material modes of nature. These pastimes are transcendental bliss to the Lord. The word *apariganya-dhāmne* is very significant. There is no limit to the Lord's appearance in different incarnations. All of these incarnations are eternal, blissful and full of knowledge.

TEXT 9

रूपं तवैतत् पुरुषर्षभेज्यं
श्रेयोऽर्थिभिर्वैदिकतान्त्रिकेण ।
योगेन धातः सह नस्त्रिलोकान्
पश्याम्यमुष्मिन्नु ह विश्वमूर्तौ ॥ ९ ॥

rūpaṁ tavaitat puruṣarṣabhejyaṁ
śreyo 'rthibhir vaidika-tāntrikeṇa
yogena dhātaḥ saha nas tri-lokān
paśyāmy amuṣminn u ha viśva-mūrtau

rūpam—form; *tava*—Your; *etat*—this; *puruṣa-ṛṣabha*—O best of all personalities; *ijyam*—worshipable; *śreyaḥ*—ultimate auspiciousness; *arthibhiḥ*—by persons who desire; *vaidika*—under the direction of Vedic instructions; *tāntrikeṇa*—realized by followers of *Tantras*, like *Nārada-pañcarātra; yogena*—by practice of mystic *yoga; dhātaḥ*—O supreme director; *saha*—with; *naḥ*—us (the demigods); *tri-lokān*—controlling the three worlds; *paśyāmi*—we see directly; *amuṣmin*—in You; *u*—oh; *ha*—completely manifested; *viśva-mūrtau*—in You, who have the universal form.

TRANSLATION

O best of persons, O supreme director, those who actually aspire for supreme good fortune worship this form of Your Lordship ac-

cording to the Vedic Tantras. My Lord, we can see all the three worlds in You.

PURPORT

The Vedic *mantras* say: *yasmin vijñāte sarvam evaṁ vijñātaṁ bhavati.* When the devotee sees the Supreme Personality of Godhead by his meditation, or when he sees the Lord personally, face to face, he becomes aware of everything within this universe. Indeed, nothing is unknown to him. Everything within this material world is fully manifested to a devotee who has seen the Supreme Personality of Godhead. *Bhagavad-gītā* (4.34) therefore advises:

tad viddhi praṇipātena
paripraśnena sevayā
upadekṣyanti te jñānaṁ
jñāninas tattva-darśinaḥ

"Just try to learn the truth by approaching a spiritual master. Inquire from him submissively and render service unto him. The self-realized soul can impart knowledge unto you because he has seen the truth." Lord Brahmā is one of these self-realized authorities (*svayambhūr nāradaḥ śambhuḥ kumāraḥ kapilo manuḥ*). One must therefore accept the disciplic succession from Lord Brahmā, and then one can understand the Supreme Personality of Godhead in fullness. Here the word *viśva-mūrtau* indicates that everything exists in the form of the Supreme Personality of Godhead. One who is able to worship Him can see everything in Him and see Him in everything.

TEXT 10

त्वय्यग्र आसीत् त्वयि मध्य आसीत्
त्वय्यन्त आसीदिदमात्मतन्त्रे ।
त्वमादिरन्तो जगतोऽस्य मध्यं
घटस्य मृत्स्नेव परः परस्मात् ॥१०॥

tvayy agra āsīt tvayi madhya āsīt
tvayy anta āsīd idam ātma-tantre

tvam ādir anto jagato 'sya madhyaṁ
ghaṭasya mṛtsneva paraḥ parasmāt

tvayi—unto You, the Supreme Personality of Godhead; *agre*—in the beginning; *āsīt*—there was; *tvayi*—unto You; *madhye*—in the middle; *āsīt*—there was; *tvayi*—unto You; *ante*—in the end; *āsīt*—there was; *idam*—all of this cosmic manifestation; *ātma-tantre*—fully under Your control; *tvam*—Your Lordship; *ādiḥ*—beginning; *antaḥ*—end; *jagataḥ*—of the cosmic manifestation; *asya*—of this; *madhyam*—middle; *ghaṭasya*—of an earthen pot; *mṛtsnā iva*—like the earth; *paraḥ*—transcendental; *parasmāt*—because of being the chief.

TRANSLATION

My dear Lord, who are always fully independent, this entire cosmic manifestation arises from You, rests upon You and ends in You. Your Lordship is the beginning, sustenance and end of everything, like the earth, which is the cause of an earthen pot, which supports the pot, and to which the pot, when broken, finally returns.

TEXT 11

त्वं माययात्माश्रयया स्वयेदं
निर्माय विश्वं तदनुप्रविष्टः ।
पश्यन्ति युक्ता मनसा मनीषिणो
गुणव्यवायेऽप्यगुणं विपश्चितः ॥११॥

tvaṁ māyayātmāśrayayā svayedaṁ
nirmāya viśvaṁ tad-anupraviṣṭaḥ
paśyanti yuktā manasā manīṣiṇo
guṇa-vyavāye 'py aguṇaṁ vipaścitaḥ

tvam—Your Lordship; *māyayā*—by Your eternal energy; *ātma-āśrayayā*—whose existence is under Your shelter; *svayā*—emanated from Yourself; *idam*—this; *nirmāya*—for the sake of creating; *viśvam*—the entire universe; *tat*—into it; *anupraviṣṭaḥ*—You enter;

paśyanti—they see; *yuktāḥ*—persons in touch with You; *manasā*—by an elevated mind; *manīṣiṇaḥ*—people with advanced consciousness; *guṇa*—of material qualities; *vyavāye*—in the transformation; *api*—although; *aguṇam*—still untouched by the material qualities; *vipaścitaḥ*—those who are fully aware of the truth of *śāstra.*

TRANSLATION

O Supreme, You are independent in Your self and do not take help from others. Through Your own potency, You create this cosmic manifestation and enter into it. Those who are advanced in Kṛṣṇa consciousness, who are fully in knowledge of the authoritative śāstra, and who, through the practice of bhakti-yoga, are cleansed of all material contamination, can see with clear minds that although You exist within the transformations of the material qualities, Your presence is untouched by these qualities.

PURPORT

The Lord says in *Bhagavad-gītā* (9.10):

mayādhyakṣeṇa prakṛtiḥ
sūyate sacarācaram
hetunānena kaunteya
jagad viparivartate

"This material nature, working under My direction, O son of Kuntī, is producing all moving and unmoving beings. By its rule this manifestation is created and annihilated again and again." The material energy creates, maintains and devastates the entire cosmic manifestation because of directions given by the Supreme Personality of Godhead, who enters this universe as Garbhodakaśāyī Viṣṇu but is untouched by the material qualities. In *Bhagavad-gītā* the Lord refers to *māyā,* the external energy, which creates this material world, as *mama māyā,* "My energy," because this energy works under the full control of the Lord. These facts can be realized only by those who are well versed in Vedic knowledge and advanced in Kṛṣṇa consciousness.

TEXT 12

यथाग्निमेधस्यमृतं च गोषु
भुव्यन्नमम्बूद्यमने च वृत्तिम् ।
योगैर्मनुष्या अधियन्ति हि त्वां
गुणेषु बुद्ध्या कवयो वदन्ति ॥१२॥

yathāgnim edhasy amṛtaṁ ca goṣu
bhuvy annam ambūdyamane ca vṛttim
yogair manuṣyā adhiyanti hi tvāṁ
guṇeṣu buddhyā kavayo vadanti

yathā—as; *agnim*—fire; *edhasi*—in wood; *amṛtam*—milk, which is like nectar; *ca*—and; *goṣu*—from cows; *bhuvi*—on the ground; *annam*—food grains; *ambu*—water; *udyamane*—in enterprise; *ca*—also; *vṛttim*—livelihood; *yogaiḥ*—by practice of *bhakti-yoga; manuṣyāḥ*—human beings; *adhiyanti*—achieve; *hi*—indeed; *tvām*—You; *guṇeṣu*—in the material modes of nature; *buddhyā*—by intelligence; *kavayaḥ*—great personalities; *vadanti*—say.

TRANSLATION

As one can derive fire from wood, milk from the milk bag of the cow, food grains and water from the land, and prosperity in one's livelihood from industrial enterprises, so, by the practice of bhakti-yoga, even within this material world, one can achieve Your favor or intelligently approach You. Those who are pious all affirm this.

PURPORT

Although the Supreme Personality of Godhead is *nirguṇa*, not to be found within this material world, the entire material world is pervaded by Him, as stated in *Bhagavad-gītā* (*mayā tatam idaṁ sarvam*). The material world is nothing but an expansion of the Lord's material energy, and the entire cosmic manifestation rests upon Him (*mat-sthāni sarva-bhūtāni*). Nonetheless, the Supreme Lord cannot be found here (*na cāhaṁ teṣv avasthitaḥ*). A devotee, however, can see the Supreme Personality of Godhead through the practice of *bhakti-yoga*. One ordinarily does not begin to practice *bhakti-yoga* unless he has practiced it in previous births. Moreover, one can begin *bhakti-yoga* only by the mercy of the spiritual master and Kṛṣṇa. *Guru-kṛṣṇa-prasāde pāya bhakti-latā-bīja.* The seed of devotional service is obtainable by the mercy of *guru,* the spiritual master, and Kṛṣṇa, the Supreme Personality of Godhead.

Only by the practice of *bhakti-yoga* can one achieve the favor of the Supreme Personality of Godhead and see Him face to face (*premāñjana-cchurita-bhakti-vilocanena santaḥ sadaiva hṛdayeṣu vilokayanti*). One cannot see the Lord by other methods, such as *karma, jñāna* or *yoga.* Under the direction of the spiritual master, one must cultivate *bhakti-yoga* (*śravaṇaṁ kīrtanaṁ viṣṇoḥ smaraṇaṁ pāda-sevanam*). Then, even within this material world, although the Lord is not visible, a devotee can see Him. This is confirmed in *Bhagavad-gītā* (*bhaktyā mām abhijānāti yāvān yaś cāsmi tattvataḥ*) and in *Śrīmad-Bhāgavatam* (*bhaktyāham ekayā grāhyaḥ*). Thus by devotional service one can achieve the favor of the Supreme Personality of Godhead, although He is not visible or understandable to materialistic persons.

In this verse, the cultivation of *bhakti-yoga* is compared to many material activities. By friction one can get fire from wood, by digging the earth one can get food grains and water, and by agitating the milk bag of the cow one can get nectarean milk. Milk is compared to nectar, which one can drink to become immortal. Of course, simply drinking milk will not make one immortal, but it can increase the duration of one's life. In modern civilization, men do not think milk to be important, and therefore they do not live very long. Although in this age men can live up to one hundred years, their duration of life is reduced because they do not drink large quantities of milk. This is a sign of Kali-yuga. In Kali-yuga, instead of drinking milk, people prefer to slaughter an animal and eat its flesh. The Supreme Personality of Godhead, in His instructions of *Bhagavad-gītā,* advises *go-rakṣya,* which means cow protection. The cow should be protected, milk should be drawn from the cows, and this milk should be prepared in various ways. One should take ample milk, and thus one can prolong one's life, develop his brain, execute devotional service, and ultimately attain the favor of the Supreme Personality of Godhead. As it is essential to get food grains and water by digging the earth, it is also essential to give protection to the cows and take nectarean milk from their milk bags.

The people of this age are inclined toward industrial enterprises for comfortable living, but they refuse to endeavor to execute devotional service, by which they can achieve the ultimate goal of life by returning home, back to Godhead. Unfortunately, as it is said, *na te viduḥ svārtha-gatiṁ hi viṣṇuṁ durāśayā ye bahir-artha-māninaḥ.* People without spiritual education do not know that the ultimate goal of life is to go back home, back to Godhead. Forgetting this aim of life, they are working very hard in disappointment and frustration (*moghāśā mogha-karmāṇo mogha-jñānā vicetasaḥ*). The so-called *vaiśyas*—the industrialists or businessmen—are involved in big, big industrial enterprises, but they are not interested in food grains and milk. However, as indicated here, by digging for water, even in the desert, we can produce food grains; when we produce food grains and vegetables, we can give protection to the cows; while giving protection to the cows, we can draw from them abundant quantities of milk; and by getting enough milk and combining it with food grains and vegetables, we can prepare hundreds of nectarean foods. We can happily eat this food and thus avoid industrial enterprises and joblessness.

Agriculture and cow protection are the way to become sinless and thus be attracted to devotional service. Those who are sinful cannot be attracted by devotional service. As stated in *Bhagavad-gītā* (7.28):

yeṣāṁ tv anta-gataṁ pāpaṁ
janānāṁ puṇya-karmaṇām
te dvandva-moha-nirmuktā
bhajante māṁ dṛḍha-vratāḥ

"Persons who have acted piously in previous lives and in this life, whose sinful actions are completely eradicated and who are freed from the duality of delusion, engage themselves in My service with determination." The majority of people in this age of Kali are sinful, short-living, unfortunate and disturbed (*mandāḥ sumanda-matayo manda-bhāgyā hy upadrutāḥ*). For them, Caitanya Mahāprabhu has advised:

harer nāma harer nāma
harer nāmaiva kevalam
kalau nāsty eva nāsty eva
nāsty eva gatir anyathā

"In this age of quarrel and hypocrisy the only means of deliverance is chanting the holy name of the Lord. There is no other way. There is no other way. There is no other way."

TEXT 13

तं त्वां वयं नाथ समुज्जिहानं
सरोजनाभातिचिरेप्सितार्थम् ।
दृष्ट्वा गता निर्वृतमद्य सर्वे
गजा दवार्ता इव गाङ्गमम्भः ॥१३॥

taṁ tvāṁ vayaṁ nātha samujjihānaṁ
saroja-nābhāticirepsitārtham
dṛṣṭvā gatā nirvṛtam adya sarve
gajā davārtā iva gāṅgam ambhaḥ

tam—O Lord; *tvām*—Your Lordship; *vayam*—all of us; *nātha*—O master; *samujjihānam*—now appearing before us with all glories; *saroja-nābha*—O Lord, whose navel resembles a lotus flower, or from whose navel grows a lotus flower; *ati-cira*—for an extremely long time; *īpsita*—desiring; *artham*—for the ultimate goal of life; *dṛṣṭvā*—seeing; *gatāḥ*—in our vision; *nirvṛtam*—transcendental happiness; *adya*—today; *sarve*—all of us; *gajāḥ*—elephants; *dava-artāḥ*—being afflicted in a forest fire; *iva*—like; *gāṅgam ambhaḥ*—with water from the Ganges.

TRANSLATION

Elephants afflicted by a forest fire become very happy when they get water from the Ganges. Similarly, O my Lord, from whose navel grows a lotus flower, since You have now appeared before us, we have become transcendentally happy. By seeing Your Lordship, whom we have desired to see for a very long time, we have achieved our ultimate goal in life.

PURPORT

The devotees of the Lord are always very eager to see the Supreme Lord face to face, but they do not demand that the Lord come before them, for a pure devotee considers such a demand to be contrary to devotional service. Śrī Caitanya Mahāprabhu teaches this lesson in His *Śikṣāṣṭaka. Adarśanān marma-hatāṁ karotu vā.* The devotee is always eager to see the Lord face to face, but if he is brokenhearted because he cannot see the Lord, even life after life, he will never command the Lord to appear. This is a sign of pure devotion. Therefore in this verse we find the word *ati-cira-īpsita-artham,* meaning that the devotee aspires for a long, long time to see the Lord. If the Lord, by His own pleasure, appears before the devotee, the devotee feels extremely happy, as Dhruva Mahārāja felt when he personally saw the Supreme Personality of Godhead. When Dhruva Mahārāja saw the Lord, he had no desire to ask the Lord for any benediction. Indeed, simply by seeing the Lord, Dhruva Mahārāja felt so satisfied that he did not want to ask the Lord for any benediction (*svāmin kṛtārtho 'smi varaṁ na yāce*). A pure devotee, whether able or unable to see the Lord, always engages in the Lord's devotional service, always hoping that at some time the Lord may be pleased to appear before him so that he can see the Lord face to face.

TEXT 14

स त्वं विधत्स्वाखिललोकपाला
वयं यदर्थास्तव पादमूलम् ।
समागतास्ते बहिरन्तरात्मन्
किं वान्यविज्ञाप्यमशेषसाक्षिणः ॥१४॥

sa tvaṁ vidhatsvākhila-loka-pālā
vayaṁ yad arthās tava pāda-mūlam
samāgatās te bahir-antar-ātman
kiṁ vānya-vijñāpyam aśeṣa-sākṣiṇaḥ

saḥ—that; *tvam*—Your Lordship; *vidhatsva*—kindly do the needful; *akhila-loka-pālāḥ*—the demigods, directors of different departments of this universe; *vayam*—all of us; *yat*—that which; *arthāḥ*—purpose; *tava*—at Your Lordship's; *pāda-mūlam*—lotus feet; *samāgatāḥ*—we have arrived; *te*—unto You; *bahiḥ-antaḥ-ātman*—O Supersoul of everyone, O constant internal and external witness; *kim*—what; *vā*—either; *anya-vijñāpyam*—we have to inform You; *aśeṣa-sākṣiṇaḥ*—the witness and knower of everything.

TRANSLATION

My Lord, we, the various demigods, the directors of this universe, have come to Your lotus feet. Please fulfill the purpose for which we have come. You are the witness of everything, from within and without. Nothing is unknown to You, and therefore it is unnecessary to inform You again of anything.

PURPORT

As stated in *Bhagavad-gītā* (13.3), *kṣetra-jñaṁ cāpi māṁ viddhi sarva-kṣetreṣu bhārata.* The individual souls are proprietors of their individual bodies, but the Supreme Personality of Godhead is the proprietor of all bodies. Since He is the witness of everyone's body, nothing is unknown to Him. He knows what we need. Our duty, therefore, is to execute devotional service sincerely, under the direction of the spiritual master. Kṛṣṇa, by His grace, will supply whatever we need in executing our devotional service. In the Kṛṣṇa consciousness movement, we simply have to execute the order of Kṛṣṇa and *guru.* Then all necessities will be supplied by Kṛṣṇa, even if we do not ask for them.

TEXT 15

अहं गिरित्रश्च सुरादयो ये
दक्षादयोऽग्नेरिव केतवस्ते ।
किं वा विदामेश पृथग्विभाता
विधत्स्व शं नो द्विजदेवमन्त्रम् ॥१५॥

ahaṁ giritraś ca surādayo ye
dakṣādayo 'gner iva ketavas te
kiṁ vā vidāmeśa pṛthag-vibhātā
vidhatsva śaṁ no dvija-deva-mantram

aham—I (Lord Brahmā); *giritraḥ*—Lord Śiva; *ca*—also; *sura-ādayaḥ*—all the demigods; *ye*—as we are; *dakṣa-ādayaḥ*—headed by Mahārāja Dakṣa; *agneḥ*—of fire; *iva*—like; *ketavaḥ*—sparks; *te*—of You; *kim*—what; *vā*—either; *vidāma*—can we understand; *īśa*—O my Lord; *pṛthak-vibhātāḥ*—independently of You; *vidhatsva*—kindly bestow upon us; *śam*—good fortune; *naḥ*—our; *dvija-deva-mantram*—the means of deliverance suitable for the *brāhmaṇas* and demigods.

TRANSLATION

I [Lord Brahmā], Lord Śiva and all the demigods, accompanied by the prajāpatis like Dakṣa, are nothing but sparks illuminated by You, who are the original fire. Since we are particles of You, what can we understand about our welfare? O Supreme Lord, please give us the means of deliverance that is suitable for the brāhmaṇas and demigods.

PURPORT

In this verse, the word *dvija-deva-mantram* is very important. The word *mantra* means "that which delivers one from the material world." Only the *dvijas* (the *brāhmaṇas*) and the *devas* (the demigods) can be delivered from material existence by the instructions of the Supreme Personality of Godhead. Whatever is spoken by the Supreme Personality of Godhead is a *mantra* and is suitable for delivering the conditioned souls from mental speculation. The conditioned souls are engaged in a struggle for existence (*manaḥ ṣaṣṭhānīndriyāṇi prakṛti-sthāni karṣati*). Deliverance from this struggle constitutes the highest benefit, but unless one gets a *mantra* from the Supreme Personality of Godhead, deliverance is impossible. The beginning *mantra* is the Gāyatrī *mantra.* Therefore, after purification, when one is qualified to become a *brāhmaṇa* (*dvija*), he is offered the Gāyatrī *mantra.* Simply by chanting the Gāyatrī *mantra,* one can be delivered. This *mantra,* however, is suitable only for the *brāhmaṇas* and demigods. In Kali-yuga, we are all in a very difficult position, in which we need a suitable *mantra* that can deliver us from the dangers of this age. Therefore the Supreme Personality of Godhead, in His incarnation as Lord Caitanya, gives us the Hare Kṛṣṇa *mantra.*

harer nāma harer nāma
harer nāmaiva kevalam
kalau nāsty eva nāsty eva
nāsty eva gatir anyathā

"In this age of quarrel and hypocrisy the only means of deliverance is chanting the holy name of the Lord. There is no other way. There is no other way. There is no other way." In His *Śikṣāṣṭaka*, Lord Caitanya says, *paraṁ vijayate śrī-kṛṣṇa-saṅkīrtanam:* "All glories to the chanting of *śrī-kṛṣṇa-saṅkīrtana!*" The *mahā-mantra*—Hare Kṛṣṇa, Hare Kṛṣṇa, Kṛṣṇa Kṛṣṇa, Hare Hare/ Hare Rāma, Hare Rāma, Rāma Rāma, Hare Hare—is directly chanted by the Lord Himself, who gives us this *mantra* for deliverance.

We cannot invent any means to be delivered from the dangers of material existence. Here, even the demigods, such as Lord Brahmā and Lord Śiva, and the *prajāpatis,* such as Dakṣa, are said to be like illuminating sparks in the presence of the Supreme Lord, who is compared to a great fire. Sparks are beautiful as long as they are in the fire. Similarly, we have to remain in the association of the Supreme Personality of Godhead and always engage in devotional service, for then we shall always be brilliant and illuminating. As soon as we fall from the service of the Lord, our brilliance and illumination will immediately be extinguished, or at least stopped for some time. When we living entities, who are like sparks of the original fire, the Supreme Lord, fall into a material condition, we must take the *mantra* from the Supreme Personality of Godhead as it is offered by Śrī Caitanya Mahāprabhu. By chanting this Hare Kṛṣṇa *mantra,* we shall be delivered from all the difficulties of this material world.

TEXT 16

श्रीशुक उवाच
एवं विरिञ्चादिभिरीडितस्तद्
विज्ञाय तेषां हृदयं यथैव ।
जगाद जीमूतगभीरया गिरा
बद्धाञ्जलीन्संवृतसर्वकारकान् ॥१६॥

śrī-śuka uvāca
evaṁ viriñcādibhir īḍitas tad
vijñāya teṣāṁ hṛdayaṁ yathaiva
jagāda jīmūta-gabhīrayā girā
baddhāñjalīn saṁvṛta-sarva-kārakān

śrī-śukaḥ uvāca—Śrī Śukadeva Gosvāmī said; *evam*—thus; *viriñca-ādibhiḥ*—by all the demigods, headed by Lord Brahmā; *īḍitaḥ*—being worshiped; *tat vijñāya*—understanding the expectation; *teṣām*—of all of them; *hṛdayam*—the core of the heart; *yathā*—as; *eva*—indeed; *jagāda*—replied; *jīmūta-gabhīrayā*—like the sound of clouds; *girā*—by words; *baddha-añjalīn*—unto the demigods, who stood with folded hands; *saṁvṛta*—restrained; *sarva*—all; *kārakān*—senses.

TRANSLATION

Śukadeva Gosvāmī continued: When the Lord was thus offered prayers by the demigods, headed by Lord Brahmā, He understood the purpose for which they had approached Him. Therefore, in a deep voice that resembled the rumbling of clouds, the Lord replied to the demigods, who all stood there attentively with folded hands.

TEXT 17

एक एवेश्वरस्तस्मिन्सुरकार्ये सुरेश्वरः ।
विहर्तुकामस्तानाह समुद्रोन्मथनादिभिः ॥१७॥

eka eveśvaras tasmin
sura-kārye sureśvaraḥ
vihartu-kāmas tān āha
samudronmathanādibhiḥ

ekaḥ—alone; *eva*—indeed; *īśvaraḥ*—the Supreme Personality of Godhead; *tasmin*—in that; *sura-kārye*—the activities of the demigods; *sura-īśvaraḥ*—the Lord of the demigods, the Supreme Personality of Godhead; *vihartu*—to enjoy pastimes; *kāmaḥ*—desiring; *tān*—unto the demigods; *āha*—said; *samudra-unmathana-ādibhiḥ*—by activities of churning the ocean.

TRANSLATION

Although the Supreme Personality of Godhead, the master of the demigods, was capable of performing the activities of the demigods by Himself, He wanted to enjoy pastimes in churning the ocean. Therefore He spoke as follows.

TEXT 18

श्रीभगवानुवाच
हन्त ब्रह्मन्नहो शम्भो हे देवा मम भाषितम् ।
शृणुतावहिताः सर्वे श्रेयो वः स्याद् यथा सुराः ॥१८॥

śrī-bhagavān uvāca
hanta brahmann aho śambho
he devā mama bhāṣitam
śṛṇutāvahitāḥ sarve
śreyo vaḥ syād yathā surāḥ

śrī-bhagavān uvāca—the Supreme Personality of Godhead said; *hanta*—addressing them; *brahman aho*—O Lord Brahmā; *śambho*—O Lord Śiva; *he*—O; *devāḥ*—demigods; *mama*—My; *bhāṣitam*—statement; *śṛṇuta*—hear; *avahitāḥ*—with great attention; *sarve*—all of you; *śreyaḥ*—good fortune; *vaḥ*—for all of you; *syāt*—shall be; *yathā*—as; *surāḥ*—for the demigods.

TRANSLATION

The Supreme Personality of Godhead said: O Lord Brahmā, Lord Śiva and other demigods, please hear Me with great attention, for what I say will bring good fortune for all of you.

TEXT 19

यात दानवदैतेयैस्तावत् सन्धिर्विधीयताम् ।
कालेनानुगृहीतैस्तैर्यावद् वो भव आत्मनः ॥१९॥

yāta dānava-daiteyais
tāvat sandhir vidhīyatām
kālenānugṛhītais tair
yāvad vo bhava ātmanaḥ

yāta—just execute; *dānava*—with the demons; *daiteyaiḥ*—and the *asuras; tāvat*—so long; *sandhiḥ*—a truce; *vidhīyatām*—execute; *kālena*—by a favorable time (or *kāvyena*—by Śukrācārya); *anugṛhītaiḥ*—receiving benedictions; *taiḥ*—with them; *yāvat*—as long as; *vaḥ*—of you; *bhavaḥ*—good fortune; *ātmanaḥ*—of yourselves.

TRANSLATION

As long as you are not flourishing, you should make a truce with the demons and asuras, who are now being favored by time.

PURPORT

One word in this verse has two readings—*kālena* and *kāvyena. Kālena* means "favored by time," and *kāvyena* means "favored by Śukrācārya," Śukrācārya being the spiritual master of the Daityas. The demons and Daityas were favored in both ways, and therefore the demigods were advised by the Supreme Lord to execute a truce for the time being, until time favored them.

TEXT 20

अरयोऽपि हि सन्धेयाः सति कार्यार्थगौरवे ।
अहिमूषिकवद् देवा ह्यर्थस्य पदवीं गतैः ॥२०॥

arayo 'pi hi sandheyāḥ
sati kāryārtha-gaurave
ahi-mūṣikavad devā
hy arthasya padavīṁ gataiḥ

arayaḥ—enemies; *api*—although; *hi*—indeed; *sandheyāḥ*—eligible for a truce; *sati*—being so; *kārya-artha-gaurave*—in the matter of an important duty; *ahi*—snake; *mūṣika*—mouse; *vat*—like; *devāḥ*—O demigods; *hi*—indeed; *arthasya*—of interest; *padavīm*—position; *gataiḥ*—so being.

TRANSLATION

O demigods, fulfilling one's own interests is so important that one may even have to make a truce with one's enemies. For the sake of one's self-interest, one has to act according to the logic of the snake and the mouse.

PURPORT

A snake and a mouse were once caught in a basket. Now, since the mouse is food for the snake, this was a good opportunity for the snake. However, since both of them were caught in the basket, even if the snake ate the mouse, the snake would not be able to get out. Therefore, the snake thought it wise to make a truce with the mouse and ask the mouse to make a hole in the basket so that both of them could get out. The snake's intention was that after the mouse made the hole, the snake would eat the mouse and escape from the basket through the hole. This is called the logic of the snake and the mouse.

TEXT 21

अमृतोत्पादने यत्नः क्रियतामविलम्बितम् ।
यस्य पीतस्य वै जन्तुर्मृत्युग्रस्तोऽमरो भवेत् ॥२१॥

amṛtotpādane yatnaḥ
kriyatām avilambitam
yasya pītasya vai jantur
mṛtyu-grasto 'maro bhavet

amṛta-utpādane—in generating nectar; *yatnaḥ*—endeavor; *kriyatām*—do; *avilambitam*—without delay; *yasya*—of which nectar; *pītasya*—anyone who drinks; *vai*—indeed; *jantuḥ*—living entity; *mṛtyu-grastaḥ*—although in imminent danger of death; *amaraḥ*—immortal; *bhavet*—can become.

TRANSLATION

Immediately endeavor to produce nectar, which a person who is about to die may drink to become immortal.

TEXTS 22–23

क्षिप्त्वा क्षीरोदधौ सर्वा वीरुत्तृणलतौषधीः ।
मन्थानं मन्दरं कृत्वा नेत्रं कृत्वा तु वासुकिम् ॥२२॥
सहायेन मया देवा निर्मन्थध्वमतन्द्रिताः ।
क्लेशभाजो भविष्यन्ति दैत्या यूयं फलग्रहाः ॥२३॥

kṣiptvā kṣīrodadhau sarvā
vīrut-tṛṇa-latauṣadhīḥ
manthānaṁ mandaraṁ kṛtvā
netraṁ kṛtvā tu vāsukim

sahāyena mayā devā
nirmanthadhvam atandritāḥ
kleśa-bhājo bhaviṣyanti
daityā yūyaṁ phala-grahāḥ

kṣiptvā—putting; *kṣīra-udadhau*—in the ocean of milk; *sarvāḥ*—all kinds of; *vīrut*—creepers; *tṛṇa*—grass; *latā*—vegetables; *auṣadhīḥ*—and drugs; *manthānam*—the churning rod; *mandaram*—Mandara Mountain; *kṛtvā*—making; *netram*—the churning rope; *kṛtvā*—making; *tu*—but; *vāsukim*—the snake Vāsuki; *sahāyena*—with a helper; *mayā*—by Me; *devāḥ*—all the demigods; *nirmanthadhvam*—go on churning; *atandritāḥ*—very carefully, without diversion; *kleśa-bhājaḥ*—sharetakers of sufferings; *bhaviṣyanti*—will be; *daityāḥ*—the demons; *yūyam*—but all of you; *phala-grahāḥ*—gainers of the actual result.

TRANSLATION

O demigods, cast into the ocean of milk all kinds of vegetables, grass, creepers and drugs. Then, with My help, making Mandara Mountain the churning rod and Vāsuki the rope for churning,

churn the ocean of milk with undiverted attention. Thus the demons will be engaged in labor, but you, the demigods, will gain the actual result, the nectar produced from the ocean.

PURPORT

It appears that when different kinds of drugs, creepers, grass and vegetables are put into this milk and the milk is churned, as milk is churned for butter, the active principles of the vegetables and drugs mix with the milk, and the result is nectar.

TEXT 24

यूयं तदनुमोदध्वं यदिच्छन्त्यसुराः सुराः ।
न संरम्भेण सिध्यन्ति सर्वार्थाः सान्त्वया यथा ॥२४॥

yūyaṁ tad anumodadhvaṁ
yad icchanty asurāḥ surāḥ
na saṁrambheṇa sidhyanti
sarvārthāḥ sāntvayā yathā

yūyam—all of you; *tat*—that; *anumodadhvam*—should accept; *yat*—whatever; *icchanti*—they desire; *asurāḥ*—the demons; *surāḥ*—O demigods; *na*—not; *saṁrambheṇa*—by being agitated in anger; *sidhyanti*—are very successful; *sarva-arthāḥ*—all desired ends; *sāntvayā*—by peaceful execution; *yathā*—as.

TRANSLATION

My dear demigods, with patience and peace everything can be done, but if one is agitated by anger, the goal is not achieved. Therefore, whatever the demons ask, agree to their proposal.

TEXT 25

न भेतव्यं कालकूटाद् विषाज्जलधिसम्भवात् ।
लोभः कार्यो न वो जातु रोषः कामस्तु वस्तुषु ॥२५॥

na bhetavyaṁ kālakūṭād
viṣāj jaladhi-sambhavāt
lobhaḥ kāryo na vo jātu
roṣaḥ kāmas tu vastuṣu

na—not; *bhetavyam*—should be afraid; *kālakūṭāt*—of *kālakūṭa; viṣāt*—from the poison; *jaladhi*—from the ocean of milk; *sambhavāt*—which will appear; *lobhaḥ*—greed; *kāryaḥ*—execution; *na*—not; *vaḥ*—unto you; *jātu*—at any time; *roṣaḥ*—anger; *kāmaḥ*—lust; *tu*—and; *vastuṣu*—in the products.

TRANSLATION

A poison known as kālakūṭa will be generated from the ocean of milk, but you should not fear it. And when various products are churned from the ocean, you should not be greedy for them or anxious to obtain them, nor should you be angry.

PURPORT

It appears that by the churning process many things would be generated from the ocean of milk, including poison, valuable gems, nectar and many beautiful women. The demigods were advised, however, not to be greedy for the gems or beautiful women, but to wait patiently for the nectar. The real purpose was to get the nectar.

TEXT 26

श्रीशुक उवाच
इति देवान्समादिश्य भगवान् पुरुषोत्तमः ।
तेषामन्तर्दधे राजन्स्वच्छन्दगतिरीश्वरः ॥२६॥

śrī-śuka uvāca
iti devān samādiśya
bhagavān puruṣottamaḥ
teṣām antardadhe rājan
svacchanda-gatir īśvaraḥ

śrī-śukaḥ uvāca—Śrī Śukadeva Gosvāmī said; *iti*—thus; *devān*—all the demigods; *samādiśya*—advising; *bhagavān*—the Supreme Personality of Godhead; *puruṣa-uttamaḥ*—the best of all persons; *teṣām*—from them; *antardadhe*—disappeared; *rājan*—O King; *svacchanda*—free; *gatiḥ*—whose movements; *īśvaraḥ*—the Personality of Godhead.

TRANSLATION

Śukadeva Gosvāmī continued: O King Parīkṣit, after advising the demigods in this way, the independent Supreme Personality of Godhead, the best of all living entities, disappeared from their presence.

TEXT 27

अथ तस्मै भगवते नमस्कृत्य पितामहः ।
भवश्च जग्मतुः स्वं स्वं धामोपेयुर्बलिं सुराः ॥२७॥

atha tasmai bhagavate
namaskṛtya pitāmahaḥ
bhavaś ca jagmatuḥ svaṁ svaṁ
dhāmopeyur baliṁ surāḥ

atha—after this; *tasmai*—unto Him; *bhagavate*—unto the Supreme Personality of Godhead; *namaskṛtya*—offering obeisances; *pitāmahaḥ*—Lord Brahmā; *bhavaḥ ca*—as well as Lord Śiva; *jagmatuḥ*—returned; *svam svam*—to their own; *dhāma*—abodes; *upeyuḥ*—approached; *balim*—King Bali; *surāḥ*—all the other demigods.

TRANSLATION

Then Lord Brahmā and Lord Śiva, after offering their respectful obeisances to the Lord, returned to their abodes. All the demigods then approached Mahārāja Bali.

TEXT 28

दृष्ट्वारीनप्यसंयत्ताञ्जातक्षोभान्स्वनायकान् ।
न्यषेधद् दैत्यराट् श्लोक्यः सन्धिविग्रहकालवित् ॥ २८ ॥

dṛṣṭvārīn apy asaṁyattāñ
jāta-kṣobhān sva-nāyakān
nyaṣedhad daitya-rāṭ ślokyaḥ
sandhi-vigraha-kālavit

dṛṣṭvā—observing; *arīn*—the enemies; *api*—although; *asaṁyattān*—without any endeavor to fight; *jāta-kṣobhān*—who became agitated; *sva-nāyakān*—his own captains and commanders; *nyaṣedhat*—prevented; *daitya-rāṭ*—the Emperor of the Daityas, Mahārāja Bali; *ślokyaḥ*—very respectable and prominent; *sandhi*—for making negotiations; *vigraha*—as well as for fighting; *kāla*—the time; *vit*—completely aware of.

TRANSLATION

Mahārāja Bali, a most celebrated king of the demons, knew very well when to make peace and when to fight. Thus although his commanders and captains were agitated and were about to kill the demigods, Mahārāja Bali, seeing that the demigods were coming to him without a militant attitude, forbade his commanders to kill them.

PURPORT

Vedic etiquette enjoins: *gṛhe śatrum api prāptaṁ viśvastam akutobhayam.* When enemies come to their opponent's place, they should be received in such a way that they will forget that there is animosity between the two parties. Bali Mahārāja was well conversant with the arts of peacemaking and fighting. Thus he received the demigods very well, although his commanders and captains were agitated. This kind of treatment was prevalent even during the fight between the Pāṇḍavas and the Kurus. During the day, the Pāṇḍavas and Kurus would fight with the utmost strength, and when the day was over they would go to each other's camps as friends and be received as such. During such friendly meetings, one enemy would offer anything the other enemy wanted. That was the system.

TEXT 29

ते वैरोचनिमासीनं गुप्तं चासुरयूथपैः ।
श्रिया परमया जुष्टं जिताशेषमुपागमन् ॥२९॥

te vairocanim āsīnaṁ
guptaṁ cāsura-yūtha-paiḥ
śriyā paramayā juṣṭaṁ
jitāśeṣam upāgaman

te—all the demigods; *vairocanim*—unto Balirāja, the son of Virocana; *āsīnam*—sitting down; *guptam*—well protected; *ca*—and; *asura-yūtha-paiḥ*—by the commanders of the *asuras; śriyā*—by opulence; *paramayā*—supreme; *juṣṭam*—blessed; *jita-aśeṣam*—who became the proprietor of all the worlds; *upāgaman*—approached.

TRANSLATION

The demigods approached Bali Mahārāja, the son of Virocana, and sat down near him. Bali Mahārāja was protected by the commanders of the demons and was most opulent, having conquered all the universes.

TEXT 30

महेन्द्रः श्लक्ष्णया वाचा सान्त्वयित्वा महामतिः ।
अभ्यभाषत तत् सर्वं शिक्षितं पुरुषोत्तमात् ॥३०॥

mahendraḥ ślakṣṇayā vācā
sāntvayitvā mahā-matiḥ
abhyabhāṣata tat sarvaṁ
śikṣitaṁ puruṣottamāt

mahā-indraḥ—the King of heaven, Indra; *ślakṣṇayā*—very mild; *vācā*—by words; *sāntvayitvā*—pleasing Bali Mahārāja very much; *mahā-matiḥ*—the most intelligent person; *abhyabhāṣata*—addressed; *tat*—that; *sarvam*—everything; *śikṣitam*—that was learned; *puruṣa-uttamāt*—from Lord Viṣṇu.

TRANSLATION

After pleasing Bali Mahārāja with mild words, Lord Indra, the King of the demigods, who was most intelligent, very politely submitted all the proposals he had learned from the Supreme Personality of Godhead, Lord Viṣṇu.

TEXT 31

तत्त्वरोचत दैत्यस्य तत्रान्ये येऽसुराधिपाः ।
शम्बरोऽरिष्टनेमिश्च ये च त्रिपुरवासिनः ॥३१॥

tat tv arocata daityasya
tatrānye ye 'surādhipāḥ
śambaro 'riṣṭanemiś ca
ye ca tripura-vāsinaḥ

tat—all those words; *tu*—but; *arocata*—were very pleasing; *daityasya*—to Bali Mahārāja; *tatra*—as well as; *anye*—others; *ye*—who were; *asura-adhipāḥ*—the chiefs of the *asuras; śambaraḥ*—Śambara; *ariṣṭanemiḥ*—Ariṣṭanemi; *ca*—also; *ye*—others who; *ca*—and; *tripura-vāsinaḥ*—all the residents of Tripura.

TRANSLATION

The proposals submitted by King Indra were immediately accepted by Bali Mahārāja and his assistants, headed by Śambara and Ariṣṭanemi, and by all the other residents of Tripura.

PURPORT

It appears from this verse that politics, diplomacy, the propensity to cheat, and everything that we find in this world in individual and social negotiations between two parties are also present in the upper planetary systems. The demigods went to Bali Mahārāja with the proposal to manufacture nectar, and the Daityas, the demons, immediately accepted it, thinking that since the demigods were already weak, when the nectar was produced the demons would take it from them and use it for their own purposes. The demigods, of course, had similar intentions. The only difference is that the Supreme Personality of Godhead, Lord Viṣṇu, was on the side of the demigods because the demigods were His devotees, whereas the demons did not care about Lord Viṣṇu. All over the universe there are two parties—the Viṣṇu party, or God-conscious party, and the godless party. The godless party is never happy or victorious, but the God-conscious party is always happy and victorious.

TEXT 32

ततो देवासुराः कृत्वा संविदं कृतसौहृदाः ।
उद्यमं परमं चक्रुरमृतार्थे परन्तप ॥३२॥

tato devāsurāḥ kṛtvā
saṁvidaṁ kṛta-sauhṛdāḥ
udyamaṁ paramaṁ cakrur
amṛtārthe parantapa

tataḥ—thereafter; *deva-asurāḥ*—both the demons and the demigods; *kṛtvā*—executing; *saṁvidam*—indicating; *kṛta-sauhṛdāḥ*—an armistice between them; *udyamam*—enterprise; *paramam*—supreme; *cakruḥ*—they did; *amṛta-arthe*—for the sake of nectar; *parantapa*—O Mahārāja Parīkṣit, chastiser of enemies.

TRANSLATION

O Mahārāja Parīkṣit, chastiser of enemies, the demigods and the demons thereafter made an armistice between them. Then, with great enterprise, they arranged to produce nectar, as proposed by Lord Indra.

PURPORT

The word *saṁvidam* is significant in this verse. The demigods and demons both agreed to stop fighting, at least for the time being, and endeavored to produce nectar. Śrīla Viśvanātha Cakravartī Ṭhākura notes in this connection:

saṁvid yuddhe pratijñāyām
ācāre nāmni toṣaṇe
sambhāṣaṇe kriyākāre
saṅketa-jñānayor api

The word *saṁvit* is variously used to mean "in fighting," "in promising," "for satisfying," "in addressing," "by practical action," "indication," and "knowledge."

TEXT 33

ततस्ते मन्दरगिरिमोजसोत्पाट्य दुर्मदाः ।
नदन्त उदधिं निन्युः शक्ताः परिघबाहवः ॥३३॥

tatas te mandara-girim
ojasotpāṭya durmadāḥ
nadanta udadhiṁ ninyuḥ
śaktāḥ parigha-bāhavaḥ

tataḥ—thereafter; *te*—all the demigods and demons; *mandara-girim*—Mandara Mountain; *ojasā*—with great strength; *utpāṭya*—extracting; *durmadāḥ*—very powerful and competent; *nadanta*—cried very loudly; *udadhim*—toward the ocean; *ninyuḥ*—brought; *śaktāḥ*—very strong; *parigha-bāhavaḥ*—having long, strong arms.

TRANSLATION

Thereafter, with great strength, the demons and demigods, who were all very powerful and who had long, stout arms, uprooted Mandara Mountain. Crying very loudly, they brought it toward the ocean of milk.

TEXT 34

दूरभारोद्वहश्रान्ताः शक्रवैरोचनादयः ।
अपारयन्तस्तं वोढुं विवशा विजहुः पथि ॥३४॥

dūra-bhārodvaha-śrāntāḥ
śakra-vairocanādayaḥ
apārayantas taṁ voḍhuṁ
vivaśā vijahuḥ pathi

dūra—for a great distance; *bhāra-udvaha*—by carrying the great load; *śrāntāḥ*—being fatigued; *śakra*—King Indra; *vairocana-ādayaḥ*—and Mahārāja Bali (the son of Virocana) and others; *apārayantaḥ*—being unable; *tam*—the mountain; *voḍhum*—to bear; *vivaśāḥ*—being unable; *vijahuḥ*—gave up; *pathi*—on the way.

TRANSLATION

Because of conveying the great mountain for a long distance, King Indra, Mahārāja Bali and the other demigods and demons became fatigued. Being unable to carry the mountain, they left it on the way.

TEXT 35

निपतन्स गिरिस्तत्र बहूनमरदानवान् ।
चूर्णयामास महता भारेण कनकाचलः ॥३५॥

nipatan sa giris tatra
bahūn amara-dānavān
cūrṇayām āsa mahatā
bhāreṇa kanakācalaḥ

nipatan—falling down; *saḥ*—that; *giriḥ*—mountain; *tatra*—there; *bahūn*—many; *amara-dānavān*—demigods and demons; *cūrṇayām āsa*—were smashed; *mahatā*—by great; *bhāreṇa*—weight; *kanaka-acalaḥ*—the golden mountain known as Mandara.

TRANSLATION

The mountain known as Mandara, which was extremely heavy, being made of gold, fell and smashed many demigods and demons.

PURPORT

By constitution, gold is heavier than stone. Since Mandara Mountain was made of gold and was therefore heavier than stone, the demigods and demons could not properly carry it to the ocean of milk.

TEXT 36

तांस्तथा भग्नमनसो भग्नबाहूरुकन्धरान् ।
विज्ञाय भगवांस्तत्र बभूव गरुडध्वजः ॥३६॥

tāṁs tathā bhagna-manaso
bhagna-bāhūru-kandharān

vijñāya bhagavāṁs tatra
babhūva garuḍa-dhvajaḥ

tān—all the demigods and demons; *tathā*—thereafter; *bhagna-manasaḥ*—being brokenhearted; *bhagna-bāhu*—with broken arms; *ūru*—thighs; *kandharān*—and shoulders; *vijñāya*—knowing; *bhagavān*—the Supreme Personality of Godhead, Viṣṇu; *tatra*—there; *babhūva*—appeared; *garuḍa-dhvajaḥ*—being carried on Garuḍa.

TRANSLATION

The demigods and demons were frustrated and disheartened, and their arms, thighs and shoulders were broken. Therefore the Supreme Personality of Godhead, who knows everything, appeared there on the back of His carrier, Garuḍa.

TEXT 37

गिरिपातविनिष्पिष्टान्विलोक्यामरदानवान् ।
ईक्षया जीवयामास निर्जरान् निर्व्रणान्यथा ॥३७॥

giri-pāta-viniṣpiṣṭān
vilokyāmara-dānavān
īkṣayā jīvayām āsa
nirjarān nirvraṇān yathā

giri-pāta—because of the falling of Mandara Mountain; *viniṣpiṣṭān*—crushed; *vilokya*—observing; *amara*—the demigods; *dānavān*—and the demons; *īkṣayā*—simply by His glance; *jīvayām āsa*—brought back to life; *nirjarān*—without aggrievement; *nirvraṇān*—without bruises; *yathā*—as.

TRANSLATION

Observing that most of the demons and the demigods had been crushed by the falling of the mountain, the Lord glanced over them and brought them back to life. Thus they became free from grief, and they even had no bruises on their bodies.

TEXT 38

गिरिं चारोप्य गरुडे हस्तेनैकेन लीलया ।
आरुह्य प्रययावब्धिं सुरासुरगणैर्वृतः ॥३८॥

giriṁ cāropya garuḍe
hastenaikena līlayā
āruhya prayayāv abdhiṁ
surāsura-gaṇair vṛtaḥ

girim—the mountain; *ca*—also; *āropya*—placing; *garuḍe*—on the back of Garuḍa; *hastena*—by the hand; *ekena*—one; *līlayā*—very easily as His pastime; *āruhya*—getting on; *prayayau*—He went; *abdhim*—to the ocean of milk; *sura-asura-gaṇaiḥ*—by the demigods and *asuras; vṛtaḥ*—surrounded.

TRANSLATION

The Lord very easily lifted the mountain with one hand and placed it on the back of Garuḍa. Then, He too got on the back of Garuḍa and went to the ocean of milk, surrounded by the demigods and demons.

PURPORT

Here is proof of the omnipotence of the Supreme Personality of Godhead, who is above everyone. There are two classes of living entities—the demons and the demigods—and the Supreme Personality of Godhead is above them both. The demons believe in the "chance" theory of creation, whereas the demigods believe in creation by the hand of the Supreme Personality of Godhead. The omnipotence of the Supreme Lord is proved here, for simply with one hand He lifted Mandara Mountain, the demigods and the demons, placed them on the back of Garuḍa and brought them to the ocean of milk. Now, the demigods, the devotees, would immediately accept this incident, knowing that the Lord can lift anything, however heavy it might be. But although demons were also carried along with the demigods, demons, upon hearing of this incident, would say that it is mythological. But if God is all-powerful, why would it be difficult for Him to lift a mountain? Since He is floating innumerable planets with many hundreds and thousands of Mandara Mountains, why can't He lift one of them with His hand? This is not mythology, but the difference between the believers and the faithless is that the devotees accept the incidents mentioned in the Vedic literatures to be true, whereas the demons simply argue and label all these historical incidents mythology. Demons would prefer to explain that everything happening in the cosmic manifestation takes place by chance, but demigods, or devotees, never consider anything to be chance. Rather, they know that everything is an arrangement of the Supreme Personality of Godhead. That is the difference between the demigods and the demons.

TEXT 39

अवरोप्य गिरिं स्कन्धात् सुपर्णः पततां वरः ।
ययौ जलान्त उत्सृज्य हरिणा स विसर्जितः ॥३९॥

avaropya giriṁ skandhāt
suparṇaḥ patatāṁ varaḥ
yayau jalānta utsṛjya
hariṇā sa visarjitaḥ

avaropya—unloading; *girim*—the mountain; *skandhāt*—from his shoulder; *suparṇaḥ*—Garuḍa; *patatām*—of all the birds; *varaḥ*—the biggest or most powerful; *yayau*—went; *jala-ante*—where the water is; *utsṛjya*—placing; *hariṇā*—by the Supreme Personality of Godhead; *saḥ*—he (Garuḍa); *visarjitaḥ*—discharged from that place.

TRANSLATION

Thereafter, Garuḍa, the chief of birds, unloaded Mandara Mountain from his shoulder and brought it near the water. Then he was asked by the Lord to leave that place, and he left.

PURPORT

Garuḍa was asked by the Lord to leave that place because the snake Vāsuki, who was to be used as the rope for churning, could not go there in the presence of Garuḍa. Garuḍa, the carrier of Lord Viṣṇu, is not a vegetarian. He eats big snakes. Vāsuki, being a great snake, would be natural food for Garuḍa, the chief of birds. Lord Viṣṇu therefore asked Garuḍa to leave so that Vāsuki could be brought to churn the ocean with Mandara Mountain, which was to be used as the churning rod. These are the wonderful arrangements of the Supreme Personality of Godhead. Nothing takes place by accident. Carrying Mandara Mountain on the back of a bird and putting it in its right position might be difficult for anyone, whether demigod or demon, but for the Supreme Personality of Godhead everything is possible, as shown by this pastime. The Lord had no difficulty lifting the mountain with one hand, and Garuḍa, His carrier, carried all the demons and demigods together by the grace of the Supreme Lord. The Lord is known as Yogeśvara, the master of all mystic power, because of His omnipotence. If He likes, He can make anything lighter than cotton or heavier than the universe. Those who do not believe in the activities of the Lord cannot explain how things happen. Using words like "accident," they take shelter of ideas that are unbelievable. Nothing is accidental. Everything is done by the Supreme Personality of Godhead, as the Lord Himself confirms in *Bhagavad-gītā* (9.10). *Mayādhyakṣeṇa prakṛtiḥ sūyate sacarācaram.* Whatever actions and reactions occur within the cosmic manifestation all take place under the superintendence of the Supreme Personality of Godhead. However, because the demons do not understand the potency of the Lord, when wonderful things are done, the demons think that they are accidental.

Thus end the Bhaktivedanta purports of the Eighth Canto, Sixth Chapter, of the Śrīmad-Bhāgavatam, *entitled "The Demigods and Demons Declare a Truce."*

CHAPTER SEVEN

Lord Śiva Saves the Universe by Drinking Poison

The summary of the Seventh Chapter is as follows. As described in this chapter, the Supreme Personality of Godhead, appearing in His incarnation as a tortoise, dove deep into the ocean to carry Mandara Mountain on His back. At first the churning of the ocean produced *kālakūṭa* poison. Everyone feared this poison, but Lord Śiva satisfied them by drinking it.

With the understanding that when the nectar was generated from the churning they would share it equally, the demigods and the demons brought Vāsuki to be used as the rope for the churning rod. By the expert arrangement of the Supreme Personality of Godhead, the demons held the snake near the mouth, whereas the demigods held the tail of the great snake. Then, with great endeavor, they began pulling the snake in both directions. Because the churning rod, Mandara Mountain, was very heavy and was not held by any support in the water, it sank into the ocean, and in this way the prowess of both the demons and the demigods was vanquished. The Supreme Personality of Godhead then appeared in the form of a tortoise and supported Mandara Mountain on His back. Then the churning resumed with great force. As a result of the churning, a huge amount of poison was produced. The *prajāpatis*, seeing no one else to save them, approached Lord Śiva and offered him prayers full of truth. Lord Śiva is called Āśutoṣa because he is very pleased if one is a devotee. Therefore he easily agreed to drink all the poison generated by the churning. The goddess Durgā, Bhavānī, the wife of Lord Śiva, was not at all disturbed when Lord Śiva agreed to drink the poison, for she knew Lord Śiva's prowess. Indeed, she expressed her pleasure at this agreement. Then Lord Śiva gathered the devastating poison, which was everywhere. He took it in his hand and drank it. After he drank the poison, his neck became bluish. A small quantity of the poison dropped from his hands to the ground, and it is because of this poison that there are poisonous snakes, scorpions, toxic plants and other poisonous things in this world.

TEXT 1

श्रीशुक उवाच
ते नागराजमामन्त्र्य फलभागेन वासुकिम् ।
परिवीय गिरौ तस्मिन् नेत्रमब्धिं मुदान्विताः ।
आरेभिरे सुरायत्ता अमृतार्थे कुरूद्वह ॥ १ ॥

śrī-śuka uvāca
te nāga-rājam āmantrya
phala-bhāgena vāsukim
parivīya girau tasmin
netram abdhiṁ mudānvitāḥ
ārebhire surā yattā
amṛtārthe kurūdvaha

śrī-śukaḥ uvāca—Śrī Śukadeva Gosvāmī said; *te*—all of them (the demigods and the demons); *nāga-rājam*—the king of the Nāgas, snakes; *āmantrya*—inviting, or requesting; *phala-bhāgena*—by promising a share of the nectar; *vāsukim*—the snake Vāsuki; *parivīya*—encircling; *girau*—Mandara Mountain; *tasmin*—unto it; *netram*—the churning rope; *abdhim*—the ocean of milk; *mudā anvitāḥ*—all surcharged with great pleasure; *ārebhire*—began to act; *surāḥ*—the demigods; *yattāḥ*—with great endeavor; *amṛta-arthe*—for gaining nectar; *kuru-udvaha*—O King Parīkṣit, best of the Kurus.

TRANSLATION

Śukadeva Gosvāmī said: O best of the Kurus, Mahārāja Parīkṣit, the demigods and demons summoned Vāsuki, king of the serpents, requesting him to come and promising to give him a share of the nectar. They coiled Vāsuki around Mandara Mountain as a churning rope, and with great pleasure they endeavored to produce nectar by churning the ocean of milk.

TEXT 2

हरिः पुरस्ताज्जगृहे पूर्वं देवास्ततोऽभवन् ॥ २ ॥

hariḥ purastāj jagṛhe
pūrvaṁ devās tato 'bhavan

hariḥ—the Supreme Personality of Godhead, Ajita; *purastāt*—from the front; *jagṛhe*—took; *pūrvam*—at first; *devāḥ*—the demigods; *tataḥ*—thereafter; *abhavan*—took the front portion of Vāsuki.

TRANSLATION

The Personality of Godhead, Ajita, grasped the front portion of the snake, and then the demigods followed.

TEXT 3

तन्नैच्छन् दैत्यपतयो महापुरुषचेष्टितम् ।
न गृह्णीमो वयं पुच्छमहेरङ्गममङ्गलम् ।
स्वाध्यायश्रुतसम्पन्नाः प्रख्याता जन्मकर्मभिः ॥ ३ ॥

tan naicchan daitya-patayo
mahā-puruṣa-ceṣṭitam
na gṛhṇīmo vayaṁ puccham
aher aṅgam amaṅgalam
svādhyāya-śruta-sampannāḥ
prakhyātā janma-karmabhiḥ

tat—that arrangement; *na aicchan*—not liking; *daitya-patayaḥ*—the leaders of the demons; *mahā-puruṣa*—of the Supreme Personality of Godhead; *ceṣṭitam*—attempt; *na*—not; *gṛhṇīmaḥ*—shall take; *vayam*—all of us (the Daityas); *puccham*—the tail; *aheḥ*—of the serpent; *aṅgam*—part of the body; *amaṅgalam*—inauspicious, inferior; *svādhyāya*—with Vedic study; *śruta*—and Vedic knowledge; *sampannāḥ*—fully equipped; *prakhyātāḥ*—prominent; *janma-karmabhiḥ*—by birth and activities.

TRANSLATION

The leaders of the demons thought it unwise to hold the tail, the inauspicious portion of the snake. Instead, they wanted to hold the

front, which had been taken by the Personality of Godhead and the demigods, because that portion was auspicious and glorious. Thus the demons, on the plea that they were all highly advanced students of Vedic knowledge and were all famous for their birth and activities, protested that they wanted to hold the front of the snake.

PURPORT

The demons thought that the front of the snake was auspicious and that catching hold of that portion would be more chivalrous. Moreover, Daityas must always do the opposite of the demigods. That is their nature. We have actually seen this in relation to our Kṛṣṇa consciousness movement. We are advocating cow protection and encouraging people to drink more milk and eat palatable preparations made of milk, but the demons, just to protest such proposals, are claiming that they are advanced in scientific knowledge, as described here by the words *svādhyāya-śruta-sampannāḥ*. They say that according to their scientific way, they have discovered that milk is dangerous and that the beef obtained by killing cows is very nutritious. This difference of opinion will always continue. Indeed, it has existed since days of yore. Millions of years ago, there was the same competition. The demons, as a result of their so-called Vedic study, preferred to hold the side of the snake near the mouth. The Supreme Personality of Godhead thought it wise to catch hold of the dangerous part of the snake and allow the demons to hold the tail, which was not dangerous, but because of a competitive desire, the demons thought it wise to hold the snake near the mouth. If the demigods were going to drink poison, the demons would resolve, "Why should we not share the poison and die gloriously by drinking it?"

In regard to the words *svādhyāya-śruta-sampannāḥ prakhyātā janma-karmabhiḥ*, another question may be raised. If one is actually educated in Vedic knowledge, is famous for performing prescribed activities and has been born in a great aristocratic family, why should he be called a demon? The answer is that one may be highly educated and may have been born in an aristocratic family, but if he is godless, if he does not listen to the instructions of God, then he is a demon. There are many examples in history of men like Hiraṇyakaśipu, Rāvaṇa and Kaṁsa who were well educated, who were born in aristocratic families and who were very powerful and chivalrous in fighting, but who, because of deriding the Supreme Personality of Godhead, were called Rākṣasas, or demons. One may be very well educated, but if he has no sense of Kṛṣṇa consciousness, no obedience to the Supreme Lord, he is a demon. That is described by the Lord Himself in *Bhagavad-gītā* (7.15):

na māṁ duṣkṛtino mūḍhāḥ
prapadyante narādhamāḥ
māyayāpahṛta-jñānā
āsuraṁ bhāvam āśritāḥ

"Those miscreants who are grossly foolish, lowest among mankind, whose knowledge is stolen by illusion, and who partake of the atheistic nature of demons, do not surrender unto Me." *Āsuraṁ bhāvam* refers to not accepting the existence of God or the transcendental instructions of the Personality of Godhead. *Bhagavad-gītā* clearly consists of transcendental instructions imparted directly by the Supreme Personality of Godhead. But *asuras,* instead of accepting these instructions directly, make commentaries according to their own whimsical ways and mislead everyone, without profit even for themselves. One should therefore be very careful of demoniac, godless persons. According to the words of Lord Kṛṣṇa, even if a godless demon is very well educated, he must be considered a *mūḍha, narādhama* and *māyayāpahṛta-jñāna.*

TEXT 4

इति तूष्णीं स्थितान्दैत्यान् विलोक्य पुरुषोत्तमः ।
स्मयमानो विसृज्याग्रं पुच्छं जग्राह सामरः ॥ ४ ॥

iti tūṣṇīṁ sthitān daityān
vilokya puruṣottamaḥ
smayamāno visṛjyāgraṁ
pucchaṁ jagrāha sāmaraḥ

iti—thus; *tūṣṇīm*—silently; *sthitān*—staying; *daityān*—the demons; *vilokya*—seeing; *puruṣa-uttamaḥ*—the Personality of Godhead; *smayamānaḥ*—smiling; *viṣṛjya*—giving up; *agram*—the front portion of the snake; *puccham*—the rear portion; *jagrāha*—grasped; *sa-amaraḥ*—with the demigods.

TRANSLATION

Thus the demons remained silent, opposing the desire of the demigods. Seeing the demons and understanding their motive, the Personality of Godhead smiled. Without discussion, He immediately accepted their proposal by grasping the tail of the snake, and the demigods followed Him.

TEXT 5

कृतस्थानविभागास्त एवं कश्यपनन्दनाः ।
ममन्थुः परमं यत्ता अमृतार्थं पयोनिधिम् ॥ ५ ॥

kṛta-sthāna-vibhāgās ta
evaṁ kaśyapa-nandanāḥ
mamanthuḥ paramaṁ yattā
amṛtārthaṁ payo-nidhim

kṛta—adjusting; *sthāna-vibhāgāḥ*—the division of the places they were to hold; *te*—they; *evam*—in this way; *kaśyapa-nandanāḥ*—the sons of Kaśyapa (both the demigods and the demons); *mamanthuḥ*—churned; *paramam*—with great; *yattāḥ*—endeavor; *amṛta-artham*—for getting nectar; *payaḥ-nidhim*—the ocean of milk.

TRANSLATION

After thus adjusting how the snake was to be held, the sons of Kaśyapa, both demigods and demons, began their activities, desiring to get nectar by churning the ocean of milk.

TEXT 6

मथ्यमानेऽर्णवे सोऽद्रिरनाधारो ह्यपोऽविशत् ।
ध्रियमाणोऽपि बलिभिर्गौरवात् पाण्डुनन्दन ॥ ६ ॥

mathyamāne 'rṇave so 'drir
anādhāro hy apo 'viśat

dhriyamāṇo 'pi balibhir
gauravāt pāṇḍu-nandana

mathyamāne—while the churning was going on; *arṇave*—in the ocean of milk; *saḥ*—that; *adriḥ*—hill; *anādhāraḥ*—without being supported by anything; *hi*—indeed; *apaḥ*—in the water; *aviśat*—drowned; *dhriyamāṇaḥ*—captured; *api*—although; *balibhiḥ*—by the powerful demigods and demons; *gauravāt*—from being very heavy; *pāṇḍu-nandana*—O son of Pāṇḍu (Mahārāja Parīkṣit).

TRANSLATION

O son of the Pāṇḍu dynasty, when Mandara Mountain was thus being used as a churning rod in the ocean of milk, it had no support, and therefore although held by the strong hands of the demigods and demons, it sank into the water.

TEXT 7

ते सुनिर्विण्णमनसः परिम्लानमुखश्रियः ।
आसन् स्वपौरुषे नष्टे दैवेनातिबलीयसा ॥ ७ ॥

te sunirviṇṇa-manasaḥ
parimlāna-mukha-śriyaḥ
āsan sva-pauruṣe naṣṭe
daivenātibalīyasā

te—all of them (the demigods and demons); *sunirviṇṇa-manasaḥ*—their minds being very disappointed; *parimlāna*—dried up; *mukha-śriyaḥ*—the beauty of their faces; *āsan*—became; *sva-pauruṣe*—with their own prowess; *naṣṭe*—being lost; *daivena*—by a providential arrangement; *ati-balīyasā*—which is always stronger than anything else.

TRANSLATION

Because the mountain had been sunk by the strength of providence, the demigods and demons were disappointed, and their faces seemed to shrivel.

TEXT 8

विलोक्य विघ्नेशविधिं तदेश्वरो
दुरन्तवीर्योऽवितथाभिसन्धिः ।
कृत्वा वपुः कच्छपमद्भुतं महत्
प्रविश्य तोयं गिरिमुज्जहार ॥ ८ ॥

vilokya vighneśa-vidhiṁ tadeśvaro
duranta-vīryo 'vitathābhisandhiḥ
kṛtvā vapuḥ kacchapam adbhutam mahat
praviśya toyaṁ girim ujjahāra

vilokya—observing; *vighna*—the obstruction (the sinking of the mountain); *īśa-vidhim*—by the providential arrangement; *tadā*—then; *īśvaraḥ*—the Supreme Personality of Godhead; *duranta-vīryaḥ*—inconceivably powerful; *avitatha*—infallible; *abhisandhiḥ*—whose determination; *kṛtvā*—expanding; *vapuḥ*—body; *kacchapam*—tortoise; *adbhutam*—wonderful; *mahat*—very great; *praviśya*—entering; *toyam*—the water; *girim*—the mountain (Mandara); *ujjahāra*—lifted.

TRANSLATION

Seeing the situation that had been created by the will of the Supreme, the unlimitedly powerful Lord, whose determination is infallible, took the wonderful shape of a tortoise, entered the water, and lifted the great Mandara Mountain.

PURPORT

Here is evidence that the Supreme Personality of Godhead is the supreme controller of everything. As we have previously described, there are two classes of men—the demons and the demigods—but neither of them are supremely powerful. Everyone has experienced that hindrances are imposed upon us by the supreme power. The demons regard these hindrances as mere accidents or chance, but devotees accept them to be acts of the supreme ruler. When faced with hindrances, therefore, devotees pray to the Lord. *Tat te 'nukampāṁ susamīkṣamāṇo bhuñjāna evātma-kṛtaṁ vipākam.* Devotees endure hindrances, accepting them to be caused by the Supreme Personality of Godhead and regarding them as benedictions. Demons, however, being unable to understand the supreme controller, regard such hindrances as accidental. Here, of course, the Supreme Personality of Godhead was present personally. It was by His will that there were hindrances, and by His will those hindrances were removed. The Lord appeared as a tortoise to support the great mountain. *Kṣitir iha vipulatare tava tiṣṭhati pṛṣṭhe.* The Lord held the great mountain on His back. *Keśava dhṛta-kūrma-śarīra jaya jagadīśa hare.* Dangers can be created by the Supreme Personality of Godhead, and they can also be removed by Him. This is known to devotees, but demons cannot understand it.

TEXT 9

तमुत्थितं वीक्ष्य कुलाचलं पुनः
समुद्यता निर्मथितुं सुरासुराः ।
दधार पृष्ठेन स लक्षयोजन-
प्रस्तारिणा द्वीप इवापरो महान् ॥ ९ ॥

tam utthitaṁ vīkṣya kulācalaṁ punaḥ
samudyatā nirmathituṁ surāsurāḥ
dadhāra pṛṣṭhena sa lakṣa-yojana-
prastāriṇā dvīpa ivāparo mahān

tam—that mountain; *utthitam*—lifted; *vīkṣya*—observing; *kulācalam*—known as Mandara; *punaḥ*—again; *samudyatāḥ*—enlivened; *nirmathitum*—to churn the ocean of milk; *sura-asurāḥ*—the demigods and the demons; *dadhāra*—carried; *pṛṣṭhena*—by the back; *saḥ*—the Supreme Lord; *lakṣa-yojana*—one hundred thousand *yojanas* (eight hundred thousand miles); *prastāriṇā*—extending; *dvīpaḥ*—a big island; *iva*—like; *aparaḥ*—another; *mahān*—very big.

TRANSLATION

When the demigods and demons saw that Mandara Mountain had been lifted, they were enlivened and encouraged to begin

churning again. The mountain rested on the back of the great tortoise, which extended for eight hundred thousand miles like a large island.

TEXT 10

सुरासुरेन्द्रैर्भुजवीर्यवेपितं
परिभ्रमन्तं गिरिमङ्ग पृष्ठतः ।
बिभ्रत् तदावर्तनमादिकच्छपो
मेनेऽङ्गकण्डूयनमप्रमेयः ॥१०॥

surāsurendrair bhuja-vīrya-vepitaṁ
paribhramantaṁ girim aṅga pṛṣṭhataḥ
bibhrat tad-āvartanam ādi-kacchapo
mene 'ṅga-kaṇḍūyanam aprameyaḥ

sura-asura-indraiḥ—by the leaders of the demons and the demigods; *bhuja-vīrya*—by the strength of their arms; *vepitam*—moving; *paribhramantam*—rotating; *girim*—the mountain; *aṅga*—O Mahārāja Parīkṣit; *pṛṣṭhataḥ*—on His back; *bibhrat*—bore; *tat*—of that; *āvartanam*—the rotating; *ādi-kacchapaḥ*—as the supreme original tortoise; *mene*—considered; *aṅga-kaṇḍūyanam*—as pleasing scratching of the body; *aprameyaḥ*—unlimited.

TRANSLATION

O King, when the demigods and demons, by the strength of their arms, rotated Mandara Mountain on the back of the extraordinary tortoise, the tortoise accepted the rolling of the mountain as a means of scratching His body, and thus He felt a pleasing sensation.

PURPORT

The Supreme Personality of Godhead is always the unlimited. Although the Supreme Personality of Godhead, in His body as a tortoise, held on His back the largest of mountains, Mandara-parvata, He did not feel any inconvenience. On the contrary, He apparently felt some itching, and thus the rotation of the mountain was certainly very pleasing.

TEXT 11

तथासुरानाविशदासुरेण
रूपेण तेषां बलवीर्यमीरयन् ।
उद्दीपयन् देवगणांश्च विष्णु-
र्दैवेन नागेन्द्रमबोधरूपः ॥११॥

tathāsurān āviśad āsureṇa
rūpeṇa teṣāṁ bala-vīryam īrayan
uddīpayan deva-gaṇāṁś ca viṣṇur
daivena nāgendram abodha-rūpaḥ

tathā—thereafter; *asurān*—unto the demons; *āviśat*—entered; *āsureṇa*—by the quality of passion; *rūpeṇa*—in such a form; *teṣām*—of them; *bala-vīryam*—strength and energy; *īrayan*—increasing; *uddīpayan*—encouraging; *deva-gaṇān*—the demigods; *ca*—also; *viṣṇuḥ*—Lord Viṣṇu; *daivena*—by the feature of goodness; *nāga-indram*—unto the King of the serpents, Vāsuki; *abodha-rūpaḥ*—by the quality of ignorance.

TRANSLATION

Thereafter, Lord Viṣṇu entered the demons as the quality of passion, the demigods as the quality of goodness, and Vāsuki as the quality of ignorance to encourage them and increase their various types of strength and energy.

PURPORT

Everyone in this material world is under the different modes of material nature. There were three different parties in the churning of Mandara Mountain—the demigods, who were in the mode of goodness, the demons, who were in the mode of passion, and the snake Vāsuki, who was in the mode of ignorance. Since they were all becoming tired (Vāsuki so much so that he was almost going to die), Lord Viṣṇu, to encourage them to continue the work of churning the ocean, entered into them according to their respective modes of nature—goodness, passion and ignorance.

TEXT 12

उपर्यगेन्द्रं गिरिराडिवान्य
आक्रम्य हस्तेन सहस्रबाहुः ।
तस्थौ दिवि ब्रह्मभवेन्द्रमुख्यै-
रभिष्टुवद्भिः सुमनोऽभिवृष्टः ॥१२॥

upary agendraṁ giri-rāḍ ivānya
ākramya hastena sahasra-bāhuḥ
tasthau divi brahma-bhavendra-mukhyair
abhiṣṭuvadbhiḥ sumano-'bhivṛṣṭaḥ

upari—on the top of; *agendram*—the big mountain; *giri-rāṭ*—the king of mountains; *iva*—like; *anyaḥ*—another; *ākramya*—catching; *hastena*—by one hand; *sahasra-bāhuḥ*—exhibiting thousands of hands; *tasthau*—situated; *divi*—in the sky; *brahma*—Lord Brahmā; *bhava*—Lord Śiva; *indra*—the King of heaven; *mukhyaiḥ*—headed by; *abhiṣṭuvadbhiḥ*—offered prayers to the Lord; *sumanaḥ*—by flowers; *abhivṛṣṭaḥ*—being showered.

TRANSLATION

Manifesting Himself with thousands of hands, the Lord then appeared on the summit of Mandara Mountain, like another great mountain, and held Mandara Mountain with one hand. In the upper planetary systems, Lord Brahmā and Lord Śiva, along with Indra, King of heaven, and other demigods, offered prayers to the Lord and showered flowers upon Him.

PURPORT

To balance Mandara Mountain while it was being pulled from both sides, the Lord Himself appeared on its summit like another great mountain. Lord Brahmā, Lord Śiva and King Indra then expanded themselves and showered flowers on the Lord.

TEXT 13

उपर्यधश्चात्मनि गोत्रनेत्रयोः
परेण ते प्राविशता समेधिताः ।
ममन्थुरब्धिं तरसा मदोत्कटा
महाद्रिणा क्षोभितनक्रचक्रम् ॥१३॥

upary adhaś cātmani gotra-netrayoḥ
pareṇa te prāviśatā samedhitāḥ
mamanthur abdhiṁ tarasā madotkaṭā
mahādriṇā kṣobhita-nakra-cakram

upari—upward; *adhaḥ ca*—and downward; *ātmani*—unto the demons and demigods; *gotra-netrayoḥ*—unto the mountain and Vāsuki, who was used as a rope; *pareṇa*—the Supreme Personality of Godhead; *te*—they; *prāviśatā*—entering them; *samedhitāḥ*—sufficiently agitated; *mamanthuḥ*—churned; *abdhim*—the ocean of milk; *tarasā*—with great strength; *mada-utkaṭāḥ*—being mad; *mahā-adriṇā*—with the great Mandara Mountain; *kṣobhita*—agitated; *nakra-cakram*—all the alligators in the water.

TRANSLATION

The demigods and demons worked almost madly for the nectar, encouraged by the Lord, who was above and below the mountain and who had entered the demigods, the demons, Vāsuki and the mountain itself. Because of the strength of the demigods and demons, the ocean of milk was so powerfully agitated that all the alligators in the water were very much perturbed. Nonetheless the churning of the ocean continued in this way.

TEXT 14

अहीन्द्रसाहस्रकठोरदृङ्मुख-
श्वासाग्निधूमाहतवर्चसोऽसुराः ।
पौलोमकालेयबलील्वलादयो
दवाग्निदग्धाः सरला इवाभवन् ॥१४॥

ahīndra-sāhasra-kaṭhora-dṛṅ-mukha-
śvāsāgni-dhūmāhata-varcaso 'surāḥ
pauloma-kāleya-balīlvalādayo
davāgni-dagdhāḥ saralā ivābhavan

ahīndra—of the King of serpents; *sāhasra*—by thousands; *kaṭhora*—very, very hard; *dṛk*—all directions; *mukha*—by the mouth; *śvāsa*—breathing; *agni*—fire coming out; *dhūma*—smoke; *āhata*—being affected; *varcasaḥ*—by the rays; *asurāḥ*—the demons; *pauloma*—Pauloma; *kāleya*—Kāleya; *bali*—Bali; *ilvala*—Ilvala; *ādayaḥ*—headed by; *dava-agni*—by a forest fire; *dagdhāḥ*—burned; *saralāḥ*—*sarala* trees; *iva*—like; *abhavan*—all of them became.

TRANSLATION

Vāsuki had thousands of eyes and mouths. From his mouths he breathed smoke and blazing fire, which affected the demons, headed by Pauloma, Kāleya, Bali and Ilvala. Thus the demons, who appeared like sarala trees burned by a forest fire, gradually became powerless.

TEXT 15

देवांश्च तच्छ्वासशिखाहतप्रभान्
धूम्राम्बरस्रग्वरकञ्चुकाननान् ।
समभ्यवर्षन्भगवद्वशा घना
ववुः समुद्रोर्म्युपगूढवायवः ॥१५॥

devāṁś ca tac-chvāsa-śikhā-hata-prabhān
dhūmrāmbara-srag-vara-kañcukānanān
samabhyavarṣan bhagavad-vaśā ghanā
vavuḥ samudrormy-upagūḍha-vāyavaḥ

devān—all the demigods; *ca*—also; *tat*—of Vāsuki; *śvāsa*—from the breathing; *śikhā*—by the flames; *hata*—being affected; *prabhān*—their bodily luster; *dhūmra*—smoky; *ambara*—dress; *srak-vara*—excellent garlands; *kañcuka*—armaments; *ānanān*—and faces; *samabhyavarṣan*—sufficiently rained; *bhagavat-vaśāḥ*—under the control of the

Supreme Personality of Godhead; *ghanāḥ*—clouds; *vavuḥ*—blew; *samudra*—of the ocean of milk; *ūrmi*—from the waves; *upagūḍha*—bearing fragments of water; *vāyavaḥ*—breezes.

TRANSLATION

Because the demigods were also affected by the blazing breath of Vāsuki, their bodily lusters diminished, and their garments, garlands, weapons and faces were blackened by smoke. However, by the grace of the Supreme Personality of Godhead, clouds appeared on the sea, pouring torrents of rain, and breezes blew, carrying particles of water from the sea waves, to give the demigods relief.

TEXT 16

मथ्यमानात् तथा सिन्धोर्देवासुरवरूथपैः ।
यदा सुधा न जायेत निर्ममन्थाजितः स्वयम् ॥१६॥

mathyamānāt tathā sindhor
devāsura-varūtha-paiḥ
yadā sudhā na jāyeta
nirmamanthājitaḥ svayam

mathyamānāt—sufficiently being churned; *tathā*—in this way; *sindhoḥ*—from the ocean of milk; *deva*—of the demigods; *asura*—and the demons; *varūtha-paiḥ*—by the best; *yadā*—when; *sudhā*—nectar; *na jāyeta*—did not come out; *nirmamantha*—churned; *ajitaḥ*—the Supreme Personality of Godhead, Ajita; *svayam*—personally.

TRANSLATION

When nectar did not come from the ocean of milk, despite so much endeavor by the best of the demigods and demons, the Supreme Personality of Godhead, Ajita, personally began to churn the ocean.

TEXT 17

मेघश्यामः कनकपरिधिः कर्णविद्योतविद्यु-
न्मूर्ध्नि भ्राजद्विलुलितकचः स्रग्धरो रक्तनेत्रः ।

जैत्रैर्दोर्भिर्जगदभयदैर्दन्दशूकं गृहीत्वा
मथ्नन् मथ्ना प्रतिगिरिरिवाशोभताथो धृताद्रिः॥

megha-śyāmaḥ kanaka-paridhiḥ karṇa-vidyota-vidyun
mūrdhni bhrājad-vilulita-kacaḥ srag-dharo rakta-netraḥ
jaitrair dorbhir jagad-abhaya-dair dandaśūkaṁ gṛhītvā
mathnan mathnā pratigirir ivāśobhatātho dhṛtādriḥ

megha-śyāmaḥ—blackish like a cloud; *kanaka-paridhiḥ*—wearing yellow garments; *karṇa*—on the ears; *vidyota-vidyut*—whose earrings shone like lightning; *mūrdhni*—on the head; *bhrājat*—gleaming; *vilulita*—disheveled; *kacaḥ*—whose hair; *srak-dharaḥ*—wearing a flower garland; *rakta-netraḥ*—with red eyes; *jaitraiḥ*—with victorious; *dorbhiḥ*—with arms; *jagat*—to the universe; *abhaya-daiḥ*—which give fearlessness; *dandaśūkam*—the snake (Vāsuki); *gṛhītvā*—after taking; *mathnan*—churning; *mathnā*—by the churning rod (Mandara Mountain); *pratigiriḥ*—another mountain; *iva*—like; *aśobhata*—He appeared; *atho*—then; *dhṛta-adriḥ*—having taken the mountain.

TRANSLATION

The Lord appeared like a blackish cloud. He was dressed with yellow garments, His earrings shone on His ears like lightning, and His hair spread over His shoulders. He wore a garland of flowers, and His eyes were pinkish. With His strong, glorious arms, which award fearlessness throughout the universe, He took hold of Vāsuki and began churning the ocean, using Mandara Mountain as a churning rod. When engaged in this way, the Lord appeared like a beautifully situated mountain named Indranīla.

TEXT 18

निर्मथ्यमानादुदधेरभूद्विषं
महोल्बणं हालहलाह्वमग्रतः ।
सम्भ्रान्तमीनोन्मकराहिकच्छपात्
तिमिद्विपग्राहतिमिङ्गिलाकुलात् ॥१८॥

nirmathyamānād udadher abhūd viṣaṁ
maholbaṇaṁ hālahalāhvam agrataḥ
sambhrānta-mīnonmakarāhi-kacchapāt
timi-dvipa-grāha-timiṅgilākulāt

nirmathyamānāt—while the activities of churning were going on; *udadheḥ*—from the ocean; *abhūt*—there was; *viṣam*—poison; *mahā-ulbaṇam*—very fierce; *hālahala-āhvam*—by the name *hālahala; agrataḥ*—at first; *sambhrānta*—agitated and going here and there; *mīna*—various kinds of fish; *unmakara*—sharks; *ahi*—different kinds of snakes; *kacchapāt*—and many kinds of tortoises; *timi*—whales; *dvipa*—water elephants; *grāha*—crocodiles; *timiṅgila*—whales that can swallow whales; *ākulāt*—being very much agitated.

TRANSLATION

The fish, sharks, tortoises and snakes were most agitated and perturbed. The entire ocean became turbulent, and even the large aquatic animals like whales, water elephants, crocodiles and timiṅgila fish [large whales that can swallow small whales] came to the surface. While the ocean was being churned in this way, it first produced a fiercely dangerous poison called hālahala.

TEXT 19

तदुग्रवेगं दिशि दिश्युपर्यधो
विसर्पदुत्सर्पदसह्यमप्रति ।
भीताः प्रजा दुद्रुवुरङ्ग सेश्वरा
अरक्ष्यमाणाः शरणं सदाशिवम् ॥१९॥

tad ugra-vegaṁ diśi diśy upary adho
visarpad utsarpad asahyam aprati
bhītāḥ prajā dudruvur aṅga seśvarā
arakṣyamāṇāḥ śaraṇaṁ sadāśivam

tat—that; *ugra-vegam*—very fierce and potent poison; *diśi diśi*—in all directions; *upari*—upward; *adhaḥ*—downward; *visarpat*—curling;

utsarpat—going upward; *asahyam*—unbearable; *aprati*—uncontrollable; *bhītāḥ*—being very much afraid; *prajāḥ*—the residents of all the worlds; *dudruvuḥ*—moved here and there; *aṅga*—O Mahārāja Parīkṣit; *sa-īśvarāḥ*—with the Supreme Lord; *arakṣyamāṇāḥ*—not being protected; *śaraṇam*—shelter; *sadāśivam*—unto the lotus feet of Lord Śiva.

TRANSLATION

O King, when that uncontrollable poison was forcefully spreading up and down in all directions, all the demigods, along with the Lord Himself, approached Lord Śiva [Sadāśiva]. Feeling unsheltered and very much afraid, they sought shelter of him.

PURPORT

One may question that since the Supreme Personality of Godhead was personally present, why did He accompany all the demigods and people in general to take shelter of Lord Sadāśiva, instead of intervening Himself. In this connection Śrīla Madhvācārya warns:

rudrasya yaśaso 'rthāya
svayaṁ viṣṇur viṣaṁ vibhuḥ
na sañjahre samartho 'pi
vāyuṁ coce praśāntaye

Lord Viṣṇu was competent to rectify the situation, but in order to give credit to Lord Śiva, who later drank all the poison and kept it in his neck, Lord Viṣṇu did not take action.

TEXT 20

विलोक्य तं देववरं त्रिलोक्या
भवाय देव्याभिमतं मुनीनाम् ।
आसीनमद्रावपवर्गहेतो-
स्तपो जुषाणं स्तुतिभिः प्रणेमुः ॥२०॥

vilokya taṁ deva-varaṁ tri-lokyā
bhavāya devyābhimataṁ munīnām

āsīnam adrāv apavarga-hetos
tapo juṣāṇaṁ stutibhiḥ praṇemuḥ

vilokya—observing; *tam*—him; *deva-varam*—the best of the demigods; *tri-lokyāḥ*—of the three worlds; *bhavāya*—for the flourishing; *devyā*—with his wife, Bhavānī; *abhimatam*—accepted by; *munīnām*—great saintly persons; *āsīnam*—sitting together; *adrau*—from the top of Kailāsa Hill; *apavarga-hetoḥ*—desiring liberation; *tapaḥ*—in austerity; *juṣāṇam*—being served by them; *stutibhiḥ*—by prayers; *praṇemuḥ*—offered their respectful obeisances.

TRANSLATION

The demigods observed Lord Śiva sitting on the summit of Kailāsa Hill with his wife, Bhavānī, for the auspicious development of the three worlds. He was being worshiped by great saintly persons desiring liberation. The demigods offered him their obeisances and prayers with great respect.

TEXT 21

श्रीप्रजापतय ऊचुः
देवदेव महादेव भूतात्मन् भूतभावन ।
त्राहि नः शरणापन्नांस्त्रैलोक्यदहनाद् विषात् ॥२१॥

śrī-prajāpataya ūcuḥ
deva-deva mahā-deva
bhūtātman bhūta-bhāvana
trāhi naḥ śaraṇāpannāṁs
trailokya-dahanād viṣāt

śrī-prajāpatayaḥ ūcuḥ—the *prajāpatis* said; *deva-deva*—O Lord Mahādeva, best of the demigods; *mahā-deva*—O great demigod; *bhūta-ātman*—O life and soul of everyone in this world; *bhūta-bhāvana*—O the cause of the happiness and flourishing of all of them; *trāhi*—deliver; *naḥ*—us; *śaraṇa-āpannān*—who have taken shelter at your lotus feet; *trailokya*—of the three worlds; *dahanāt*—which is causing the burning; *viṣāt*—from this poison.

TRANSLATION

The prajāpatis said: O greatest of all demigods, Mahādeva, Supersoul of all living entities and cause of their happiness and prosperity, we have come to the shelter of your lotus feet. Now please save us from this fiery poison, which is spreading all over the three worlds.

PURPORT

Since Lord Śiva is in charge of annihilation, why should he be approached for protection, which is given by Lord Viṣṇu? Lord Brahmā creates, and Lord Śiva annihilates, but both Lord Brahmā and Lord Śiva are incarnations of Lord Viṣṇu and are known as *śaktyāveśa-avatāras.* They are endowed with a special power like that of Lord Viṣṇu, who is actually all-pervading in their activities. Therefore whenever prayers for protection are offered to Lord Śiva, actually Lord Viṣṇu is indicated, for otherwise Lord Śiva is meant for destruction. Lord Śiva is one of the *īśvaras*, or the controllers known as *śaktyāveśa-avatāras.* Therefore he can be addressed as having the qualities of Lord Viṣṇu.

TEXT 22

त्वमेकः सर्वजगत ईश्वरो बन्धमोक्षयोः ।
तं त्वामर्चन्ति कुशलाः प्रपन्नार्तिहरं गुरुम् ॥२२॥

tvam ekaḥ sarva-jagata
īśvaro bandha-mokṣayoḥ
taṁ tvām arcanti kuśalāḥ
prapannārti-haraṁ gurum

tvam ekaḥ—Your Lordship is indeed; *sarva-jagataḥ*—of the three worlds; *īśvaraḥ*—the controller; *bandha-mokṣayoḥ*—of both bondage and liberation; *tam*—that controller; *tvām arcanti*—worship you; *kuśalāḥ*—persons who want good fortune; *prapanna-ārti-haram*—who can mitigate all the distresses of a sheltered devotee; *gurum*—you who act as a good advisor to all fallen souls.

TRANSLATION

O lord, you are the cause of bondage and liberation of the entire universe because you are its ruler. Those who are advanced in spiritual consciousness surrender unto you, and therefore you are the cause of mitigating their distresses, and you are also the cause of their liberation. We therefore worship Your Lordship.

PURPORT

Actually Lord Viṣṇu maintains and accomplishes all good fortune. If one has to take shelter of Lord Viṣṇu, why should the demigods take shelter of Lord Śiva? They did so because Lord Viṣṇu acts through Lord Śiva in the creation of the material world. Lord Śiva acts on behalf of Lord Viṣṇu. When the Lord says in *Bhagavad-gītā* (14.4) that He is the father of all living entities (*ahaṁ bīja-pradaḥ pitā*), this refers to actions performed by Lord Viṣṇu through Lord Śiva. Lord Viṣṇu is always unattached to material activities, and when material activities are to be performed, Lord Viṣṇu performs them through Lord Śiva. Lord Śiva is therefore worshiped on the level of Lord Viṣṇu. When Lord Viṣṇu is untouched by the external energy He is Lord Viṣṇu, but when He is in touch with the external energy, He appears in His feature as Lord Śiva.

TEXT 23

गुणमय्या स्वशक्त्यास्य सर्गस्थित्यप्ययान्विभो ।
धत्से यदा स्वदृग् भूमन्ब्रह्मविष्णुशिवाभिधाम् ॥२३॥

guṇa-mayyā sva-śaktyāsya
sarga-sthity-apyayān vibho
dhatse yadā sva-dṛg bhūman
brahma-viṣṇu-śivābhidhām

guṇa-mayyā—acting in three modes of activity; *sva-śaktyā*—by the external energy of Your Lordship; *asya*—of this material world; *sarga-sthiti-apyayān*—creation, maintenance and annihilation; *vibho*—O lord; *dhatse*—you execute; *yadā*—when; *sva-dṛk*—you manifest yourself; *bhūman*—O great one; *brahma-viṣṇu-śiva-abhidhām*—as Lord Brahmā, Lord Viṣṇu or Lord Śiva.

TRANSLATION

O lord, you are self-effulgent and supreme. You create this material world by your personal energy, and you assume the names Brahmā, Viṣṇu and Maheśvara when you act in creation, maintenance and annihilation.

PURPORT

This prayer is actually offered to Lord Viṣṇu, the *puruṣa*, who in His incarnations as the *guṇa-avatāras* assumes the names Brahmā, Viṣṇu and Maheśvara.

TEXT 24

त्वं ब्रह्म परमं गुह्यं सदसद्भावभावनम् ।
नानाशक्तिभिराभातस्त्वमात्मा जगदीश्वरः ॥२४॥

tvaṁ brahma paramaṁ guhyaṁ
sad-asad-bhāva-bhāvanam
nānā-śaktibhir ābhātas
tvam ātmā jagad-īśvaraḥ

tvam—Your Lordship; *brahma*—impersonal Brahman; *paramam*—supreme; *guhyam*—confidential; *sat-asat-bhāva-bhāvanam*—the cause of varieties of creation, its cause and effect; *nānā-śaktibhiḥ*—with varieties of potencies; *ābhātaḥ*—manifest; *tvam*—you are; *ātmā*—the Supersoul; *jagat-īśvaraḥ*—the Supreme Personality of Godhead.

TRANSLATION

You are the cause of all causes, the self-effulgent, inconceivable, impersonal Brahman, which is originally Parabrahman. You manifest various potencies in this cosmic manifestation.

PURPORT

This prayer is offered to the impersonal Brahman, which consists of the effulgent rays of Parabrahman. Parabrahman is the Supreme Personality of Godhead (*paraṁ brahma paraṁ dhāma pavitraṁ paramaṁ bhavān*). When Lord Śiva is worshiped as Parabrahman, the worship is meant for Lord Viṣṇu.

TEXT 25

त्वं शब्दयोनिर्जगदादिरात्मा
प्राणेन्द्रियद्रव्यगुणः स्वभावः ।
कालः क्रतुः सत्यमृतं च धर्म-
स्त्वय्यक्षरं यत् त्रिवृदामनन्ति ॥२५॥

tvaṁ śabda-yonir jagad-ādir ātmā
prāṇedriya-dravya-guṇaḥ svabhāvaḥ
kālaḥ kratuḥ satyam ṛtaṁ ca dharmas
tvayy akṣaraṁ yat tri-vṛd-āmananti

tvam—Your Lordship; *śabda-yoniḥ*—the origin and source of Vedic literature; *jagat-ādiḥ*—the original cause of material creation; *ātmā*—the soul; *prāṇa*—the living force; *indriya*—the senses; *dravya*—the material elements; *guṇaḥ*—the three qualities; *sva-bhāvaḥ*—material nature; *kālaḥ*—eternal time; *kratuḥ*—sacrifice; *satyam*—truth; *ṛtam*—truthfulness; *ca*—and; *dharmaḥ*—two different types of religion; *tvayi*—unto you; *akṣaram*—the original syllable, *oṁkāra; yat*—that which; *tri-vṛt*—consisting of the letters *a, u* and *m; āmananti*—they say.

TRANSLATION

O lord, you are the original source of Vedic literature. You are the original cause of material creation, the life force, the senses, the five elements, the three modes and the mahat-tattva. You are eternal time, determination and the two religious systems called truth [satya] and truthfulness [ṛta]. You are the shelter of the syllable oṁ, which consists of three letters "a-u-m."

TEXT 26

अग्निर्मुखं तेऽखिलदेवतात्मा
क्षितिं विदुर्लोकभवाङ्घ्रिपङ्कजम् ।

कालं गतिं तेऽखिलदेवतात्मनो
दिशश्च कर्णौ रसनं जलेशम् ॥२६॥

agnir mukhaṁ te 'khila-devatātmā
kṣitiṁ vidur loka-bhavāṅghri-paṅkajam
kālaṁ gatiṁ te 'khila-devatātmano
diśaś ca karṇau rasanaṁ jaleśam

agniḥ—fire; *mukham*—mouth; *te*—of Your Lordship; *akhila-devatā-ātmā*—the origin of all demigods; *kṣitim*—the surface of the globe; *viduḥ*—they know; *loka-bhava*—O origin of all planets; *aṅghri-paṅka-jam*—your lotus feet; *kālam*—eternal time; *gatim*—progress; *te*—of Your Lordship; *akhila-devatā-ātmanaḥ*—the total aggregate of all the demigods; *diśaḥ*—all directions; *ca*—and; *karṇau*—your ears; *rasanam*—taste; *jala-īśam*—the demigod controller of the water.

TRANSLATION

O father of all planets, learned scholars know that fire is your mouth, the surface of the globe is your lotus feet, eternal time is your movement, all the directions are your ears, and Varuṇa, master of the waters, is your tongue.

PURPORT

In the *śruti-mantras* it is said, *agniḥ sarva-devatāḥ:* "Fire is the aggregate of all demigods." Agni is the mouth of the Supreme Personality of Godhead. It is through Agni, or fire, that the Lord accepts all sacrificial oblations.

TEXT 27

नाभिर्नभस्ते श्वसनं नभस्वान्
सूर्यश्च चक्षूंषि जलं स्म रेतः ।
परावरात्माश्रयणं तवात्मा
सोमो मनो द्यौर्भगवन् शिरस्ते ॥२७॥

nābhir nabhas te śvasanaṁ nabhasvān
sūryaś ca cakṣūṁṣi jalaṁ sma retaḥ

parāvarātmāśrayaṇaṁ tavātmā
somo mano dyaur bhagavan śiras te

nābhiḥ—navel; *nabhaḥ*—the sky; *te*—of Your Lordship; *śvasanam*—breathing; *nabhasvān*—the air; *sūryaḥ ca*—and the sun globe; *cakṣūṁṣi*—your eyes; *jalam*—the water; *sma*—indeed; *retaḥ*—semen; *para-avara-ātma-āśrayaṇam*—the shelter of all living entities, low and high; *tava*—your; *ātmā*—self; *somaḥ*—the moon; *manaḥ*—mind; *dyauḥ*—the higher planetary systems; *bhagavan*—O Your Lordship; *śiraḥ*—head; *te*—of you.

TRANSLATION

O lord, the sky is your navel, the air is your breathing, the sun is your eyes, and the water is your semen. You are the shelter of all kinds of living entities, high and low. The god of the moon is your mind, and the upper planetary system is your head.

TEXT 28

कुक्षिः समुद्रा गिरयोऽस्थिसङ्घा
रोमाणि सर्वौषधिवीरुधस्ते ।
छन्दांसि साक्षात् तव सप्त धातव-
स्त्रयीमयात्मन् हृदयं सर्वधर्मः ॥२८॥

kukṣiḥ samudrā girayo 'sthi-saṅghā
romāṇi sarvauṣadhi-vīrudhas te
chandāṁsi sākṣāt tava sapta dhātavas
trayī-mayātman hṛdayaṁ sarva-dharmaḥ

kukṣiḥ—abdomen; *samudrāḥ*—the oceans; *girayaḥ*—the mountains; *asthi*—bones; *saṅghāḥ*—combination; *romāṇi*—the hairs of the body; *sarva*—all; *auṣadhi*—drugs; *vīrudhaḥ*—plants and creepers; *te*—your; *chandāṁsi*—Vedic *mantras; sākṣāt*—directly; *tava*—your; *sapta*—seven; *dhātavaḥ*—layers of the body; *trayī-maya-ātman*—O three *Vedas* personified; *hṛdayam*—core of the heart; *sarva-dharmaḥ*—all kinds of religion.

TRANSLATION

O lord, you are the three Vedas personified. The seven seas are your abdomen, and the mountains are your bones. All drugs, creepers and vegetables are the hairs on your body, the Vedic mantras like Gāyatrī are the seven layers of your body, and the Vedic religious system is the core of your heart.

TEXT 29

मुखानि पञ्चोपनिषदस्तवेश
यैस्त्रिंशदष्टोत्तरमन्त्रवर्गः ।
यत् तच्छिवाख्यं परमात्मतत्त्वं
देव स्वयंज्योतिरवस्थितिस्ते ॥२९॥

mukhāni pañcopaniṣadas taveśa
yais trimśad-aṣṭottara-mantra-vargaḥ
yat tac chivākhyaṁ paramātma-tattvaṁ
deva svayaṁ-jyotir avasthitis te

mukhāni—faces; *pañca*—five; *upaniṣadaḥ*—Vedic literatures; *tava*—your; *īśa*—O lord; *yaiḥ*—by which; *trimśat-aṣṭa-uttara-mantra-vargaḥ*—in the category of thirty-eight important Vedic *mantras; yat*—that; *tat*—as it is; *śiva-ākhyam*—celebrated by the name Śiva; *parama-ātma-tattvam*—which ascertain the truth about Paramātmā; *deva*—O lord; *svayam-jyotiḥ*—self-illuminated; *avasthitiḥ*—situation; *te*—of Your Lordship.

TRANSLATION

O lord, the five important Vedic mantras are represented by your five faces, from which the thirty-eight most celebrated Vedic mantras have been generated. Your Lordship, being celebrated as Lord Śiva, is self-illuminated. You are directly situated as the supreme truth, known as Paramātmā.

PURPORT

The five *mantras* mentioned in this connection are as follows: (1) *Puruṣa,* (2) *Aghora,* (3) *Sadyojāta,* (4) *Vāmadeva,* and (5) *Īśāna.*

These five *mantras* are within the category of thirty-eight special Vedic *mantras* chanted by Lord Śiva, who is therefore celebrated as Śiva or Mahādeva. Another reason why Lord Śiva is called Śiva, which means "all-auspicious," is that he is self-illuminated, exactly like Lord Viṣṇu, who is the Paramātmā. Because Lord Śiva is directly an incarnation of Lord Viṣṇu, he is situated as Lord Viṣṇu's direct representative. This fact is corroborated by a Vedic *mantra: patiṁ viśvasyātmeśvaraṁ śāśvataṁ śivam acyutam.* The Supersoul is called by many names, of which Maheśvara, Śiva and Acyuta are especially mentioned.

TEXT 30

छाया त्वधर्मोर्मिषु यैर्विसर्गो
नेत्रत्रयं सत्त्वरजस्तमांसि ।
सांख्यात्मनः शास्त्रकृतस्तवेक्षा
छन्दोमयो देव ऋषिः पुराणः ॥३०॥

chāyā tv adharmormiṣu yair visargo
netra-trayaṁ sattva-rajas-tamāṁsi
sāṅkhyātmanaḥ śāstra-kṛtas tavekṣā
chandomayo deva ṛṣiḥ purāṇaḥ

chāyā—shadow; *tu*—but; *adharma-ūrmiṣu*—in the waves of irreligion, like *kāma, krodha, lobha* and *moha; yaiḥ*—by which; *visargaḥ*—so many varieties of creation; *netra-trayam*—three eyes; *sattva*—goodness; *rajaḥ*—passion; *tamāṁsi*—and darkness; *sāṅkhya-ātmanaḥ*—the origin of all Vedic literatures; *śāstra*—scriptures; *kṛtaḥ*—made; *tava*—by you; *īkṣā*—simply by glancing; *chandaḥ-mayaḥ*—full of Vedic verses; *deva*—O lord; *ṛṣiḥ*—all Vedic literatures; *purāṇaḥ*—and the *Purāṇas*, the supplementary *Vedas.*

TRANSLATION

O lord, your shadow is seen in irreligion, which brings about varieties of irreligious creations. The three modes of nature—goodness, passion and ignorance—are your three eyes. All the Vedic literatures, which are full of verses, are emanations from

you because their compilers wrote the various scriptures after receiving your glance.

TEXT 31

न ते गिरित्राखिललोकपाल-
विरिञ्चवैकुण्ठसुरेन्द्रगम्यम् ।
ज्योतिः परं यत्र रजस्तमश्च
सत्त्वं न यद् ब्रह्म निरस्तभेदम् ॥३१॥

na te giri-trākhila-loka-pāla-
viriñca-vaikuṇṭha-surendra-gamyam
jyotiḥ paraṁ yatra rajas tamaś ca
sattvaṁ na yad brahma nirasta-bhedam

na—not; *te*—of Your Lordship; *giri-tra*—O King of the mountains; *akhila-loka-pāla*—all the directors of departments of material activities; *viriñca*—Lord Brahmā; *vaikuṇṭha*—Lord Viṣṇu; *sura-indra*—the King of heaven; *gamyam*—they can understand; *jyotiḥ*—effulgence; *param*—transcendental; *yatra*—wherein; *rajaḥ*—the mode of passion; *tamaḥ ca*—and the mode of ignorance; *sattvam*—the mode of goodness; *na*—not; *yat brahma*—which is impersonal Brahman; *nirasta-bhedam*—without distinction between demigods and human beings.

TRANSLATION

O Lord Girīśa, since the impersonal Brahman effulgence is transcendental to the material modes of goodness, passion and ignorance, the various directors of this material world certainly cannot appreciate it or even know where it is. It is not understandable even to Lord Brahmā, Lord Viṣṇu or the King of heaven, Mahendra.

PURPORT

The *brahmajyoti* is actually the effulgence of the Supreme Personality of Godhead. As stated in *Brahma-saṁhitā* (5.40):

yasya prabhā prabhavato jagad-aṇḍa-koṭi-
koṭiṣv aśeṣa-vasudhādi-vibhūti-bhinnam
tad brahma niṣkalam anantam aśeṣa-bhūtaṁ
govindam ādi-puruṣaṁ tam ahaṁ bhajāmi

"I worship Govinda, the primeval Lord, who is endowed with great power. The glowing effulgence of His transcendental form is the impersonal Brahman, which is absolute, complete and unlimited and which displays the varieties of countless planets, with their different opulences, in millions and millions of universes." Although the impersonal feature of the Absolute is an expansion of the rays of the Supreme Personality of Godhead, He does not need to take care of the impersonalists who enter the *brahmajyoti.* Kṛṣṇa says in *Bhagavad-gītā* (9.4), *mayā tatam idaṁ sarvaṁ jagad avyakta-mūrtinā:* "In My impersonal feature I pervade this entire universe." Thus the *avyakta-mūrti,* the impersonal feature, is certainly an expansion of Kṛṣṇa's energy. Māyāvādīs, who prefer to merge into this Brahman effulgence, worship Lord Śiva. The *mantras* referred to in text 29 are called *mukhāni pañcopaniṣadas taveśa.* Māyāvādīs take all these *mantras* seriously in worshiping Lord Śiva. These *mantras* are as follows: (1) *tat puruṣāya vidmahe śāntyai,* (2) *mahā-devāya dhīmahi vidyāyai,* (3) *tan no rudraḥ pratiṣṭhāyai,* (4) *pracodayāt dhṛtyai,* (5) *aghorebhyas tamā . . . ,* (6) *atha ghorebhyo mohā . . . ,* (7) *aghorebhyo rakṣā . . . ,* (8) *aghoratarebhyo nidrā . . . ,* (9) *sarvebhyaḥ sarva-vyādhyai,* (10) *sarva-sarvebhyo mṛtyave,* (11) *namas te 'stu kṣudhā . . . ,* (12) *rudra-rūpebhyas tṛṣṇā . . . ,* (13) *vāmadevāya rajā . . . ,* (14) *jyeṣṭhāya svāhā . . . ,* (15) *śreṣṭhāya ratyai,* (16) *rudrāya kalyāṇyai,* (17) *kālāya kāmā . . . ,* (18) *kala-vikaraṇāya sandhinyai,* (19) *bala-vikaraṇāya kriyā . . . ,* (20) *balāya vṛddhyai,* (21) *balacchāyā . . . ,* (22) *pramathanāya dhātryai,* (23) *sarva-bhūta-damanāya bhrāmaṇyai,* (24) *manaḥ-śoṣiṇyai,* (25) *unmanāya jvarā . . . ,* (26) *sadyojātaṁ prapadyāmi siddhyai,* (27) *sadyojātāya vai namaḥ ṛddhyai,* (28) *bhave dityai,* (29) *abhave lakṣmyai,* (30) *nātibhave medhā . . . ,* (31) *bhajasva māṁ kāntyai,* (32) *bhava svadhā . . . ,* (33) *udbhavāya prabhā . . . ,* (34) *īśānaḥ sarva-vidyānāṁ śaśinyai,* (35) *īśvaraḥ sarva-bhūtānām abhaya-dā . . . ,* (36) *brahmādhipatir brahmaṇodhipatir brahman brahmeṣṭa-dā . . . ,*(37) *śivo me astu marīcyai,* (38) *sadāśivaḥ jvālinyai.*

The impersonal Brahman is unknown even to the other directors of the material creation, including Lord Brahmā, Lord Indra and even Lord Viṣṇu. This does not mean, however, that Lord Viṣṇu is not omniscient. Lord Viṣṇu is omniscient, but He does not need to understand what is going on in His all-pervading expansion. Therefore in *Bhagavad-gītā* the Lord says that although everything is an expansion of Him (*mayā tatam idaṁ sarvam*), He does not need to take care of everything (*na cāhaṁ teṣv avasthitaḥ*), since there are various directors like Lord Brahmā, Lord Śiva and Indra.

TEXT 32

कामाध्वरत्रिपुरकालगराद्यनेक-
भूतद्रुहः क्षपयतः स्तुतये न तत् ते ।
यस्त्वन्तकाल इदमात्मकृतं स्वनेत्र-
वह्निस्फुलिङ्गशिखया भसितं न वेद॥३२॥

kāmādhvara-tripura-kālagarādy-aneka-
bhūta-druhaḥ kṣapayataḥ stutaye na tat te
yas tv anta-kāla idam ātma-kṛtaṁ sva-netra-
vahni-sphuliṅga-śikhayā bhasitaṁ na veda

kāma-adhvara—sacrifices for sense gratification (like Dakṣa-yajña, the sacrifices performed by Dakṣa); *tripura*—the demon named Tripurāsura; *kālagara*—Kālagara; *ādi*—and others; *aneka*—many; *bhūta-druhaḥ*—who are meant for giving trouble to the living entities; *kṣapayataḥ*—being engaged in their destruction; *stutaye*—your prayer; *na*—not; *tat*—that; *te*—speaking to you; *yaḥ tu*—because; *anta-kāle*—at the time of annihilation; *idam*—in this material world; *ātma-kṛtam*—done by yourself; *sva-netra*—by your eyes; *vahni-sphuliṅga-śikhayā*—by the sparks of fire; *bhasitam*—burned to ashes; *na veda*—I do not know how it is happening.

TRANSLATION

When annihilation is performed by the flames and sparks emanating from your eyes, the entire creation is burned to ashes. Nonetheless, you do not know how this happens. What then is to

be said of your destroying the Dakṣa-yajña, Tripurāsura and the kālakūṭa poison? Such activities cannot be subject matters for prayers offered to you.

PURPORT

Since Lord Śiva considers the great acts he performs to be very unimportant, what was to be said of counteracting the strong poison produced by the churning? The demigods indirectly prayed that Lord Śiva counteract the *kālakūṭa* poison, which was spreading throughout the universe.

TEXT 33

ये त्वात्मरामगुरुभिर्हृदि चिन्तिताङ्घ्रि-
द्वन्द्वं चरन्तमुमया तपसाभितप्तम् ।
कत्थन्त उग्रपरुषं निरतं श्मशाने
ते नूनमूतिमविदंस्तव हातलज्जाः ॥३३॥

ye tv ātma-rāma-gurubhir hṛdi cintitāṅghri-
dvandvaṁ carantam umayā tapasābhitaptam
katthanta ugra-paruṣaṁ nirataṁ śmaśāne
te nūnam ūtim avidaṁs tava hāta-lajjāḥ

ye—persons who; *tu*—indeed; *ātma-rāma-gurubhiḥ*—by those who are self-satisfied and who are considered to be spiritual masters of the world; *hṛdi*—within the heart; *cintita-aṅghri-dvandvam*—thinking of your two lotus feet; *carantam*—moving; *umayā*—with your consort, Umā; *tapasā abhitaptam*—highly advanced through practice of austerity and penance; *katthante*—criticize your acts; *ugra-paruṣam*—not a gentle person; *niratam*—always; *śmaśāne*—in the crematorium; *te*—such persons; *nūnam*—indeed; *ūtim*—such activities; *avidan*—not knowing; *tava*—your activities; *hāta-lajjāḥ*—shameless.

TRANSLATION

Exalted, self-satisfied persons who preach to the entire world think of your lotus feet constantly within their hearts. However,

when persons who do not know your austerity see you moving with Umā, they misunderstand you to be lusty, or when they see you wandering in the crematorium they mistakenly think that you are ferocious and envious. Certainly they are shameless. They cannot understand your activities.

PURPORT

Lord Śiva is the topmost Vaiṣṇava (*vaiṣṇavānāṁ yathā śambhuḥ*). It is therefore said, *vaiṣṇavera kriyā-mudrā vijñe nā bujhaya.* Even the most intelligent person cannot understand what a Vaiṣṇava like Lord Śiva is doing or how he is acting. Those who are conquered by lusty desires and anger cannot estimate the glories of Lord Śiva, whose position is always transcendental. In all the activities associated with lusty desires, Lord Śiva is an implement of *ātma-rāma.* Ordinary persons, therefore, should not try to understand Lord Śiva and his activities. One who tries to criticize the activities of Lord Śiva is shameless.

TEXT 34

तत् तस्य ते सदसतोः परतः परस्य
नाञ्जः स्वरूपगमने प्रभवन्ति भूम्नः ।
ब्रह्मादयः किमुत संस्तवने वयं तु
तत्सर्गसर्गविषया अपि शक्तिमात्रम् ॥३४॥

tat tasya te sad-asatoḥ parataḥ parasya
nāñjaḥ svarūpa-gamane prabhavanti bhūmnaḥ
brahmādayaḥ kim uta saṁstavane vayaṁ tu
tat-sarga-sarga-viṣayā api śakti-mātram

tat—therefore; *tasya*—of that; *te*—of Your Lordship; *sat-asatoḥ*—of the living entities, moving and not moving; *parataḥ*—transcendentally situated; *parasya*—very difficult to understand; *na*—nor; *añjaḥ*—as it is; *svarūpa-gamane*—to approach your reality; *prabhavanti*—it is possible; *bhūmnaḥ*—O great one; *brahma-ādayaḥ*—even such persons as Lord Brahmā; *kim uta*—what to speak of others; *saṁstavane*—in offering prayers; *vayam tu*—as far as we are concerned; *tat*—of you; *sarga-*

sarga-viṣayāḥ—creations of the creation; *api*—although; *śakti-mātram*—to our ability.

TRANSLATION

Even personalities like Lord Brahmā and other demigods cannot understand your position, for you are beyond the moving and nonmoving creation. Since no one can understand you in truth, how can one offer you prayers? It is impossible. As far as we are concerned, we are creatures of Lord Brahmā's creation. Under the circumstances, therefore, we cannot offer you adequate prayers, but as far as our ability allows, we have expressed our feelings.

TEXT 35

एतत् परं प्रपश्यामो न परं ते महेश्वर ।
मृडनाय हि लोकस्य व्यक्तिस्तेऽव्यक्तकर्मणः ॥३५॥

etat paraṁ prapaśyāmo
na paraṁ te maheśvara
mṛḍanāya hi lokasya
vyaktis te 'vyakta-karmaṇaḥ

etat—all these things; *param*—transcendental; *prapaśyāmaḥ*—we can see; *na*—not; *param*—the actual transcendental position; *te*—of Your Lordship; *mahā-īśvara*—O great ruler; *mṛḍanāya*—for the happiness; *hi*—indeed; *lokasya*—of all the world; *vyaktiḥ*—manifested; *te*—of Your Lordship; *avyakta-karmaṇaḥ*—whose activities are unknown to everyone.

TRANSLATION

O greatest of all rulers, your actual identity is impossible for us to understand. As far as we can see, your presence brings flourishing happiness to everyone. Beyond this, no one can appreciate your activities. We can see this much, and nothing more.

PURPORT

When the demigods offered these prayers to Lord Śiva, their inner purpose was to please him so that he would rectify the disturbing situation created by the *hālahala* poison. As stated in *Bhagavad-gītā* (7.20), *kāmais tais tair hṛta-jñānāḥ prapadyante 'nya-devatāḥ:* when one worships demigods, this is certainly because of deep-rooted desires he wants fulfilled by the mercy of those demigods. People are generally attached to the worship of demigods for some motive.

TEXT 36

श्रीशुक उवाच

तद्वीक्ष्य व्यसनं तासां कृपया भृशपीडितः ।
सर्वभूतसुहृद् देव इदमाह सतीं प्रियाम् ॥३६॥

śrī-śuka uvāca
tad vīkṣya vyasanaṁ tāsāṁ
kṛpayā bhṛśa-pīḍitaḥ
sarva-bhūta-suhṛd deva
idam āha satīṁ priyām

śrī-śukaḥ uvāca—Śrī Śukadeva Gosvāmī said; *tat*—this situation; *vīkṣya*—seeing; *vyasanam*—dangerous; *tāsām*—of all the demigods; *kṛpayā*—out of compassion; *bhṛśa-pīḍitaḥ*—greatly aggrieved; *sarva-bhūta-suhṛt*—the friend of all living entities; *devaḥ*—Mahādeva; *idam*—this; *āha*—said; *satīm*—unto Satīdevī; *priyām*—his very dear wife.

TRANSLATION

Śrīla Śukadeva Gosvāmī continued: Lord Śiva is always benevolent toward all living entities. When he saw that the living entities were very much disturbed by the poison, which was spreading everywhere, he was very compassionate. Thus he spoke to his eternal consort, Satī, as follows.

TEXT 37

श्रीशिव उवाच

अहो बत भवान्येतत् प्रजानां पश्य वैशसम् ।
क्षीरोदमथनोद्भूतात् कालकूटादुपस्थितम् ॥३७॥

śrī-śiva uvāca
aho bata bhavāny etat
prajānāṁ paśya vaiśasam
kṣīroda-mathanodbhūtāt
kālakūṭād upasthitam

śrī-śivaḥ uvāca—Śrī Śiva said; *aho bata*—how pitiable; *bhavāni*—my dear wife, Bhavānī; *etat*—this situation; *prajānām*—of all living entities; *paśya*—just see; *vaiśasam*—very dangerous; *kṣīra-uda*—of the ocean of milk; *mathana-udbhūtāt*—produced by the churning; *kālakūṭāt*—because of the production of poison; *upasthitam*—the present situation.

TRANSLATION

Lord Śiva said: My dear Bhavānī, just see how all these living entities have been placed in danger because of the poison produced from the churning of the ocean of milk.

TEXT 38

आसां प्राणपरीप्सूनां विधेयमभयं हि मे ।
एतावान्हि प्रभोरर्थो यद् दीनपरिपालनम् ॥३८॥

āsāṁ prāṇa-parīpsūnāṁ
vidheyam abhayaṁ hi me
etāvān hi prabhor artho
yad dīna-paripālanam

āsām—all of these living entities; *prāṇa-parīpsūnām*—very strongly desiring to protect their lives; *vidheyam*—something must be done; *abhayam*—safety; *hi*—indeed; *me*—by me; *etāvān*—this much; *hi*—indeed; *prabhoḥ*—of the master; *arthaḥ*—duty; *yat*—that which; *dīna-paripālanam*—to give protection to suffering humanity.

TRANSLATION

It is my duty to give protection and safety to all living entities struggling for existence. Certainly it is the duty of the master to protect his suffering dependents.

TEXT 39

प्राणैः स्वैः प्राणिनः पान्ति साधवः क्षणभङ्गुरैः ।
बद्धवैरेषु भूतेषु मोहितेष्वात्ममायया ॥३९॥

prāṇaiḥ svaiḥ prāṇinaḥ pānti
sādhavaḥ kṣaṇa-bhaṅguraiḥ
baddha-vaireṣu bhūteṣu
mohiteṣv ātma-māyayā

prāṇaiḥ—by lives; *svaiḥ*—their own; *prāṇinaḥ*—other living entities; *pānti*—protect; *sādhavaḥ*—devotees; *kṣaṇa-bhaṅguraiḥ*—temporary; *baddha-vaireṣu*—unnecessarily engaged in animosity; *bhūteṣu*—unto living entities; *mohiteṣu*—bewildered; *ātma-māyayā*—by the external energy of the Lord.

TRANSLATION

People in general, being bewildered by the illusory energy of the Supreme Personality of Godhead, are always engaged in animosity toward one another. But devotees, even at the risk of their own temporary lives, try to save them.

PURPORT

This is the characteristic of a Vaiṣṇava. *Para-duḥkha-duḥkhī:* a Vaiṣṇava is always unhappy to see the conditioned souls unhappy. Otherwise, he would have no business teaching them how to become happy. In materialistic life, people must certainly engage in activities of animosity. Materialistic life is therefore compared to *saṁsāra-dāvānala,* a blazing forest fire that automatically takes place. Lord Śiva and his followers in the *paramparā* system try to save people from this dangerous condition of materialistic life. This is the duty of devotees following the principles of Lord Śiva and belonging to the Rudra-sampradāya. There are four Vaiṣṇava *sampradāyas,* and the Rudra-sampradāya is one of them because Lord Śiva (Rudra) is the best of the Vaiṣṇavas (*vaiṣṇavānāṁ yathā śambhuḥ*). Indeed, as we shall see, Lord Śiva drank all the poison for the benefit of humanity.

TEXT 40

पुंसः कृपयतो भद्रे सर्वात्मा प्रीयते हरिः ।
प्रीते हरौ भगवति प्रीयेऽहं सचराचरः ।
तस्मादिदं गरं भुञ्जे प्रजानां स्वस्तिरस्तु मे ॥४०॥

puṁsaḥ kṛpayato bhadre
sarvātmā prīyate hariḥ
prīte harau bhagavati
prīye 'haṁ sacarācaraḥ
tasmād idaṁ garaṁ bhuñje
prajānāṁ svastir astu me

puṁsaḥ—with a person; *kṛpayataḥ*—engaged in benevolent activities; *bhadre*—O most gentle Bhavānī; *sarva-ātmā*—the Supersoul; *prīyate*—becomes pleased; *hariḥ*—the Supreme Personality of Godhead; *prīte*—because of His pleasure; *harau*—the Supreme Lord, Hari; *bhagavati*—the Personality of Godhead; *prīye*—also become pleased; *aham*—I; *sa-cara-acaraḥ*—with all others, moving and nonmoving; *tasmāt*—therefore; *idam*—this; *garam*—poison; *bhuñje*—let me drink; *prajānām*—of the living entities; *svastiḥ*—welfare; *astu*—let there be; *me*—by me.

TRANSLATION

My dear gentle wife Bhavānī, when one performs benevolent activities for others, the Supreme Personality of Godhead, Hari, is very pleased. And when the Lord is pleased, I am also pleased, along with all other living creatures. Therefore, let me drink this poison, for all the living entities may thus become happy because of me.

TEXT 41

श्रीशुक उवाच

एवमामन्त्र्य भगवान्भवानीं विश्वभावनः ।
तद् विषं जग्धुमारेभे प्रभावज्ञान्वमोदत ॥४१॥

śrī-śuka uvāca
evam āmantrya bhagavān
bhavānīṁ viśva-bhāvanaḥ
tad viṣaṁ jagdhum ārebhe
prabhāva-jñānvamodata

śrī-śukaḥ uvāca—Śrī Śukadeva Gosvāmī said; *evam*—in this way; *āmantrya*—addressing; *bhagavān*—Lord Śiva; *bhavānīm*—Bhavānī; *viśva-bhāvanaḥ*—the well-wisher of all the universe; *tat viṣam*—that poison; *jagdhum*—to drink; *ārebhe*—began; *prabhāva-jñā*—mother Bhavānī, who perfectly knew the capability of Lord Śiva; *anvamodata*—gave her permission.

TRANSLATION

Śrīla Śukadeva Gosvāmī continued: After informing Bhavānī in this way, Lord Śiva began to drink the poison, and Bhavānī, who knew perfectly well the capabilities of Lord Śiva, gave him her permission to do so.

TEXT 42

ततः करतलीकृत्य व्यापि हालाहलं विषम् ।
अभक्षयन्महादेवः कृपया भूतभावनः ॥४२॥

tataḥ karatalī-kṛtya
vyāpi hālāhalaṁ viṣam
abhakṣayan mahā-devaḥ
kṛpayā bhūta-bhāvanaḥ

tataḥ—thereafter; *karatalī-kṛtya*—taking in his hand; *vyāpi*—widespread; *hālāhalam*—called *hālahala; viṣam*—poison; *abhakṣayat*—drank; *mahā-devaḥ*—Lord Śiva; *kṛpayā*—out of compassion; *bhūta-bhāvanaḥ*—for the welfare of all living entities.

TRANSLATION

Thereafter, Lord Śiva, who is dedicated to auspicious, benevolent work for humanity, compassionately took the whole quantity of poison in his palm and drank it.

PURPORT

Although there was such a great quantity of poison that it spread all over the universe, Lord Śiva had such great power that he reduced the poison to a small quantity so that he could hold it in his palm. One should not try to imitate Lord Śiva. Lord Śiva can do whatever he likes, but those who try to imitate Lord Śiva by smoking *gañja* and other poisonous things will certainly be killed because of such activities.

TEXT 43

तस्यापि दर्शयामास स्ववीर्यं जलकल्मषः ।
यच्चकार गले नीलं तच्च साधोर्विभूषणम् ॥४३॥

tasyāpi darśayām āsa
sva-vīryaṁ jala-kalmaṣaḥ
yac cakāra gale nīlaṁ
tac ca sādhor vibhūṣaṇam

tasya—of Lord Śiva; *api*—also; *darśayām āsa*—exhibited; *sva-vīryam*—its own potency; *jala-kalmaṣaḥ*—that poison born of the water; *yat*—which; *cakāra*—made; *gale*—on the neck; *nīlam*—bluish line; *tat*—that; *ca*—also; *sādhoḥ*—of the saintly person; *vibhūṣaṇam*—ornament.

TRANSLATION

As if in defamation, the poison born from the ocean of milk manifested its potency by marking Lord Śiva's neck with a bluish line. That line, however, is now accepted as an ornament of the Lord.

TEXT 44

तप्यन्ते लोकतापेन साधवः प्रायशो जनाः ।
परमाराधनं तद्धि पुरुषस्याखिलात्मनः ॥४४॥

tapyante loka-tāpena
sādhavaḥ prāyaśo janāḥ
paramārādhanaṁ tad dhi
puruṣasyākhilātmanaḥ

tapyante—voluntarily suffer; *loka-tāpena*—because of the suffering of people in general; *sādhavaḥ*—saintly persons; *prāyaśaḥ*—almost always; *janāḥ*—such persons; *parama-ārādhanam*—the topmost method of worshiping; *tat*—that activity; *hi*—indeed; *puruṣasya*—of the Supreme Person; *akhila-ātmanaḥ*—who is the Supersoul of everyone.

TRANSLATION

It is said that great personalities almost always accept voluntary suffering because of the suffering of people in general. This is considered the highest method of worshiping the Supreme Personality of Godhead, who is present in everyone's heart.

PURPORT

Here is an explanation of how those engaged in activities for the welfare of others are very quickly recognized by the Supreme Personality of Godhead. The Lord says in *Bhagavad-gītā* (18.68–69), *ya idaṁ paramaṁ guhyaṁ mad-bhakteṣv abhidhāsyati . . . na ca tasmān manuṣyeṣu kaścin me priya-kṛttamaḥ:* "One who preaches the message of *Bhagavad-gītā* to My devotees is most dear to Me. No one can excel him in satisfying Me by worship." There are different kinds of welfare activities in this material world, but the supreme welfare activity is the spreading of Kṛṣṇa consciousness. Other welfare activities cannot be effective, for the laws of nature and the results of *karma* cannot be checked. It is by destiny, or the laws of *karma*, that one must suffer or enjoy. For instance, if one is given a court order, he must accept it, whether it brings suffering or profit. Similarly, everyone is under obligations to *karma* and it reactions. No one can change this. Therefore the *śāstra* says:

tasyaiva hetoḥ prayateta kovido
na labhyate yad bhramatām upary adhaḥ
(*Bhāg.* 1.5.18)

One should endeavor for that which is never obtained by wandering up and down the universe as a result of the reactions of *karma*. What is that? One should endeavor to become Kṛṣṇa conscious. If one tries to spread Kṛṣṇa consciousness all over the world, he should be understood to be performing the best welfare activity. The Lord is automatically very pleased with him. If the Lord is pleased with him, what is left for him to achieve? If one has been recognized by the Lord, even if he does not ask the Lord for anything, the Lord, who is within everyone, supplies him whatever he wants. This is also confirmed in *Bhagavad-gītā* (*teṣāṁ nityābhiyuktānāṁ yoga-kṣemaṁ vahāmy aham*). Again, as stated here, *tapyante loka-tāpena sādhavaḥ prāyaśo janāḥ.* The best welfare activity is raising people to the platform of Kṛṣṇa consciousness, since the conditioned souls are suffering only for want of Kṛṣṇa consciousness. The Lord Himself also comes to mitigate the suffering of humanity.

yadā yadā hi dharmasya
glānir bhavati bhārata
abhyutthānam adharmasya
tadātmānaṁ sṛjāmy aham

paritrāṇāya sādhūnāṁ
vināśāya ca duṣkṛtām
dharma-saṁsthāpanārthāya
sambhavāmi yuge yuge

"Whenever and wherever there is a decline in religious practice, O descendant of Bharata, and a predominant rise of irreligion—at that time I descend Myself. To deliver the pious and to annihilate the miscreants, as well as to reestablish the principles of religion, I advent Myself millennium after millennium." (Bg. 4.7–8) All the *śāstras* conclude, therefore, that spreading the Kṛṣṇa consciousness movement is the best welfare activity in the world. Because of the ultimate benefit this bestows upon people in general, the Lord very quickly recognizes such service performed by a devotee.

TEXT 45

निशम्य कर्म तच्छम्भोर्देवदेवस्य मीढुषः ।
प्रजा दाक्षायणी ब्रह्मा वैकुण्ठश्च शशंसिरे ॥४५॥

niśamya karma tac chambhor
deva-devasya mīḍhuṣaḥ

prajā dākṣāyaṇī brahmā
vaikuṇṭhaś ca śaśaṁsire

niśamya—after hearing; *karma*—the act; *tat*—that; *śambhoḥ*—of Lord Śiva; *deva-devasya*—who is worshipable even for the demigods; *mīḍhuṣaḥ*—he who bestows great benedictions upon people in general; *prajāḥ*—the people in general; *dākṣāyaṇī*—Bhavānī, the daughter of Dakṣa; *brahmā*—Lord Brahmā; *vaikuṇṭhaḥ ca*—Lord Viṣṇu also; *śaśaṁsire*—praised very much.

TRANSLATION

Upon hearing of this act, everyone, including Bhavānī [the daughter of Mahārāja Dakṣa], Lord Brahmā, Lord Viṣṇu, and the people in general, very highly praised this deed performed by Lord Śiva, who is worshiped by the demigods and who bestows benedictions upon the people.

TEXT 46

प्रस्कन्नं पिबतः पाणेर्यत् किञ्चिज्जगृहुः स्म तत् ।
वृश्चिकाहिविषौषध्यो दन्दशूकाश्च येऽपरे ॥४६॥

praskannaṁ pibataḥ pāṇer
yat kiñcij jagṛhuḥ sma tat
vṛścikāhi-viṣauṣadhyo
dandaśūkāś ca ye 'pare

praskannam—scattered here and there; *pibataḥ*—of Lord Śiva while drinking; *pāṇeḥ*—from the palm; *yat*—which; *kiñcit*—very little; *jagṛhuḥ*—took the opportunity to drink; *sma*—indeed; *tat*—that; *vṛścika*—the scorpions; *ahi*—the cobras; *viṣa-auṣadhyaḥ*—poisonous drugs; *dandaśūkāḥ ca*—and animals whose bites are poisonous; *ye*—who; *apare*—other living entities.

TRANSLATION

Scorpions, cobras, poisonous drugs and other animals whose bites are poisonous took the opportunity to drink whatever little

poison had fallen and scattered from Lord Śiva's hand while he was drinking.

PURPORT

Mosquitoes, jackals, dogs and other varieties of *dandaśūka*, or animals whose bites are poisonous, drank the poison of the *samudra-manthana*, the churned ocean, since it was available after it fell from the palms of Lord Śiva.

Thus end the Bhaktivedanta purports of the Eighth Canto, Seventh Chapter, of the Śrīmad-Bhāgavatam, *entitled "Lord Śiva Saves the Universe by Drinking Poison."*

CHAPTER EIGHT

The Churning of the Milk Ocean

This chapter describes how the goddess of fortune appeared during the churning of the ocean of milk and how she accepted Lord Viṣṇu as her husband. As described later in the chapter, when Dhanvantari appeared with a pot of nectar the demons immediately snatched it from him, but Lord Viṣṇu appeared as the incarnation Mohinī, the most beautiful woman in the world, just to captivate the demons and save the nectar for the demigods.

After Lord Śiva drank all the poison, both the demigods and demons took courage and resumed their activities of churning. Because of this churning, first a *surabhi* cow was produced. Great saintly persons accepted this cow to derive clarified butter from its milk and offer this clarified butter in oblations for great sacrifices. Thereafter, a horse named Uccaiḥśravā was generated. This horse was taken by Bali Mahārāja. Then there appeared Airāvata and other elephants that could go anywhere in any direction, and she-elephants also appeared. The gem known as Kaustubha was also generated, and Lord Viṣṇu took that gem and placed it on His chest. Thereafter, a *pārijāta* flower and the Apsarās, the most beautiful women in the universe, were generated. Then the goddess of fortune, Lakṣmī, appeared. The demigods, great sages, Gandharvas and others offered her their respectful worship. The goddess of fortune could not find anyone to accept as her husband. At last she selected Lord Viṣṇu to be her master. Lord Viṣṇu gave her a place to stay everlastingly at His chest. Because of this combination of Lakṣmī and Nārāyaṇa, all who were present, including the demigods and people in general, were very pleased. The demons, however, being neglected by the goddess of fortune, were very depressed. Then Vāruṇī, the goddess of drinking, was generated, and by the order of Lord Viṣṇu the demons accepted her. Then the demons and demigods, with renewed energy, began to churn again. This time a partial incarnation of Lord Viṣṇu called Dhanvantari appeared. He was very beautiful, and he carried a jug containing nectar. The demons immediately snatched the jug from

Dhanvantari's hand and began to run away, and the demigods, being very morose, took shelter of Viṣṇu. After the demons snatched the jug from Dhanvantari, they began to fight among themselves. Lord Viṣṇu solaced the demigods, who therefore did not fight, but remained silent. While the fighting was going on among the demons, the Lord Himself appeared as the incarnation Mohinī, the most beautiful woman in the universe.

TEXT 1

श्रीशुक उवाच
पीते गरे वृषाङ्केण प्रीतास्तेऽमरदानवाः ।
ममन्थुस्तरसा सिन्धुं हविर्धानी ततोऽभवत् ॥ १ ॥

śrī-śuka uvāca
pīte gare vṛṣāṅkeṇa
prītās te 'mara-dānavāḥ
mamanthus tarasā sindhuṁ
havirdhānī tato 'bhavat

śrī-śukaḥ uvāca—Śrī Śukadeva Gosvāmī said; *pīte*—was drunk; *gare*—when the poison; *vṛṣa-aṅkeṇa*—by Lord Śiva, who sits on a bull; *prītāḥ*—being pleased; *te*—all of them; *amara*—the demigods; *dānavāḥ*—and the demons; *mamanthuḥ*—again began to churn; *tarasā*—with great force; *sindhum*—the ocean of milk; *havirdhānī*—the *surabhi* cow, who is the source of clarified butter; *tataḥ*—from that churning; *abhavat*—was generated.

TRANSLATION

Śukadeva Gosvāmī continued: Upon Lord Śiva's drinking the poison, both the demigods and the demons, being very pleased, began to churn the ocean with renewed vigor. As a result of this, there appeared a cow known as surabhi.

PURPORT

The *surabhi* cow is described as *havirdhānī*, the source of butter. Butter, when clarified by melting, produces ghee, or clarified butter, which is inevitably necessary for performing great ritualistic sacrifices. As stated in *Bhagavad-gītā* (18.5), *yajña-dāna-tapaḥ-karma na tyājyaṁ kāryam eva tat:* sacrifice, charity and austerity are essential to keep human society perfect in peace and prosperity. *Yajña,* the performance of sacrifice, is essential; to perform *yajña,* clarified butter is absolutely necessary; and to get clarified butter, milk is necessary. Milk is produced when there are sufficient cows. Therefore in *Bhagavad-gītā* (18.44), cow protection is recommended (*kṛṣi-go-rakṣya-vāṇijyaṁ vaiśya-karma svabhāva-jam*).

TEXT 2

तामग्निहोत्रीमृषयो जगृहुर्ब्रह्मवादिनः ।
यज्ञस्य देवयानस्य मेध्याय हविषे नृप ॥ २ ॥

tām agni-hotrīm ṛṣayo
jagṛhur brahma-vādinaḥ
yajñasya deva-yānasya
medhyāya haviṣe nṛpa

tām—that cow; *agni-hotrīm*—absolutely necessary for the production of yogurt, milk and ghee to offer as oblations in the fire; *ṛṣayaḥ*—sages who perform such sacrifices; *jagṛhuḥ*—took in charge; *brahma-vādinaḥ*—because such sages know the Vedic ritualistic ceremonies; *yajñasya*—of sacrifice; *deva-yānasya*—which fulfills the desire to be elevated to the higher planetary systems and to Brahmaloka; *medhyāya*—fit for offering oblations; *haviṣe*—for the sake of pure clarified butter; *nṛpa*—O King.

TRANSLATION

O King Parīkṣit, great sages who were completely aware of the Vedic ritualistic ceremonies took charge of that surabhi cow, which produced all the yogurt, milk and ghee absolutely necessary for offering oblations into the fire. They did this just for the sake of pure ghee, which they wanted for the performance of sacrifices to elevate themselves to the higher planetary systems, up to Brahmaloka.

PURPORT

Surabhi cows are generally found on the Vaikuṇṭha planets. As described in *Brahma-saṁhitā,* Lord Kṛṣṇa, on His planet, Goloka Vṛndāvana, engages in tending the *surabhi* cows (*surabhīr abhipālayantam*). These cows are the Lord's pet animals. From the *surabhi* cows one can take as much milk as one needs, and one may milk these cows as many times as he desires. In other words, the *surabhi* cow can yield milk unlimitedly. Milk is necessary for the performance of *yajña.* Sages know how to use milk to elevate human society to the perfection of life. Since cow protection is recommended everywhere in the *śāstras,* the *brahmavādīs* took charge of the *surabhi* cow, in which the demons were not very interested.

TEXT 3

तत उच्चैःश्रवा नाम हयोऽभूच्चन्द्रपाण्डुरः ।
तस्मिन्बलिः स्पृहां चक्रे नेन्द्र ईश्वरशिक्षया ॥ ३ ॥

tata uccaiḥśravā nāma
hayo 'bhūc candra-pāṇḍuraḥ
tasmin baliḥ spṛhāṁ cakre
nendra īśvara-śikṣayā

tataḥ—thereafter; *uccaiḥśravāḥ nāma*—by the name Uccaiḥśravā; *hayaḥ*—a horse; *abhūt*—was generated; *candra-pāṇḍuraḥ*—being as white as the moon; *tasmin*—unto it; *baliḥ*—Mahārāja Bali; *spṛhām cakre*—desired to possess; *na*—not; *indraḥ*—the King of the demigods; *īśvara-śikṣayā*—by the previous advice of the Lord.

TRANSLATION

Thereafter, a horse named Uccaiḥśravā, which was as white as the moon, was generated. Bali Mahārāja desired to possess this horse, and Indra, the King of heaven, did not protest, for he had previously been so advised by the Supreme Personality of Godhead.

TEXT 4

तत ऐरावतो नाम वारणेन्द्रो विनिर्गतः ।
दन्तैश्चतुर्भिः श्वेताद्रेर्हरन्भगवतो महिम् ॥ ४ ॥

tata airāvato nāma
vāraṇendro vinirgataḥ
dantaiś caturbhiḥ svetādrer
haran bhagavato mahim

tataḥ—thereafter; *airāvataḥ nāma*—of the name Airāvata; *vāraṇa-indraḥ*—the king of elephants; *vinirgataḥ*—was generated; *dantaiḥ*—with its tusks; *caturbhiḥ*—four; *śveta*—white; *adreḥ*—of the mountain; *haran*—defying; *bhagavataḥ*—of Lord Śiva; *mahim*—the glories.

TRANSLATION

As the next result of the churning, the king of elephants, named Airāvata, was generated. This elephant was white, and with its four tusks it defied the glories of Kailāsa Mountain, the glorious abode of Lord Śiva.

TEXT 5

ऐरावणादयस्त्वष्टौ दिग्गजा अभवंस्ततः ।
अभ्रमुप्रभृतयोऽष्टौ च करिण्यस्त्वभवन्नृप ॥५॥

airāvaṇādayas tv aṣṭau
dig-gajā abhavaṁs tataḥ
abhramu-prabhṛtayo 'ṣṭau ca
kariṇyas tv abhavan nṛpa

airāvaṇa-ādayaḥ—headed by Airāvaṇa; *tu*—but; *aṣṭau*—eight; *dik-gajāḥ*—elephants that could go in any direction; *abhavan*—were generated; *tataḥ*—thereafter; *abhramu-prabhṛtayaḥ*—headed by the she-elephant named Abhramu; *aṣṭau*—eight; *ca*—also; *kariṇyaḥ*—female elephants; *tu*—indeed; *abhavan*—also generated; *nṛpa*—O King.

TRANSLATION

Thereafter, O King, eight great elephants, which could go in any direction, were generated. They were headed by Airāvaṇa. Eight she-elephants, headed by Abhramu, were also generated.

PURPORT

The names of the eight elephants were Airāvaṇa, Puṇḍarīka, Vāmana, Kumuda, Añjana, Puṣpadanta, Sārvabhauma and Supratīka.

TEXT 6

कौस्तुभाख्यमभूद् रत्नं पद्मरागो महोदधेः ।
तस्मिन् मणौ स्पृहां चक्रे वक्षोऽलङ्करणे हरिः ।
ततोऽभवत् पारिजातः सुरलोकविभूषणम् ।
पूरयत्यर्थिनो योऽर्थैः शश्वद् भुवि यथा भवान् ॥ ६ ॥

kaustubhākhyam abhūd ratnaṁ
padmarāgo mahodadheḥ
tasmin maṇau spṛhāṁ cakre
vakṣo-'laṅkaraṇe hariḥ
tato 'bhavat pārijātaḥ
sura-loka-vibhūṣaṇam
pūrayaty arthino yo 'rthaiḥ
śaśvad bhuvi yathā bhavān

kaustubha-ākhyam—known as Kaustubha; *abhūt*—was generated; *ratnam*—a valuable gem; *padmarāgaḥ*—another gem, named Padmarāga; *mahā-udadheḥ*—from that great ocean of milk; *tasmin*—that; *maṇau*—jewel; *spṛhām cakre*—desired to possess; *vakṣaḥ-alaṅkaraṇe*—to decorate His chest; *hariḥ*—the Lord, the Supreme Personality of Godhead; *tataḥ*—thereafter; *abhavat*—was generated; *pārijātaḥ*—the celestial flower named *pārijāta; sura-loka-vibhūṣaṇam*—which decorates the heavenly planets; *pūrayati*—fulfills; *arthinaḥ*—giving persons desiring material wealth; *yaḥ*—that which; *arthaiḥ*—by what is desired; *śaśvat*—always; *bhuvi*—on this planet; *yathā*—as; *bhavān*—Your Lordship (Mahārāja Parīkṣit).

TRANSLATION

Generated thereafter from the great ocean were the celebrated gems Kaustubha-maṇi and Padmarāga-maṇi. Lord Viṣṇu, to decorate His chest, desired to possess them. Generated next was the pārijāta flower, which decorates the celestial planets. O King, as you fulfill the desires of everyone on this planet by fulfilling all ambitions, the pārijāta fulfills the desires of everyone.

TEXT 7

ततश्चाप्सरसो जाता निष्ककण्ठ्यः सुवाससः ।
रमण्यः स्वर्गिणां वल्गुगतिलीलावलोकनैः ॥ ७ ॥

tataś cāpsaraso jātā
niṣka-kaṇṭhyaḥ suvāsasaḥ
ramaṇyaḥ svargiṇāṁ valgu-
gati-līlāvalokanaiḥ

tataḥ—thereafter; *ca*—also; *apsarasaḥ*—the residents of Apsaroloka; *jātāḥ*—were generated; *niṣka-kaṇṭhyaḥ*—decorated with golden necklaces; *su-vāsasaḥ*—dressed with fine clothing; *ramaṇyaḥ*—extremely beautiful and attractive; *svargiṇām*—of the inhabitants of the heavenly planets; *valgu-gati-līlā-avalokanaiḥ*—moving very softly, they attract everyone's heart.

TRANSLATION

Next there appeared the Apsarās [who are used as prostitutes on the heavenly planets]. They were fully decorated with golden ornaments and lockets and were dressed in fine and attractive clothing. The Apsarās move very slowly in an attractive style that bewilders the inhabitants of the heavenly planets.

TEXT 8

ततश्चाविरभूत् साक्षाच्छ्री रमा भगवत्परा ।
रञ्जयन्ती दिशः कान्त्या विद्युत् सौदामनी यथा॥८॥

tataś cāvirabhūt sākṣāc
chrī ramā bhagavat-parā
rañjayantī diśaḥ kāntyā
vidyut saudāmanī yathā

tataḥ—thereafter; *ca*—and; *āvirabhūt*—manifested; *sākṣāt*—directly; *śrī*—the goddess of fortune; *ramā*—known as Ramā; *bhagavat-parā*—absolutely inclined to be possessed by the Supreme Personality of Godhead; *rañjayantī*—illuminating; *diśaḥ*—all directions; *kāntyā*—by luster; *vidyut*—lightning; *saudāmanī*—Saudāmanī; *yathā*—as.

TRANSLATION

Then there appeared the goddess of fortune, Ramā, who is absolutely dedicated to being enjoyed by the Supreme Personality of Godhead. She appeared like electricity, surpassing the lightning that might illuminate a marble mountain.

PURPORT

Śrī means opulence. Kṛṣṇa is the owner of all opulences.

bhoktāraṁ yajña-tapasāṁ
sarva-loka-maheśvaram
suhṛdaṁ sarva-bhūtānāṁ
jñātvā māṁ śāntim ṛcchati

This peace formula for the world is given in *Bhagavad-gītā* (5.29). When people know that the Supreme Lord, Kṛṣṇa, is the supreme enjoyer, the supreme proprietor and the most intimate well-wishing friend of all living entities, peace and prosperity will ensue all over the world. Unfortunately, the conditioned souls, being placed into illusion by the external energy of the Lord, want to fight with one another, and therefore peace is disturbed. The first prerequisite for peace is that all the wealth presented by Śrī, the goddess of fortune, be offered to the Supreme Personality of Godhead. Everyone should give up his false proprietorship over worldly possessions and offer everything to Kṛṣṇa. This is the teaching of the Kṛṣṇa consciousness movement.

TEXT 9

तस्यां चक्रुः स्पृहां सर्वे ससुरासुरमानवाः ।
रूपौदार्यवयोवर्णमहिमाक्षिप्तचेतसः ॥ ९ ॥

tasyāṁ cakruḥ spṛhāṁ sarve
sasurāsura-mānavāḥ
rūpaudārya-vayo-varṇa-
mahimākṣipta-cetasaḥ

tasyām—unto her; *cakruḥ*—did; *spṛhām*—desire; *sarve*—everyone; *sa-sura-asura-mānavāḥ*—the demigods, the demons and the human beings; *rūpa-audārya*—by the exquisite beauty and bodily features; *vayaḥ*—youth; *varṇa*—complexion; *mahimā*—glories; *ākṣipta*—agitated; *cetasaḥ*—their minds.

TRANSLATION

Because of her exquisite beauty, her bodily features, her youth, her complexion and her glories, everyone, including the demigods, the demons and the human beings, desired her. They were attracted because she is the source of all opulences.

PURPORT

Who in this world does not want to possess wealth, beauty and the social respectability that come from these opulences? People generally desire material enjoyment, material opulence and the association of aristocratic family members (*bhogaiśvarya-prasaktānām*). Material enjoyment entails money, beauty and the reputation they bring, which can all be achieved by the mercy of the goddess of fortune. The goddess of fortune, however, never remains alone. As indicated in the previous verse by the word *bhagavat-parā*, she is the property of the Supreme Personality of Godhead and is enjoyable only by Him. If one wants the favor of the goddess of fortune, mother Lakṣmī, because she is by nature *bhagavat-parā* one must keep her with Nārāyaṇa. The devotees who always engage in the service of Nārāyaṇa (*nārāyaṇa-parāyaṇa*) can easily achieve the favor of the goddess of fortune without a doubt, but materialists who try to get the favor of the goddess of fortune only to possess her for personal enjoyment are frustrated. Theirs is not a good policy. The celebrated demon Rāvaṇa, for example, wanted to deprive Rāmacandra of Lakṣmī, Sītā, and thus be victorious, but the result was just the opposite. Sītā, of course, was taken by force by Lord Rāmacandra, and Rāvaṇa and his entire material empire were vanquished. The goddess of fortune is desirable for everyone, including human beings, but one should understand that the goddess of fortune is the exclusive property of the Supreme Personality of Godhead. One cannot achieve the mercy of the goddess of fortune unless one prays both to her and to the supreme enjoyer, the Personality of Godhead.

TEXT 10

तस्या आसनमानिन्ये महेन्द्रो महदद्भुतम् ।
मूर्तिमत्यः सरिच्छ्रेष्ठा हेमकुम्भैर्जलं शुचि ॥१०॥

tasyā āsanam āninye
mahendro mahad-adbhutam
mūrtimatyaḥ saric-chreṣṭhā
hema-kumbhair jalaṁ śuci

tasyāḥ—for her; *āsanam*—a sitting place; *āninye*—brought; *mahā-indraḥ*—the King of heaven, Indra; *mahat*—glorious; *adbhutam*—wonderful; *mūrti-matyaḥ*—accepting forms; *sarit-śreṣṭhāḥ*—the best of various sacred waters; *hema*—golden; *kumbhaiḥ*—with waterpots; *jalam*—water; *śuci*—pure.

TRANSLATION

The King of heaven, Indra, brought a suitable sitting place for the goddess of fortune. All the rivers of sacred water, such as the Ganges and Yamunā, personified themselves, and each of them brought pure water in golden waterpots for mother Lakṣmī, the goddess of fortune.

TEXT 11

आभिषेचनिका भूमिराहरत् सकलौषधीः ।
गावः पञ्च पवित्राणि वसन्तो मधुमाधवौ ॥११॥

ābhiṣecanikā bhūmir
āharat sakalauṣadhīḥ
gāvaḥ pañca pavitrāṇi
vasanto madhu-mādhavau

ābhiṣecanikāḥ—paraphernalia required for installing the Deity; *bhūmiḥ*—the land; *āharat*—collected; *sakala*—all kinds of; *auṣadhīḥ*—drugs and herbs; *gāvaḥ*—the cows; *pañca*—five different varieties of products from the cow, namely milk, yogurt, clarified butter, cow dung and cow urine; *pavitrāṇi*—uncontaminated; *vasantaḥ*—personified springtime; *madhu-mādhavau*—flowers and fruits produced during spring, or in the months of Caitra and Vaiśākha.

TRANSLATION

The land became a person and collected all the drugs and herbs needed for installing the Deity. The cows delivered five products, namely milk, yogurt, ghee, urine and cow dung, and spring personified collected everything produced in spring, during the months of Caitra and Vaiśākha [April and May].

PURPORT

Pañca-gavya, the five products received from the cow, namely milk, yogurt, ghee, cow dung and cow urine, are required in all ritualistic ceremonies performed according to the Vedic directions. Cow urine and cow dung are uncontaminated, and since even the urine and dung of a cow are important, we can just imagine how important this animal is for human civilization. Therefore the Supreme Personality of Godhead, Kṛṣṇa, directly advocates *go-rakṣya,* the protection of cows. Civilized men who follow the system of *varṇāśrama,* especially those of the *vaiśya* class, who engage in agriculture and trade, must give protection to the cows. Unfortunately, because people in Kali-yuga are *mandāḥ,* all bad, and *sumanda-matayaḥ*, misled by false conceptions of life, they are killing cows in the thousands. Therefore they are unfortunate in spiritual consciousness, and nature disturbs them in so many ways, especially through incurable diseases like cancer and through frequent wars and among nations. As long as human society continues to allow cows to be regularly killed in slaughterhouses, there cannot be any question of peace and prosperity.

TEXT 12

ऋषयः कल्पयाञ्चक्रुराभिषेकं यथाविधि ।
जगुर्भद्राणि गन्धर्वा नट्यश्च ननृतुर्जगुः ॥१२॥

ṛṣayaḥ kalpayāṁ cakrur
ābhiṣekaṁ yathā-vidhi
jagur bhadrāṇi gandharvā
naṭyaś ca nanṛtur jaguḥ

ṛṣayaḥ—the great sages; *kalpayām cakruḥ*—executed; *ābhiṣekam*—the *abhiṣeka* ceremony, which is required during the installation of the Deity; *yathā-vidhi*—as directed in the authorized scriptures; *jaguḥ*—chanted Vedic *mantras; bhadrāṇi*—all good fortune; *gandharvāḥ*—and the inhabitants of Gandharvaloka; *naṭyaḥ*—the women who were professional dancers; *ca*—also; *nanṛtuḥ*—very nicely danced on the occasion; *jaguḥ*—and sang authorized songs prescribed in the *Vedas.*

TRANSLATION

The great sages performed the bathing ceremony of the goddess of fortune as directed in the authorized scriptures, the Gandharvas chanted all-auspicious Vedic mantras, and the professional women dancers very nicely danced and sang authorized songs prescribed in the Vedas.

TEXT 13

मेघा मृदङ्गपणवमुरजानकगोमुखान् ।
व्यनादयन् शङ्खवेणुवीणास्तुमुलनिःस्वनान् ॥१३॥

meghā mṛdaṅga-paṇava-
murajānaka-gomukhān
vyanādayan śaṅkha-veṇu-
vīṇās tumula-niḥsvanān

meghāḥ—personified clouds; *mṛdaṅga*—drums; *paṇava*—kettledrums; *muraja*—another kind of drum; *ānaka*—another type of drum; *gomukhān*—a type of bugle; *vyanādayan*—vibrated; *śaṅkha*—conchshells; *veṇu*—flutes; *vīṇāḥ*—stringed instruments; *tumula*—tumultuous; *niḥsvanān*—vibration.

TRANSLATION

The clouds in personified form beat various types of drums, known as mṛdaṅgas, paṇavas, murajas and ānakas. They also blew conchshells and bugles known as gomukhas and played flutes and stringed instruments. The combined sound of these instruments was tumultuous.

TEXT 14

ततोऽभिषिषिचुर्देवीं श्रियं पद्मकरां सतीम् ।
दिगिभाः पूर्णकलशैः सूक्तवाक्यैर्द्विजेरितैः ॥१४॥

tato 'bhiṣiṣicur devīṁ
śriyaṁ padma-karāṁ satīm
digibhāḥ pūrṇa-kalaśaiḥ
sūkta-vākyair dvijeritaiḥ

tataḥ—thereafter; *abhiṣiṣicuḥ*—poured all-auspicious water on the body; *devīm*—the goddess of fortune; *śriyam*—very beautiful; *padma-karām*—with a lotus in her hand; *satīm*—she who is most chaste, not knowing anyone but the Supreme Personality of Godhead; *digibhāḥ*—the great elephants; *pūrṇa-kalaśaiḥ*—by completely full waterjugs; *sūkta-vākyaiḥ*—with Vedic *mantras; dvi-ja*—by *brāhmaṇas; īritaiḥ*—chanted.

TRANSLATION

Thereafter, the great elephants from all the directions carried big water jugs full of Ganges water and bathed the goddess of

fortune, to the accompaniment of Vedic mantras chanted by learned brāhmaṇas. While thus being bathed, the goddess of fortune maintained her original style, with a lotus flower in her hand, and she appeared very beautiful. The goddess of fortune is the most chaste, for she does not know anyone but the Supreme Personality of Godhead.

PURPORT

The goddess of fortune, Lakṣmī, is described in this verse as *śriyam*, which means that she has six opulences—wealth, strength, influence, beauty, knowledge and renunciation. These opulences are received from the goddess of fortune. Lakṣmī is addressed here as *devī*, the goddess, because in Vaikuṇṭha she supplies all opulences to the Supreme Personality of Godhead and His devotees, who in this way enjoy natural life in the Vaikuṇṭha planets. The Supreme Personality of Godhead is pleased with His consort, the goddess of fortune, who carries a lotus flower in her hand. Mother Lakṣmī is described in this verse as *satī*, the supremely chaste, because she never diverts her attention from the Supreme Personality of Godhead to anyone else.

TEXT 15

समुद्रः पीतकौशेयवाससी समुपाहरत् ।
वरुणः स्रजं वैजयन्तीं मधुना मत्तषट्पदाम् ॥१५॥

samudraḥ pīta-kauśeya-
vāsasī samupāharat
varuṇaḥ srajaṁ vaijayantīṁ
madhunā matta-ṣaṭpadām

samudraḥ—the ocean; *pīta-kauśeya*—yellow silk; *vāsasī*—both the upper and lower portions of a garment; *samupāharat*—presented; *varuṇaḥ*—the predominating deity of the water; *srajam*—garland; *vaijayantīm*—the most decorated and the biggest; *madhunā*—with honey; *matta*—drunken; *ṣaṭ-padām*—bumblebees, which have six legs.

TRANSLATION

The ocean, which is the source of all valuable jewels, supplied the upper and lower portions of a yellow silken garment. The predominating deity of the water, Varuṇa, presented flower garlands surrounded by six-legged bumblebees, drunken with honey.

PURPORT

When bathing the Deity in the *abhiṣeka* ceremony with various liquids, such as milk, honey, yogurt, ghee, cow dung and cow urine, it is customary to supply yellow garments. In this way the *abhiṣeka* ceremony for the goddess of fortune was performed according to the regular Vedic principles.

TEXT 16

भूषणानि विचित्राणि विश्वकर्मा प्रजापतिः ।
हारं सरस्वती पद्ममजो नागाश्च कुण्डले ॥१६॥

bhūṣaṇāni vicitrāṇi
viśvakarmā prajāpatiḥ
hāraṁ sarasvatī padmam
ajo nāgāś ca kuṇḍale

bhūṣaṇāni—varieties of ornaments; *vicitrāṇi*—all very nicely decorated; *viśvakarmā prajāpatiḥ*—Viśvakarmā, one of the *prajāpatis*, the sons of Lord Brahmā who generate progeny; *hāram*—garland or necklace; *sarasvatī*—the goddess of education; *padmam*—a lotus flower; *ajaḥ*—Lord Brahmā; *nāgāḥ ca*—the inhabitants of Nāgaloka; *kuṇḍale*—two earrings.

TRANSLATION

Viśvakarmā, one of the prajāpatis, supplied varieties of decorated ornaments. The goddess of learning, Sarasvatī, supplied a necklace, Lord Brahmā supplied a lotus flower, and the inhabitants of Nāgaloka supplied earrings.

TEXT 17

ततः कृतस्वस्त्ययनोत्पलस्रजं
नदद्द्विरेफां परिगृह्य पाणिना ।
चचाल वक्त्रं सुकपोलकुण्डलं
सव्रीडहासं दधती सुशोभनम् ॥१७॥

tataḥ kṛta-svastyayanotpala-srajaṁ
nadad-dvirephāṁ parigṛhya pāṇinā
cacāla vaktraṁ sukapola-kuṇḍalaṁ
savrīḍa-hāsaṁ dadhatī suśobhanam

tataḥ—thereafter; *kṛta-svastyayanā*—being worshiped regularly by all-auspicious ritualistic ceremonies; *utpala-srajam*—a garland of lotuses; *nadat*—humming; *dvirephām*—surrounded by bumblebees; *parigṛhya*—capturing; *pāṇinā*—by the hand; *cacāla*—went on; *vaktram*—face; *su-kapola-kuṇḍalam*—her cheeks decorated with earrings; *sa-vrīḍa-hāsam*—smiling with shyness; *dadhatī*—expanding; *su-śobhanam*—her natural beauty.

TRANSLATION

Thereafter, mother Lakṣmī, the goddess of fortune, having been properly celebrated with an auspicious ritualistic ceremony, began moving about, holding in her hand a garland of lotus flowers, which were surrounded by humming bumblebees. Smiling with shyness, her cheeks decorated by her earrings, she looked extremely beautiful.

PURPORT

The goddess of fortune, mother Lakṣmījī, accepted the ocean of milk as her father, but she perpetually rests on the bosom of Nārāyaṇa. She offers benedictions even to Lord Brahmā and other living entities in this material world, yet she is transcendental to all material qualities. Although she appeared to have been born of the ocean of milk, she immediately resorted to her eternal place on the bosom of Nārāyaṇa.

TEXT 18

स्तनद्वयं चातिकृशोदरी समं
निरन्तरं चन्दनकुङ्कुमोक्षितम् ।
ततस्ततो नूपुरवल्गुशिञ्जितै-
र्विसर्पती हेमलतेव सा बभौ ॥१८॥

stana-dvayaṁ cātikṛśodarī samaṁ
nirantaraṁ candana-kuṅkumokṣitam
tatas tato nūpura-valgu śiñjitair
visarpatī hema-lateva sā babhau

stana-dvayam—her two breasts; *ca*—also; *ati-kṛśa-udarī*—the middle portion of her body being very thin; *samam*—equally; *nirantaram*—constantly; *candana-kuṅkuma*—with sandalwood pulp and *kuṅkuma*, a reddish powder; *ukṣitam*—smeared; *tataḥ tataḥ*—here and there; *nūpura*—of ankle bells; *valgu*—very beautiful; *śiñjitaiḥ*—with the light resounding; *visarpatī*—walking; *hema-latā*—a golden creeper; *iva*—exactly like; *sā*—the goddess of fortune; *babhau*—appeared.

TRANSLATION

Her two breasts, which were symmetrical and nicely situated, were covered with sandalwood pulp and kuṅkuma powder, and her waist was very thin. As she walked here and there, her ankle bells jingling softly, she appeared like a creeper of gold.

TEXT 19

विलोकयन्ती निरवद्यमात्मनः
पदं ध्रुवं चाव्यभिचारिसद्गुणम् ।
गन्धर्वसिद्धासुरयक्षचारण-
त्रैपिष्टपेयादिषु नान्वविन्दत ॥१९॥

vilokayantī niravadyam ātmanaḥ
padaṁ dhruvaṁ cāvyabhicāri-sad-guṇam

gandharva-siddhāsura-yakṣa-cāraṇa-
traipiṣṭapeyādiṣu nānvavindata

vilokayantī—observing, examining; *niravadyam*—without any fault; *ātmanaḥ*—for herself; *padam*—position; *dhruvam*—eternal; *ca*—also; *avyabhicāri-sat-guṇam*—without any change of qualities; *gandharva*—among the inhabitants of Gandharvaloka; *siddha*—the inhabitants of Siddhaloka; *asura*—the demons; *yakṣa*—the Yakṣas; *cāraṇa*—the inhabitants of Cāraṇaloka; *traipiṣṭapeya-ādiṣu*—and among the demigods; *na*—not; *anvavindata*—could accept any one of them.

TRANSLATION

While walking among the Gandharvas, Yakṣas, asuras, Siddhas, Cāraṇas and denizens of heaven, Lakṣmīdevī, the goddess of fortune, was scrutinizingly examining them, but she could not find anyone naturally endowed with all good qualities. None of them was devoid of faults, and therefore she could not take shelter of any of them.

PURPORT

The goddess of fortune, Lakṣmīdevī, having been generated from the ocean of milk, was the daughter of the ocean. Thus she was allowed to select her own husband in a *svayaṁvara* ceremony. She examined every one of the candidates, but she could not find anyone suitably qualified to be her shelter. In other words, Nārāyaṇa, the natural husband of Lakṣmī, cannot be superseded by anyone in this material world.

TEXT 20

नूनं तपो यस्य न मन्युनिर्जयो
ज्ञानं क्वचित् तच्च न सङ्गवर्जितम् ।
कश्चिन्महांस्तस्य न कामनिर्जयः
स ईश्वरः किं परतोव्यपाश्रयः ॥२०॥

nūnaṁ tapo yasya na manyu-nirjayo
jñānaṁ kvacit tac ca na saṅga-varjitam

kaśin mahāṁs tasya na kāma-nirjayaḥ
sa īśvaraḥ kiṁ parato vyapāśrayaḥ

nūnam—certainly; *tapaḥ*—austerity; *yasya*—of someone; *na*—not; *manyu*—anger; *nirjayaḥ*—conquered; *jñānam*—knowledge; *kvacit*—in some saintly person; *tat*—that; *ca*—also; *na*—not; *saṅga-varjitam*—without the contamination of association; *kaścit*—someone; *mahān*—a very great exalted person; *tasya*—his; *na*—not; *kāma*—material desires; *nirjayaḥ*—conquered; *saḥ*—such a person; *īśvaraḥ*—controller; *kim*—how can he be; *parataḥ*—of others; *vyapāśrayaḥ*—under the control.

TRANSLATION

The goddess of fortune, examining the assembly, thought in this way: Someone who has undergone great austerity has not yet conquered anger. Someone possesses knowledge, but he has not conquered material desires. Someone is a very great personality, but he cannot conquer lusty desires. Even a great personality depends on something else. How, then, can he be the supreme controller?

PURPORT

Here is an attempt to find the supreme controller, or *īśvara.* Everyone may be accepted as an *īśvara,* or controller, but still such controllers are controlled by others. For example, one may have undergone severe austerities but still be under the control of anger. By a scrutinizing analysis, we find that everyone is controlled by something else. No one, therefore, can be the true controller but the Supreme Personality of Godhead, Kṛṣṇa. This is supported by the *śāstras. Īśvaraḥ paramaḥ kṛṣṇaḥ:* the supreme controller is Kṛṣṇa. Kṛṣṇa is never controlled by anyone, for He is the controller of everyone (*sarva-kāraṇa-kāraṇam*).

TEXT 21

धर्मः क्वचित् तत्र न भूतसौहृदं
त्यागः क्वचित् तत्र न मुक्तिकारणम्।

वीर्यं न पुंसोऽस्त्यजवेगनिष्कृतं
न हि द्वितीयो गुणसङ्गवर्जितः ॥२१॥

dharmaḥ kvacit tatra na bhūta-sauhṛdaṁ
tyāgaḥ kvacit tatra na mukti-kāraṇam
vīryaṁ na puṁso 'sty aja-vega-niṣkṛtaṁ
na hi dvitīyo guṇa-saṅga-varjitaḥ

dharmaḥ—religion; *kvacit*—one may have full knowledge of; *tatra*—therein; *na*—not; *bhūta-sauhṛdam*—friendship with other living entities; *tyāgaḥ*—renunciation; *kvacit*—one may possess; *tatra*—therein; *na*—not; *mukti-kāraṇam*—the cause of liberation; *vīryam*—power; *na*—not; *puṁsaḥ*—of any person; *asti*—there may be; *aja-vega-niṣkṛtam*—no release from the power of time; *na*—nor; *hi*—indeed; *dvitīyaḥ*—the second one; *guṇa-saṅga-varjitaḥ*—completely freed from the contamination of the modes of nature.

TRANSLATION

Someone may possess full knowledge of religion but still not be kind to all living entities. In someone, whether human or demigod, there may be renunciation, but that is not the cause of liberation. Someone may possess great power and yet be unable to check the power of eternal time. Someone else may have renounced attachment to the material world, yet he cannot compare to the Supreme Personality of Godhead. Therefore, no one is completely freed from the influence of the material modes of nature.

PURPORT

The statement *dharmaḥ kvacit tatra na bhūta-sauhṛdam* is very important in this verse. We actually see that there are many Hindus, Muslims, Christians, Buddhists and religionists of other cults who adhere to their religious principles very nicely but are not equal to all living entities. Indeed, although they profess to be very religious, they kill poor animals. Such religion has no meaning. *Śrīmad-Bhāgavatam* (1.2.8) says:

dharmaḥ svanuṣṭhitaḥ puṁsāṁ
viṣvaksena-kathāsu yaḥ
notpādayed yadi ratiṁ
śrama eva hi kevalam

One may be very expert in following the religious principles of his own sect, but if he has no tendency to love the Supreme Personality of Godhead, his observance of religious principles is simply a waste of time. One must develop a sense of loving Vāsudeva (*vāsudevaḥ sarvam iti sa mahātmā sudurlabhaḥ*). The sign of a devotee is that he is a friend to everyone (*suhṛdaṁ sarva-bhūtānām*). A devotee will never allow a poor animal to be killed in the name of religion. This is the difference between a superficially religious person and a devotee of the Supreme Personality of Godhead.

We find that there have been many great heroes in history, but they could not escape from the cruel hands of death. Even the greatest hero cannot escape from the ruling power of the Supreme Personality of Godhead when Kṛṣṇa comes as death. That is described by Kṛṣṇa Himself: *mṛtyuḥ sarva-haraś cāham.* The Lord, appearing as death, takes away a hero's so-called power. Even Hiraṇyakaśipu could not be saved when Nṛsiṁhadeva appeared before him as death. One's material strength is nothing before the strength of the Supreme Personality of Godhead.

TEXT 22

क्वचिच्चिरायुर्न हि शीलमङ्गलं
क्वचित् तदप्यस्ति न वेद्यमायुषः ।
यत्रोभयं कुत्र च सोऽप्यमङ्गलः
सुमङ्गलः कश्च न काङ्क्षते हि माम् ॥२२॥

kvacic cirāyur na hi śīla-maṅgalaṁ
kvacit tad apy asti na vedyam āyuṣaḥ
yatrobhayaṁ kutra ca so 'py amaṅgalaḥ
sumaṅgalaḥ kaśca na kāṅkṣate hi mām

kvacit—someone; *cira-āyuḥ*—has a long duration of life; *na*—not; *hi*—indeed; *śīla-maṅgalam*—good behavior or auspiciousness; *kvacit*—

someone; *tat api*—although possessing good behavior; *asti*—is; *na*—not; *vedyam āyuṣaḥ*—aware of the duration of life; *yatra ubhayam*—if there are both (behavior and auspiciousness); *kutra*—somewhere; *ca*—also; *saḥ*—that person; *api*—although; *amaṅgalaḥ*—a little inauspicious in some other detail; *su-maṅgalaḥ*—auspicious in every respect; *kaśca*—someone; *na*—not; *kāṅkṣate*—desires; *hi*—indeed; *mām*—me.

TRANSLATION

Someone may have longevity but not have auspiciousness or good behavior. Someone may have both auspiciousness and good behavior, but the duration of his life is not fixed. Although such demigods as Lord Śiva have eternal life, they have inauspicious habits like living in crematoriums. And even if others are well qualified in all respects, they are not devotees of the Supreme Personality of Godhead.

TEXT 23

एवं विमृश्याव्यभिचारिसद्गुणै-
वरं निजैकाश्रयतयागुणाश्रयम् ।
वव्रे वरं सर्वगुणैरपेक्षितं
रमा मुकुन्दं निरपेक्षमीप्सितम् ॥२३॥

evaṁ vimṛśyāvyabhicāri-sad-guṇair
varaṁ nijaikāśrayatayāguṇāśrayam
vavre varaṁ sarva-guṇair apekṣitaṁ
ramā mukundaṁ nirapekṣam īpsitam

evam—in this way; *vimṛśya*—after full deliberation; *avyabhicāri-sat-guṇaiḥ*—with extraordinary transcendental qualities; *varam*—superior; *nija-eka-āśrayatayā*—because of possessing all good qualities without depending on others; *aguṇa-āśrayam*—the reservoir of all transcendental qualities; *vavre*—accepted; *varam*—as a bridegroom; *sarva-guṇaiḥ*—with all transcendental qualities; *apekṣitam*—qualified; *ramā*—the goddess of fortune; *mukundam*—unto Mukunda; *nirapekṣam*—although He did not wait for her; *īpsitam*—the most desirable.

TRANSLATION

Śukadeva Gosvāmī continued: In this way, after full deliberation, the goddess of fortune accepted Mukunda as her husband because although He is independent and not in want of her, He possesses all transcendental qualities and mystic powers and is therefore the most desirable.

PURPORT

The Supreme Personality of Godhead, Mukunda, is self-sufficient. Since He is fully independent, He was not in want of the support or association of Lakṣmīdevī. Nonetheless, Lakṣmīdevī, the goddess of fortune, accepted Him as her husband.

TEXT 24

तस्यांसदेश उशतीं नवकञ्जमालां
माद्यन्मधुव्रतवरूथगिरोपघुष्टाम् ।
तस्थौ निधाय निकटे तदुरः स्वधाम
सव्रीडहासविकसन्नयनेन याता ॥२४॥

tasyāṁsa-deśa uśatīṁ nava-kañja-mālāṁ
mādyan-madhuvrata-varūtha-giropaghuṣṭām
tasthau nidhāya nikaṭe tad-uraḥ sva-dhāma
savrīḍa-hāsa-vikasan-nayanena yātā

tasya—of Him (the Supreme Personality of Godhead); *aṁsa-deśe*—on the shoulders; *uśatīm*—very beautiful; *nava*—new; *kañja-mālām*—garland of lotus flowers; *mādyat*—maddened; *madhuvrata-varūtha*—of bumblebees; *girā*—with the vibrating; *upaghuṣṭām*—surrounded by their humming; *tasthau*—remained; *nidhāya*—after placing the garland; *nikaṭe*—nearby; *tat-uraḥ*—the bosom of the Lord; *sva-dhāma*—her real resort; *sa-vrīḍa-hāsa*—smiling with shyness; *vikasat*—glittering; *nayanena*—with the eyes; *yātā*—so situated.

TRANSLATION

Approaching the Supreme Personality of Godhead, the goddess of fortune placed upon His shoulders the garland of newly grown

lotus flowers, which was surrounded by humming bumblebees searching for honey. Then, expecting to get a place on the bosom of the Lord, she remained standing by His side, her face smiling in shyness.

TEXT 25

तस्याः श्रियस्त्रिजगतो जनको जनन्या
वक्षोनिवासमकरोत् परमं विभूतेः ।
श्रीः स्वाः प्रजाः सकरुणेन निरीक्षणेन
यत्र स्थितैधयत साधिपतींस्त्रिलोकान् ॥२५॥

tasyāḥ śriyas tri-jagato janako jananyā
vakṣo nivāsam akarot paramaṁ vibhūteḥ
śrīḥ svāḥ prajāḥ sakaruṇena nirīkṣaṇena
yatra sthitaidhayata sādhipatīṁs tri-lokān

tasyāḥ—of her; *śriyaḥ*—the goddess of fortune; *tri-jagataḥ*—of the three worlds; *janakaḥ*—the father; *jananyāḥ*—of the mother; *vakṣaḥ*—bosom; *nivāsam*—residence; *akarot*—made; *paramam*—supreme; *vibhūteḥ*—of the opulent; *śrīḥ*—the goddess of fortune; *svāḥ*—own; *prajāḥ*—descendants; *sa-karuṇena*—with favorable mercy; *nir-īkṣaṇena*—by glancing over; *yatra*—wherein; *sthitā*—staying; *aidhayata*—increased; *sa-adhipatīn*—with the great directors and leaders; *tri-lokān*—the three worlds.

TRANSLATION

The Supreme Personality of Godhead is the father of the three worlds, and His bosom is the residence of mother Lakṣmī, the goddess of fortune, the proprietor of all opulences. The goddess of fortune, by her favorable and merciful glance, can increase the opulence of the three worlds, along with their inhabitants and their directors, the demigods.

PURPORT

According to the desire of Lakṣmīdevī, the goddess of fortune, the Supreme Personality of Godhead made His bosom her residence so that by her glance she could favor everyone, including the demigods and ordinary human beings. In other words, since the goddess of fortune stays on the bosom of Nārāyaṇa, she naturally sees any devotee who worships Nārāyaṇa. When the goddess of fortune understands that a devotee is in favor of devotional service to Nārāyaṇa, she is naturally inclined to bless the devotee with all opulences. The *karmīs* try to receive the favor and mercy of Lakṣmī, but because they are not devotees of Nārāyaṇa, their opulence is flickering. The opulence of devotees who are attached to the service of Nārāyaṇa is not like the opulence of *karmīs*. The opulence of devotees is as permanent as the opulence of Nārāyaṇa Himself.

TEXT 26

शङ्खतूर्यमृदङ्गानां वादित्राणां पृथुः स्वनः ।
देवानुगानां सस्त्रीणां नृत्यतां गायतामभूत् ॥२६॥

śaṅkha-tūrya-mṛdaṅgānāṁ
vāditrāṇāṁ pṛthuḥ svanaḥ
devānugānāṁ sastrīṇāṁ
nṛtyatāṁ gāyatām abhūt

śaṅkha—conchshells; *tūrya*—bugles; *mṛdaṅgānām*—and of different types of drums; *vāditrāṇām*—of the musical instruments; *pṛthuḥ*—very great; *svanaḥ*—sound; *deva-anugānām*—the inhabitants of the upper planets like the Gandharvas and Cāraṇas, who follow the demigods; *sa-strīṇām*—as along with their own wives; *nṛtyatām*—engaged in dancing; *gāyatām*—singing; *abhūt*—became.

TRANSLATION

The inhabitants of Gandharvaloka and Cāraṇaloka then took the opportunity to play their musical instruments, such as conchshells, bugles and drums. They began dancing and singing along with their wives.

TEXT 27

ब्रह्मरुद्राङ्गिरोमुख्याः सर्वे विश्वसृजो विभुम् ।
ईडिरेऽवितथैर्मन्त्रैस्तल्लिङ्गैः पुष्पवर्षिणः ॥२७॥

brahma-rudrāṅgiro-mukhyāḥ
sarve viśva-sṛjo vibhum
īḍire 'vitathair mantrais
tal-liṅgaiḥ puṣpa-varṣiṇaḥ

brahma—Lord Brahmā; *rudra*—Lord Śiva; *aṅgiraḥ*—the great sage Aṅgirā Muni; *mukhyāḥ*—headed by; *sarve*—all of them; *viśva-sṛjaḥ*—the directors of universal management; *vibhum*—the very great personality; *īḍire*—worshiped; *avitathaiḥ*—real; *mantraiḥ*—by chanting; *tat-liṅgaiḥ*—worshiping the Supreme Personality of Godhead; *puṣpa-varṣiṇaḥ*—throwing flowers like showers.

TRANSLATION

Lord Brahmā, Lord Śiva, the great sage Aṅgirā, and similar directors of universal management showered flowers and chanted mantras indicating the transcendental glories of the Supreme Personality of Godhead.

TEXT 28

श्रियावलोकिता देवाः सप्रजापतयः प्रजाः ।
शीलादिगुणसम्पन्ना लेभिरे निर्वृतिं पराम् ॥२८॥

śriyāvalokitā devāḥ
saprajāpatayaḥ prajāḥ
śīlādi-guṇa-sampannā
lebhire nirvṛtiṁ parām

śriyā—by the goddess of fortune, Lakṣmī; *avalokitāḥ*—being seen favorably with mercy; *devāḥ*—all the demigods; *sa-prajāpatayaḥ*—with all the *prajāpatis; prajāḥ*—and their generations; *śīla-ādi-guṇa-sampannāḥ*—all blessed with good behavior and good characteristics; *lebhire*—achieved; *nirvṛtim*—satisfaction; *parām*—the ultimate.

TRANSLATION

All the demigods, along with the prajāpatis and their descendants, being blessed by Lakṣmījī's glance upon them, were im-

mediately enriched with good behavior and transcendental qualities. Thus they were very much satisfied.

TEXT 29

निःसत्त्वा लोलुपा राजन् निरुद्योगा गतत्रपाः ।
यदा चोपेक्षिता लक्ष्म्या बभूवुर्दैत्यदानवाः ॥२९॥

niḥsattvā lolupā rājan
nirudyogā gata-trapāḥ
yadā copekṣitā lakṣmyā
babhūvur daitya-dānavāḥ

niḥsattvāḥ—without strength; *lolupāḥ*—very greedy; *rājan*—O King; *nirudyogāḥ*—frustrated; *gata-trapāḥ*—shameless; *yadā*—when; *ca*—also; *upekṣitāḥ*—neglected; *lakṣmyā*—by the goddess of fortune; *babhūvuḥ*—they became; *daitya-dānavāḥ*—the demons and Rākṣasas.

TRANSLATION

O King, because of being neglected by the goddess of fortune, the demons and Rākṣasas were depressed, bewildered and frustrated, and thus they became shameless.

TEXT 30

अथासीद् वारुणी देवी कन्या कमललोचना ।
असुरा जगृहुस्तां वै हरेरनुमतेन ते ॥३०॥

athāsīd vāruṇī devī
kanyā kamala-locanā
asurā jagṛhus tāṁ vai
harer anumatena te

atha—thereafter (after the appearance of the goddess of fortune); *āsīt*—there was; *vāruṇī*—Vāruṇī; *devī*—the demigoddess who controls drunkards; *kanyā*—a young girl; *kamala-locanā*—lotus-eyed; *asurāḥ*—the demons; *jagṛhuḥ*—accepted; *tām*—her; *vai*—indeed;

hareḥ—of the Supreme Personality of Godhead; *anumatena*—by the order; *te*—they (the demons).

TRANSLATION

Next appeared Vāruṇī, the lotus-eyed goddess who controls drunkards. With the permission of the Supreme Personality of Godhead, Kṛṣṇa, the demons, headed by Bali Mahārāja, took possession of this young girl.

TEXT 31

अथोदधेर्मथ्यमानात् काश्यपैरमृतार्थिभिः ।
उदतिष्ठन्महाराज पुरुषः परमाद्भुतः ॥३१॥

athodadher mathyamānāt
kāśyapair amṛtārthibhiḥ
udatiṣṭhan mahārāja
puruṣaḥ paramādbhutaḥ

atha—thereafter; *udadheḥ*—from the ocean of milk; *mathyamānāt*—while being churned; *kāśyapaiḥ*—by the sons of Kaśyapa, namely the demigods and the demons; *amṛta-arthibhiḥ*—anxious to get nectar from the churning; *udatiṣṭhat*—there appeared; *mahārāja*—O King; *puruṣaḥ*—a male person; *parama*—highly; *adbhutaḥ*—wonderful.

TRANSLATION

O King, thereafter, while the sons of Kaśyapa, both demons and demigods, were engaged in churning the ocean of milk, a very wonderful male person appeared.

TEXT 32

दीर्घपीवरदोर्दण्डः कम्बुग्रीवोऽरुणेक्षणः ।
श्यामलस्तरुणः स्रग्वी सर्वाभरणभूषितः ॥३२॥

dīrgha-pīvara-dor-daṇḍaḥ
kambu-grīvo 'ruṇekṣaṇaḥ
śyāmalas taruṇaḥ sragvī
sarvābharaṇa-bhūṣitaḥ

dīrgha—long; *pīvara*—stout and strong; *doḥ-daṇḍaḥ*—the arms; *kambu*—like a conchshell; *grīvaḥ*—the neck; *aruṇa-īkṣaṇaḥ*—reddish eyes; *śyāmalaḥ*—blackish complexion; *taruṇaḥ*—very young; *sragvī*—wearing a flower garland; *sarva*—all; *ābharaṇa*—with ornaments; *bhūṣitaḥ*—decorated.

TRANSLATION

He was strongly built; his arms were long, stout and strong; his neck, which was marked with three lines, resembled a conchshell; his eyes were reddish; and his complexion was blackish. He was very young, he was garlanded with flowers, and his entire body was fully decorated with various ornaments.

TEXT 33

पीतवासा महोरस्कः सुमृष्टमणिकुण्डलः ।
स्निग्धकुञ्चितकेशान्तसुभगः सिंहविक्रमः ।
अमृतापूर्णकलसं बिभ्रद् वलयभूषितः ॥३३॥

pīta-vāsā mahoraskaḥ
sumṛṣṭa-maṇi-kuṇḍalaḥ
snigdha-kuñcita-keśānta-
subhagaḥ siṁha-vikramaḥ
amṛtāpūrṇa-kalasaṁ
bibhrad valaya-bhūṣitaḥ

pīta-vāsāḥ—wearing yellow garments; *mahā-uraskaḥ*—his chest very broad; *su-mṛṣṭa-maṇi-kuṇḍalaḥ*—whose earrings were well polished and made of pearls; *snigdha*—polished; *kuñcita-keśa*—curling hair; *anta*—at the end; *su-bhagaḥ*—separated and beautiful; *siṁha-vikramaḥ*—strong like a lion; *amṛta*—with nectar; *āpūrṇa*—filled to the top; *kalasam*—a jar; *bibhrat*—moving; *valaya*—with bangles; *bhūṣitaḥ*—decorated.

TRANSLATION

He was dressed in yellow garments and wore brightly polished earrings made of pearls. The tips of his hair were anointed with oil, and his chest was very broad. His body had all good features, he was stout and strong like a lion, and he was decorated with bangles. In his hand he carried a jug filled to the top with nectar.

TEXT 34

स वै भगवतः साक्षाद्विष्णोरंशांशसम्भवः ।
धन्वन्तरिरिति ख्यात आयुर्वेददृगिज्यभाक् ॥३४॥

sa vai bhagavataḥ sākṣād
viṣṇor aṁśāṁśa-sambhavaḥ
dhanvantarir iti khyāta
āyur-veda-dṛg ijya-bhāk

saḥ—he; *vai*—indeed; *bhagavataḥ*—of the Supreme Personality of Godhead; *sākṣāt*—directly; *viṣṇoḥ*—of Lord Viṣṇu; *aṁśa-aṁśa-sambhavaḥ*—incarnation of the plenary portion of a plenary portion; *dhanvantariḥ*—Dhanvantari; *iti*—thus; *khyātaḥ*—celebrated; *āyuḥ-veda-dṛk*—fully conversant in the medical science; *ijya-bhāk*—one of the demigods eligible to share the benefits of sacrifices.

TRANSLATION

This person was Dhanvantari, a plenary portion of a plenary portion of Lord Viṣṇu. He was very conversant with the science of medicine, and as one of the demigods he was permitted to take a share in sacrifices.

PURPORT

Śrīla Madhvācārya remarks:

teṣāṁ satyāc cālanārthaṁ
harir dhanvantarir vibhuḥ

samartho 'py asurāṇāṁ tu
sva-hastād amucat sudhām

Dhanvantari, who was carrying the jug containing nectar, was a plenary incarnation of the Supreme Personality of Godhead, but although he was very strong, the *asuras* were able to take the jug of nectar from his hands.

TEXT 35

तमालोक्यासुराः सर्वे कलसं चामृताभृतम् ।
लिप्सन्तः सर्ववस्तूनि कलसं तरसाहरन् ॥३५॥

tam ālokyāsurāḥ sarve
kalasaṁ cāmṛtābhṛtam
lipsantaḥ sarva-vastūni
kalasaṁ tarasāharan

tam—him; *ālokya*—seeing; *asurāḥ*—the demons; *sarve*—all of them; *kalasam*—the container of nectar; *ca*—also; *amṛta-ābhṛtam*—filled with nectar; *lipsantaḥ*—desiring strongly; *sarva-vastūni*—all objects; *kalasam*—the jug; *tarasā*—immediately; *aharan*—snatched away.

TRANSLATION

Upon seeing Dhanvantari carrying the jug of nectar, the demons, desiring the jug and its contents, immediately snatched it away by force.

TEXT 36

नीयमानेऽसुरैस्तस्मिन्कलसेऽमृतभाजने ।
विषण्णमनसो देवा हरिं शरणमाययुः ॥३६॥

nīyamāne 'surais tasmin
kalase 'mṛta-bhājane
viṣaṇṇa-manaso devā
hariṁ śaraṇam āyayuḥ

nīyamāne—being carried; *asuraiḥ*—by the demons; *tasmin*—that; *kalase*—jug; *amṛta-bhājane*—containing nectar; *viṣaṇṇa-manasaḥ*—

aggrieved in mind; *devāḥ*—all the demigods; *harim*—unto the Supreme Lord; *śaraṇam*—to take shelter; *āyayuḥ*—went.

TRANSLATION

When the jug of nectar was carried off by the demons, the demigods were morose. Thus they sought shelter at the lotus feet of the Supreme Personality of Godhead, Hari.

TEXT 37

इति तद्दैन्यमालोक्य भगवान्भृत्यकामकृत् ।
मा खिद्यत मिथोऽर्थं वः साधयिष्ये स्वमायया ॥३७॥

iti tad-dainyam ālokya
bhagavān bhṛtya-kāma-kṛt
mā khidyata mitho 'rthaṁ vaḥ
sādhayiṣye sva-māyayā

iti—in this way; *tat*—of the demigods; *dainyam*—moroseness; *ālokya*—seeing; *bhagavān*—the Supreme Personality of Godhead; *bhṛtya-kāma-kṛt*—who is always ready to fulfill the desires of His servants; *mā khidyata*—do not be aggrieved; *mithaḥ*—by a quarrel; *artham*—to get nectar; *vaḥ*—for all of you; *sādhayiṣye*—I shall execute; *sva-māyayā*—by My own energy.

TRANSLATION

When the Supreme Personality of Godhead, who always desires to fulfill the ambitions of His devotees, saw that the demigods were morose, He said to them, "Do not be aggrieved. By My own energy I shall bewilder the demons by creating a quarrel among them. In this way I shall fulfill your desire to have the nectar."

TEXT 38

मिथः कलिरभूत्तेषां तदर्थे तर्षचेतसाम् ।
अहं पूर्वमहं पूर्वं न त्वं न त्वमिति प्रभो ॥३८॥

mithaḥ kalir abhūt teṣāṁ
tad-arthe tarṣa-cetasām
ahaṁ pūrvam ahaṁ pūrvaṁ
na tvaṁ na tvaṁ iti prabho

mithaḥ—among themselves; *kaliḥ*—disagreement and quarrel; *abhūt*—there was; *teṣām*—of all of them; *tat-arthe*—for the sake of nectar; *tarṣa-cetasām*—bewildered in heart and soul by the illusory energy of Viṣṇu; *aham*—I; *pūrvam*—first; *aham*—I; *pūrvam*—first; *na*—not; *tvam*—you; *na*—not; *tvam*—you; *iti*—thus; *prabho*—O King.

TRANSLATION

O King, a quarrel then arose among the demons over who would get the nectar first. Each of them said, "You cannot drink it first. I must drink it first. Me first, not you!"

PURPORT

This is the symptom of demons. The first concern of a nondevotee is how to enjoy his personal sense gratification at once, whereas the devotee's first concern is to satisfy the Lord. This is the distinction between the nondevotee and the devotee. In this material world, since most people are nondevotees, they regularly compete, fight, disagree and war among themselves, for everyone wants to enjoy and satisfy his own senses. Therefore, unless such demons become Kṛṣṇa conscious and are trained to satisfy the senses of the Lord, there can be no question of peace in human society or any society, even that of the demigods. The demigods and devotees, however, always surrender to the lotus feet of the Lord, and thus the Lord is always anxious to satisfy their ambitions. While the demons fight to satisfy their own senses, devotees engage in devotional service to satisfy the senses of the Lord. The members of the Kṛṣṇa consciousness movement must be alert in regard to this point, and then their preaching of the Kṛṣṇa consciousness movement will be successful.

TEXTS 39–40

देवाः स्वं भागमर्हन्ति ये तुल्यायासहेतवः ।
सत्रयाग इवैतस्मिन्नेष धर्मः सनातनः ॥३९॥

इति स्वान्प्रत्यषेधन्वै दैतेया जातमत्सराः ।
दुर्बलाः प्रबलान् राजन् गृहीतकलसान् मुहुः ॥४०॥

devāḥ svaṁ bhāgam arhanti
ye tulyāyāsa-hetavaḥ
satra-yāga ivaitasminn
eṣa dharmaḥ sanātanaḥ

iti svān pratyaṣedhan vai
daiteyā jāta-matsarāḥ
durbalāḥ prabalān rājan
gṛhīta-kalasān muhuḥ

devāḥ—the demigods; *svam bhāgam*—their own share; *arhanti*—deserve to take; *ye*—all of them who; *tulya-āyāsa-hetavaḥ*—who made an equal endeavor; *satra-yāge*—in the performance of sacrifices; *iva*—similarly; *etasmin*—in this matter; *eṣaḥ*—this; *dharmaḥ*—religion; *sanātanaḥ*—eternal; *iti*—thus; *svān*—among themselves; *pratyaṣedhan*—forbade one another; *vai*—indeed; *daiteyāḥ*—the sons of Diti; *jāta-matsarāḥ*—envious; *durbalāḥ*—weak; *prabalān*—by force; *rājan*—O King; *gṛhīta*—possessing; *kalasān*—the jug containing nectar; *muhuḥ*—constantly.

TRANSLATION

Some of the demons said, "All the demigods have taken part in churning the ocean of milk. Now, as everyone has an equal right to partake in any public sacrifice, according to the eternal religious system it is befitting that the demigods now have a share of the nectar." O King, in this way the weaker demons forbade the stronger demons to take the nectar.

PURPORT

Desiring to take the nectar, those among the demons who were less strong spoke in favor of the demigods. The weaker Daityas naturally pleaded on behalf of the demigods to stop the stronger Daityas from drinking the nectar without sharing it. In this way, disagreement and trouble arose as they forbade one another to drink the nectar.

TEXTS 41–46

एतस्मिन्नन्तरे विष्णुः सर्वोपायविदीश्वरः ।
योषिद्रूपमनिर्देश्यं दधार परमाद्भुतम् ॥४१॥
प्रेक्षणीयोत्पलश्यामं सर्वावयवसुन्दरम् ।
समानकर्णाभरणं सुकपोलोन्नसाननम् ॥४२॥
नवयौवननिर्वृत्तस्तनभारकृशोदरम् ।
मुखामोदानुरक्तालिझङ्कारोद्विग्नलोचनम् ॥४३॥
बिभ्रत् सुकेशभारेण मालामुत्फुल्लमल्लिकाम् ।
सुग्रीवकण्ठाभरणं सुभुजाङ्गदभूषितम् ॥४४॥
विरजाम्बरसंवीतनितम्बद्वीपशोभया ।
काञ्च्या प्रविलसद्वल्गुचलच्चरणनूपुरम् ॥४५॥
सव्रीडस्मितविक्षिप्तभ्रूविलासावलोकनैः ।
दैत्ययूथपचेतःसु काममुद्दीपयन् मुहुः ॥४६॥

etasminn antare viṣṇuḥ
sarvopāya-vid īśvaraḥ
yoṣid-rūpam anirdeśyaṁ
dadhāra paramādbhutam

prekṣaṇīyotpala-śyāmaṁ
sarvāvayava-sundaram
samāna-karṇābharaṇaṁ
sukapolonnasānanam

nava-yauvana-nirvṛtta-
stana-bhāra-kṛśodaram
mukhāmodānuraktāli-
jhaṅkārodvigna-locanam

bibhrat sukeśa-bhāreṇa
mālām utphulla-mallikām
sugrīva-kaṇṭhābharaṇaṁ
su-bhujāṅgada-bhūṣitam

virajāmbara-saṁvīta-
nitamba-dvīpa-śobhayā
kāñcyā pravilasad-valgu-
calac-caraṇa-nūpuram

savrīḍa-smita-vikṣipta-
bhrū-vilāsāvalokanaiḥ
daitya-yūtha-pa-cetaḥsu
kāmam uddīpayan muhuḥ

etasmin antare—after this incident; *viṣṇuḥ*—Lord Viṣṇu; *sarva-upāya-vit*—one who knows how to deal with different situations; *īśvaraḥ*—the supreme controller; *yoṣit-rūpam*—the form of a beautiful woman; *anirdeśyam*—no one could ascertain who She was; *dadhāra*—assumed; *parama*—supremely; *adbhutam*—wonderful; *prekṣaṇīya*—pleasing to look at; *utpala-śyāmam*—blackish like a newly grown lotus; *sarva*—all; *avayava*—parts of the body; *sundaram*—very beautiful; *samāna*—equally adjusted; *karṇa-ābharaṇam*—ornaments on the ears; *su-kapola*—very beautiful cheeks; *unnasa-ānanam*—a raised nose on Her face; *nava-yauvana*—newly youthful; *nirvṛtta-stana*—breasts not agitated; *bhāra*—weight; *kṛśa*—very lean and thin; *udaram*—waist; *mukha*—face; *āmoda*—creating pleasure; *anurakta*—attracted; *ali*—bumblebees; *jhaṅkāra*—making a humming sound; *udvigna*—from anxiety; *locanam*—Her eyes; *bibhrat*—moving; *su-keśa-bhāreṇa*—by the weight of beautiful hair; *mālām*—with a flower garland; *utphulla-mallikām*—made of fully grown *mallikā* flowers; *su-grīva*—a nice neck; *kaṇṭha-ābharaṇam*—ornamented with beautiful jewelry; *su-bhuja*—very beautiful arms; *aṅgada-bhūṣitam*—decorated with bangles; *viraja-ambara*—very clean cloth; *saṁvīta*—spread; *nitamba*—breast; *dvīpa*—appearing like an island; *śobhayā*—by such beauty; *kāñcyā*—the belt on the waist; *pravilasat*—spreading over; *valgu*—very beautiful; *calat-caraṇa-nūpuram*—moving ankle bells; *sa-vrīḍa-smita*—smiling with shyness; *vikṣipta*—glancing; *bhrū-vilāsa*—activities of the eyebrows; *avalokanaiḥ*—glancing over; *daitya-yūtha-pa*—the leaders of the demons; *cetaḥsu*—in the core of the heart; *kāmam*—lusty desire; *uddīpayat*—awakening; *muhuḥ*—constantly.

TRANSLATION

The Supreme Personality of Godhead, Viṣṇu, who can counteract any unfavorable situation, then assumed the form of an extremely beautiful woman. This incarnation as a woman, Mohinī-mūrti, was most pleasing to the mind. Her complexion resembled in color a newly grown blackish lotus, and every part of Her body was beautifully situated. Her ears were equally decorated with earrings, Her cheeks were very beautiful, Her nose was raised and Her face full of youthful luster. Her large breasts made Her waist seem very thin. Attracted by the aroma of Her face and body, bumblebees hummed around Her, and thus Her eyes were restless. Her hair, which was extremely beautiful, was garlanded with mallikā flowers. Her attractively constructed neck was decorated with a necklace and other ornaments, Her arms were decorated with bangles, Her body was covered with a clean sari, and Her breasts seemed like islands in an ocean of beauty. Her legs were decorated with ankle bells. Because of the movements of Her eyebrows as She smiled with shyness and glanced over the demons, all the demons were saturated with lusty desires, and every one of them desired to possess Her.

PURPORT

Because of the Supreme Lord's assuming the form of a beautiful woman to arouse the lusty desires of the demons, a description of Her complete beauty is given here.

Thus end the Bhaktivedanta purports of the Eighth Canto, Eighth Chapter, of the Śrīmad-Bhāgavatam, *entitled "The Churning of the Milk Ocean."*

Appendixes

The Author

His Divine Grace A. C. Bhaktivedanta Swami Prabhupāda appeared in this world in 1896 in Calcutta, India. He first met his spiritual master, Śrīla Bhaktisiddhānta Sarasvatī Gosvāmī, in Calcutta in 1922. Bhaktisiddhānta Sarasvatī, a prominent devotional scholar and the founder of sixty-four Gauḍīya Maṭhas (Vedic institutes), liked this educated young man and convinced him to dedicate his life to teaching Vedic knowledge. Śrīla Prabhupāda became his student, and eleven years later (1933) at Allahabad he became his formally initiated disciple.

At their first meeting, in 1922, Śrīla Bhaktisiddhānta Sarasvatī Ṭhākura requested Śrīla Prabhupāda to broadcast Vedic knowledge through the English language. In the years that followed, Śrīla Prabhupāda wrote a commentary on the *Bhagavad-gītā*, assisted the Gauḍīya Maṭha in its work and, in 1944, without assistance, started an English fortnightly magazine, edited it, typed the manuscripts and checked the galley proofs. He even distributed the individual copies freely and struggled to maintain the publication. Once begun, the magazine never stopped; it is now being continued by his disciples in the West.

Recognizing Śrīla Prabhupāda's philosophical learning and devotion, the Gauḍīya Vaiṣṇava Society honored him in 1947 with the title "Bhaktivedanta." In 1950, at the age of fifty-four, Śrīla Prabhupāda retired from married life, and four years later he adopted the *vānaprastha* (retired) order to devote more time to his studies and writing. Śrīla Prabhupāda traveled to the holy city of Vṛndāvana, where he lived in very humble circumstances in the historic medieval temple of Rādhā-Dāmodara. There he engaged for several years in deep study and writing. He accepted the renounced order of life (*sannyāsa*) in 1959. At Rādhā-Dāmodara, Śrīla Prabhupāda began work on his life's masterpiece: a multivolume translation and commentary on the eighteen thousand verse *Śrīmad-Bhāgavatam* (*Bhāgavata Purāṇa*). He also wrote *Easy Journey to Other Planets.*

After publishing three volumes of *Bhāgavatam*, Śrīla Prabhupāda came to the United States, in 1965, to fulfill the mission of his spiritual master. Since that time, His Divine Grace has written over forty volumes of authoritative translations, commentaries and summary studies of the philosophical and religious classics of India.

In 1965, when he first arrived by freighter in New York City, Śrīla Prabhupāda was practically penniless. It was after almost a year of great difficulty that he established the International Society for Krishna Consciousness in July of 1966. Under his careful guidance, the Society has grown within a decade to a worldwide confederation of almost one hundred *āśramas*, schools, temples, institutes and farm communities.

In 1968, Śrīla Prabhupāda created New Vṛndāvana, an experimental Vedic community in the hills of West Virginia. Inspired by the success of New Vṛndāvana, now a thriving farm community of more than one thousand acres, his students have since founded several similar communities in the United States and abroad.

In 1972, His Divine Grace introduced the Vedic system of primary and secondary education in the West by founding the Gurukula school in Dallas, Texas. The school began with 3 children in 1972, and by the beginning of 1975 the enrollment had grown to 150.

Śrīla Prabhupāda has also inspired the construction of a large international center at Śrīdhāma Māyāpur in West Bengal, India, which is also the site for a planned Institute of Vedic Studies. A similar project is the magnificent Kṛṣṇa-Balarāma Temple and International Guest House in Vṛndāvana, India. These are centers where Westerners can live to gain firsthand experience of Vedic culture.

Śrīla Prabhupāda's most significant contribution, however, is his books. Highly respected by the academic community for their authoritativeness, depth and clarity, they are used as standard textbooks in numerous college courses. His writings have been translated into eleven languages. The Bhaktivedanta Book Trust, established in 1972 exclusively to publish the works of His Divine Grace, has thus become the world's largest publisher of books in the field of Indian religion and philosophy. Its latest project is the publishing of Śrīla Prabhupāda's most recent work: a seventeen-volume translation and commentary—completed by Śrīla Prabhupāda in only eighteen months—on the Bengali religious classic *Śrī Caitanya-caritāmṛta.*

In the past ten years, in spite of his advanced age, Śrīla Prabhupāda has circled the globe twelve times on lecture tours that have taken him to six continents. In spite of such a vigorous schedule, Śrīla Prabhupāda continues to write prolifically. His writings constitute a veritable library of Vedic philosophy, religion, literature and culture.

References

The purports of *Śrīmad-Bhāgavatam* are all confirmed by standard Vedic authorities. The following authentic scriptures are specifically cited in this volume:

Bhagavad-gītā, 5, 8, 12, 13, 16, 17, 21, 22, 23, 24, 25, 63, 64, 66, 67, 71, 75, 80, 83, 85, 87, 89, 91, 93, 95, 97, 100, 102, 104–105, 113, 114, 115–116, 158, 158–159, 160–161, 163, 169, 170, 172, 174, 174–175, 178, 179, 191, 195, 197, 200, 209, 211, 213, 214, 215, 216, 219, 239, 245, 261, 269, 270, 274, 280, 281, 287, 292

Bhakti-rasāmṛta-sindhu, 104

Brahma-saṁhitā, 18–19, 76, 93, 111, 184–185, 268–269, 288

Brahma-vaivarta Purāṇa, 61–62

Caitanya-candrodaya-nāṭaka, 28

Caitanya-caritāmṛta, 28

Gautamīya Tantra, 16, 108

Gopāla-tāpanī Upaniṣad, 86

Īśopaniṣad, 99, 169

Padma Purāṇa, 165, 199

Śikṣāṣṭaka, 20, 218, 221

Śrīmad-Bhāgavatam, 14, 21, 22, 22–23, 44, 46, 65, 87, 93, 95, 98, 101, 111, 113–114, 116, 119, 131, 133, 134, 161, 162, 170–171, 172–173, 176, 198, 199, 215, 280, 304–305

Glossary

A

Ācārya—a spiritual master who teaches by example.

Ārati—a ceremony for greeting the Lord with offerings of food, lamps, fans, flowers and incense.

Arcanā—the devotional process of Deity worship.

Āśrama—the four spiritual orders of life: celibate student, householder, retired life and renounced life.

Asuras—atheistic demons.

Avatāra—a descent of the Supreme Lord.

B

Bhagavad-gītā—the basic directions for spiritual life spoken by the Lord Himself.

Bhakta—a devotee.

Bhakti-mārga—the path of developing devotion to Kṛṣṇa.

Bhakti-yoga—linking with the Supreme Lord by devotional service.

Brahmacarya—celibate student life; the first order of Vedic spiritual life.

Brahman—the Absolute Truth; especially the impersonal aspect of the Absolute.

Brāhmaṇa—one wise in the *Vedas* who can guide society; the first Vedic social order.

C

Cakra—the wheel held by Lord Viṣṇu.

D

Devas—demigods.

Dharma—eternal occupational duty; religious principles.

Dvijas—*brāhmaṇas.*

E

Ekādaśī—a special fast day for increased remembrance of Kṛṣṇa, which comes on the eleventh day of both the waxing and waning moon.

G

Gadā—the club held by Lord Viṣṇu.

Goloka (Kṛṣṇaloka)—the highest spiritual planet, containing Kṛṣṇa's personal abodes, Dvārakā, Mathurā and Vṛndāvana.

Gopīs—Kṛṣṇa's cowherd girl friends who are His most confidential servitors.

Gṛhastha—regulated householder life; the second order of Vedic spiritual life.

Guṇa-avatāras—the three incarnations of Viṣṇu who control the three modes of material nature; Viṣṇu controls goodness, Brahmā passion and Śiva ignorance.

Guru—a spiritual master.

H

Hare Kṛṣṇa mantra—*See: Mahā-mantra*

J

Jīva-tattva—the living entities, atomic parts of the Lord.

Jīvātmā—the infinitesimal soul, the living entity.

Jñāna—knowledge of matter, spirit and the controller of both.

K

Kali-yuga (Age of Kali)—the present age, which is characterized by quarrel. It is last in the cycle of four, and began five thousand years ago.

Karatālas—hand cymbals used in *kīrtana.*

Karma—fruitive action, for which there is always reaction, good or bad.

Karmī—a person satisfied with working hard for flickering sense gratification.

Kīrtana—chanting the glories of the Supreme Lord.

Kṛṣṇaloka—*See:* Goloka

Kṣatriyas—a warrior or administrator; the second Vedic social order.

L

Līlā-avatāras—innumerable incarnations of the Lord who descend to the material world to display spiritual pastimes.

M

Mahājanas—great souls, spiritual authorities.
Mahā-mantra—the great chanting for deliverance:
Hare Kṛṣṇa, Hare Kṛṣṇa, Kṛṣṇa Kṛṣṇa, Hare Hare
Hare Rāma, Hare Rāma, Rāma Rāma, Hare Hare.
Mahat-tattva—the total material energy.
Mantra—a sound vibration that can deliver the mind from illusion.
Manvantara-avatāras—the Manu incarnations, administrators of the universe.
Mathurā—Lord Kṛṣṇa's abode, surrounding Vṛndāvana, where He took birth and later returned to after performing His Vṛndāvana pastimes.
Māyā—(*mā*—not; *yā*—this), illusion; forgetfulness of one's relationship with Kṛṣṇa.
Māyāvādīs—impersonal philosophers who say that the Lord cannot have a transcendental body.
Mṛdaṅga—a clay drum used for congregational chanting.
Muni—a great thinker.

N

Nirguṇa—transcendental to the modes of material nature; free from all material contamination.

P

Padma—the lotus flower held by Lord Viṣṇu.
Paramahaṁsa—the highest stage of the *sannyāsa* order; a topmost devotee of the Lord.
Paramparā—the chain of spiritual masters in disciplic succession.
Prajāpatis—the demigods in charge of populating the universe.
Prasāda—the Lord's mercy; anything first offered to the Lord and then utilized by His devotees.
Puruṣa—the Supreme Personality of Godhead, the supreme enjoyer.

R

Ṛṣis—great sages.

S

Sac-cid-ānanda-vigraha—the Lord's transcendental form, which is eternal, full of knowledge and bliss.

Śakti-tattva—the various energies of the Lord.

Sampradāya—a chain of spiritual masters.

Śaṅkha—the conchshell held by Lord Viṣṇu.

Saṅkīrtana—public chanting of the names of God, the approved *yoga* process for this age.

Sannyāsa—renounced life; the fourth order of Vedic spiritual life.

Śāstras—revealed scriptures.

Śravaṇaṁ kīrtanaṁ viṣṇoḥ—the devotional processes of hearing and chanting about Lord Viṣṇu.

Śruti-mantra—the hymns of the *Vedas* and *Upaniṣads.*

Stotra—a prayer.

Śūdra—a laborer; the fourth of the Vedic social orders.

Svāmī—one who controls his mind and senses; title of one in the renounced order of life.

T

Tantras—Vedic literatures consisting mostly of dialogues between Lord Śiva and Durgā.

Tapasya—austerity; accepting some voluntary inconvenience for a higher purpose.

Tattvas—the Absolute Truth's multifarious categories.

Tilaka—auspicious clay marks that sanctify a devotee's body as a temple of the Lord.

V

Vaikuṇṭha—the spiritual world.

Vaiṣṇava—a devotee of Lord Viṣṇu, Kṛṣṇa.

Vaiśyas—farmers and merchants; the third Vedic social order.

Vānaprastha—one who has retired from family life; the third order of Vedic spiritual life.

Varṇāśrama—the Vedic social system of four social and four spiritual orders.

Vedas—the original revealed scriptures, first spoken by the Lord Himself.

Virāṭ-rūpa—the all-pervading universal form of the Lord.

Viṣṇu, Lord—Kṛṣṇa's first expansion for the creation and maintenance of the material universes.

Viṣṇu-tattva—personal expansions of the Lord which are equal in power to Him.

Vṛndāvana—Kṛṣṇa's personal abode, where He fully manifests His quality of sweetness.

Vyāsadeva—Kṛṣṇa's incarnation, at the end of Dvāpara-yuga, for compiling the *Vedas*.

Y

Yajña—sacrifice; work done for the satisfaction of Lord Viṣṇu.

Yoga—the process of linking with the Supreme.

Yogamāyā—internal spiritual potency of the Lord.

Yogī—a transcendentalist who, in one way or another, is striving for union with the Supreme.

Yuga-avatāras—the four incarnations of the Lord which appear in the four *yugas* or millenniums to prescribe the appropriate method of spiritual realization for that age.

Yugas—ages in the life of a universe, occurring in a repeated cycle of four.

Sanskrit Pronunciation Guide

Vowels

अ a आ ā इ i ई ī उ u ऊ ū ऋ ṛ ॠ ṝ
ऌ ḷ ए e ऐ ai ओ o औ au
ं ṁ *(anusvāra)* ः ḥ *(visarga)*

Consonants

Gutturals:	क ka	ख kha	ग ga	घ gha	ङ ṅa
Palatals:	च ca	छ cha	ज ja	झ jha	ञ ña
Cerebrals:	ट ṭa	ठ ṭha	ड ḍa	ढ ḍha	ण ṇa
Dentals:	त ta	थ tha	द da	ध dha	न na
Labials:	प pa	फ pha	ब ba	भ bha	म ma
Semivowels:	य ya	र ra	ल la	व va	
Sibilants:	श śa	ष ṣa	स sa		
Aspirate:	ह ha	ऽ ' *(avagraha)* – the apostrophe			

The vowels above should be pronounced as follows:

a – like the *a* in org*a*n or the *u* in b*u*t.
ā – like the *a* in f*a*r but held twice as long as short *a*.
i – like the *i* in p*i*n.
ī – like the *i* in p*i*que but held twice as long as short *i*.
u – like the *u* in p*u*sh.
ū – like the *u* in r*u*le but held twice as long as short *u*.

ṛ – like the *ri* in *ri*m.
ṝ – like *ree* in *ree*d.
ḷ – like *l* followed by ṛ (*lṛ*).
e – like the *e* in th*ey*.
ai – like the *ai* in *ai*sle.
o – like the *o* in g*o*.
au – like the *ow* in h*ow*.
ṁ (*anusvāra*) – a resonant nasal like the *n* in the French word *bon*.
ḥ (*visarga*) – a final *h*-sound: *aḥ* is pronounced like *aha; iḥ* like *ihi*.

The consonants are pronounced as follows:

k – as in *k*ite
kh – as in Ec*kh*art
g – as in *g*ive
gh – as in di*g-h*ard
ṅ – as in si*ng*
c – as in *ch*air
ch – as in staun*ch-h*eart
j – as in *j*oy
jh – as in he*dgeh*og
ñ – as in ca*ny*on
ṭ – as in *t*ub
ṭh – as in ligh*t-h*eart
ḍ – as in *d*ove
ḍha- as in re*d-h*ot
ṇ – as r*na* (prepare to say the *r* and say *na*).

Cerebrals are pronounced with tongue to roof of mouth, but the following dentals are pronounced with tongue against teeth:

t – as in *t*ub but with tongue against teeth.
th – as in ligh*t-h*eart but with tongue against teeth.
d – as in *d*ove but with tongue against teeth.
dh – as in re*d-h*ot but with tongue against teeth.
n – as in *n*ut but with tongue between teeth.

p – as in *p*ine
ph – as in u*ph*ill (not *f*)
b – as in *b*ird
bh – as in ru*b-h*ard
m – as in *m*other
y – as in *y*es
r – as in *r*un
l – as in *l*ight
v – as in *v*ine
ś (palatal) – as in the *s* in the German word *sprechen*
ṣ (cerebral) – as the *sh* in *sh*ine
s – as in *s*un
h – as in *h*ome

There is no strong accentuation of syllables in Sanskrit, only a flowing of short and long (twice as long as the short) syllables.

Index of Sanskrit Verses

This index constitutes a complete listing of the first and third lines of each of the Sanskrit poetry verses of this volume of *Śrīmad-Bhāgavatam*, arranged in English alphabetical order. The first column gives the Sanskrit transliteration, and the second and third columns, respectively, list the chapter-verse reference and page number for each verse.

B

C

D

E

O

P

R

General Index

Numerals in boldface type indicate references to translations of the verses of *Śrīmad-Bhāgavatam.*

A

Abhiṣeka ceremony
for goddess of fortune, 299
ingredients for, 299
Abhramu, **290**
Abhyutthānam adharmasya
verse quoted, 87, 195, 209, 281
Ābrahma-bhuvanāl lokāḥ
quoted, 163
Absolute Truth
Lord as, 19, **20,** 175
as personal, 74
spiritual master sees, 211
See also: Reality; Supreme Lord
Ācārya. See: Spiritual master, *all entries*
Acintya-bhedābheda, defined, 19
Activities
fruitive. *See:* Fruitive activities
of Kṛṣṇa. *See:* Incarnations of the Supreme Lord; Pastimes of the Supreme Lord
in Kṛṣṇa consciousness, 22
material vs. spiritual, 22, 85
Activities, material
bondage to, 22, 25
impersonalist falls to, 134
spiritual activities vs., 22, 85
by Viṣṇu via Śiva, 261
See also: Fruitive activities; *Karma*
Adarśanān marma-hatāṁ karotu vā
quoted, 218
Adhikaṁ yo 'bhimanyeta
verse quoted, 14
Āditya-varṇaṁ tamasaḥ parastāt
quoted, 78
Advaita, Lord, as Caitanya's associate, 173
African devotee in Māyāpura, 24
Agastya Muni
curse by, as benediction, 122–123, 130
Indradyumna neglected, **129,** 130
quoted on Indradyumna, **129–130**
Age of Kali. *See:* Kali-yuga
Agni
as fire, 264
as Lord's mouth, 264
as Svārociṣa Manu's father, 30
Agniḥ sarva-devatāḥ
quoted, 264
Agriculture. *See:* Cow protection; Food; *Vaiśyas*
Aham ādir hi devānām
quoted, 97
Ahaṁ bīja-pradaḥ pitā
quoted, 89, 261
Ahaṁ sarvasya prabhavaḥ
quoted, 97
Ahaṁ tvāṁ sarva-pāpebhyo
verse quoted, 160
Air(s)
in body wheel, **174**
from God, **186**
living entities sustained by, 186
as Lord's breathing, **265**
Airāvaṇa, **290**
Airāvata (elephant king), **289**
Ajāmila, Nārāyaṇa's name saved, 72, 83, 197
Ajo 'pi sann avyayātmā
verse quoted, 209
Akāmaḥ sarva-kāmo vā
verse quoted, 93, 101, 198
Ākūti, **7, 8**
Alakṣyaṁ sarva-bhūtānām
quoted, 16
Āmāra ājñāya guru hañā tāra' ei deśa
verse quoted, 28
Anādir ādir govindaḥ
verse quoted, 19, 76, 93
Aṇḍa-ja, defined, 180
Aṇḍāntara-stha-paramāṇu-cayāntara-stham
quoted, 16, 97
Anejad ekaṁ manaso javīyo
verse quoted, 169

E

Gṛhe śatrum api prāptaṁ
quoted, 230
Guṇa-avatāra, Brahmā as, **157**, 262
Guṇāṁś ca doṣāṁś ca mune vyatīta
quoted, 82
Guṇas. See: Modes of material nature
Guru. See: Spiritual master
Guru-kṛṣṇa-prasāde pāya bhakti-latā-bīja
quoted, 215

H

Happiness
fruitive activities lack, 22
via the Lord, 218
in material world absent, 108, 163
See also: Bliss; Enjoyment, material
Hare Kṛṣṇa *mantra*
Caitanya delivered, 221
for devotees, 25
as essential, 72
for Kali-yuga, 161–162, 221
liberation by, 83
potency of, 20, 161–162
śāstras recommend, 20
as song in Hare Kṛṣṇa movement, 167
See also: Chanting the Lord's holy names; Names of the Supreme Lord; *Saṅkīrtana* movement
Hare Kṛṣṇa movement. *See:* Kṛṣṇa consciousness movement
Harer nāma harer nāma
verse quoted, 217, 221
Hari, Lord, Gajendra saved by, **37, 38**
Haridāsa Ṭhākura, imitating, condemned, 23, 24
Harimedhā, **37**
Hariṁ vinā naiva mṛtiṁ taranti
quoted, 115
Hariṇī, **37**
Haris, **36**
Haviṣmān, **149**
Hearing about the Supreme Lord
by pure devotee, **103**
seeing Lord vs., 167
Hearing about the Supreme Lord
sins absolved by, **144**
from Vedic authority, **166,** 167
Heaven, King of. *See:* Indra, King
Heavenly planets
animals on, **45**
Apsarās in, **291**
elevation to, **287**
landscape of, 45
from Lord's universal form, **188**
residents of. *See:* Demigods
women beautiful in, 47–48
Hell, Yudhiṣṭhira saw, 136
Hetunānena kaunteya
verse quoted, 170, 213
Hindus as sectarian, 304
Hiraṇyakaśipu
as *asura,* 165
as atheist No. 1, 179
as educated demon, 244
Nṛsiṁhadeva killed, 179, 305
Hiraṇyākṣa
Jaya as, 148
as Varāha's opponent, 148
Hiraṇyaromā, **145**
Holy name of the Lord. *See:* Chanting the Lord's holy names; Hare Kṛṣṇa *mantra;* Names of the Supreme Lord; Supreme Lord, *appropriate entries*
Householders. *See:* Family; *Gṛhastha*
Hṛd-vāg-vapurbhir vidadhan namas te
verse quoted, 133
Hūhū, King
as crocodile, **124**
Devala cursed, **124**
Gandharva status regained by, **124, 125**
Lord merciful to, **124, 125**
prayed to the Lord, **124**
Human being(s)
animalistic, 98
demigods vs., 45, 47
in Kali-yuga degraded, 216, 295–296
opulences desired by, 293
pious, turn to God, 63, 216
types of, three listed, 101

N

Na cāhaṁ teṣv avasthitah
quoted, 214, 270
Na ca tasmān manuṣyeṣu
quoted, 280
Nāgas, **299**
Naimiṣāraṇya, 22
Naiṣkarmya
defined, 85
as impractical without Kṛṣṇa consciousness, 23
Naiṣkarmyam apy acyuta-bhāva-varjitaṁ
quoted, 22, 85
Na māṁ duṣkṛtino mūḍhāḥ
quoted, 65, 67
verse quoted, 245
Names of the Supreme Lord
for creation, maintenance, annihilation, **262**
as God Himself, 83
pastimes according to, 20
potency of, 20
See also: Chanting the Lord's holy names; Hare Kṛṣṇa *mantra;* Supreme Lord, *specific names*
Nāmnām akāri bahudhā nija-sarva-śaktiḥ
quoted, 20
Nāpnuvanti mahātmānaḥ
verse quoted, 191
Nara, **35**
Nārada Muni
curse by, as benediction, 122–123
quoted on proprietorship, 14
Nārāyaṇa, Lord
Ajāmila saved by name of, 72, 83, 197
Gajendra rescued by, **118**
as Lakṣmī's lord, 293, 300, 302, 309
as soul of universe, 116
See also: Supreme Lord
Narottama dāsa Ṭhākura, songs of, 167
Na sañjahre samartho 'pi
verse quoted, 258
Nāśayāmy ātma-bhāva-stho
verse quoted, 95
Na tasya kāryaṁ karaṇaṁ ca vidyate
quoted, 107, 193
Na tat-samaś cābhyadhikaś ca dṛśyate
quoted, 107, 169
Na te viduḥ svārtha-gatiṁ hi viṣṇum
quoted, 177, 216
Nature, material
as inimitable, 44
living entity under, 174
Lord above, 44, 89, 170, 193, 213, 239
as mother, 89
See also: Body, material; Elements, material; Modes of material nature
Nectar
demons quarreled over, **317, 318**–319
demons stole, **315, 316**
Dhanvantari carried, **315**
for immortality, 226
milk compared to, 216
from milk ocean, **150, 151, 227, 228**
Nectar of Devotion as auspicious, 38–39
Nirguṇa defined, 83
Nirguṇa guṇa-bhoktṛ ca
quoted, 200
Nityānanda, Lord, as Caitanya's associate, 173
Nityo nityānāṁ cetanaś cetanānām
quoted, 5, 10
Nondevotees
creator denied by, 110
devotees vs., 317
Lord disfavors, 112
sense gratification pursued by, 317
See also: Atheists; Demons; Materialists
Notpādayed yadi ratiṁ
verse quoted, 305
Nṛsiṁhadeva, Lord, Hiraṇyakaśipu killed by, 179, 305
Nṛsiṁha prayer recommended, 72

O

Ocean(s)
fire in, **183**
goddess of fortune served by, **299**
in universe, 44
Ocean of milk. *See:* Milk, ocean of

T

U

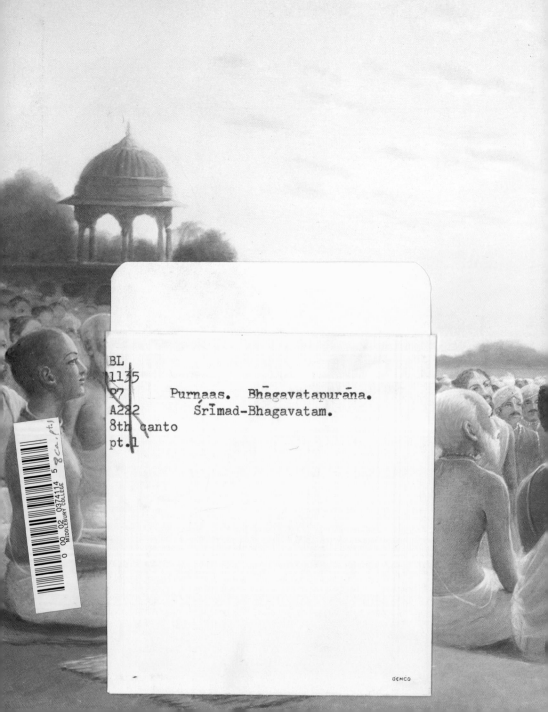